Watching THE Lord OF THE RINGS

Sut Jhally & Justin Lewis
General Editors

Vol. 3

PETER LANG
New York • Washington, D.C./Baltimore • Bern
Frankfurt am Main • Berlin • Brussels • Vienna • Oxford

Watching THE LORD OF THE RINGS

TOLKIEN'S WORLD AUDIENCES

MARTIN BARKER & ERNEST MATHIJS,

EDITORS

PETER LANG
New York • Washington, D.C./Baltimore • Bern
Frankfurt am Main • Berlin • Brussels • Vienna • Oxford

Library of Congress Cataloging-in-Publication Data

Watching the Lord of the rings: Tolkien's world audiences /
edited by Martin Barker, Ernest Mathijs.
p. cm. — (Media and culture; v. 3)
Includes bibliographical references and index.
1. Lord of the Rings films—History and criticism.
2. Tolkien, J. R. R. (John Ronald Reuel), 1892–1973.
Lord of the rings. I. Title.
PN1995.9.L58B37   791.43'75—dc22   2007024352
ISBN: 978-0-8204-6397-1 (hard cover)
ISBN 978-0-8204-6396-4 (paperback)
ISSN 1098-4208

Bibliographic information published by **Die Deutsche Bibliothek**.
Die Deutsche Bibliothek lists this publication in the "Deutsche
Nationalbibliografie"; detailed bibliographic data is available
on the Internet at http://dnb.ddb.de/.

Cover design by Clear Point Designs

The paper in this book meets the guidelines for permanence and durability
of the Committee on Production Guidelines for Book Longevity
of the Council of Library Resources.

Printed in the United States of America

Contents

Tables and Figure

Acknowledgments

This project owes debts of gratitude to very many people who in large and small ways made it possible for us to achieve so much of our grandiose ambitions. We hope very much that we have not forgotten to thank anyone in print. Many people helped us in more than one way—we mention you once, and hope that will do for all your contributions!

First, in the U.K. hobbit hub, we must thank Janet Jones, who was involved in the original proposal to the Economic and Social Research Council and in the early days of the project before having to withdraw for personal reasons; Kate Egan, our brilliant research assistant, who not only held the project together nationally and internationally, but also saved us from at least two major disasters; Dave Gregory, for his excellent work on the design and construction of our web questionnaire, with all its complexities. Thanks also to Gwen Bouvier, Angelina Karpovich, and Kerstin Leder, doctoral students at Aberystwyth, particularly for the organisational help with our closing Project Conference at Gregynog.

We record our appreciation of the Economic and Social Research Council for Research Grant No. RES-000-22-0323—a project of this kind is simply unthinkable without this kind of support. Our thanks also to the University of Wales, Aberystwyth, which made an additional award to our project, enabling us to lengthen and thereby deepen it.

To our research partners in all of our collaborating countries: first, thank you for trusting us sufficiently to become involved in what may have looked to you a hare-brained scheme. Not all of you made it right through to the end of the project, and not all of you are directly represented in the writing of this book. But without all the levels of contribution that people were able to make, the overall outcomes would have been so much more restricted. Our thanks to: Austria/Norway—Hege Rossa; Australia—Sue Turnbull; Belgium—Daniel Biltereyst, Philippe Meers, and Ann Leysen; Canada—Barbara Loh; China—Liu Jun; Colombia—Jair Vega; Denmark—Ann Jerslev and Dan Pedersen; France—Divina Frau-Meigs; Germany—Lothar Mikos (to whom special thanks for organising the early conference on methodology, in Potsdam in 2004), Susanne Eichner, Elizabeth Prommer, and Michael Wedel; Greece—Yannis Skarpelos; Italy—Alberto Trobia and Mariano Longo (and Marco Centorrino, who enabled us to form our Italian links); The Netherlands—Giselinde Kuipers and Jeroen De Kloet; New Zealand—Stan Jones, Geoff Lealand, and Sean Cubitt; Russia—Christina Stojanova; Slovenia—Breda Luthar and Dejan Jontes; Spain—José Javier Sánchez Aranda, Joseba Bonaut, and Maria del Mar Grandío; Turkey—Ahmed Gurata; United States—Barbara Klinger, Janet Wasko, and Peggy Tally.

A number of people outside the research network helped us with translations of the questionnaire, and of sample sets of responses in particular languages. Thanks to Jamie Medhurst, Sabina Mihelji, Noel Parker, and Xin Zhang.

Thank you to the 24,739 people who filled out our questionnaire and in some cases allowed us to interview you as well. Without you there would not have been any research. The knowledge produced here is ultimately yours: you gave it to us, and we are happy to give it back.

We also extend our thanks to Damon Zucca and Sophie Appel at Peter Lang, for their insistent support of this project.

Both Martin and Ernest owe a series of personal debts, which they will fulfil privately and fully!

Martin Barker
Ernest Mathijs
March 2007

Contributors

MARTIN BARKER is professor of film and television studies at the University of Wales, Aberystwyth. He has published widely, including on censorship campaigns and controversial cultural forms, on film audiences, and on issues of methods. His main publications include: *The Crash Controversy* (2001, with Jane Arthurs and Ramaswami Harindranath); *Ill Effects: The Media/Violence Debate* (2001, edited with Julian Petley); and *From Antz to Titanic: Reinventing Film Analysis* (2000, with Thomas Austin). He is co-editor of *Participations,* the online journal of audience and reception studies.

DANIEL BILTEREYST is professor of film, television, and cultural media studies at the Ghent University, Belgium, where he leads the Research Group Film and Television Studies. His work is on screen studies and the public debate, recently mainly on the historical reception and censorship of controversial film and television. He has published in various journals (for example, *Media, Culture & Society, European Journal of Cultural Studies, Studies in French Cinema*) and readers (*Youth Culture in Global Cinema, Communication Theory and Research, Rebel without a Cause*).

JOSEBA BONAUT is doctor of communication by the University of Navarra, Spain. His Ph.D. concerned television and sports in Spain. He loves sport, cinema, and *The Lord of the Rings.*

JEROEN DE KLOET is assistant professor of media studies at the University of Amsterdam and affiliated with the Amsterdam School for Cultural Analysis

(ASCA) and the International Institute for Asian Studies (IIAS). His work on contemporary Chinese culture has appeared in several journals, including *The China Quarterly, Visual Anthropology,* and *Critical Studies in Media Communication.* A volume he edited together with Edwin Jurriens, titled *Cosmopatriots,* is forthcoming from Rodopi Press.

KATE EGAN is a lecturer in film and television studies at the University of Wales, Aberystwyth. Her main research interests are in the areas of historical reception studies, horror and genre study, film censorship, and media collecting. Her monographs on the history of the "video nasties," and *The Evil Dead* as a cult text, are forthcoming from Manchester University Press and Wallflower.

SUSANNE EICHNER is scientific assistant and lecturer at the Academy of Film and Television, Potsdam-Babelsberg in media studies (analysis, aesthetics, audience). She is currently working on her Ph.D., focusing on the reception and reception aesthetics of interactive formats, particularly video games. She has published articles on computer games and on reception aesthetics in various journals and anthologies.

MARÍA DEL MAR GRANDÍO is lecturer at the School of Communication of the Universidad Católica San Antonio in Spain. Her Ph.D. was about the reception of the TV sitcom *Friends* in Spain. She researches into audiences, fandom, and entertainment.

STAN JONES is a senior lecturer in screen and media at the University of Waikato, New Zealand. He has published on Wim Wenders and on German and NZ film in several volumes, including *European Cinema: Inside Out* (eds. G. Rings and R. Morgan-Tamosunas, 2003), *Lord of the Rings: Popular Culture in a Global Context* (ed. Ernest Mathijs, 2006), and the *Schirmer Encyclopaedia of Film* (ed. B. Grant, 2006). He is currently researching cross-cultural influence and identity questions in contemporary cinema.

BARBARA KLINGER is a professor in the Department of Communication and Culture at Indiana University in Bloomington, where she teaches film and media studies. Her research focuses on reception studies, fan studies, and cinema's relationship to new media. In addition to numerous articles, she is author of *Melodrama and Meaning: History, Culture, and the Films of Douglas Sirk* (Indiana University Press, 1994) and *Beyond the Multiplex: Cinema, New Technologies, and the Home* (University of California Press, 2006).

GISELINDE KUIPERS is assistant professor of sociology at the University of Amsterdam, The Netherlands. She has published in English and Dutch on humour, media, and cultural globalisation. Her work has been published in *Media, Culture and Society, New Media and Society,* and the *European Journal of Cultural Studies.* Her book *Good Humor, Bad Taste: A Sociology of the Joke* (Berlin and New York: Mouton de Gruyter) appeared in 2006.

BREDA LUTHAR is an associate professor of media studies at the Faculty of Social Sciences, University of Ljubljana, Slovenia. Her research focuses on popular media, popular culture, and consumer culture. Her recent publications in English include "Food, Ethics and Aesthetics" (*Appetite*) and "Remembering Socialism: On Desire, Consumption and Surveillance" (*Journal of Consumer Culture*). She is currently co-editing a book on popular culture and everyday life in socialism (*Remembering Utopia: The Culture of Everyday Life in Socialist Yugoslavia*) for New Academia Publishing (forthcoming).

ERNEST MATHIJS is assistant professor of film and theatre studies at the University of British Columbia, Canada. He researches the reception of cult and alternative cinema. He has published in *Screen* and *Cinema Journal,* and edited *The Lord of the Rings: Popular Culture in Global Context* (2006), *From Hobbits to Hollywood* (with Murray Pomerance, 2006), and *The Cult Film Reader* (with Xavier Mendik, 2007). His monograph *The Cinema of David Cornenberg* is forthcoming.

PHILIPPE MEERS is assistant professor in film and media studies at the University of Antwerp, Belgium, where he is a member of the Visual Culture Research Group. His research on popular media culture and film audiences appears in *Media, Culture and Society, Journal of Popular Film and Television.* He edited a reader on genre with Daniel Biltereyst and has contributed to several readers (*Big Brother International,* 2004; *Hollywood Abroad: Audiences and Cultural Relations,* 2004; and *The Lord of the Rings: Popular Culture in Global Context,* 2006). He is co-editor of a book series *Film & TV Studies* and promoter of *The "Enlightened" City* project on the history of film exhibition and film culture in Flanders and Brussels (SRC, 2005–2007, with Daniel Biltereyst and Marnix Beyen). Meers is the chair of the ECREA film studies section.

LOTHAR MIKOS is professor of television studies at the University of Film and Television "Konrad Wolf" in Potsdam-Babelsberg, Germany. He is head of the Department of Audio-Visual Media Studies and responsible for a master programme in media studies—Analysis, Aesthetics, Audiences. His main research interests are popular media and everyday life, qualitative methodology, audience research, and film and TV analysis. He has published widely on film and TV, popular culture, and mediated sport.

ELIZABETH PROMMER is assistant professor for media studies and media research at the Hochschule für Film und Fernsehen in Potsdam-Babelsberg, Germany. Her research interests are audience and reception studies, and film and media marketing. She has published a mediabiographical study on cinema audiences, *Kinobesuch im Lebenslauf: Eine Historische und Medianbiographische Studie* (1999), and co-edited a book about converging media use, *Mediennutzung in konvergierenden Medienumgebungen* (2004). Her monograph on television taste, lifestyle, and comedy is forthcoming.

JOSÉ JAVIER SÁNCHEZ ARANDA is professor at the School of Communication of the University of Navarra, Spain. His area of expertise is methodology of communication research. He has participated in several research projects, such as a survey among Spanish and Iberoamerican journalists, a study about the representation of women in advertising and television news in Spain.

ALBERTO TROBIA is professor of sociology and social research at the University of Palermo, Italy. His main research interests are in the field of complexity theories (in particular, multiagent simulation), the micro-macro link, quali-quantitative research, and textual analysis. His main publications include: *La sociologia come scienza rigorosa* (2001) and *La ricerca sociale quali-quantitativa* (2005). He has also written some entries for the *Encyclopedia of Survey Research Methods* (Sage Publications, forthcoming).

SUE TURNBULL is an associate professor in media studies at La Trobe University, Australia. She has published broadly in the fields of audience studies, media education, and television. With Martin Barker, she is co-editor of the journal *Participations.* Her current research project with Felicity Collins at La Trobe is concerned with the history and reception of Australian screen comedy, and is funded by an Australian Research Council Discovery Grant.

SOFIE VAN BAUWEL is lecturer at the Department of Communication Studies and is a member of the Working Group Film and Television of the Ghent University, Belgium. She researches popular culture, film and television, and gender. She has published on gender bending in visual culture, gender representations in the media, and feminist media theory.

JANET WASKO is the Knight Chair for Communication Research at the University of Oregon. She is the author of *How Hollywood Works* (Sage, 2003), *Understanding Disney: The Manufacture of Fantasy* (Polity Press, 2001), and *Hollywood in the Information Age: Beyond the Silver Screen* (Polity Press, 1994), and editor of *A Companion to Television* (Blackwell, 2005) and *Dazzled by Disney? The Global Disney Audience Project* (Leicester University Press, 2001), as well as other volumes on the political economy of communication and democratic media.

MICHAEL WEDEL is assistant professor of film at the University of Amsterdam, The Netherlands. His publications on German and Hollywood cinema have appeared in edited collections and in journals such as *Film History* and *New German Critique.* He is the author of *Der Deutsche Musikfilm* (2007), and co-edited *The BFI Companion to German Cinema* (with Thomas Elsaesser, 1999) and *Die Spur durch den Spiegel: Der Film in der Kultur der Moderne* (with Malte Hagener and Johann N. Schmidt, 2004).

Researching
The Lord of the Rings

Audiences and Contexts

MARTIN BARKER, KATE EGAN, STAN JONES,
AND ERNEST MATHIJS

This book tells the story and presents the core findings of a major international research project. The project, conducted across 2003 and 2004, was crazily simple: its aim was to explore audience responses across the world to *The Return of the King*, the final part of the film trilogy adapted from J. R. R. Tolkien's *The Lord of the Rings* (henceforth *LotR*). We have no embarrassment in claiming that it represented the largest and most complex attempt to date to study audience responses to a film.

Film audiences have long received attention from researchers and policy makers, in two main ways. Questions about the medium's potential dangers for untrained viewers and the impact of its popularity have kept institutions from Hollywood to censor boards preoccupied for over a hundred years. And film producers have wanted to find out just enough about their audiences to be able to persuade them to buy tickets (and associated products, of course). The problems with these two traditions are well known: the culture-control approach has always, despite its "scientism," been heavily moralistic. And producers' research has been limited to that persuasive purpose—and mostly kept secret.

So, at the beginning of the twenty-first century, we still do not know that much about *how* actual film audiences watch films. By way of illustration: in Pierre Bourdieu's paradigmatic work on the sociology of taste, film hardly features at all, and only in the context of a rather crude distinction between artistic and popular cinema.[1] In 1992, Janet Staiger could still maintain that the study of film audiences was a serious lacuna.[2] At the heart of that is what Thomas Austin has identified as the "disciplinary fire wall" between traditions concerned with studying audiences: mass communication studies, cultural studies, film studies, and even, to some extent, literary reception studies.[3] Each nurtures its own institutional traditions and core concepts. Kim Schrøder and colleagues, and Staiger provide excellent overviews of the mass communications tradition, showing its lack of interest in the specificity of films, their form, and semiotic operations. Conversely, Robert Holub and Arild Fetveit, in giving good overviews of literary reception theory, show its almost exclusive reliance on the "text" as central hub of analysis.[4]

Film studies, presumably the discipline with the most interest in films' impact on actual viewers, hardly acknowledges them. It only rarely proceeds beyond the notion of an individual embedded viewer, located in the fuzzy space between text and context, who is either struggling with the consequences of forced identification or prowling the text as an untouchable all-seeing puzzle solver (to paraphrase the paradigmatic formulations of the stances exemplified by Laura Mulvey and David Bordwell, respectively).[5] The exceptions—and there is a growing number of these— are some valuable but small-scale studies of fans, critics, cult and art-house audiences, audiences of violent or controversial films, and star-gazers.[6] But even here, it is hard to find studies that have tried to catch audience involvements in flight, close to when they are actually taking place, and with attention to all the complexities of where, when, and with what preparations viewing takes place.

To go beyond these limitations requires an integrated approach, one that starts from the actual conditions of film watching, and responds to Barbara Klinger's proposal to integrate both synchronic and diachronic processes of reception.[7] This means devoting attention to the accompanying materials to which audiences are exposed even before they reach the theatre. It means addressing the precise ways in which films are brought to audiences. It means focusing on the social and individual conditions under which the films are accessed, watched, appreciated, and digested, and how cultural values and worldviews are used as active points of reference in these processes. And it means investigating people's senses of community, legacy, and affiliation, all of which influence the longer term settling of the viewing experience. Such a complex approach has to be based upon rigorously gathered and transparently analysed empirical evidence. This was our project's goal.

THE LORD OF THE RINGS AS A PHENOMENON

The film that allowed us to attempt these things was the most significant (be it in terms of revenue, visibility, or labour effort) film event of the twenty-first century so far: New Line Cinema and Peter Jackson's film adaptation of Tolkien's trilogy. There is little point in dwelling on the history of *LotR,* since much of this has been told and retold, not least in the welter of talk that accompanied the films' launches. But some elaboration is necessary. First published in 1953 and 1954, after a long gestation from the 1930s, Tolkien's trilogy of Middle-earth, and of the alliance of hobbits, elves, men, dwarves, and others to defeat the evil Sauron by destroying his Ring of Power, has remained in print ever since, and is still a big seller. Translated into all major and many minor languages in the world, it has reputedly sold over 50 million copies, and been read by more than 100 million people.[8] As the advert on the back of the 1999 edition boasts, "the English speaking world is divided into those who have read *The Hobbit* and *The Lord of the Rings* and those who are going to read them." There are also, of course, determined refusers.

The books' success has been discussed from many angles. A first wave of critical debates concerned the books' status within/as literature, with huge disagreements between proponents and opponents. Neatly captured by Neil Isaacs and Rose Zimbardo in their study of Tolkien and his critics, this body of works demonstrates how public and expert opinion on *LotR* is carved along partisan lines of aesthetic and political criticism, with opponents denouncing the books' populism and conservatism, and proponents championing their accessibility and idealist utopianism.[9] The issue of the books' generic denominator "fantasy" is a key topic, with fantasy's unsettled reputation in taste cultures generating both critiques and defences.[10] The dispute around *LotR*'s qualities settled remarkably slowly, and, while there is now a general acknowledgement of the book's esteem, there are still occasional outbursts of indignation.[11]

A second wave of studies has addressed the cultural value and impact of *LotR*. These more recent efforts seek to channel the merits or flaws of the books as fantasy into claims about its place in culture. They usually come in one of two forms: as studies of how Tolkien's books address particular cultural systems (mythologies, religions, philosophies, worldviews), or as studies of its fandoms and uses in contemporary popular culture (what Isaacs and Zimbardo call its suitability for "faddism and fannism, cultism and clubbism").[12] The first form emphasises the cultural value of the text, and is exemplified by a wide range of authors perusing the book for a hidden social or political agenda, signs of how it can be seen as a manifesto of certain beliefs, with the tropes of friendship, belonging, and journey as its key metaphors for contemporary culture.[13] The second form stresses the text's reception, how it sparked a particularly vivid fandom in 1960s counterculture, and how it has since been used by generations of fans (most prominently represented by the Tolkien Society and *theonering.net*, but also in serious fan publications like *Mythlore*, *Mallorn*, *Orcrist*, *Amon Hen*, and the *Minas Tirith Evening Star*).[14] As accounts of these fandoms demonstrate, *LotR* has taken on a wide range of meanings for people, from escapist devotion to musical inspiration to imaginative political potential.[15]

The importance of these debates is not to be underestimated. Their liveliness meant that as far back as the late 1960s and early 1970s, the issue of the books' popularity infiltrated most discussions, forcing critics to address why audiences like it. This situation continues today. So when, as recently as 2003, Brian Rosebury chided critics for still maintaining that only "hard-core Tolkien addicts who've elevated the book to the status of a cult" are responsible for its inclusion in any canons, both he and the critics he cites have to devote several pages to the phenomenon.[16] It has led to a situation in which virtually every consideration of *LotR* is required to spice its account with some facts, and many more speculations, about the books' audiences, and why they are so attached to it. But there's been no solid research on these audiences.

THE LORD OF THE RINGS FILM TRILOGY

These debates around *LotR* increased exponentially with the news that New Line Cinema was to adapt the books into a film trilogy. It also created a new reach in terms of territory and intellectual breadth, some manufactured by the film producers, some seemingly erupting spontaneously.

Of particular interest is the way in which "Hollywood" encountered "New Zealand" in the making of *LotR*, particularly because of the way this illustrates the interweaving of economic forces and cultural rhetorics. Innumerable accounts have rehearsed how the films shifted the books' international reputation and success onto a global scale.[17] By disseminating the *LotR* story into territories relatively unaware of it, like Japan and China, New Line ensured its global reception, which has in turn cemented an "epic" status for the phenomenon in cinema history.[18] The effects of this must include the impact on New Zealand itself, a location amongst the most remote both geographically and in the distance of its indigenous filmmaking economy from the trilogy's legal, financial, and distributive "centre" in Hollywood. Yet while the project's production history demonstrates how Peter Jackson's homeland provided a particularly suitable locale, it also ironically highlights New Zealand's inherent weakness in the global mediascape, not least because it consumes from abroad far more product that it can ever produce indigenously.

What sorts of suitability do we mean? At one extreme, a definition of local suitability lies in the pride in a special "local character," well expressed by the New Zealand filmmaker Costa Botes: "This show couldn't have been made anywhere else in the world . . . because it was so bloody hard."[19] By implication, a distinctive character or spirit predisposes New Zealand to be the location for such arduous projects. Botes' claim merits attention, as he was invited by Peter Jackson to document the production process on video. Such "spin-offs" abound notoriously in tourism and PR through efforts to create a local "heritage" from *LotR*, chiefly by seeking to brand New Zealand permanently as "Middle-earth."

At the other extreme lies the theory of "cultural industries," as proposed by Richard A. Petersen and Narasimhan Anand, who emphasise "six facets of production (technology, law and regulation, industry structure, organisation structure, occupational careers, and market)."[20] Applied to New Zealand, these illuminate the function of its "cultural industries," including film production. But, while Kiwi "film culture" may be almost as old as cinema itself, its scale has always been that of a miniscule "second cinema,"[21] with limited local production and exhibition supported, since the mid-1970s, by various forms of state subsidy and incentive for private producers. No transnational distribution, exhibition, or promotion originates here, except for the sales and promotion activities of the two state-funded bodies, the Film Commission and Film New Zealand. Understood within David Hesmondhalgh's historical categories for the "cultural industries," New Zealand film culture therefore still displays a "patronage"[22] by the state to enable film as cultural expression and as promoter of new talent. There has never been a "corporate professional" level to match Hollywood. Filmmaking in New Zealand has never achieved any vertical integration resembling Hollywood structures. Rather, it has always operated horizontally by variously integrating individuals and individual firms into particular projects—as it did with *LotR*.

Support from the New Zealand State for the *LotR* project figured notably in the naming of a designated minister to work with the production team, and in the New Zealand army furnishing logistical support and extras, whilst public funds supported PR abroad as well as the refurbishing of the venue for the *Return of the King* premiere in Wellington. Less well known is the role of the Inland Revenue and the New Zealand dollar itself. Economically, when the project arrived in 1998, the comparative weakness of the New Zealand dollar favoured the location, but the production gained most from its favourable tax status. This was so favourable that the minister of finance commented publicly, "It would be very reasonable if the New Zealand taxpayer got free seats."[23] Subsequently, he has resolutely refused to extend the same tax provisions to filmmaking or any other occupation, leaving *LotR* with a unique status, with the state effectively indemnifying its overseas producers against significant loss.

It is true that, post-*LotR*, in 2004–5 New Zealand filmmaking enjoyed its most productive year ever, as far as the release of films either substantially made in New Zealand (*King Kong*, Peter Jackson, 2005) or about the place (*The World's Fastest Indian*, Roger Donaldson, 2005) goes.[24] Yet despite these, the question still remains whether the *LotR* phenomenon has achieved for New Zealand "film culture" anything more than a "Frodo economy,"[25] a brief brushfire illuminating the familiar vicissitudes of small-scale screen production. Or, as Helen Martin and Geoff Lealand asked in their recent survey, "What is the relationship between the local (indigenous film) and the global (New Zealand as all-purpose film location)? Are there negative outcomes as well as positive? Will the prevailing fashion for New Zealand last beyond the next few years?" Although their account recognises the post-*LotR* activity, Martin and Lealand stress how it is dictated by offshore interests, and carefully leave the long-term prospects for New Zealand filmmaking open: "In this climate, any discussion of New Zealand film must be characterised by all kinds of qualifications, reservations and ambiguity."[26] Any shift caused by *LotR* in the status of New Zealand's "film culture" remains at best uncertain.

Given these parameters, the decision by New Line Cinema to fund Peter Jackson may not have been quite as risky as it first appeared. And the production benefited greatly from carefully managed advance publicity, as Bertha Chin and Jonathan Gray demonstrate in their study of prefigurations of the first film in the trilogy, *The Fellowship of the Ring*, which was executed in a culture of high anticipation.[27] All this paid off in spades. The trilogy made about $3 billion worldwide in theatrical revenue only. That income, coupled with huge earnings from tie-ins and merchandising[28] (some of which also included officially endorsed publications adding their own perspective to the *Lord of the Rings* critical discourse),[29] and highly successful sales of DVDs and videos, along with runaway success in the 2004 Oscars, made what could have been a death-knell commitment by New Line into an astonishing success for the company.[30]

DEBATES ON *THE LORD OF THE RINGS* PHENOMENON AFTER THE FILM RELEASE

As could be expected, one wave of discussions concentrated on the comparison between book and film, often employing the same highbrow-lowbrow distinctions as had been present in the pre-film debates, but enriching them with the "faithfulness" argument actually typical of an older, and now passing, style of adaptation studies.[31] A second wave of discussions decided to ignore the source material and instead concentrate on the films *as films*. In such discussions, the main foci tend to be aesthetics and genre, with ample attention for the auteur Peter Jackson, his past as a cult-horror filmmaker, and the value of "filmic fantasy" in an era of digital special effects.[32] But a third type of discussion is perhaps the most intriguing. *LotR* became a focus of interest for a renewed wish, especially from religious quarters, to look upon films almost as sermons, to be mined for their moral and philosophical potentials.[33] Alongside these, and in some respects their pessimistic equivalent, there soon followed considerations of cultural impact, significance, and appeal. Such studies often concentrate on curious parallels between the stories and contemporary real-life politics and culture (like terrorism or the war in Iraq), on the changes in its fandoms, or on particular instances of its critical reception.[34] Among these are investigations of the challenges posed by dealing with a story that spreads itself out over book, film, DVD, games, and myriads of other different media platforms.[35]

THE *LORD OF THE RINGS* RESEARCH PROJECT

But amidst all this, the actual audiences, their interaction with the films and all this attendant noise, were again sadly overlooked—or better, taken as something that observers and critics could fairly speculate on.

An understanding of these actual, natural audiences is what our project aimed for. The project had small, very local and personal beginnings. Martin Barker, who became its director, read and loved the books back in the late 1950s, and carried that pleasure forward to the BBC's 1981 radio version. But he didn't fall in love with the films, for complicated reasons that made him wonder about other people's responses.[36] He started exploring the films' surrounding contexts: production companies and systems, marketing practices, merchandising, reviews, and other cultural "noise" that typically accompanies Hollywood films. Then came a circulating email, with its image of George Bush wearing the One Ring, and the tag-line "Frodo Has Failed." This provoked in him thoughts about the ways in which a film generates wider cultural resonances. With colleagues Ernest Mathijs and Janet Jones, a proposal for an ambitious multinational project was developed and submitted to the British Economic and Social Research Council for core funding.[37] At a very early point, colleagues at Waikato University in New Zealand, who were already researching the impact of the *LotR* production on their country, became involved in the project. Together, we issued a call for interested researchers anywhere in the world to join us.

Ultimately, researchers connected with twenty countries "signed up" to play a part in the project, all of them with their own mix of personal, academic, and "political" reasons for wanting to do so.[38] What held everyone together was the question of the impact of a Hollywood product on actual local audiences, with particular emphasis on three key issues:

1. the cross-national reception of international communications;
2. the functions and role of fantasy within contemporary culture; and
3. the role of marketing and publicity regimes in prefiguring a film's reception.

There has been a long debate about "Hollywoodisation," "cultural imperialism," and the impact on national cultures of industrialised cultural production. One side in this debate, exemplified by Armand Mattelart, focuses on media content as the conveyor of imperialist messages. Another, championed by Harold Innis, stresses the imperialistic potential of media export in itself, regardless of the message transmitted.[39] But this debate has been ill served with actual studies of audiences. Sonia Livingstone and Annabelle Sreberny have written on some of the dangers involved in doing cross-cultural research, and it is difficult not to read in their warnings a resignation that such research is practically unachievable.[40] In the main it has been conducted as a series of semiseparate studies in a number of individual countries that are then compared. It is hard to find a study that has generated *cross-country* and therefore *cross-cultural* data and materials. Moreover, the few attempts we found exclude film: they focus on television formats or are not medium specific.[41] *LotR* provided a great potential case study because of its complexities: a very "English" story and origins; a filming process celebrating New Zealand, with funding from a subsidiary of Hollywood's largest company, Time-Warner. How might audiences' responses be affected by these, and what could this reveal about the ways local, national, and cross-national cultures are formed.

LotR belongs to the "fantasy" genre. It constructs an alternate world, and there plays out enlarged human dilemmas. The problem is that much talk about the concept of "fantasy" seems to veer among unhelpful poles: the pole of irrelevance ("it's only sheer fantasy"), the pole of absorption ("people can become lost in their fantasy worlds, lose the distinction between reality and fantasy"), and the psychoanalytic pole ("people's selves are constructs out of their childhood fantasies" and "fantasy harbours the fears of our selves").[42] As ever, there has been little attempt to test the claims in these. We needed to operationalise the concept of "fantasy." This is beginning to be done, especially in relation to children, in a small number of cases.[43] What might a substantial, sophisticated study of audience responses to a fantasy film reveal that could contribute to this debate, or perhaps change its terms of reference?

In recent years, within film studies, there has been a shift of attention from primarily examining films as "texts" to recognising the ways in which they are prefigured by a welter of publicity and marketing, and mediated by many other kinds of talk. Some good work has been done on particular films, but little comparative work yet exists.[44] That was the challenge for us. How could we research the ways in which, in different country contexts, varied ways of thinking about the film emerged, and, from there, move to capturing the impact of these on various audience groups within those countries?

METHODOLOGICAL CHALLENGES

Tackling these was a considerable methodological test. But while there were individual studies and methods upon which we could draw, we estimated the broader shape and direction of our field to be distinctly unhelpful. Audience research is, in fact, in a complicated state. On the one hand, American mass communications research—still the clear favourite among opinion leaders and policy makers—combines a veneer of sophistication that it obtains from its statistical strictness with a real barrenness of questions ("Do films affect us?"; "Why do people like them?"; "Are they safe or harmful?") and concepts (for example, "mood," "arousal," "entertainment").[45] These questions and concepts couple with a resolute refusal to take any account of how audiences may characterise their own experiences. Analysts will decide what the appropriate categories are, and will conduct content analyses to determine the risks. So, even if children say that they do not see cartoons as "violent," they are, because analysts say so. The audiences are not only wrong, they are simply not to be trusted.[46] Instead, they are to be "reduced" to virtual automata, untouched by culture and history.

On the other hand, there has been the cultural studies tradition. This has very valuably, and productively, committed itself to unpacking the complexities in cultural forms (against the naïveté of mass communications' content analyses), and in audiences' responses to them (against mass communications' simplistic notions of cumulative and passively absorbed "effects"). But it has become stuck in at least two ways. First, an overwhelming adherence to Stuart Hall's encoding-decoding model has led to a search for and celebration of responses that may be classed as "resistant" (while, in the background, lurks the silhouette figure of the "unresistant"). Second, methodologically, this research rarely transcends the snapshot. The considerable problems of managing large numbers of responses, each of which must be respected for its semiotic richness, has made it very hard indeed to see how any rigorous propositions could be advanced or tested.[47]

We therefore faced a series of linked theoretical and methodological challenges. Although closely interrelated, they can, for sake of argument, be separated into four concerns.

Integrating Quantitative and Qualitative Investigations

Consider this tiny fragment, the answer by one person to two questions in our questionnaire database:

> This is a film for which I had been waiting breathlessly for two years. On the day of the release itself my body felt numb (except for my stomach where a herd of Mumakil were rampaging!). I experienced a mixture of extreme joy that I was going to see *Return* coupled with sadness that the journey's at an end. . . . In a time when it is all too easy to become disillusioned with the world around us it was beautiful and uplifting to see how millions around the world took this tale of honour love and duty to their hearts. Through the film I have come into contact with generous honourable people who give me a real hope for the future.

To our eyes, just on its own, this fragment is rich beyond measure in possibilities and implications. Audience responses to films are complex, even when they are short. They can include feelings, views, and opinions that are not easily condensed into numerical codes—try it on the above. But some sort of quantification of data is needed if we are to pass beyond snapshots. The trouble is that the requirements of coding in quantitative research *reduces* materials into its categories. Any aspect of the materials not fitting the categories, distinctions, oppositions, and other sorting operations used primarily on quantitative information falls outside the frame of analysis. It is not just that it is ignored; it is unwanted, annoying noise. We needed to preserve the complexity, but still be able to generalise from it (map the whole terrain of audience responses, distinguish different groups, demonstrate patterned connections, even show trends over time).

So the first, crucial challenge was to combine quantitative and qualitative methods. This has been an ambition of audience research for some time, but it is not easy. Even one of the best attempts known to us, a cross-cultural study by Sonia Livingstone and colleagues, in the end really only uses the qualitative materials to *illustrate* conclusions arrived at by quantitative means.[48]

Our solution was to build into the structure of our investigation ways of combining quantifiable responses. An example: the multiple-choice question "How much did you enjoy the film?" was coupled with asking people to explain what their answer *means* ("What did you think of the film?"). In itself such a procedure is not new: several library search engines and text-mining procedures use it (the most obvious example being Lexis-Nexis). But as a route to analysing audiences, we do not think it has been used before. By configuring our collected materials so that they would fit a relational database, we would allow quantitative and qualitative data to play equally important roles as sorting devices for trends.

But that was just a first stage. We also needed questions that, in combination, would enable us to look for patterns across both quantitative and qualitative responses. Putting it crudely, suppose we found that young females, irrespective of country, tended to choose the same favourite character; we needed then to be able to explore their answers to other questions if we were to discover *why* this might be the case. We were also operating globally, and eventually gathered responses in fourteen languages. If we wanted to gather even minimal demographic information (for example, about occupations), we had to work with the fact that there are no universal definitions for job categories. Indeed, ideally, we wanted to know not just *what* people did, but *what sort of work they considered it to be.* For all these, we drew initially on a matrix system that had been developed by Barker, and tested on *Crash, Straw Dogs,* and (with Mathijs) *A Clockwork Orange.*[49] The principle here was to get audiences to assign themselves along key dimensions (in these cases, Enjoyment and Approval), and then explore the ways people within each combination of responses talk about the film. What do those within each "cell" see in the film? How alike or unalike are responses within each "cell"? How do they view each other? And so on. But of course our choice of dimensions for self-allocation is critical. In the case of *LotR,* our key self-allocation question gave people a list of twelve ways they might characterise the story, asking them to choose up to three. Once we had struggled with the nature of this list, and the complicated translation issues, this became our most productive tool, as the rest of this book will hopefully demonstrate.

Reception Trajectory: Contexts of Viewing

The second challenge concerns timing, in this case the structuring of the collection of data according to trajectories of reception. As audiences have access to, and might consider their own viewing in the light of, materials previously (or subsequently) available in the public sphere, the points at which such materials become available, and how they interrelate, becomes quintessential for finding out how audiences' views are informed by them. Since the late 1990s, some good research has been carried out into the publicity run-ups to theatrical releases.[50] But if it considers it at all, this research still tends to assume a homogeneous and uniform reception process. This is because most reception research uses either a synchronic or a diachronic approach to materials available in the public sphere. A diachronic approach investigates how different phases of reception *follow* each other, from the very beginning until months or even years after the release of a film. A synchronic approach researches all the elements of a film's reception at a given point in time. Diachronic approaches show evolutions; synchronic approaches show debates. The combination of the two approaches is described by Fernand Braudel of the *Annales* school as an essential step toward "total history," capturing the move through time of a work and its surroundings.[51]

The integration of the two approaches for contemporary materials is complicated by two theoretical problems. The first is determining the content and status of the materials to be collected. It can be solved by considering all materials—news reports, advertisements, reviews, essays, DVD extras, interviews, and so on—as having the same semiotic value as *talk*, within particular specific political-economical perspectives. In a post-Marxist sense, this means seeing the materials as equipped with "sign value." But this does not mean one needs to resign to the ultimate incompatibility and incommensurability of such materials (a position taken by Jean Baudrillard).[52] They are not un-researchable. Given that their *public presence* is what all these types of "talk" have in common, careful attention to the contexts within which such "talk" is uttered makes their content comparable, hence providing a set point of reference for their analysis. Barker has attempted to address this by going over the possibilities of analysing them as *ancillary materials* that carry significant information about, and indeed some of the core characteristics *of,* the film texts they are supposed to accompany. In fact, as Barker notes, the realisation that such ancillary materials have come to play an essential role in setting up avenues of interpretation for films necessitates giving them as much scrutiny as the films themselves, if not more. In addition, treating these materials as "talk" also enables comparisons with the kinds of talk produced by actual audiences when they express their opinions about a film.[53]

The second problem was defining a starting point for collecting materials. Given the myriad ways in which films get released, this is a recurrent problem in film studies. In the case of *RotK*, the release dates are straightforward enough, and the fact that they are—following blockbuster opening weekend and general market saturation strategies—released quasi-simultaneously, makes it not that difficult to get a firm and fixed point of reference. But "talk" about the film had been present in the public sphere since years before the films' releases.[54] How does one structure this jungle of materials? The solution suggested by Mathijs was again to take the public presence of such talk as determining its validity (it needs to be accessible), and to see the run-up period, the actual release period, and the aftermath of the release as a *reception trajectory,* turning the point of release into one of several key points along a road of receptions.[55]

Modality: Ways of Viewing

The third challenge involves a problem we have already touched upon, how to deal with the issue of *modalities of perception:* How do different audiences attach a *kind of reality* to the film? In part our thinking about this is a response to some recent attempts to theorise perceptions of audiovisual representations, especially those by Rick Altman (whose account of how genres originate, historically, has much to teach, but who stops short on the role of the audience), David Bordwell (whose account of different levels of film comprehension invites us to explore how theoretically articulated different responses may be), Kendall Walton (who, along with others, has tackled the issue of how "real" films become for audiences), and David Lewis and Nicholas Rescher (who have approached Walton's issue from the point of view of the "construction of possible worlds").[56] The questions these works address are vital, since they address the issue of what it means to engage in a fictional world. Aside from these approaches, valuable work on modality has been done by semiotic theoreticians such as Gunther Kress and Theo van Leeuwen.[57] From these researchers come not only some of the richest understandings of the issues involved, but also some of the most articulated methods of researching them. But they are still not applied to audiences.

Our task was to conceive ways of drawing out from audiences all the complexities of how they think the relationship between Middle-earth and our world works, and then have the means to analyse that talk. This required, we think, attention to four aspects of people's responses: the *degree*, the *kind*, the *context*, and the *salience* of the "reality" attached to them. A mile and more away from the persistent concerns about whether people can tell, or might lose, the distinction between "fantasy" and "reality," *modality* addresses the immensely varied ways in which we accord trusted status to ideas, stories, characters, and images.

Degree

Modality considerations first arose in relation to sentences like, say, "It's a monster." Sententially, this is a propositional claim. But it can be, and often is, modified in important ways ("It might be a monster"; "It's some kind of monster"; "It's a really scary monster"; "He's a monster if you get him angry"). Each of these alters the force of monstrousness, qualifies the implied risk in some way. This is the first level of operation of modality: to increase or decrease the definiteness associated with a propositional claim. One or two of these assertions begin to put conditions on when and how "monsterhood" might show itself—because, after all, monsters are things that concern us. Their meaning is partly in the reactions we might have to them. Things get more complicated at the moment when we begin to state or imply contexts to propositions about monsters ("Let's pretend it's a monster"—or even "Let's pretend you're a monster"). The moment we point to these features, new elements begin to intrude—for example, Who is doing this, with whom? What "figures" of monster-ness are they drawing on?—and we have to pass beyond the level of the sentence.

Kind

At the second level, the isolated claim about "monsterhood" begins to gain a wider context. Consider the proposition: "Gollum is the real monster." This sentence is not about the *literal* status of Gollum, but about something that requires us to see wider. It invokes a set of criteria: Against what measures should we evaluate Gollum? By comparison with whom is he to be judged? What is a monster in this situation, and what, indeed, *is* "this situation"? The answers could be very varied. It could just be Gollum's physical appearance—he is almost, but not quite, human, and that could make him more abhorrent than the Orcs, who are outrageously ugly. It could be his scheming, his deceitfulness and double persona. The first of these is, of course, film specific: Tolkien does not provide that much description of Gollum, while the films clearly embody him. The second belongs to both books and films, albeit with some different emphases. But it could also, with ease, outrun books and films. Gollum may be measured against criteria, against figures, real people and situations outside the story-world. To call a politician a "real Gollum" is to highlight characteristics and, perhaps, to clarify by imaginative exaggeration a tendency we see in them. They are sneaky, untrustworthy, deceitful, slimy on the inside. So, at the second level, modality addresses the *kinds of criteria* against which we measure things.

Context

The child who says to his or her parent, "Pretend you are a monster" is doing something extraordinarily complex. He or she is summoning up a set of rules of engagement. (I want to play, and I want you to be scary, but not too scary, just enough that I will be really mock-frightened. I can do this with you, because you are my dad, and you do this kind of thing well. I think you know what I mean by "monster" because you read me that story, and I told you about that dream I had. We both know what play-monsters *do* [they raise their hands and pretend to catch me—maybe do catch me—and then they hug me or something like that] because we know what "play" is. But if I was to do this with one of my friends, we would play differently. And so on.) A context of reality and imagination is invoked, along with a set of shared, stock figures, which are borrowed from personal past histories and culturally encountered materials. This point is important. Stories are always set within contexts, which combine the real and the imaginary, the known and the guessed at, the rule-governed and the unknown. We have to know how to share contexts, but of course they are always changing. So, the *LotR* film trilogy comes out within a whole range of contexts that may shape the criteria we use for responding to and evaluating it. Contexts of: the books, and knowledge of and feelings about them; the cinema, and where, how, and with whom we watch the films; the other films the trilogy is in competition with; the "hype" accompanying the films; the actors who appear in them; and, of course, a host of things beyond—Hollywood, America, New Zealand, the state of the world into which the films emerge, and on which they might even be seen to be commenting (recall that email of Bush as virtual Sauron).

Salience

All these *matter* to us more or less. The child who does not often play with her father may invest more in the opportunity for fierce play than one who routinely does this most days, because it involves physical, even risky, contact. Going through a difficult transition (entering school, for example) could even give metaphorical meaning to "scary monsters," to be worked through by play. A person going to the cinema to see the *LotR* films might just not want to miss out on something that she or he knows will be water-cooler topic of the week. It might be the end of a twenty-year wait, to see someone else's visualisation of a story frequently revisited, built into a repertoire of emotions and cognitions and imaginative parallels—so that much is at stake.

These four aspects make up what we mean by the term *modality*. They cannot operate independently of each other. Separately and together, they are just what make people's reactions to films like the *LotR* trilogy so very interesting, complicated, and worthwhile.

The challenge for our project was to bring into view the ways in which people were (or weren't) convinced of the "truth" of the film they were watching; the kind of world they saw Middle-earth as constituting; within what real and imaginative contexts they set their responses (and that includes other people "with whom" they felt they were watching); and why and how much it all *mattered* to them. In short, what criteria were applied to the film, what "rules" (like the child's rules for monster-play) were enacted, and were they met and adhered to by the film?

Strategies of Viewing

The fourth challenge is the most complicated, because it puts to work the three preceding ones. Nobody ever just "happens" to watch a film in the cinema. Everybody—sometimes more, sometimes less—is *prepared* to watch and respond to a film. And that makes a difference in how we do these things, and how we do them again next time. The concept of "viewing strategy" is our summarising phrase for three processes audiences go through:

Preparation

It might be for ten minutes, a week, a month, or twenty years, but audiences generally know in advance that they are going to see a film. And they learn things about it. With greater or lesser intensity, these processes prepare and shape our expectations: What can I expect from this film? What do I hope for? Who should I go with, and perhaps to which cinema? What do I want to know about reviews, about the film's story, its production, its stars, their stories, gossip, and so on? What do I *not* want to know—what should be avoided? Some things audiences would find hard to avoid—posters, trailers, headlines, and cover images, for example. And the sheer weight and omnipresence of talk and pictures generate a buzz that it is hard to miss. All these, and much more, help develop images of what kind of an experience might be hoped for and expected from seeing the film. In addition, the fact that *RotK* was the closing segment of the trilogy further strengthens the presumption that most of the audience were well primed to see it.

The Cinematic Experience

Only recently has there been much attention to the complexities of seeing a film.[58] For instance, we know, because we saw and heard it, we were repeatedly told about it, and we did it ourselves, that in many cinemas the opening titles of the third film produced a deep collective sigh as people settled in for what they hoped and expected to be a powerful experience. (Some, of course, would be carrying fears and existing disappointments into their viewing.) But those sighs were the beginning of a rich brew of sensory experiences, emotional responses, cognitive struggles with what is happening and where it is going, and the imaginative creation of a "world" into which people more or less fully enter. From these come half-formed overall responses, things being put into memory for later retelling and discussion. There are moments of irritation, things not quite right—an often-heard comment when adaptations are concerned. What is clear is that however much people may know, they still need to experience it, and they want the physical and emotional "shocks" and surprises that are part of the film. What is also clear, but more controversial since its implications have rarely been followed through, is that in any film, but perhaps particularly in films as richly sensuous, finely crafted, and imaginatively wrought as the *LotR* trilogy, there is simply always too much to take in. People attend first to the elements that are most important to them, that become pushed to the forefront. They follow, in other words, a *strategy* of engaging and following. Of course that can be interrupted or stalled. One strategy can be, of course, to "lie back and think of England," to allow the film to come at you in a multisensory way, to "fill you up." This might be called "strategic passivity." But it is still a strategy, and as a result some features will be less attended to, and therefore less responded to as a participant begins to move to grasping the "whole" that is his or her experience of the film, and to formulating a first judgement on its nature and quality.

Sedimentation

Many people enjoy talking about things as intense as film experiences. It is one reason for going in company. But shared physical presence aside, there are also people for whom we ready conversations afterwards. And there is our self, too, that part of our mind with whom we hold an internal conversation: What did I think of that? Did it close the trilogy effectively? Which parts of the book did it treat properly? What's my estimation of the battle scenes? Why did that bit remind me of another film? It can take quite a while, and we should not underestimate the importance of people saying (as many did to us) that they were lost for words. The experience is still being savoured, like a new taste. From "Wow!" to lists of superlatives, the experience is still the predominant thing. But over time, the experience is worked over with significant others. The "sense of the whole," and of a judgment on it, becomes more articulated. We have tried out words, and often shared them, and measured them against other peoples.'

The routes across these three are what we mean by a "viewing strategy." But what previous research has shown, convincingly, is that the more patterned and grounded the expectations with which people go, the more there are principles shaping selection and attention, the more the urge to construct a "sense of the whole" and to arrive at evaluations.[59] Our goal was to reach into the fabric of these strategies, and to draw out their nature and implications.

This is a sample of the problems we needed to tackle. Others emerged later. For instance, we were committed to using discourse analytic approaches to our audiences' talk. But, as we revisited this domain and came to try to use its procedures, it became clear, first, that as currently practised, most versions (and there are many) are unsuited to being used on large data sets. Further, many versions of discourse analysis incorporate assumptions about discursive power that, for us as audience researchers, were precisely what we wanted to *test*. We could not presume one way in which either the films or their accompanying materials might be powerful.[60] Our solutions to these dilemmas are hopefully displayed clearly enough in subsequent chapters.

RESEARCH METHODOLOGY: FROM PRINCIPLES TO METHODS

There is no such thing as perfect research. There are only better or worse ways of tackling questions under the conditions given and constraining the project. We set ourselves these very ambitious goals—big questions, wide reach—and, within the resources available to us, looked to gather as much as we could, in forms that could get us furthest toward being able to answer at least some of our questions.

It was fairly easy to write down the big intentions that drove our project, but it was quite another matter to do the things that have to follow from saying them. We had to think through what these questions entail: What kinds of understanding of Tolkien's story, of the film, and of audiences' relations to them, are indicated by these questions, and what types of methods are the consequences of asking them? Here was an exceptional opportunity, a film being released in three parts, giving us two years to get ready for the worldwide launch of *RotK* on December 17, 2003. This gave us the time to work toward solutions, and plan the course of the research. In the end, we worked through three stages:

1. exhaustive collection of prefigurative and reception materials;
2. a worldwide audience questionnaire; and
3. in-depth follow-up interviews with some questionnaire respondents.

STAGE 1: PREFIGURATION AND RECEPTION

From October 1, 2003, to January 1, 2004, we gathered as wide an array of ancillary materials as we could. We wanted to be able to study the fullest possible range of the materials that prefigure the film for audiences: publicity and marketing, merchandise and other licensed materials, press, magazine, radio, and television coverage, and Internet materials. Essentially, we had the (of course, unachievable) ambition to gather every public item, of any kind, that made mention of *LotR* in any context. This meant that we were interested in anything that mentioned the films or books, even if this was just a passing mention. In the United Kingdom alone, this gave us more than 2,500 items, gathered by a combination of systematic searches in the national press, radio, and television and in a wide range of magazines, and just hoovering up every other kind of material (from acquiring postcards, to clipping articles from free magazines, to photographing store displays, and so on). Managing these required a structured approach, so that the significant features of these materials could be entered into a quantitative/qualitative database parallel to the one containing our audiences' responses. How we did this, exactly, is explained in the closing methodology chapter.

Of course the mere presence of materials does not guarantee their use, or even their visibility among the masses of other circulating materials. We needed to be able to find out which materials were actually drawn upon by audiences. This first stage was therefore complemented, and checked, by data from the second stage, in the questionnaire. There, we asked audiences to tell us which top three sources they had particularly consulted to learn about the film in the run-up to its release. Some of the results of this are set out in chapter 2.[61]

STAGE 2: THE AUDIENCE QUESTIONNAIRE

The second and most crucial stage would be a questionnaire. This was broadly modelled on a combination of two prior projects: first, a project on the British controversy over David Cronenberg's film *Crash*.[62] The questionnaire for that project trialled the method of asking audiences to assign themselves along some key dimensions, while simultaneously asking them to say what those self-allocations meant to them. But in this case, we also wanted to make this primarily a web-based questionnaire because of some benefits accruing from this:

1. that all the web-completed questionnaires could be compiled automatically into a database, allowing us to manage very large numbers, and thence making many kinds of automated analysis possible;
2. that the questionnaire could be publicised worldwide, and even appear in many different languages;
3. that we should be able to generate large numbers of responses quite "cheaply," through reaching people via email lists, web sites, and other electronic communication routes.

We therefore drew on Janet Jones' experience of using such a questionnaire in research on responses to *Big Brother*. Of course, the risk was that we would too easily recruit enthusiasts in this way, and might have more problems attracting the reluctant, the critical, and the hostile. To mitigate this, we therefore also prepared paper versions of the questionnaire, and in a number of countries we were able to recruit helpers to approach people at cinemas. The data from the resultant completed forms—more than two thousand across the world—of course had then to be manually entered.

The questionnaire combined several different kinds of questions:

1. We asked respondents to allocate themselves via multiple-choice questions on several dimensions: their degree of enjoyment, and the importance of the film to them (using five-point Likert scales), on the *kind of story* it was for them (our key modality question), and the main source of their expectations about the film (eight choices or their own nomination). In among these we asked people to tell us the meanings of their answers in their own words.
2. We asked additional open questions about: where in their imagination Middle-earth exists; their favourite character; the most memorable, and most disappointing, moment in the film, and whether they felt that viewing the film had been primarily a personal or a social experience. (A final question gave an opportunity to add anything they felt we had missed.)
3. We also sought some sociodemographic and general background information: age, sex, and occupation (for the important debate on this, see our methodology chapter); how often they had seen the other parts of the film trilogy; how much they had read the books; and in what country they were living. Finally, our questionnaire automatically recorded which of the fourteen language options people were using.[63]

The questionnaire went online on the day of *RotK*'s general release, and, over the next six months, 24,739 people completed it.[64] In the United Kingdom, having committed ourselves to attracting 2,000 responses, we ultimately achieved 3,115 (of which more than 500 were completed on paper). These questionnaires are crucial. They are the common resource of the whole international project network. We believe this book shows how much has already been achieved through analysing them. Considering the richness of these questionnaire responses, much more is surely possible. They are now freely available, via the British Economic and Social Data Services, to any other researcher who wishes to use them.

STAGE 3: INTERVIEWS

The final stage was a very challenging one. The idea was to conduct an early round of analysis of the questionnaire responses in order to identify emergent patterns and groupings, and then to conduct follow-up interviews with individuals who appeared to typify these, in order to flesh out their meaning. This was demanding, and expensive. Because only some of our research teams had funding, only a few participating countries were able to complete this stage. In the United Kingdom, we managed 107 telephone interviews, averaging an hour in length. This alone is a formidable body of materials. Essentially, we asked people to tell us more about their answers to all areas of the questionnaire, but supplemented these by getting them to tell us how, when, and with whom they had seen the film, their sense of the event at the cinema, their feelings about the film trilogy's worldwide success (this produced some very striking answers), how long they had known Tolkien's story, and its importance in their lives. We encountered overwhelming delight from just about everyone at being given the chance to talk about these things.

THE OUTCOMES OF THE PROJECT

We do not talk in this introduction about the kinds and directions of analysis that we have deployed on our big body of materials. The rest of the book should do this. We would say only two things about this.

In the design and conduct of this project, it could actually be a problem that our fellow researchers in this project came from quite different research backgrounds and traditions. But when it came to the *analysis,* the problem became a virtue. Different individuals and groups tackled varying questions and problems, exploring sections and aspects of the materials in contrasting ways. Different software preferences allowed diverse challenges to be met. Different conceptions of the film-audience relationship prompted people to deal with different topics and aspects. The sheer richness of what we gathered has enabled a real confluence of methods—each one adding something genuinely new to our knowledge and understanding of audiences generally, of the functions of film fantasy, and specifically of the place of J. R. R. Tolkien's story-world in contemporary culture.

A project of this size also fans out in different sorts of disseminations. One of the features of this research was that it was taking some quite global concepts ("fantasy," "Hollywoodisation," and so on) and seeking to develop operational means of exploring them. That meant that there was no simple direct-testing relationship between our research implements and our founding questions. The downside of that was that we could, if we were not careful, lose sight of our original purposes. But the upside (which could also of course be a problem) was that in the course of gathering such complex and wide-ranging materials and data, inevitably, a host of other questions and possibilities might emerge. And they did. Aside from this book, which has sought to stay close to the core motivating topics of the project, many other publications are emerging in different places, presenting outcomes from the project. It was agreed among the teams that different avenues of publication and presentation were available to all members of the project, as long as due reference was given to the project and to this—the core book. The fact that we are already seeing a wide diversity in such publications speaks of the project's potential for academically generated knowledge. The fact that much of these publications seem to share a common attitude toward film audience research testifies to the necessity of the endeavour.[65] If we are all now a bit exhausted, the mountain has been definitely worth climbing.

CHAPTER ONE

The Lord of the Rings

Selling the Franchise

JANET WASKO

> For sheer commerciality, Rings has arguably become the most profitable fictional work of all time.
>
> —ETHAN GILSDORF

INTRODUCTION

By most accounts, New Line Cinema's version of *The Lord of the Rings* was a huge success. The three films attracted over $3 billion at the worldwide box office, plus other revenue still rolling in from other media outlets and merchandise. The films won seventeen Academy Awards and the praise of fans and critics around the world. This chapter will discuss *LotR* as a franchise, the background and ownership of the property, and the marketing and merchandising connected to the New Line films, especially *The Return of the King*.[1]

LOTR AS A FRANCHISE

New Line Cinema claims that it is "a pioneer in franchise filmmaking and its *LotR* trilogy . . . is one of the most successful and most honored film franchises in history."[2]

The concept of a *franchise,* as it relates to film or entertainment, has been defined by some to mean simply sequels. However, a better description is a property or concept that is repeatable in multiple media platforms or outlets with merchandising and tie-in potential. *Merchandise* includes commodities that derive from a film, while *tie-ins* represent already existing products featuring (that is, tied to) a film. (*Product placements,* not relevant here, are products that are featured in a film.) It works particularly well if the franchise includes reoccurring and copyrightable characters and story elements. The *LotR* trilogy represents an ideal franchise for a diversified entertainment conglomerate for three reasons:

1. *Its already established popularity.* The three *LotR* films draw on an already successful set of books and thus tap into a huge potential audience already familiar with the story and characters. The books are sometimes considered children's literature (or what *Variety* calls "kiddie lit"), which has become a common standby for Hollywood blockbusters or franchises (an obvious example is the *Harry Potter* franchise). As *Variety* explains, these types of films "are the perfect fuel for the synergy machine(s)" that characterise the vertically integrated companies that own the Hollywood studios.[3]

2. *Its appeal across demographic groups.* Even though *Variety* may characterise *LotR* as "kiddie lit," it is obvious that the books have a much wider appeal. Indeed, *LotR* is a film franchise that hoped to appeal to a wide range of age groups—and succeeded. According to a New Line executive, the only audience group that wasn't particularly attracted is the "50+ woman," the "Achilles heel" of the franchise.[4]

3. *Its merchandise potential.* The movies offer countless merchandising possibilities due to this wide appeal, as well as the huge numbers of characters with costumes, jewelry, swords, and other weapons.

All of these points are captured rather well in a statement by the CEO of Toy Biz (one of *LotR*'s key merchandisers): "With its intricately detailed fantasy world, incredible range of highly-unique fantasy characters, and a story that has captivated kids and adults alike for more than 40 years, *The Lord of the Rings* has enormous potential in the marketplace."[5] Indeed, *LotR* lived up to its potential. The franchise is considered the fourth most successful film franchise of all time, according to Box Office Mojo (see table 1.1).

BACKGROUND OF THE *LORD OF THE RINGS* TRILOGY

The ownership of the rights to *LotR* is important in order to understand who controls and benefits from the franchise. Initially, J. R. R. Tolkien signed a contract to publish *LotR* with George Allen and Unwin, which included a 50/50 profit-sharing deal. Because of the length, the book was published in three parts. In August 1954, 3,500 copies of the first installment, *The Fellowship of the Rings*, were released.

Table 1.1: Box Office Mojo's Top Franchises

Franchise	Total Gross* (in millions $)	No. of Films	Average per Ffilm (in millions $)
Star Wars	$1,882.8	6	$313.8
James Bond	$1,435.8	22	$65.3
Harry Potter	$1,119.1	4	$279.8
Lord of the Rings	$1,060.7	4	$265.2
Batman	$ 916.3	6	$152.7
Spider-Man	$ 777.3	2	$388.6
Jurassic Park	$ 767.3	3	$255.8
Star Trek	$ 755.6	10	$75.6

Source: http://www.boxofficemojo.com/franchises/ (accessed 1/15/07).
*These figures report domestic theatrical box office grosses only.

Table 1.2: *Lord of the Rings:* The Movies

Title	Gross	Theatres	Opening	Theatres	Date
The Return of the King	$377,027,325	3,703	$72,629,713	3,703	12/17/03
The Two Towers	$339,789,881	3,622	$62,007,528	3,622	12/18/02
Fellowship of the Ring	$313,364,114	3,381	$47,211,490	3,359	12/19/01
The Lord of the Rings	$30,471,420	31	$626,649	31	11/15/78 (UA/1978)
Lifetime gross total:	$1,060,652,740				

Source: http://www.boxofficemojo.com/franchises/chart/?id=lordoftherings.htm.

It was republished six weeks later because of its initial success. The second installment, *Two Towers*, was published in November 1954, and the third and final installment, *RotK*, in October 1955.[6]

In 1967, Tolkien sold the film and other merchandising rights for *LotR* to United Artists.[7] In 1976, United Artists sold the movie and merchandising rights to a Hollywood producer, Saul Zaentz.[8] In 1977, Rankin/Bass Productions created an animated television movie titled *The Hobbit*, which aired on ABC-TV and was subsequently distributed on video. The next year, Ralph Bakshi produced a $10 million animated version of *LotR*, which was distributed by United Artists. The film received cool critical reviews and attracted relatively paltry box office receipts (see table 1.2).

Hollywood's reintroduction to *LotR* began in 1998, when the Saul Zaentz Company, doing business as Tolkien Enterprises, granted a license to film the trilogy to New Line Cinema, a subsidiary of Time Warner (which will be discussed below).[9] Three films were produced over a period of fifteen months at a reported cost of $300 million, and released in theatres in December 2001, 2002, and 2003. Under the terms of the contract, New Line Cinema also received the license for renderings based on the movie depictions of the characters—in other words, merchandise. However, Tolkien Enterprises still held the rights to *LotR* characters in a more general sense. For instance, merchandisers who want to use a likeness of a character in the film must go through New Line. However, a more generic depiction of the character must be licensed through Tolkien Enterprises.[10] The Tolkien family receives nothing from the films or any of the merchandising, with the exception of 50 percent of profits from book sales.[11]

While the exact terms of New Line's contract are unavailable, it is reported that the arrangement involved a complex profit-sharing scheme. However, some of the parties involved have not been satisfied with their share of the enormous pie. In 2004, Zaentz filed a suit against New Line for £11 million, claiming that his share of the profits from the first movie, *The Fellowship of the Rings*, was based on net profits rather than gross receipts.[12] Then in 2005, Peter Jackson's company filed suit against New Line, asking for an accounting of all revenue, not only international box office, but also TV, DVD sales, merchandising, and so on.[13]

NEW LINE AND TIME WARNER

Founded in 1967, New Line Cinema claims to be an "independent" film company, even though it is fully owned by Time Warner. In 2003, New Line generated the highest revenue in its existence and accounted for 10 percent of the U.S. film market with $924 million in box-office grosses, making it the fifth-ranked studio in the United States for the second year in a row. The success of the *LotR* trilogy obviously contributed a good deal to New Line's success.

Time Warner, Inc., is generally considered to be the world's largest media company, with revenues in 2003 of $39.6 billion. The company is the result of the merger of Time Warner and America Online in January 2001, becoming AOL Time Warner. The name was changed back to Time Warner in October 2003.[14] The company is currently divided into five segments: America Online, Cable, Filmed Entertainment, Networks, and Publishing. But these five categories do not fully capture the size of the company. AOL is still the leading provider of Internet access in the United States, and operates in many other countries around the world. AOL also operates Mapquest.com and Moviefone, while Time Warner Cable serves 10.9 million U.S. customers. Meanwhile, the Filmed Entertainment division includes Warner Brothers Studios, Castle Rock Entertainment, and New Line Cinema. The Networks division includes the Turner Broadcasting System, which itself includes CNN, TBS Superstation, TNT, Turner Classic Movies, and the Cartoon Network. Also included are the WB Network, HBO, and Cinemax. Finally, the Publishing division is comprised of many of the largest circulating magazines, including *Time, Sports Illustrated, People, InStyle, Fortune, Entertainment Weekly, Real Simple, Money, Southern Living, Sunset, Golf, Field and Stream, Ideal Home,* and *Country Life,* as well as many more niche publications.

In other words, the company is a classic vertically and horizontally integrated corporation with possibilities for synergy between segments, as exemplified by the marketing of *LotR,* which will be discussed below.

BUILDING MARKETS: PUBLICITY, PROMOTION, AND ADVERTISING

The *LotR* films (and other products associated with the film) did not sell themselves; their releases were accompanied by extensive promotional activities. Marketing any Hollywood film involves strategies to gain the attention of potential buyers in various markets. Although efforts to influence these markets often overlap, films are sold to distributors, theatrical exhibitors, and audiences, as well as other media markets such as home video, cable, and network television. In addition, merchandising and tie-ins often are involved.

However, the launch of a trilogy such as *LotR* became an even more complex process, with planning over a longer time period than most projects for the three films released between 2001 and 2003. In other words, the marketing and promotion involved an integrated process of "sequelisation" around the three movies.[15] Biltereyst and Meers have discussed *LotR* as an example of a "constructed event," similar to other blockbuster films. They distinguish between a film's development as a *marketing event* ("concrete initiatives by a producer/distributor to attract attention"), a *media event* ("discourses produced by the media around a blockbuster"), and a *societal event* ("wider discourses in society with reference to the movie").[16]

The focus here will be on the marketing—in other words, the deliberate efforts by New Line to promote the final film, *RotK,* although some discussion of the initial launch of the trilogy is included. It also might be noted that, as Biltereyst and Meers explain, these marketing activities contributed in various ways to build the media and social events that surrounded the film.

In Hollywood, distinctions are made between various marketing activities. *Media buys* refer to expenditures made on advertising (television, billboards, and so on), while *marketing* involves the overhead, premieres, and publicity events associated with a project. However, these terms are often used rather imprecisely, and *marketing* usually refers to all of these activities. Marketing costs have been a major target for criticism in Hollywood over the years, as these costs continue to grow. Though the average cost for producing a studio picture was around $60 million in 2005, marketing expenses added another $36.2 million. However, event movies almost always involve more marketing expenditures. Overall, the major studios reportedly spent $3.5 billion for marketing and advertising in 2005.[17]

It is often difficult to find accurate information on how much is expended for marketing specific films, and the *LotR* trilogy is no exception. Estimates of the amount that New Line budgeted for marketing the three films range from $145 to $180 million, although it is likely that the amount was much higher.[18] For instance, New Line spent $192.7 million on advertising in 2004 and reported that *RotK* "was a significant piece of our advertising."[19] As a global marketing event, the project involved centralised planning, as well as decentralised or local strategies.[20] For instance, more groundwork needed to be done in Japan, since the Tolkien books were not known as well there as they were in other markets.[21] Indeed, *LotR* represents a good example of the way that global marketing often adjusts to local nuances. Biltereyst and Meers explain these promotional strategies for *RotK* in Belgium, where Cinéart distributed the films:

> Overall, the patterns of the launch of *The Return of the King* indicate how Cinéart's and New Line Cinema's publicity and wider marketing strategies were successful in gradually building up media and public attention, leading to three peaks in terms of the amount of time and space spent on it by local news media. Closely following New Line Cinema's script, the local distributor used a wide arsenal of typical blockbuster means to obtain this attention and participation from partners—from specific distribution strategies and market saturation release, through multiple level advertising, merchandising, tie-ins, and press strategies, to the creation of marathons and other events.[22]

However, while promotion involved different strategies in different regions, there was careful centralised control. *Variety* reported before the first film was released that "No foreign distribs will be designing marketing of their own."[23]

It is also interesting that the marketing itself became a promotional device, as indicated in the following excerpt from a press report: "From the strategic partnerships to the innovative promotions to the scores of licensees already on board, the studio's film trilogy . . . is being developed as one of the marketing world's biggest, largest, and most unique productions ever."[24]

The discussion that follows briefly outlines some of the deliberate efforts to market *RotK,* including selling to distributors, publicity and advertising activities, the use of the Internet and tie-ins, as well as how these efforts were integrated by/within Time Warner synergy. The chapter will conclude with a discussion of the merchandise and merchandise sites that helped promote the films.

SELLING THE DISTRIBUTORS

Theatrical films are typically sold first to distributors in order to reach theatres and audiences. New Line produced the trilogy, but also distributed the films in the

United States. Distribution rights were sold in other regions of the world, where some foreign distributors also invested in the film's production.

At Cannes 2000, potential distributors were shown twenty minutes of dramatic scenes without any effects. Most of the global sales were closed at that time. The distribution companies that signed on included "market-leading outfits" in various territories, including Entertainment in the United Kingdom, Nippon Herald in Japan, Village Roadshow in Australia/NZ, Metropolitan in France, Medusa in Italy, Kinowelt in Germany and eastern Europe, and Aurum in Spain. Distributors were told that "the target is for all of them to outdo the previous top grosser in their territory." In some countries that meant spending as much on P&A (prints and advertising) as it cost to purchase the films. In addition, New Line's Rolf Mittweg insisted that foreign exhibitors wanting the first movie had to buy rights to all three, sight unseen. Also, huge advances were required to book all three films. [25]

Even though the films had not been completed, Cannes 2001 was used to launch the first film, as well as to preview the film for cast, crew, and foreign distributors. New Line's Mittweg reported that Cannes would serve as "our official worldwide media launch for *The Lord of the Rings.* As the global press converge on the Croissette, New Line will pull out all the stops to ensure that movie fans everywhere discover the first installment of this epic cinematic event." [26] The first glimpse of the epic, however, was only for the cast and crew. The company rented a castle located one hour from Cannes, then used the design team who worked on the film to turn it into "a fantastic scene from Middle Earth," where members of the cast and crew were treated to a short preview of the film. [27]

The twenty-six-minute clip then was shown to press representatives, distributors, and exhibitors. The company had specifically arranged for 150 selected magazine journalists to be flown to Cannes from around the world to see the preview and meet the stars for three days. They were asked not to disclose any details of the preview. *Variety* reported an "enthusiastic" response, even though questions about the length and the film's rating were still pending. "New Line is believed to have spent more than 1 million pounds to launch the project in Cannes in a careful strategy to obtain the maximum publicity." [28]

PUBLICITY

As with most blockbusters, publicity for the film began even before cameras rolled, and continued through the films' theatrical and video release, as well as during the various awards periods. The publicity and promotional activities in most markets accelerated dramatically around the release dates as the films became "media events." (Interestingly, some of these events were by media owned by the same corporation that planned the marketing events, as will be discussed in a later section.)

As with many films, a slick press kit was distributed digitally by New Line and contributed to extensive press coverage and numerous magazine cover stories.

Guest appearances by the cast and director were ubiquitous across the media. While all these activities are typical of blockbuster events, *LotR* seemed to receive endless coverage and promotion. It is impossible to recount all of these efforts here, but the campaigns included a wide range of special parties, competitions and contests, giveaways, marathons, and so on. An especially interesting example was an arrangement with the entertainment promotions agency Planet Report to distribute Rings bookmarks and posters to millions of junior high and high school students.[29] Planet Report distributed 26 million *RotK* bookmarks, which the company claimed "provided enormous buzz among nation's youth in the two weeks prior to the film's release."[30]

Movie premieres also should be considered part of publicity, and the examples for *LotR* were stunning. The world premiere of *RotK* was in Wellington on December 1, 2003, at the newly refurbished Embassy Theatre. The event featured Maori warriors, 100,000 fans (3 percent of the country's population), and the prime minister of New Zealand in chain mail. A parade featured elves, hobbits, orcs, and other Middle-earth inhabitants.

The Los Angeles premiere on December 3 seemed to pale in comparison, including a mere two thousand guests for a typical "mega-premiere" in Westwood. The after-party, however, featured two gigantic Australian fig trees and three interlocking themed tents that covered forty thousand square feet of grass.[31] The theatrical release strategy for *RotK* was especially interesting. New Line re-released the first two films in their DVD versions (with extra footage) at 100 to 150 U.S. and Canadian theatres a few weeks before the final film's theatrical opening. While theatres were told "that these events are produced as a marketing/publicity stunt and not as a revenue-generating opportunity," the screenings also were thought to "bode well for DVD sales."[32] Nevertheless, the theatre screenings of the extended editions of the movies were reportedly sold out in less than an hour at most theatres.[33]

On December 16 ("Trilogy Tuesday"), a worldwide twelve-hour marathon featuring the three films shown back-to-back was offered at select theatres. Many theatres reported that tickets for the marathon screening were immediately sold out, resulting in eBay auctions in which tickets sold for up to $200.[34]

ADVERTISING

The first sign of advertising for a film might be considered the theatrical trailer. New Line delivered the first teaser trailer for the first film as early as May 25 in the United States. Other trailers followed, with a three-minute version in September.[35]

Promotion of *RotK* included trailers in theatres, as well as on DVDs of *The Two Towers*,[36] and a wide range of typical advertising, including newspaper and magazine ads, television and radio commercials, and billboards. One report claims that from 2001 through December 2003, $164 million was reportedly spent on advertising for all the films, with more than $131 spent in the United States.[37] However, because advertising is arranged by both the distributors and the theatres, it is a real challenge to find data on total advertising costs.

INTERNET

Another important component of New Line's marketing of *LotR* involved the Internet, which deserves special attention here. New Line's use of the Internet has been somewhat unique compared to studios' online strategies for other block-busters and is especially interesting in regards to the promotion of *LotR*. Even before *LotR,* New Line had established itself "at the forefront of new-media marketing." The company created one of the earliest interactive marketing departments, using "guerilla marketing" with American Online, Compuserve, and Prodigy before the World Wide Web, and developed new ways of delivering news and screen savers to journalists using floppy disks.[38]

The company uses techniques that have become common in online marketing. For instance, QEIB (quantifiable early Internet buzz) involves early planning and timing for the launch of a buzz campaign. As Gordon Paddison, New Line's director of interactive marketing, explains,

> In my world we call the key multipliers "Avids." These are people who attend movies four times a month. They are the people who help influence their peer group. People who generally end up at your Website early are key multipliers because they have a pre-awareness and they are seeking your brand versus your brand seeking them. The great thing about the Internet is that it represents the entire base of marketing—from awareness to exploration to conversion.[39]

The *LotR* producers developed unique relationships with fans, even before the actual production of the films. As Elana Shefrin concludes, "Lord of the Rings fans have been actively courted by Jackson and New Line Cinema throughout all aspects of authoring, casting, filming, and marketing the trilogy."[40] Jackson participated in several key online interviews in 1998 and 1999, in a deliberate effort to connect with *LotR* fans, specifically discussing the scripts and casting decisions. Shefrin observes, "Both as an intuitive motivation and as a conscious strategy, he [Jackson] focused on the Tolkien Websites and alliance possibilities with online fans."[41]

New Line Cinema's official website (lordoftherings.net) was launched in 1999, two and a half years before release of the first film. The site was available in ten languages and included a wide array of features—seemingly endless pages of information about the films, the characters, the actors and the effects, photos and video clips, and interactive activities, plus desktop images, screen savers, maps, electronic cards, America Online buddy icons, and so on.[42] New Line's website generated more than 350 million hits worldwide between January and April 2001.[43] According to the Nielsen/NetRatings, the site attracted over 2 million unique visitors during both of the months in which the first two films were released.[44]

Paddison maintained the website, networked with other Tolkien fan sites,[45] handled all Internet publicity, and dealt with online copyright issues. Paddison dispensed information about the film, provided web access to online clips, and gave away merchandise. He also kept track of the use of unauthorised material on other sites, as well as monitoring chat rooms and discussion boards.[46] Again, a careful relationship was developed with Internet fans, as noted by New Line's executive producer, Mark Odesky: "it's just such a contrast to other big-budget blockbusters where the fans and the Internet are seen as things to be kept away."[47]

Even though Paddison admits that "embracing the fans was a risky strategy,"[48] the Internet was a key component in New Line's marketing activities for the trilogy.[49] Paddison explains New Line's plans before the release of *RotK:*

> The strategy was to develop a dialogue and give a continuous flow of information that was unique to the production and not reactive to the gossip surrounding the production. The best part of the "Lord of the Rings" campaign is the fact it was done with the passion of this project and the passion of the audience in mind. Although we are constantly recalibrating timing, the way the program was laid out in '99 is exactly what worked throughout and will work throughout the next two years. . . . A nice thing about this campaign is there is not a need for new strategy going forward. There is nothing that we have to do new and breakout that will garner an audience. I think we now have a 98–99% consumer awareness of the brand, which is amazing.[50]

Online ticket sales were also emphasised in this process. The tactic seemed to work, with nearly 14 percent of the opening weekend's ticket sales for *RotK* reportedly purchased online. In addition, according to theatre exit polls, 45 percent of the opening weekend audience for the first film said that they had learned about the movie from web promotions.

TIE-INS

In addition to advertising placed directly by New Line and theatres, tie-ins and merchandising deals with other companies were extremely important in promoting the film. Indeed, many of the events and contests promoting the trilogy were tied in to these products. Again, most tie-in deals were negotiated at least a year before the first film was released. *Variety* reported, "The global marketing machine has been cranking up since last September [2000], with an NL hit squad touring the world to close merchandising tie-in and promotional deals."[51]

New Line arranged licensing deals with approximately a hundred companies worldwide. While this may seem like a significant number, it is actually lower than for the typical blockbuster. David Imhoff, director of licensing and merchandise at New Line, explains that this was intentional. "Over-proliferation of licenses was not in our plan."[52] Yet it still seemed that there was a proliferation of promotional activities surrounding the films. The various deals involved promotion of the film with a wide range of products, advertising arrangements, and links between company and film websites.

The first film involved a deal with Burger King with a global marketing plan that included over 100,000 restaurants worldwide and a $30 million advertising campaign in the United States. However, the arrangement did not continue for the second or third films, as the tie-ins were said to be taking away from the "high-class image" of the film (or perhaps, as one reporter observed, because "there are no Whoppers in Middle Earth"). Meanwhile, Verizon arranged a two-year deal and helped promote the films and the Verizon products associated with the film. Verizon gave all new subscribers a free video and a chance to win a trip to New Zealand, as well as offering *LotR* ring tones, games, text message alerts, and other products. A Verizon ad was included on the *Two Towers* video. A company representative explains: "We see 'Lord of the Rings' as a phenomenon—a community of raving fans that also has mass-market appeal."[53]

JVC's arrangement was reported to be a $40 million deal that featured DVD players and VCRs loaded with movie trailers, behind-the-scenes footage, and film stickers.[54] Other tie-in products and services involved Pringles, Cheerios, A&W, Cadbury, Bassett's Candy, HP Baked Beans, Air New Zealand, JVC, and France Telecomm. In addition, *National Geographic* produced several programs and featured the film on a National Geographic Special. The programs also are sold on video/DVD.

One of the biggest promotions involving tie-ins consisted of an "Adventure Card" in conjunction with the second and third films. The promotional partners included Dr. Pepper/7-Up, Chrysler, Duracell, Verizon Wireless, America Online, and EA Games, as well as the retail partners Target, Best Buy, and Circuit City. Adventure Cards were packed in more than 10 million DVDs and single VHS copies of the movies, and consumers were directed to the website (www.lotradventurecard.com), where they were required to enter a PIN included on the card. At the site, there were coupons for everything from $5 off Duracell batteries to a $500 "cash allowance good towards the purchase" of a new minivan. Dr. Pepper and 7-Up featured *LotR* imagery on their products and "Liquidloot" points, which customers could use to bid on merchandise on the Adventure Card website, presented by eBay.

Air New Zealand participated in the worldwide marketing campaign, with four of its aircraft depicting characters from the film appearing at key locations around the world. By the time that *RotK* was released, the first two aircraft were reported to have flown "the equivalent of 250 times around the globe displaying their giant billboards."[55] Air New Zealand's marketing campaign also featured a New Zealand vacation package that included round-trip airfare, accommodations, car rental, and Rings Location Guidebook for purchase at the website.[56]

VIDEO/DVD RELEASES

The release of the video and DVD versions also deserves some attention. The various releases, which were "orchestrated in minute detail"[57] over a three-year period, were coordinated to promote the films' box-office releases. The company used a "dual video release strategy," involving a video version of the original theatrical versions of the films, followed by extended editions hitting the market immediately before the theatrical release of the next installment of the series. For instance, *The Two Towers* DVD/VHS was released in its theatrical version in August 2003, followed by an extended DVD version with additional footage in November, two weeks before the theatrical release of *RotK*.[58]

Additional advertising and promotion accompanied the video releases. For instance, the first film's video release involved a $45 million marketing campaign by New Line and its promotional partners, and included massive TV and print advertising.[59] The release of the extended version of the film in November involved a second wave of ads.

THE JOYS OF SYNERGY

Time Warner is similar to other diversified entertainment conglomerates in attempting to cross-promote its products throughout its organisation in synergistic fashion. *Synergy* has been defined as "the cooperative action of different parts for a greater effect,"[60] and companies such as Time Warner are not shy about explaining this line of attack. In fact, Time Warner's 2003 Factbook states that "AOL Time Warner is more than a random collection of great brands and businesses. Each and every franchise plays an important role in helping people be informed, entertained and connected. Our focus is on developing, strengthening and taking advantage of the natural overlaps to make each part stronger than it would be alone, and the whole greater than the sum of its parts."[61] A few examples of how this worked for *LotR* included a TV special on the Time Warner–owned WB network on the making of the film and the first airing of the trailer; a nine-page cover story in *Time* (December 9, 2002), featuring Aragorn, Frodo, and Gandalf on the cover; a cover story in *Entertainment Weekly* (December 26, 2003/January 2, 2004), with the cover featuring Aragorn and Frodo, as well as a competition to win figurines based on the characters; and CNN's Larry King interview of Ian McKellen (Gandalf), in February 2004.

An advance clip of the film was available on AOL in April 2000, and was downloaded over 1.7 million times. AOL subscribers were offered a chance to enter a competition to be flown to the movie's world premiere in New Zealand, if they upgraded to AOL 7.0. In two weeks, 800,000 community members signed up.[62] Thus, for a company such as Time Warner, *LotR* offered "the perfect fuel for the synergy machine"—in other words, a franchise that the company continues to promote across its various businesses.

MERCHANDISE FOR THEM ALL

Before New Line/Jackson, there was already a significant amount of merchandise associated with *LotR*. However, with the New Line trilogy, the floodgates opened even wider. The merchandise helped promote the film, but also garnered additional revenues for the franchise. Movie merchandise is not unusual and represents a huge global market, with $2.5 billion in royalties from entertainment properties reported in 2001.[63] However, many, if not most, movies do not translate well into merchandise. In addition, studios and licensees have been cautious after some significant losses in the past.

The merchandise for the *LotR* trilogy was marketed as carefully as the films, as explained by a trade magazine writer: "The film producer has made an unprecedented effort to maintain artistic integrity of the products. Every font, every drawing, every logo, every image on every product has to adhere to strict style guides, consistent with the film."[64]

Another assertion was that "the range of merchandise launched to tie-in with the new *Lord of the Rings* film [*sic*] is almost unprecedented in the movie world."[65] Allegedly, the merchandise was released rather slowly. One reporter states that New Line "held back a merchandise blitz at the start of the trilogy in 2000 to build the property slowly"; New Line's Imhoff explains, "It was about letting the marketplace build on its own, and it's worked out wonderfully."[66]

While there was apparently less *RotK*-tied merchandise, new products were released around *RotK* and another new range of products was offered for 2004, with the release of *RotK* in video/DVD formats, including fifty new action figures, new games and collectibles, and more.[67] One source has noted that the merchandising of *LotR* is an example of "dual merchandising"the classic book-related products as well as the movie-tied products. There seemed to be some kind of agreement not to overlap in some areas, but there still was quite a bit of duplication. While the movie-tied products promoted connections to the films, the movies also increased the revenues for classic products.[68] One store owner explains, "*Lord of the Rings* is popular with both young and old," and observes that parents were introducing their kids to the trilogy through the films. Furthermore, "customers have included people not normally associated with the purchase of science-fiction and fantasy paraphernalia."[69]

It is nearly impossible to obtain accurate accounts of the amount of revenues or profits that are associated with film merchandise, as companies rarely report such revenues. The *Hollywood Reporter* noted that from $1 billion to $1.2 billion was generated from the worldwide sale of *LotR* merchandise.[70] More recently, New Line reported on its website that the *LotR* DVDs and videos, plus "related merchandise," had attracted $2.5 billion. Another indication of trilogy's merchandise clout is the award that one of the films received for best entertainment brand license of the year at the 2003 Licensing Show sponsored by LIMA.[71]

It also is difficult to accurately assess the number of licensees or the amount of merchandise. Mark Rahner states that there were more than three hundred licensees worldwide, while other reports are much lower.[72] Typically, a producer or distributor receives an advance payment for such products, as well as royalty payments, often between 5 and 10 percent of gross revenues from sales to retailers (that is, the wholesale price). However, royalties for *LotR* properties were reported to be between 10 and 15 percent of the wholesale price.[73] Whatever the revenues or profits have been, New Line has expressed satisfaction with the results. As Imhoff explains, "We are tremendously pleased with the dedication and commitment Toy Biz, Burger King, and the other licensees have brought to this process and thrilled to see their work being embraced across the globe. They never lost sight of the history and intricacies of the books, as well as the characters of Tolkien and Peter Jackson's Middle-earth."[74] Merchandising was even involved in the budgeting of the films. It is claimed that 10 percent of the budget was raised by selling rights to "video games, toys and merchandise companies."[75] Another source says that "$11 million came from Burger King, JVC Electronics, Barnes & Noble, and other toy and merchandising companies."[76]

LotR involved what seemed like an endless number of the typical products associated with film franchises, but also introduced some unique categories of merchandise. Only a brief overview will be offered here.[77]

Again, many of the products are similar to those associated with other Hollywood blockbuster films. A wide variety of toys have been available, with Marvel's Toy Biz alone, as the "master licensee," producing 450 to 500 items.[78] Many sets of action figures continue to be produced, as well as other toys, including the *LotR* version of Barbie (as Galadriel) and Ken (as Legolas). Other products include paper supplies, trading cards, household items, party supplies, clothing items, Halloween costumes, and other holiday fare.

It is not unusual for films to be accompanied by a wide range of books. Of course, the Tolkien texts are the source of the film, and not necessarily products initiated by the film. However, they still might be considered merchandise in this context, in addition to the wide range of books that have been inspired by the films. The success of the films undoubtedly influenced the sale of the "classic" books. But there are also countless books and other publications that are directly linked with the film. With the release of *RotK,* for instance, Houghton Mifflin's various tie-in editions and books about the films filled four pages in its 2004 catalogue.

Again, the *LotR* films are not unique in inspiring more expensive merchandise, as other films that attract avid fans also offer high-end products. However, there seemed to be a wide range of high-end products available from the trilogy, everything from high-priced goblets, shot glasses, mugs, flasks, and pipes to exclusive clothing such as Elven cloaks (at $600) or aviator jackets ($249). The films also inspired a wide range of weaponry and jewelry (including not One Ring, but many).

As with many blockbuster or film franchises, there are many products called "collectibles"—which could include anything from original artwork to decorative plates. Weta Digital, the company that helped create the visual effects for *LotR,* sold many collectible products, including "polystone environments," statues, figures, plaques, busts, weapon sets, and medallions.

The wide range of games that are tied to the *LotR* films is representative of the "richness" of the *LotR* franchise. Traditional board games were converted to *LotR* formats, and video and computer games (in many formats) were created for each film. Meanwhile, role-playing games, including strategy or tabletop battle games, tradeable miniatures games, and trading card games, sometimes also included online activities.

THE MERCHANDISE SITES

Not only did New Line's website for the trilogy promote the film, but it also sold products based on the film. New Line continues to sell a long list of merchandise at the New Line Cinema Studio Store (http://shop.newline.com). In an attempt to promote the products (and the films), New Line also offered an affiliate program to merchandisers. If they placed banners and links to NewLineShop.com on their websites, they would receive 10 percent commissions on items sold as a result of someone clicking on those banners/links.

In addition, many of the fan sites still include shops that sell merchandise or lists/links to merchandise. There also was continuous promotion of these sites via email for customers who ordered products or signed up for further information. While other sites included this feature, the OneRing.Net has been a notable site for the proliferation of information about almost everything relating to the trilogy. The site still has extensive archives with photos sent of fans displaying their *LotR* merchandise (see www.theonering.net/scrapbook).

CONCLUSION

The marketing and promotional strategies surrounding New Line's trilogy demonstrate the ability of integrated entertainment conglomerates (such as Time Warner) to promote their products across their various businesses in synergistic fashion through building markets and creating events. As Biltereyst and Meers conclude,

> This is not to say, of course, that the tremendous financial, box-office and audience success of blockbusters such as *The Lord of the Rings* is completely reducible to marketing, publicity or the industry's professional skills in creating events. Many authors have been looking at textual, aesthetic or technical features of this extraordinary picture, or at the audience and wider societal reception of it. These various analyses of the blockbuster phenomenon, however, should not overlook a critical political economy approach towards the discursive power of the Hollywood marketing machine. This includes the power to *create* events (what we see

as a connecting issue), and through these events eventually *guide* expectations, imagination and reception.[79]

This discussion also suggests the ideal nature of the *LotR* franchise for a diversified entertainment conglomerate such as Time Warner. It is obvious that Time Warner (despite the company's claims to the contrary), Jackson, and others continue to make buckets of money from the trilogy.[80]

It is not surprising that the motivations of the movies' creators have been interrogated by some observers. In an interesting and thoughtful piece about the implications of the commercialisation of Tolkien's work, *Boston Globe* reporter Ethan Gilsdorf offers the following comments: "Make no mistake. Rings is serious, and the money-grubbing and hype do not jibe with Tolkien's medieval aesthetic or his sober themes. Commercialisation degrades his creation to a lowest-common-denominator enterprise. Market forces pare down a nuanced story to its superficial aspects, confusing the experience of literature with buying mass-produced plastic junk."[81] As we consider the significance and reception of the *LotR* trilogy, it seems clear that we also need to understand that the companies that control these films and attempt to control the events that surround them ultimately make decisions based on the potential for profit, not necessarily for artistic, creative, or communicative goals.

How these decisions influence audience reception may be an important part of the story revealed by others in this volume. In other words, the marketing and promotion of the *LotR* films discussed in this chapter hopefully sets the stage for further analysis of the reception of the films. For instance, it could be interesting to find how this tidal wave of marketing and merchandising may have influenced the experiences of the films. Did the participatory websites, with their leaks and advance information, influence audiences' reception of the films? Were there avid *LotR* fans who would have seen the films even without being exposed to any advertising or promotion? On the other hand, did the abundance of marketing and merchandise have a negative influence (similar to Gilsdorf's comments above) on some potential audience members, especially fans of the "classic" *LotR?* And how did different marketing campaigns around the world influence audiences' reception of the films? For answers to these queries, and many other related questions, read on . . .

CHAPTER TWO

An Avalanche of Attention

The Prefiguration and Reception
of *The Lord of the Rings*

DANIEL BILTEREYST, ERNEST MATHIJS, AND PHILIPPE MEERS

Hype easily self-assassinates, but *The Lord of the Rings* may be immune to excess. . . . [B]ecause of its extra-cinematic life, it can't escape being a monument to its own built-in cult, which is roughly the size of humanity.

—MICHAEL ATKINSON[1]

This quotation gives a rough idea of the scale of the prefiguration in the run-in to the premiere of the first part of the *LotR* trilogy. And unless you were on a different planet from the beginning of 2001 until the summer of 2004, you too will have been part of that hype, reluctantly or voluntarily. But its sheer size should not deter us from analyzing its most apparent properties.

This chapter starts from the assumption that a film's public presence is its primary condition for existing. Mirroring in crude terms a well-known saying—"If a tree falls in the woods and no one is around, does it make a sound?"—we maintain that it is through its interaction with mechanisms of production, distribution, reception, and consumption that a film acquires meaning. Those mechanisms are grouped under the umbrella of a film's "public presence." As a concept, "public presence" relates to the public sphere, conceptualised most prominently by Jürgen Habermas as a zone between the private environment of the family and the official state environment of governance and judiciary that form the two most recognisable poles of cultures and societies.[2] But while Habermas reserves "public sphere" for an arena of debates among equals, we use "public presence" to include commercial conditions as well as the larger cultural and economic frameworks within which they operate.[3]

In the preceding chapter, Janet Wasko lays out the core characteristics of the production, promotion, and franchising of *LotR* and explains how they frame its public understanding. Other works too have highlighted levels of production, distribution, and reception.[4] These concerns lie at the heart of this chapter.

WAVES OF PREFIGURATION: INVOLVEMENT, AWARENESS, PENETRATION, AND SATURATION

In true reflexive fashion, fans, critics, and academics were reflecting upon the film's reception even before its release—and ever since. Discounting official and tie-in sites, speculations about how *LotR* was going to be received appeared across a range of media, each of which boasted some sort of involvement with the production, and expressed some concern about its reception. By and large, speculation about the reception of *LotR* came in three waves.[5]

THE FIRST WAVE OF PREFIGURATION: FROM LOCAL AND PERSONAL INVOLVEMENT TO GLOBAL AWARENESS AND ONLINE HAVOC (1998–2001)

Late Summer 1998. Those closest to the action know first, cheer first, worry first, and report first—and also predict first. A first strand of speculations and predictions about *LotR* followed the announcement by New Line/Peter Jackson that the film was going to be made, in New Zealand, by a Hollywood company. The involvement here was, then, by the country of New Zealand, by Hollywood, and by Tolkien's fans.

According to Davinia Thornley, reports predicting the impact of the film appeared in the New Zealand newspapers the *Dominion* and the *Evening Post* as early as late summer 1998 (when Jackson landed the contract from New Line). Unsurprisingly, the New Zealand media were extremely positive, though there was some caution as to the possible effect of the enterprise upon their cultural economy.[6] Hollywood's corporate reporting media all published brief reports, including predictions, around the same time, stressing box-office opportunities and tentpole franchising, but also slightly worrying about what that might mean for the "content" and "look" of the actual films.

The fan press, too, reported on the possible receptions, though its output was fairly small. The One Ring (theonering.net), widely credited as the most comprehensive fan site on *LotR*, was not launched until 1999. From then on, the site reported almost daily on the films, giving it a huge reputation (it was soon rated the number one *LotR* fan site by the Tolkien Society) but also generating some suspicion (its activity seemed to be running remarkably parallel to New Line's efforts to manage audiences' prefigurations of the films). Typical for the "involved" fan press response were the speculations by Hollywood watcher Harry Knowles' Aint-It-Cool site (aint-it-cool.com).[7] There was faith that Jackson would pull it off because of his credentials as a "geek" and "cult" filmmaker, one whose allegiance with *Famous Monsters of Filmland* and Ray Harryhausen types of fantasy guarantee respect for the original story and "excellent filmmaking." As Knowles puts it, in reply to forty-two threads of talkback,

> Me, I'm out to get a place in line. Sure I've seen these films, we all have, each and every one of us that have read those tomes. We have that film right in front of that sparkling silver screen in front of our mind's eye. But you know what, I haven't seen Peter Jackson's version. But I will, and for that I rejoice. I cheer as loud as I can, I dance myself a hole all the way to New Zealand. I'm happy, I'm excited. Why? Because this is new. This is not something I've seen in a movie theater. Am I setting myself up for the biggest disappointment ever? Could be, but damn if my head ain't going to be throwing three-dimensional images from The Fellowship Of The Ring, Two Towers and Return of the King, all around. Damned if my friends and cohorts won't get into extensive friggin dialogues about how cool, how sucky, how right these films will be.[8]

The frame of reference of this first wave, then, contains four elements: (1) opportunities for New Zealand, (2) a concern about faithfulness towards the story, (3) an acknowledgement of New Line's massive economic gamble from the endeavour, plus the likely benefits to them, and (4) faith in Peter Jackson the Hero to bring it all to fruition. Those seem to be the issues that mattered in locally involved prefigurations three years before the premiere of the first installment.

In the two years between this and the avalanche of attention in the final year before release, a gradual increase in volume and tenor slowly lead to "hype."[9] This hype of speculation was fuelled by a virtual media blackout by New Line, imposed to protect the shooting schedule from any interference, running through most of 2000 to May 2001, and ending with the presentation of a twenty-minute edited clip of the films at the Cannes film festival. The only significant puncture in this period of "official silence" was the mid-2000 release of an online trailer. The ironic, or perhaps calculated, effect of that blackout was an avalanche of speculation, pre-interpretation, guessing, and in some cases spying (The One Ring set up a special unit to report on the proceedings of the shoot and any *LotR*-related activities). Factual reporting was replaced by the creation of "myths."

During 1999 and 2000, the local New Zealand media, online fan press, and international media gradually stepped up their coverage. Speculation in the truest sense, most of these articles ventured guesses about how the films would be made. One recurrent topic was the "transfer" of book into film: Which characters would be cut? Who would play which parts? Whose parts would be highlighted? Which locations would be used? In the "local" New Zealand media this mostly took the form of minutely detailed reports on New Zealand's involvement in shaping

Middle-earth: the use of military personnel, the in-house special effects of Weta workshop, the casting of extras, location scouting, and the "messianic" figure of Jackson. In more than one sense, this amounted to a joint effort to appropriate *LotR* into New Zealand's cultural economy, making it Middle-earth's physical "home." The *Evening Post,* the *Sunday Star Times,* and the *Christchurch Press* were among the most active participants in this endeavour, as were specialist magazines *Onfilm* and *Infotech Weekly* (both of which have evident interests). The culmination of this effort was, no doubt, a series of reports from the Ministries of Tourism, Culture, and Economy championing the films as a boost for New Zealand's economy and global image. But, as time progressed, dissenting voices also appeared, mostly in the form of political and policy documents, and, sporadically, in letters to editors of citizens concerned about New Zealand's "selling out."[10]

Both the fan press and the international press were more concerned with speculation about the casting and general news about the shooting, and how that would inform the reception of the films. The fan press' interest makes obvious sense, but the volume of reports was remarkable, not so much in the paper-based genre press and fan mags (like *SFX, Starlog,* and *Cinefantastique,* all of which carried regular reports but didn't really show much appetite), but especially on the Internet. By the middle of 2000, no fewer than four hundred fan sites were discussing *LotR* on a daily basis. The most active sites were Aint-It-Cool, then at the zenith of its involvement, boasting at one point a Q&A session with Jackson about the project (this was right before the media blackout), and The One Ring, whose activity grew exponentially as official news dried up. The One Ring also found itself at the centre of a developing network of online fan communities, each with its own site and/or speciality and effortlessly crossing language boundaries (a good example is the immensely popular Spanish-language fan site elfenomeno.com). Added to these were numerous general Internet providers with discussion boards and chat rooms (Yahoo!, MSN Hotmail), leading to what soon became known as "general online havoc." In an interesting development, the Internet craze about *LotR* became a newsworthy event in itself, the first hyperbolic conflation of the story of the event with the event of the story. Canada's prime newspaper the *Globe and Mail*'s article "The Lord of the Web" and *Fox News*'s short feature on "record breaking Internet traffic" are typical in that they merge a prediction about the film's reception with an observation about its impact on online chat and traffic (both volume and tone).[11] The event that most sparked these peaks of attention was the "sneak preview" of an online trailer featuring the first images from the films. From the point of view of New Line, which had organised the online trailer, it was a first triumph of "control" of the films' public presence.

International media attention also increased, particularly emphasising the general scale of the enterprise (remarked upon in, for instance, the *International Herald Tribune* and *Vanity Fair,* and through news wires like AP, Reuters, DPA, and AFP). Similarly, Hollywood's media gradually increased the volume of reporting, but without profiling their news in any direction. One notable development, however, was the increased involvement of those British- and Australian-based newspapers with a decided international news slant. For Australian media, like the *Sidney Morning Herald*, a "spillover" factor explains its relatively higher number of speculations: watching little neighbour New Zealand hosting such an enterprise led several pundits to speculate about the place of "South Pacific" film culture—obvious references are the Australian shooting of *Star Wars* and the *Matrix* films.

The British interest is probably best explained by what one would call a "heritage" factor: Tolkien, his estate, the Tolkien Society, the origin of the books and the cultural context within which they are grounded, substantial parts of its original fandom, the BBC radio version, and the recurrent presence of *The Lord of the Rings* in debates about "the nation's best books" have given it firm British roots. In that respect the reports in the British papers can be seen as a combination of local and internationalist perspectives. And in their articles, the local element does shine through, not just in references to Tolkien, but also in specific connections. So, for instance, the *Guardian*'s first article on the films starts by establishing a connection between British cinema and Tolkien, by invoking British director John Boorman (of *Excalibur*, 1981) whose career-long dream it was to film *LotR*, by reminding everyone that Ian Holm has played a Hobbit before, and that Ian McKellen is, indeed, *Sir* Ian.[12] Similar side references abound in the *Daily Telegraph*, the *Times*, and the *Sunday Times* (which stands out because of its volume of reports).[13]

The British and Australian interest and the explosion of online fan discussions have one involvement in common—their speculation almost always concerns casting, actors, and characters. This should remind us that regardless of contemporary blockbusters' reliance on spectacle, it is the "people" involved, and the "personal" and "professional" connotations they embody, who are still the preferred ways into discussions about the films. The casting of *LotR* did lead to fierce debates, especially concerning the roles played by Liv Tyler (on whose hiring there was much disagreement among fans); Ian Holm, Ian McKellen, Christopher Lee, and Cate Blanchett (whose casting met with high approval as "typically Tolkienesque" and testifying to the "British origin" and "Australian" interest, respectively, Holm having been featured in the BBC radio version, McKellen and Lee having previously expressed their affiliations with the books, and Blanchett being an Australian citizen).[14] In other cases, reports on the casting of actors led to conjectures about how their performances would please/surprise/impress audiences, and how it would push their characters' parts into the limelight (Elijah Wood, Sean Bean, Viggo Mortensen). Occasionally, casting news would lead to extraordinary stories: the casting of "lean, mean" Sean Astin to play the chubby Sam is one such example, as is the "making" of new heartthrob Orlando Bloom.[15]

By the end of 2000, with the first premiere still a year away, global speculation about *LotR*'s reception had found a firm grounding in fan media, especially online ones, and had achieved a general, somewhat lurking presence in international and screen trade media. It is necessary to point out that the language of speculation so far was almost uniquely English. In fact, when asked how they became acquainted with the films, even non-English-speaking communities point to English-language sites, especially Aint-It-Cool and The One Ring. Even notable exception Elfenomeno (elfenomeno.com) credits The One Ring as a source of inspiration and information (and as "ringleader" of the fan network). In short, *LotR* seemed to be, by the end of 2000, an Anglophone global phenomenon.

THE SECOND WAVE: FROM GLOBAL AWARENESS TO TOTAL LOCAL PENETRATION (EARLY 2001–DECEMBER 2001)

During 2001, the scope changed dramatically. The public presence of *LotR* reached total penetration of all media. Whether they were local radio, student newspapers, community news services, or free house-to-house magazines, all media managed to feature stories and speculations about the upcoming releases of the films several months before the first film premiered. Two aspects of this are worth a closer look, especially their relationship to the films' "localisation" within two spheres: the generic and the geographical.

The Generic Sphere

The *generic sphere* refers to the textual properties of the films as "films," "fantasy," and "adaptations." Although all these markers were already well known, they only became regularly employed in the last year. They offer media with an interest in *LotR*'s generic traits a "hook" for their reports and speculations.

First, the film press, up until now reluctant, joined the developing hype. British magazine *Empire* became the first to put *LotR* on its cover, as part of the "major films of 2001" preview. Other magazines followed suit, and each sought to find a "rationale" for its reporting: previewing the year in the case of *Empire,* or mentioning *LotR* in the course of an essay on John Boorman in the British Film Institute's major publication *Sight and Sound.*[16] These are symptomatic of two strands in the film press, and their respective attitudes toward *LotR.* The first strand, exemplified by *Empire* or the German *Cinema,* joined the hype fully, and became partners in New Line's attempts to "steer" news on the films. They reported and speculated at every opportunity, and their reports were consistently positive—there was not one false note in the entire eleven months leading to the premiere. The second strand, exemplified by *Sight and Sound,* or the American *Cineaste,* was more skeptical, but the publications found themselves reporting on the films in spite of their reservations—news was presented with ironic overtones, but nevertheless presented.

But another part of the film press did not go overboard in its speculations. *SFX, Starlog,* and other genre presses did step up their efforts—but only gradually. After all, *LotR* did not readily fit their categories (horror, science fiction, emphasis on television). Feature fantasy still had, for some, a smell of the 1980s and an association with kids' movies (for example, *Legend, Krull, Willow, Labyrinth, Dark Crystal*). So, where other corners of the press were able to find reasons to localise *LotR,* the genre press resisted. This explains its unusually slow progress. A final consideration is the adverse attitude of much of the genre press to all too overt alliances with Hollywood hype. *The Phantom Menace* debacle, when the genre press received a lambasting by its readership for "promoting" what turned out to be a "bad" movie, was a fair warning against premature alignment. As editorials in *Cinefantastique* demonstrated, "realignment" with the readers was more important than access to "prefigurative" materials. New Line simply could not control the genre press' momentum.

The third aspect of the first sphere, "adaptation," primarily showed itself in online reports about the devotion and faith of the actors and director in "keeping true to the spirit" of Tolkien's original. A huge topic in online fan writings, it also became a means to test the waters. Throughout 2001, bits of information were released about the ways in which the films would be different from, or true to, the original. All of these, from the removal of Bombadil and Glorfindel, through concerns over the parts of Arwen and Saruman, to guesswork on the special effects ("What does an Uruk-Hai really look like?") were heavily debated, especially online. Interestingly, parts of this speculation took place in what appears to be a close connection with the production. Across 2001, Jackson gave a few interviews to address matters of adaptation (in *E Online,* for instance), and in several online journals people associated with the production commented on them (John Rhys-Davies in the *National Post,* Cate Blanchett in *Ananova,* for example). Probably the best example is Ian McKellen's logbook of the shooting and his subsequent posts (www.mckellen.com), which became a source of authority for other media: McKellen's notes and musings were eagerly printed by the *Guardian* and the *Independent* (which jumped at the chance to use the "British legitimacy" of McKellen's cultural status). In all these cases, New Line maintained much control over the momentum of the speculation.

The Geographical Sphere

The *geographical sphere* refers to the way, gradually, local media with no investment or involvement in the films also displayed a significant increase in their reporting and speculating. In itself this is not so unusual. Local media will report on blockbusters, even beyond the rationale that such films will play at local theatres, because film news (especially news about stars, news from Hollywood) is seen as copy that sells well. But in this case, local media did not have the biggest possible stars, or the closest possible connection to Hollywood to hold on to. Instead, local media adopted the strategy of localising the films at every opportunity.

Here are some examples. The Spanish newspaper *El Pais* grabbed the chance to speculate on *LotR* on the occasion of Christopher Lee visiting Barcelona in February 2001 to promote a documentary about European genre (horror) cinema. *El Pais* is generally considered a Madrid paper, with an antagonistic connection with Barcelona's Catalonia. It would also not usually consider horror films, or Lee, worthy of much attention. But because it provided the opportunity to connect to the *LotR* hype, the paper covered it. Similar opportunities were used in the French *Le Monde*, which took the opportunity of an April 2001 retrospective of Ralph Bakshi's films to elaborate on *LotR*'s public presence. The retrospective itself of course could not have been timed better to attract attention of media wanting to link into the hype around *LotR*. In November 2001, the Dutch paper *De Volkskrant* found no less than ten reasons to report on the upcoming releases in less than three weeks, one of which involved relating it to the upcoming release of locally produced fantasy film *Minoes* (2001). And in November, the South African *Africa News* used the fact that the Harmony Gold Mining company teamed up with New Line "to produce 18-carat gold rings with text from the JRR Tolkien novel on which the film is based" to establish its own hype.[17] The gross result is a veritable explosion of reporting and speculation, a tenfold increase in attention between January 2001 and October 2001.

The process of localisation also occurred online. During 2001, more locally organised fan sites emerged, like the Dutch-language site The Fellowship (thefellowship.nl) and the German-based Herr-der-ringe-film) (herr-der-ringe-film.de), and became increasingly active and popular. To some extent these sites duplicated, and sometimes translated, news from other sites—with The One Ring serving as the prime source. But there were also local debates, discussions of cultural sensitivities, and links to local events and activities. These covered not just fan gatherings but also local distribution, venues, sources for collectibles, and, above all, speculations about issues that local fan communities felt strongly about.

In such a context the clear-cut distinction between New Line control and chaotic diversity seems no longer to hold. It becomes difficult to discover which reports are fuelled by either media partnerships with New Line (in the form of deals) or manipulated (incited) by New Line or its partners' release of information. Still, by and large, the situation we sketched on the international level seems to hold on the local level as well: preferred partners lead the way in feeding information and starting speculation on the reception, and other media follow suit, either by being caught up in the hype, or by being forced to address it (which, ironically, means joining it).

Two Key Moments

The mechanisms involved here are best laid out through two key moments in 2001 that functioned as triggers for the local media—and the film press, for that matter—to start reporting on *LotR*. Both moments were instigated by New Line, but both had implications beyond the studio's control—which is of course a perfect description of hype.

The first moment was the release of the trailer. Although bits and pieces had been available before, at selected sites and venues, January 2001 marks the month when the trailers became a full-blown phenomenon. Within a few weeks the online trailer was downloaded 1.7 million times.[18] In the meantime, the trailer was also shown in cinemas. This became a phenomenon in its own right. In the United Kingdom, for instance, Virgin Radio urged people to go to the cinema (to any film) to see the new trailer, an encouragement that led other media to report on it (the *Guardian* for one, but also *Empire*). In the United States, a similar pattern was followed (with *Entertainment News Daily* among the many media picking up the story). By the end of January, the announcements of the trailer, media reporting on the trailer, and media reporting on the media attention to the trailer had become indistinguishable. So even when some media reported on the trailer frenzy in a not-so-positive fashion, this did not affect its flow as free publicity. Moreover, it did not seem to rub off on the mentioning of the trailers themselves. Even when reports seemed to express worry about the degree of hype the trailer caused, the commodities behind it all were considered well made, promising, and exciting.

The second key moment was the screening, at the Cannes film festival in May 2001, of a twenty-six-minute trailer of the three films. This screening served several functions. *LotR*'s presence in Cannes was not only one of ceremonial and publicity presence; as detailed reports in the trade press (*Variety* and *Screen International*) demonstrate, the business of finding distributors for the films preceded all other functions. The decision of New Line to prefer many smaller distribution deals per territory above a few bigger distributors (and their decision to choose, in several instances, as in The Netherlands and Belgium, distributors known as "alternative," "art house," or "fringe") needs to be seen within the context of this more general localisation. It offered, almost forced, local involvement in a way that made it virtually impossible for local media to ignore: the trailer created a buzz that would attract local distributors (who wouldn't normally bid for something with such hype attached), and the interest of local distributors made local headlines.[19]

As with the theatrical trailer, the buzz became newsworthy in itself, even without the deals attached. In France and Europe more widely, news about Cannes always attracts attention, but in the United States and Canada, for instance, two territories removed from the Cannes context, the *LotR* event received separate, extensive attention, even in outlets that had until now remained relatively mute (the critical press, like *Salon.com* and the *Age,* or the regional press in North America). To indicate how "special" this buzz was, reporters wrote more about the "sets shipped from New Zealand" (*USA Today*), or the "gargantuan bash" (the *New York Post*) that was thrown to celebrate the distribution-deal making, or the "standing ovation" the long trailer was greeted with by critics (*Ottawa Citizen*). If it seems, in hindsight, only logical that media all over the world would devote attention to a twenty-six-minute trailer of *LotR* after so much preparatory hyping, we need to bear in mind that at this point in time nothing would guarantee the impact of the films (and the stars and director were not the big names they are now). So from New Line's point of view there was still a risk involved, and spreading that risk across many distributors reduced it, especially when distributors could be asked to bear part of the burden by taking active stakes.

Several aspects of the speculations changed, and the way the hype became embedded within cultural communities led us to believe that New Line's control and its clever dealing with distributors are not the only reasons for its effectiveness. *LotR* resonated with and within cultural practices beyond New Line's control. Beyond being publicity fodder, both the theatrical trailer and the longer one shown at Cannes are crucial in prefigurating the films' releases because they offered the press the chance to report on a "text," albeit a truncated one. In his discussion of the *LotR* trailer Erik Hedling argues that they need to be seen as texts in their own right, and the attention accorded to them is akin to the one proper film texts receive.[20] Though there may be various differences, it does seem that the way the two are treated by world news media is not just as a basis for speculating on the releases, but also simultaneously as news events and aesthetic "texts" in their own right—a sort of dress rehearsal for the real thing later that year. This is one thing New Line could not control (in spite of organised leaks, preferential media partnerships, and the "screening" of critics attending the Cannes showings). If the trailer had not been applauded, the hype would have lacked a boost. And the reason it was applauded lies in the cultural appeal of *The Lord of the Rings*—and its properties (at that time, at least) as a contemporary text for a contemporary culture. The total local penetration of news on *The Lord of the Rings* can be seen as moving from a hype to a "cult." As Julian Dibell points out in the *Village Voice*, the concerns over "adaptation," "faithfulness," "location," and general "care" Jackson found himself forced to answer to at every occasion demonstrate Tolkien's story's firm basis within certain aspects of contemporary culture:

> The Tolkienite hordes have been flooding Web sites for months with gossip and debate about the film. Add in every online discussion about the genealogy of the kings of Gondor, every argument over the syntax of the Elven Quenya dialect, and the monthly textual output of the world's Tolkien-flavored chat rooms and message boards probably exceeds, kilobyte for kilobyte, the 1400 pages of *The Lord of the Rings* itself. In short, the year 2001 finds Tolkien's following bigger and busier than at any other period in the four decades since Philip Toynbee wrote its obituary. What that amounts to in the greater pop cultural scheme of things, of course, is harder to say than it used to be.[21]

For Dibell, the culture it is grounded in is "geekdom," which he sees not as a subculture but as a formative force in the cultural imagination of our times. Tolkien appeals to geekdom, and because geekdom is so significant in our world *LotR* found a cultural niche that just happened to be the biggest one a film can tap into. It gave the films a cultural weight unlike any other product. A good example of this weight is a report in *De Volkskrant*, one month before the release of the first film, in which the cultural impact of the upcoming event is measured against the heaviest possible pop-cultural references: the Beatles. With such powerful comparisons, even before the first film went into release, the battle had been won.

As such, the theatrical trailer and Cannes screening can be seen as both the culmination of New Line's control over the prefiguration and, simultaneously, the moments when it became clear to news media that there was indeed a cultural base for the trilogy's prefigurative popularity. As always, this observation became part of the news flow, and so by December 2001 there was as much speculation about the films' impact as there was about *how* (not *if*) the fans, geeks, cult members, and every one else would relate to what was already being seen as a cultural phenomenon—before it even happened. The speculation was as much about the success of the films as it was about the audiences.

THE THIRD WAVE: SERIALISATION AND SUSTAINED SATURATION (DECEMBER 2001–DECEMBER 2003)

Once *FotR* had been released, the prefiguration was, technically at least, over. But because of the serialised nature of the trilogy (one film every year), the period between the first premiere and the last was one in which reception (of the first films) and prefiguration (of the later films) met. This led, unsurprisingly, to a continued saturation. Between December 2001 and December 2003, there was not one single month in which *LotR* was not at the front of the news.

We will not go into the details of this period, for reasons of space.[22] But it is necessary to single out a few general characteristics. The first is the unprecedentedly positive tenor of the critical reception of the film and DVD releases. Unlike *Star Wars* or *Titanic*, there were no seriously dissenting voices (the few token ones were often exactly that: token). Each and every reviewer, critic, journalist, and blogger praised the effort and/or the achievement. There was not too much complaining about the deletion of Bombadil or Glorfindel, or even about the role of Arwen being played by Liv Tyler. Every concern about, say, the way the conflict between Gandalf and Saruman is resolved (through a fight, not a debate) was balanced with praise for the rest of the movie, and often accompanied by an admission of being an all-too-invested fan of the books (as if that were an obstacle for which audiences are to blame, not the makers). It seemed critical reviews would not have made a difference anyway. Audiences had already made up their minds to go see the films. No reviews would change that.[23] Moreover, and confirming speculation on the reputation of *LotR* as a cult, audiences kept returning for encores, with generational visits (parents with their children), pal visits (with friends), immersion visits (return visits for a "private" immersion into the story after, or before, one goes to see it with others), and event visits (*LotR* as a "night out," even after having seen the film before). In all these instances the films are part of a ritualised attendance, demonstrating their cultural currency among audiences.

The best proof of this lies in the ways in which the films generated spontaneous debates—penetrating even the few spheres that had been immune to its public presence, small-scale communities such as classrooms, maternity mailing lists, or newsletters. Frequently, such debates crossed borders between previously unconnected discourses, forging links, and hence becoming a "common currency," a nodal point through which conversations across cultural spheres and networks could be opened, sustained, and organised. *LotR* became a topic like "the weather" or, previously, *Dallas* or *Big Brother:* a subject one could safely broach in casual conversation and that might function as what Roman Jakobson has called *phatic communication:* talk designed to keep the channel of communication open so that other information can pass more easily.[24] Such communication needs to be available to everyone, to have achieved a general sense of consensus. Usually this type of communication to some extent relies upon disagreement, but the disagreement should not jeopardise the rest of the communication process. *LotR* fit this description perfectly: any disagreement about its achievement was relegated to details, and the global awareness of its existence was total. Indeed, the phrase *casual talk* was explicitly mentioned 547 times (out of a total of 11,629 English questionnaires) as one of the three most important means of information about *LotR*. That means that roughly 1 out of 20 English speakers found out about the films through phatic talk.

As a result of its overwhelming public presence, *LotR* quickly became a shorthand topic in casual conversations on other issues, and within a few weeks of the releases mentions of Peter Jackson, *FotR,* Weta workshop, Frodo, and other markers popped up in media reports on the most divergent issues, from sports reports (London football team Arsenal's defence line was described as being composed of Orc lookalikes, and David Beckham was compared to Legolas), through politics (the link between 9/11 and "the two towers" is an obvious invite), the comparison of Bush with Sauron (in a widespread, infamous pun that spread like wildfire), to use of *LotR*-related terminology to report on astronomy (especially Saturn's, you got it, *rings*). By the middle of 2002, eager editors around the world were using any chance they got to "frame" news items by coining phrases involving "ring" or "lord of."

Finally, there is the tension between a controlled presence, one governed by New Line and its partners, and a chaotic diversity of presence, one that is the result of *LotR*'s public presence fanning out across all sorts of platforms, appearing as a point of reference (not just "shorthand") in reports ranging from jazz reviews (in the *Village Voice*), over travel writing, to the sports pages (especially in relation to rugby, football/soccer, and cricket). The controlled presences seem to be having the upper hand in the months in which commodities or official appraisals are staged, like the DVD release, the BAFTA Awards, the Academy Awards, or MTV awards. At such times, we notice a concentration of argument and opinion: the films, stories, actors, stars, director, and production. But in periods in which there is no abundance of such events or stagings available, less official presences garner more visibility. One possibility is of course that these less official presences never really disappear but are drowned out, as it were, whenever official stagings occur. Another explanation is the "topical habit" of the press. Used, by now, to be reporting on *LotR*-related materials, and aware that future releases and official events will warrant attention, editors and writers are more keen to insert references to the films and their ancillary discourses into news stories than would otherwise be the case. This, in turn, inflates the significance of the films even further.

Throughout this all, two types of presences remain relentlessly productive: the fan sites and the critical debate. In 2002 and 2003, fan discussions reached unprecedented levels of intensity. Next to the now well-known sites, a plethora of new sites entered the debates, often with very specific briefs (such as defining themselves around one or two characters, or around an approach). Below is a list of fan sites mentioned as a source of information by audiences in our questionnaire (the most popular in italics):

Table 2.1: Fan Sites as Source of Information

theonering.net	councilofelrond.com
elfenomeno.com	Tolkienonline.com
thefellowship.nl	Tolkien-movies.com
herr-der-ringe-film.de	chiletolkien.tk
thelostalliance.com	waroftherring.net
elbakin.net	yuzuklerinefendisi.com
jrr-tolkien.de	faszination-tolkien.de
minastirith.com	elbenwald.de
unquendor.com	lotrplaza.com
orlandomultimedia.net	

For Elana Shefrin, such a wide variety of sources indicates a "participatory" fandom, one that attempts to exercise control over the "text" by putting it at the centre of intense debate. Using Henry Jenkins' notion of "poaching," Shefrin argues that these fan communities also engage in activities of appropriation, with the creation of "fan art" and "fan fiction" prominent among them.[25] A good example is the biweekly cartoon of Dutch cartoonist Philippe Collin (nickname Philbo and based at The Fellowship.nl). In the summer of 2002, his drawings attracted wide attention, and became a source of debate within the fan communities—actually displaying the close-knit relationships among the online sites (his work was referenced widely on The One Ring and achieved visibility across a wide range of sites, Council of Elrond (councilofelrond.com) being a prominent promoter of his work).[26]

The critical debate is relentlessly productive because of the ongoing publication of reviews, but also because of its reflexive nature. A first major stream of reviews of the films appeared, unsurprisingly, in the few weeks after December 19, 2001, and, if one includes monthly magazines, this stream lasted until the beginning of February. It then morphed into critical debates about awards (with the Academy Award nominations and the BAFTA nominations and ceremony, as well as New Zealand's numerous smaller ceremonial awards bestowed upon Jackson) during most of February and March, to come to a lull in April. From June onwards the momentum picked up again (with the MTV awards and the DVD release as prime markers), to smoothly move into the prefiguration of *The Two Towers*, via reviews of the extended DVD and the soundtrack.

Most noticeable about this flow is not so much its occurrence (after all, the film's phenomenal success clearly warrants scrutiny), but the consistent tone of admiration and praise for every new "textual" element the films brought up. The most important ones among these are the special effects, the acting, and the "blockbuster aesthetics." The special effects debate is interesting because, for one of the first times in non-genre film criticism, they are discussed not as a side effect of the story, but as an aesthetic achievement in their own right. With acting, the complex relationship between "fixed character" (often seen as a shortcoming of fantasy) and "acting skills" is debated. The general agreement was that, for the first time, fantasy cinema managed to get the acting right. Ian McKellen's BAFTA Award for acting in a fantasy film was hotly debated, as it was seen to pull the genre out of its "infantility complex," and the "Gollum sketch" for the MTV awards, in which the character Gollum launches a tirade against Andy Serkis, the actor who inspired his performance, was discussed for its clever representation of the tensions between "digital" and "live" acting. The "blockbuster" argument was usually entered via comparisons with other hugely successful films (*Titanic, Star Wars*) and stressed the stylistic aspects of the blockbuster as a new genre. Throughout, the stream of reviews employed a seriousness not usually accorded to fantasy cinema.

A SYSTEMATIC VIEW ON THE PUBLIC PRESENCE
OF *THE LORD OF THE RINGS*

To provide a systematic analysis of the public presence of *LotR*, in all its forms (speculation, penetration, saturation, and the conflation between prefiguration and reception), we have singled out one period (October 1, 2003, to January 1, 2004). We collected all press and publicity materials relating to the films that appeared in that period, as well as all materials that contained the search terms "Peter Jackson," "Lord of the Rings," and "Return of the King" (the third film, which was nearing its release at the time); see table 2.2.

This table demonstrates the quantitative dominance of website materials, and press materials (dailies and magazines) in relation to more publicity-oriented

Table 2.2: Press and Publicity Materials (United Kingdom)

Marketing	193
Merchandise (info + samples)	147
National press coverage	946
National magazine coverage	542
National radio coverage	22
Terrestrial TV coverage	64
Official/unofficial websites	647
TOTAL	**2,512**

materials, which make up only 13.5 percent of all materials. It seems, then, that those materials under less direct control of New Line and its partners massively predominate. This is a good indication of the independent momentum that the public presence of the films had acquired. Of course, New Line's role in initiating this should not be underestimated. But it appears that the steered prefiguration is, by October 2003, at least, replaced by overall news interest (in an age of corporate convergence), opportunistic poaching, and even some resistant threads.

SOURCES OF INFORMATION FOR PREFIGURATION AND RECEPTION: BREAKDOWN PER MEDIUM

In our online questionnaire, 24,739 respondents gave up to "three main sources of information about the film before they saw it." Ranked by popularity, they are listed in table 2.3.

Table 2.3: Main Sources of Information

Source	First Source of Information	Among Three Most Important Sources of Information
Internet/websites	6,357	11,617
Trailers	4,271	8,317
Friends	3,093	7,597
TV program/show	1,466	4,387
Posters	1,401	3,105
Magazines	834	2,996
Reviews	1,029	2,731
Books	1,523	2,364
Conversations/word of mouth	825	2,247
Newspaper	652	1,814
Advertising	283	687
Fans	191	499
Family	160	359
Attending pre- or gala premiere	16	23

While each medium is only one of three sources, there is ample reason to consider them individually, for they do not appear in any great number as set strings. The most prominent string is the combination of "friends, Internet, trailer," which occurs only 528 out of 24,739 times (2 percent). This does not give any strong support for any theory on, say, new media users' views on social life. At the broadest level, there is a prevalence of electronic media over paper-based media, but the significance of oral communication cuts through that distinction. At best, we see a preference for the use of "hybrid" electronic media, which could encompass news, critical opinion, and advertising in media like the Internet or television.

When viewed per medium, the first place of the "Internet" corroborates observations that much of the speculation, local penetration, and saturation of *LotR*'s public presence happened through online media.

Table 2.4: Online Media as Sources of Information

Source	First Source of Information	Among Three Most Important Sources of Information
Internet/websites	6,357	11,617
theonering.net	883	1,175
Official LotR site	341	796
elfenomeno.com	190	222
aint-it-cool.com	53	144
Internet Movie Database/ imdb.com	67	128
livejournal.com	23	110
thefellowship.nl	79	102
herr-der-ringe-film.de	62	81
yahoo.com	21	60
comingsoon.net	4	13
google.com	1	8

Among the online media, fan sites take up the majority of the mentions, with *theonering.net* and the larger *LotR* online fan-network as the most prominently featured sites (see table 2.4). Given the privileged relationship between The One Ring and New Line, the popularity of these sites must be seen as a sign that New Line's attempts to "feed" information or generate debate was successful, especially since sites not associated with New Line in any way (or even critical of the entire enterprise) are far less mentioned. Similarly, the popularity of Aint-It-Cool and Coming Soon is the result of these sites' reputation for having "scoops" and "inside contacts." Still, the substantial difference between The One Ring and the official site indicates that, even if associated with the production, the fan site is nevertheless more likely to be used as a prime source of information. Direct corporate communication on the Internet is less likely to be trusted than information posted on a site with a shared commitment.

Next to that, many audiences seem to value person-to-person communication almost as much as online mediation. "Conversations/word of mouth" is seen by almost 10 percent of the audience as one of their major three sources of information (see table 2.5). "Friends" tellingly outranks "family," but if we bear in mind that the demographic of our population is representative for that of the filmgoing audience (teenagers, young adults, people under thirty-five) such an emphasis need not surprise. Mates, buddies, pals, amigos, and comrades are preferred over colleagues (who are mentioned only sixty times). And mentions of "family" and "colleagues" are virtually always accompanied by mentions of "friends."

Table 2.5: Social Networks as Sources of Information

	SOURCE OF INFORMATION			Overall Age
Age	"Family" (n=359)	"Friends" (n=7,595)	"Colleagues" (n=60)	Representation (n=24,739)
Under 16	21%	11.3%	0%	10%
16–25	43.5%	50%	20%	47%
26–35	16.5%	22.5%	38%	24%
36–45	10%	9%	28%	10.5%
46–55	5%	4.5%	12.5%	5%
56–65	3%	1%	1.5%	1.5%
Over 65	1%	0.5%	0%	0.5%

This table maps the social and personal networks within which views on and information about cinema are communicated and appreciated. "Friends" are the most significant source of information in the age brackets most commonly associated with film attendance. "Family" becomes a prime source for young and older cohorts, and colleagues' views matter at the age when they are virtually part of your family anyway.

When looked at by region, the "friendship" theme is, in essence, *the* core "textual" argument in the American reception of *RotK*—one of the terms most often used to describe the appeal of the films. In the case of the American media, "friendship" is also, simultaneously, an "extratextual" trope, one that allows critics to report on *LotR*'s cultural embedding. In a similar vein as the *Village Voice* report we quoted above, American media seem to realise how much *LotR* was sedimented within American popular culture, and how wide its fandom has spread—beyond clichéd views of hippiedom, heavy metal, and geek culture. It is almost as if American media suddenly realised that *LotR* had become somewhat of a "national cultural symbol"— part of the nation's mythology, like Sleepy Hollow or Paul Revere. A perfect illustration of this is Bruce Westwood's laboured attempt to use the theme of "friendship" to link arguments about the cast's camaraderie, the story's cohesiveness and emotional appeal, and the endearing and encouraging sight of hordes of teens sharing a passion with other generations.[27] Through the theme of "friendship," the "cult" of *LotR* graduated to "culture," from marginal to relevant.

The books take up a curious place in this list. They are the fourth most popular source of information, and often seen as an obvious one (many mentions of the book as prime source accompanied by a "what else" or "obviously" remark). But audiences listing the books tend *only* to see them as their prime source; there is not the same level of mentions when all three sources are included. In other words, those who mention the book tend to mention it as first source, or not at all. It leads us to think that the "book mentioners" are the die-hard insular fans, those who would see the films as extensions of their book reading.

It is surprising to see how few respondents mention "fans" as a major source of information, especially considering the huge significance of fandom in the instigation of the public presence of the films. Only 191 respondents list "fans" as their primary source of information for the prefiguration and reception, and only 499 as one of their three most important sources. It leads us to think that by the time of our survey (well into the total saturation) fandom had become a less distinct marker. Family had become almost as important as fandom. And friends had become much more significant: the clique-ish "involvement" along a shared interest and the vanguard attitude that are so typical of fandom had been replaced by a general topicality: casual talk with friends and not just committed posts.

Table 2.6: Magazines as Sources of Information

Source	First Source of Information	Among Three Most Important Sources of Information
Magazines	834	2,996
Empire (U.K.)	163	336
Newsweek (U.S.)	24	92
Entertainment Weekly (U.S.)	24	84
Total Film (U.K.)	27	65
SFX (U.S.)	21	43
Premiere (U.S.)	7	28
Studio Magazine (French)	6	12

Table 2.7: Newspapers as Sources of Information

Source	First Source of Information	Among Three Most Important Sources of Information
Newspapers	612	1,680
Times/Sunday Times	43	74
Guardian/Observer	34	70
New York Times	16	32

If we turn our attention to "traditional" media,[28] *Empire*'s decision to lead the film press into abundant reporting and speculating on the impact of *LotR* gave it a strong currency with audiences: 366 respondents specifically cited *Empire* as one of their three most important sources of information, substantially more than the general press, or than any competition, even more than online media such as the Internet Movie Database and Aint-It-Cool, or genre press like *SFX*. (See tables 2.6 and 2.7.) Of course, the alliance of *Empire* with New Line goes back to the very beginning of the prefiguration of the films, and New Line's partnerships with the *Times,* the *New York Times,* and *Newsweek* are also longstanding—such connections are, in fact, frequently mentioned as explanations for why audiences think these outlets are a "good" source of information for prefiguration and reception. Among the newspapers, the *Times/Sunday Times* (U.K.) receives the most mentions.[29] The *Guardian*'s place among important sources defies the overall trend. However, its mention is probably more the result of its own profile than of its stand on *The Lord of the Rings*. A paper with a very strong (and free!) Internet presence, the *Guardian* is generally accessed by Internet users as a source of information. And its popularity is particularly high among the socioeconomic group that shares a long-standing affiliation with "utopian thought," "liberalism," and "tolerance" with an appreciation of the books—an affiliation that long predates the films.

Surprising in the list of important sources is the prevalence of "reviews" (929 respondents cited it as their first source of information, without even counting those respondents who only mentioned specific reviews). This runs contrary to complaints that reviews have lost their impact on drawing audiences to, or away from, movies. Our data seem to call for some qualification to this worry. Audiences do use reviews in their information-seeking process, indicating that reviews are not superfluous. What reviews will not do is deter audiences from attending a screening. For Philip French, the relevance of reviews lies in offering arguments for the word of mouth that can make or break the long-term reception of a film, its cult status, or its potential for return visits. For Jay Stone, the relevance of reviews lies in the "sound bites," shorthand arguments in the form of slogans or "star rankings" that distributors and audiences alike can employ to support their arguments. Our research suggests that reviews offer audiences a point of reference for their decision-making processes, not so much economically but culturally. They offer an argument as to how the films can be (and should be) placed. Audiences seek out reviews for those arguments, and they are used for partisan cultural alignment. In Pierre Bourdieu's terms, they offer an opportunity for discrimination and distinction.[30]

PREMIERES, PREVIEWS, AND "CONSPICUOUS COINCIDENCES" IN THE PREFIGURATION OF *THE RETURN OF THE KING*

Two elements that need stressing when discussing the prefiguration and reception of *RotK* are "premieres" and "previews." In a climate obsessed with hype, buzz, and saturation, it is expected that contemporary reviewers will be the first to espouse what will become the prevailing opinion, or to trumpet that opinion louder and more elaborately than anyone else. Newspaper reviewing is especially sensitive to these pressures, as it sees itself as threatened by the fickleness of its audience. On the one hand, it must compete with new(er) media like television and the Internet in getting word out first. On the other, it sees itself, traditionally (because of the place newspapers still hold in the public sphere), in competition with weekly and monthly publications for delineating relevance in a society. Consequently, newspaper reviewers need to be fast and they need to be "right." This has led to the advent of what we propose to call previewing: securing access to the product before its actual release, thus being forced to guess its cultural impact (rather than observing it), getting the message out among a frenzy of publicity hyping, carefully mimicking preapproved languages so as not to jeopardise that access for future use, and to admit that same message for repackaging in subsequent publicity efforts.

The paradox of reviewing a film before it is released is conveniently solved by the gala premiere. Once an important aspect of classical Hollywood, the premiere had seemingly lost much of its appeal in a world of global multiplex releases. But the move of making blockbusters into media events has allowed them a comeback.[31] Respective premieres in Wellington, New Zealand, or London function themselves as newsworthy events. We counted no less than 122 reports in the North American daily press of the Wellington premiere. They also, importantly, function to generate that high-status coverage known as "critical review," even prior to general release, so that it can be recuperated for further publicity use.

Next to these structural efforts to conflate pre- and postrelease discourses across the date of the general release (why else organise a premiere?), there exist a number of what one would call "random" events that are recruited into the larger discussion in the run-in to the release. Such events seem unplanned, or at least unrelated to the more overt attempts to influence the direction of prefigurative coverage. But because their timing is so convenient they become "conspicuous or opportunistic coincidences." The way in which teaching curricula suddenly featured more examples of *LotR*, the way in which the "leaked" story about the deletion of Saruman from the theatrical version of *RotK* coincided with the increase in debate about how much Christopher Lee enjoyed participating in the project, the sudden outburst of *LotR* posts on academic mailing lists, and even the appearance in the news of our own research initiatives add to the amount of talk, but they do not answer to an overall scheme. Rather, they are the results of smaller schemes (a school board aiming to profile a curriculum, Lee's fans wanting to exercise pressure to retain his part for the DVDs, academics attempting to spice up lectures, or our own efforts to publicise our questionnaire). For sure, how can one be suspicious of book publishers Houghton Mifflin and Ballantine when they collaborate with the Los Angeles County juvenile probation system to offer seventeen thousand Los Angeles kids free copies of the books, and offer them free attendance to a preopening screening of *RotK*?[32]

CONCLUSION: CONTROLLED TENT-POLING
AND CHAOTIC DIVERSITY

It is impossible to ignore the wide diversity of ways in which *LotR* was prefigured for audiences, and how varied its receptions were in countries and regions around the world. But a few characteristics were shared by all territories:

1. the move in prefiguration from initial involvement via global awareness through local penetration to saturation;
2. the tension between concerted efforts to manage the public presence of the film and the "chaotic diversity" of opportunistic, accidental, and "conspicuously coincidental" occurrences;
3. the growing importance of online media as a source of information for upcoming events, and the Internet's trustworthiness as a means of communication shared with allies;
4. the centrality of the concept of friendship in any approach towards *LotR* as a meaningful text, for individuals as well as nations;
5. the challenge that the reach and omnipresence of *LotR* posed for traditional practices of film criticism, and the tendencies it highlights of a conflation between criticism and publicity.

It is, by now, common to approach the public presence of *LotR* from a political economy perspective, and a lot of our findings confirm the validity of such an approach. But besides all the corporate efforts to instigate and control, we observed much room for maneuvering. This requires additional perspectives, borrowed from reception studies, cultural studies, audience research, and media studies. If our chapter has one theoretical aim, it is a plea for these perspectives to start listening to each other. Maybe one day they can become, like Frodo and Sam, bickering, inseparable friends.

CHAPTER THREE

Promotional Frame Makers and the Meaning of the Text

The Case of *The Lord of the Rings*

BREDA LUTHAR[1]

INTRODUCTION

The underlying assumption of this chapter is that the meaning of a text does not arise solely from the text-object, "the thing in itself." I shall seek to show how the meaning of *The Lord of the Rings: The Return of the King*, launched in Slovenia in January 2004, was not the exclusive consequence of the inherent characteristics of the film as an aesthetic object itself, but rather that the meaning of the film-object, or its public face, was co-constituted by the strategies of representation of the film in the local media.[2] These strategies created the discursive framing for the reading of the film. The meaning of the film and, consequently, the reception and interpretation of the film, is therefore shaped in large measure by the different discourses of representation, from advertising or unpaid publicity to journalism and critical reviews by other cultural intermediaries within the media industry. Our case study addresses the issue of the prefiguration of the film and the role of promotional framing for the meaning formation. The promotional framing of the film is understood as a discursive process that together with textual meaning defines and constructs an event or an issue and, consequently, shapes its meaning.[3] A frame as a structural device of cultural narratives supplies a context and suggests what the issue is through the "media package" of different devices: exclusion, emphasis, metaphors, stock phrases, rhetorics, narrativisation. I do not address the entire spectrum of the representational and promotional strategies for *LotR* in Slovene media; my particular focus is the publicity or unpaid media attention that supports the paid promotion and advertising. The features of the film, its textual and aesthetic properties, and the role of pleasure, gratification, and fantasy in the reception and use of the film will thus be put to one side. My primary consideration thus moves from the text as object and from the reader as a product of historical context and discourses, or the process of reception, to selected aspects of the promotional context of the film.

All three parts of the film trilogy *LotR* were based on the books by J. R. R. Tolkien, first published in English in 1953 and 1954. Tolkien's fantasy epic, which acquired a cult following and became a symbol of the British counterculture, was translated into Slovene in 1995, forty-one years after the publication of the British original. It was then again published in a different translation just before the premiere of the third part of the trilogy at the end of 2002. As a consequence of the late publication of the books, a large proportion of our Slovene respondents/viewers (40.9 percent) had not read the books prior to the local film premiere. Only China has a larger share of nonreaders among its responding audience (44.5 percent), whereas in the other direction only 6.5 percent of U.S. respondents and 16.6 percent of British interviewees had not read the books prior to viewing the film (see the introduction in this volume).[4] In addition, the data on the level of pleasure shows that, comparatively, a significantly smaller proportion of Slovene respondents found the film extremely enjoyable: while 82.3 percent of U.S. viewers, 70.5 percent of British viewers, and 61.4 percent of Danish viewers found the film extremely enjoyable, only 46.4 percent of Slovene viewers enjoyed the film. The late publication of the trilogy and the unsuccessful first translation in 1995 meant that the following of Tolkien's books, or, broadly defined, fan culture, as a cultural and interpretative institution, did not develop independently of the filmic interpretation of Tolkien's work. Marketing of the film and the promotion of the second, more successful translation of the Tolkien books were interdependent and intertwined. The publication of the books was thus part of the local promotional strategies for the film, while at the same time the film helped to promote the book. The promotional entanglement of book and film has contributed to the lesser role of fan productivity (semiotic productivity, enunciative productivity, textual output such as online discussion groups, and so on) and thus to the absence of "skilled audience."[5] Consequently, the absence of the significant number of audience members who would have a history of engagement with Tolkien's imaginary world contributed to the lack of symbolic resources available for the construction of the meaning of *LotR* that would develop independently of the filmic and promotional interpretation.

Due to the lack of symbolic resources mobilised by fans, enthusiasts, and the interested public, the construction of audiences' expectations and the appropriation of the text was to a greater extent than in other national contexts left to the powerful role of industrial framing of the film. Textually productive fans necessarily move the fan text out of framing produced by the media industry and, as argued by John

Fiske, constitute the ground on which mass culture is transformed into popular culture through the creation of meaning.[6] Although there is no guarantee that the tactics of fan reading would be oppositional to the strategies of industrial production of culture, textual productivity can be subversive, and thus "invite emancipation from, and resistance to, such frames."[7] It could be argued that the colonisation of imagination by the promotional/industrial discourse is the more or less direct consequence of the absence of a "skilled audience" or knowledgeable community of readers. Furthermore, publicity relies for its existence on the local mass media. The discursive independence of local journalism from the promotional regimes of the global film industry and its local distributors will be addressed. The second important factor that contributed to the power of promotional discourse in the framing of the film is thus the characteristics of local journalism (its textual conventions, routinised practices, professional ideology, culture of production, its relationship to the political and economic field, and uncritical mythological partnership or strategic alliance with local cultural entrepreneurs) that will be addressed further in this chapter. In our study we thus first address the "framing" and prefiguration of *The Return of the King* through free publicity and analyze the discursive centers of commentaries about the film in the local media.[8] In short, we try to address the gendered and class nature of different framing strategies revealed in the existence of different "discursive worlds" in different media and their imagined audiences.[9]

THE CONTEXT OF THE TEXT

Before a major Hollywood film such as *LotR* makes it to a local cinema, various promotional and publicity strategies are applied in order to shape/frame the meaning and, consequently, the reading of the film. The financial interests at stake require a carefully planned publicity campaign for the film, not susceptible to the vagaries and unpredictability of independent journalism. The industrial framing is thus crucial for the financial success of any major film; moreover, it is also semiotically important for its meaning. In order to understand how industrial framing works semiotically, we would like to conceptualise film as a textual process or "textual event." A textual event consists of the text-object along with the discourses that surround and interpret it. Or, as argued by Nick Couldry, "The 'textual event' is inherently multitextual and involves multiple media."[10] The interpretive event thus occurs at the intersection of multiple determinations.[11] *The Return of the King* was framed by various promotional discourses that were the result of the producer's industrial strategy as well as by independent critical discourses of cultural intermediaries—cultural critics and journalists. The "prefiguration" in the local media (marketing, publicity, independent reviews) creates a referential frame for the "consumption" of the film and contributes to the meaning of the film. The meaning is thus also context-activated, not just text- or reader-activated, and is to be searched for in that "contextual intersection."[12] This means that the way in which the film is represented—categorised, labeled, interpreted, criticised, celebrated—plays an important role in the activation of the meaning of the film and in the formation of the background of expectation that influences the interpretation. Although the film-object is not a "floating signifier" that can take on any meaning independently of its symbolic properties, the reading experience is thus potentially shaped by the way the film is framed and by the kind of experience and pleasure that is promised. Promotional discourses can shape the meaning of the objects and put it in poten-tially arbitrary relationship to its aesthetic properties. The unpaid publicity was in our case understood as a context that "inscribed the text within a specific ideology of consumption."[13] *LotR* was thus made meaningful to the audience before it actu-ally reached the movie theatres and long before they could see it. In short, the process of representation becomes a crucial element in the production of the meaning of the film, so that it is no longer possible to consider it as an additional element indepen-dent of the film and external to the text.[14]

However, the expansion of the concept of text is not just a question of the the-oretical approach, but also the consequence of changes in film production and in the organisation of the film industry from the 1970s onwards. One of the reasons why the promotional framing has become perceived as important for the meaning formation is the changes in the Hollywood film industry. When television in the 1970s rapidly took on the cultural role of a daily storyteller and a cultural forum in a national context, mainstream film had to change. One of the changes is an inten-sive orientation towards conglomeration and cross-promotion, new methods of mar-keting, and, in the context of ever greater synergy and commercialisation, production of blockbusters and high-concept films. This style became central to many high-concept films and is shaped by economic and institutional factors.[15] As a result of the growth of television and its rapid takeover of film audiences, films from the 1970s onwards had to become more spectacular and grandiose, and the film indus-try had to develop new distributional and promotional strategies.[16] The promotion of a Hollywood blockbuster had become so intensive that the publicity had to be so carefully planned that independent discourse on the film, either critical or cele-bratory, became more the exception than the rule. As a result of the colonisation of the media by the promotional strategy of cultural industries, independent journal-istic discussion has been marginalised. Another consequence of the changes with-in the film industry is the (re)shaping of the content and the form of the film in keeping with a preplanned strategy of promotion.[17] The marketing strategy thus became a crucial element in the production of the film, so that the plot of the film, the selection of characters, the iconography of the film—that is, its thematic, nar-rative, and aesthetic aspects—became dependent on the promotional strategy and not the other way around. According to Justin Wyatt again, high-concept films are differentiated within the marketplace through an emphasis on style and an integra-tion with their marketing. The meaning of the film itself, once it arrives at a local cinema, is thus the result, first, of the meaning of the film-object and the relationship of the film towards other films and, second, of the discursive prefiguration of the film.

PROMOTIONAL INTERPRETERS

Public relations in cultural industries are experienced "frame makers." Their framing power comes from their material resources, their strategic alliances or mythological partnership with the media, and their cultural capital and skills. The information on the aspects of the film, images of events, and the categorisation of the film in Slovene media as either an "epic trilogy" or a "fight of good versus evil" were to a great extent supplied by the producers and distributors.[18] The entire reporting was based on pseudo-events that triggered and guided unpaid publicity: the world premiere of the film, the Golden Globe nomination, the local premiere, the awarding of a Golden Globe, the Oscar nominations, the awarding of the Oscars, the release of a new Slovene translation of the Tolkien books, and, finally, pseudo-events associated with the launching of merchandise on the market (CD of the film soundtrack, board games, computer games, and so on), and celebrity promotion (weight gain by one of the actresses, discovery of the biological father of one of the actors, and so on). One of the first and most crucial promotional events that was supposed to stimulate the media coverage of *LotR* was the grandiose December premiere in New Zealand. Almost a month prior to the local premiere a world premiere triggered a global wave of publicity for the film: "Thousands of ecstatic fans of The Lord of the Rings trilogy attended the premiere of the last part of the fantastic trilogy The Lord of the Rings in New Zealand, where the film spectacle was also filmed. Like a mighty general at the head of his armed forces, the director of the film."[19]

A new opportunity for publicity was offered by the local premiere in Slovenia in the first week of January 2004. The same newspaper reported about the local premiere:

> Many fans of the fantasy tales eagerly awaited the last part of the trilogy of one of the greatest film spectacles in recent time—The Lord of the Rings: The Return of the King. Wednesday evening was reserved in advance for a select few (the Kolosej Cinema held a media premiere), but the number of impatient fans was clearly huge, since 7000 tickets were sold in advance at Ljubljana theaters. Like many others, outspoken Slovene politician Zmago Jeličnič decided to spend the evening with "the Ring."[20]

It could be argued that the majority of the Slovene media in fact outsourced the entire journalistic coverage of the *LotR* film.

In what follows we will take a look at the relationship between independent journalistic texts in Slovene media on the one hand, and unpaid publicity based on press releases, press conferences, pseudo-events, and press kits provided to the media by the local distributor on the other. We monitored Slovene print media in

December 2003 and January 2004—a month before the local film premiere at the beginning of January and a month after it. Contributions on the *LotR* film in December and January can be divided into (1) independently authored journalistic texts of different genres—commentaries, critics' reviews, and interviews—and (2) unpaid publicity—that is, journalists' reports that are based on staged promotional events or are inspired by organised promotional discourse. The promotional material relentlessly tries to label the film, "give it a name," and accumulate keywords that are constitutive for its meaning and interpretation. An article was thus classified as independently authored if, first, the author interprets, selects, and combines existing information rather than just compiling facts about the film that are provided by the producer and/or distributor in promotional materials. Its goal was therefore the production of new knowledge or an original interpretation rather than mere mediation of information provided by the producer or local distributor.[21] Second, the metaphors, keywords, and stock phrases provided by industrial discourse shape the film's meaning and guide its reception. The independent authorial reviews, on the other hand, invent new labels and metaphors and offer an innovative genre identification of *LotR*. And third, the writer has the status of a cultural intermediary in the local journalistic field and has his or her own individualised style, which testifies to the author's self-referential presence within the media narrative.

Thus those articles that were an individual stylistic and interpretative appropriation of the existing information and an individual reinterpretation of the industrial promotional framing of the film were classified as independent media articles. The ratio of independent to commercial or promotional contributions on *LotR* was strongly weighted towards the latter. Unpaid publicity predominated in all media, with the exception of the left-wing weekly magazine *Mladina,* with its charismatic and influential in-house film critic, and the pop-culture pages of the quality daily *Delo.* Altogether, of 125 contributions of different types, there were only 8 independent texts, less than 10 percent of the total. Different forms of publicity discourse were thus characteristic for various genres and different media. In general, all could be merged into two categories of promotional prefiguration: celebrity discourse (approximately 35 percent of all stories) and "factism" (55 percent).[22]

CELEBRITY AS A CULTURAL AND PROMOTIONAL CATEGORY

Of a total of 125 articles published on *The Return of the King* in the Slovene print media in December 2003 and January 2004, 40—that is, more than one-third of all stories published—were celebrity stories. The celebrity framing of *LotR* was typical of women's magazines, teenage girls' magazines, and weekly tabloids, media with the largest audience share. The alliance of the celebrity system and journalism has produced specific forms of representation of the film in which any reference to the plot, thematics, production process, or generic or technical aspects of the film is absent. The film itself is hardly mentioned, and we find only a passing mention of the local premiere and a brief standardised description of the story taken from promotional press releases. The entire discussion of the film is thus limited to the celebrity gossip and the discussion of the constructed private personae of film stars. Magazines constantly conflate celebrity as commodity and celebrity as fantasy and offer a convergence with the promotional discourses of the film industry. The celebrity system thus is part of the information production that moves from promotion, publicity, and public relations of the film industry into the discourses of journalism.[23] Consequently, the editorial content is in reality nonexistent.

The code of film in women's and teen magazines is the code of celebrity intertwined with the "romantic code." Celebrity content in women's and teen magazines is just one aspect of the ethos of romantic individualism as the central discourse of magazines and an instance of their ideological work: the construction of male and female roles that are as separate and distinct as possible.[24] The discourse on popular culture is thus in these magazines reduced to a romantic code, offering romance, dreams, and fantasies as the central preoccupation of the teenage girl, and frequently also of the woman reader, and emotionality through the figure of the celebrity, particularly male stars as potential romantic objects.

The types of masculinity represented by the stars of *LotR* correspond to the classification of romanticised male figures in teen magazines as done by Angela McRobbie in her analysis of the language and ideology of teen magazines.[25] According to her study, the representation of boys/men in teen magazines can generally be classified into four types of masculinity: the irresistible, fun-loving cool guy (in our case Orlando Bloom); the confused "zany" boy who arouses maternal feelings in girls (Elijah Wood and Sean Astin); the emotional, shy, and somewhat artistic type (also Elijah Wood); and the mysterious, and at first glance emotionally aloof, but sexy real man who has to be tamed by the girl (Viggo Mortensen).[26] Liv Tyler, who plays Arwen in the film and is the only systematically promoted female star of the film, is humanised through reporting on her weight problems, a typical strategy that allows the construction of a shared woman/girl experience and a false unity among all women with no regard for class differences: "Liv Tyler says that she will no longer subject herself to Hollywood standards according to which she is supposed to be too fat. . . . Because Liv is entirely happy with herself and her husband also says that she is even more beautiful when she is fuller, and she intends to stay the way she is."[27] Magazines offer themselves as intermediaries between celebrities and audiences, who are continually addressed as "you" in an "idealised teen speech," in the cozy tone of a casual conversation, and let the reader know "all about the great time 'we' are having hanging out with celebrities on 'your' behalf."[28] In this way women's and teen magazines create the illusion of an intimate relationship between readers and celebrities. A characteristic of celebrity discourse in teen magazines is the communicative ethos of friendliness and the complete absence of any sort of joking irony or critical or uncomplimentary remarks, however indirect, at the expense of the stars of the film. In contrast to what Turner calls a happy, breathless tone of idealised "teen speech" in teen magazines or the friendly babbling of women's magazines is the occasional irony and friendly gossip of "gee whiz" stories in tabloids for a general public.

The culture of celebrity is clearly a promotional discourse and part of the commodification of culture. It had a clear economic function for the producers and local distributors of the film. However, celebrity discourse in popular media cannot be understood as solely the realisation of the promotional strategy of the film producer and distributor. The promotional role of celebrity gossip can be realised if the celebrity discourse is culturally meaningful for the audiences.[29] Celebrities here are thus on the one hand a promotional category and on the other the central points for the discussion of a wide scope of personal concerns (love, femininity, masculinity, relationships, and so on). The magazines we studied did not provide any sources for "critical reading" of *LotR* and encouraged "referential reading,"[30] which directly connects the story of *LotR* to real life and takes the text as a guide for real life. Viewers relate to the characters or to the constructed private personae of celebrities as real people and relate them to their own real-life concerns. Critical reading, however, is more cognitive and treats the popular text as a fictional construction and as a formal game with aesthetic rules. The reader learns to transfer knowledge from one genre to another and from one medium to another. The question arises of the consequences of the dominance of celebrity framing of the film in public discourse and of the kind of reading that is encouraged by the reduction of the discussion of the film to personal concerns and within the horizons of the everyday. One of the consequences is the total absence of "training" in critical framing of the popular texts. Celebrity discourse as promotional and at the same time cultural discourse offers to the readers a subject position of privatised consumers of popular culture. The media thus offer a very restricted repertoire of interpretation and transmit a limited understanding and knowledge of film and, as a result, reproduce and enhance cultural but also gender inequality. Gendered oppositions between reason and affect and hard news and popular entertainment are thus reinforced.[31] Although I do not want to assume at all that media cultures can be exclusively captured by commodification and privatisation, promotion through celebrity discourse has in this case a colonising effect.

THE FALLACY OF FACTUALITY

The descriptive stories do a better job of hiding their promotional nature than does the celebrity framing of the film, since they fit in well with the professional culture and ideology of the factual/informational role of journalism and ritualised practices of "objective" journalism. It is in line with the professional codes, rituals, and conventions such as news values, objectivity as a journalistic ideal, routinised everydayness of the media, construction of authenticity by evidence, and so on that are characteristic of the news production in mainstream journalism. Promotional articles of this type have continuously provided an abundance of factual data on technological and commercial novelty and the extraordinariness and grandiosity of the film and thereby provided their accounts the credibility and a factual status: "Let's look at some numbers regarding the successes and records set by the greatest adventure film of all time. The trilogy cost a record 300 million dollars. The first part brought in 60 million dollars during the first weekend of showing. With the success of the film 50 million copies of Tolkien's trilogy have been sold all over the world.[32] Media were reproducing the labeling, keywords, and stock phrases offered by the promotional material and were enabling the activation of the meaning of the film first as absolute novelty and second as unparalleled "success story." The factual promotional discourse was dominant in the mass-market popular magazines aimed at a general audience or men, middle-brow daily newspapers, and on both television stations (low-middle culture). In addition, the informative/factual articles about the superlative qualities and novelty of the film were also part of the promotional mix in media where otherwise celebrity framing reigned. Framing in terms of absolute novelty and unparalleled success was addressing neophiliacs and technophiles, lovers of the new in the field of technology who are mostly young males. The film was conventionally presented as the most serious candidate for an Oscar, well before the national premiere. In order to define the film, the metaphorics of superlatives was used and media repeatedly framed the film-event as "one of the most successful films of all time," "an incredible success," "a spectacle," "absolute record-setter of all time," as the book of the century and the film of the decade, "a film destined to win an Oscar," "an experience of epic dimensions," "grandiose," "monumental," "an unbelievably emotionally charged film," "brilliant," "one of the most anticipated titles in 2004," "the most successful brand-name," "a trilogy which is setting new viewing records," "a commercial success which is rated as highly by critics as by audiences."

The spectacular novelty of *LotR* was an important aspect of the superlative qualities of a film that was promoted as the most expensive film in history, a new cult film, a film using the latest computer technology, a film with special effects unparalleled in the history of film, a film with the largest team of actors in the history of film, and so on. In this instance the promotion of the film as an absolute novelty, therefore offering a completely new viewing experience, is a crucial integral part of the film as a text-event and of the experience it promises to offer. The enjoyment in novelty lies, according to Colin Campbell, in imaginative, not actual, pleasures, and is central to the self-illusory hedonism of modern subjectivity.[33] Novelty as a value and a norm at the same time and the institutionalisation of desire for the new are integral parts of a strategy for encouraging the dynamics of consumption of material as well as cultural goods. The promotion of a cultural commodity as novelty, as "never before" and "unparalleled," is one of the key strategies contributing to the commercial success of the film. The audience thus knew of the grandiosity, success, and monumentality of the film long before its local premiere. The prefiguration of the film as an incredible success and absolute novelty has performative-ly worked as a self-fulfilling prophecy that contributed to the actual financial success of the film. By promising a novel and different experience it attracted potential audiences to come and see it.

Descriptive discourse of "unparalleled novelty/unprecedented success" framing is in accord with the journalistic ideology of objectivity, which subordinates discursive commentary to factuality. Precisely because of the conformity with existing journalistic conventions, the promotional role of factual information on the film is less obvious. The idea of journalistic objectivity is based on a naïve empiricism that believes that the facts concerning a phenomenon or an event are the meaning of that event. The truth meaning of the event or phenomenon is to be discovered through the impartial facts, and facts can be separated from values at the level of discourse: "hard" facts (numbers) are believed to be unambiguous and epistemologically transparent facts. But facts are, as H. White argues, "a function of the meaning assigned to events, not some primitive data that determine what meaning an event can be."[34] Furthermore, a promotional pseudo-event (a press conference, a local VIP premiere) fits the news values of contemporary journalism with frequency and continuity as two of the main criteria for the newsworthiness of events. Typically, a phenomenon is newsworthy if it is marked by a one-time event: an increase in cinema-going, for example, must be marked by the release of statistics on cinema-going; the excellence of the film is marked by an award ceremony. The frequency or the time frame of an event is one of the principal news values in journalism and is closely associated with the daily nature of the mass media—that is, the routine daily production and consumption of news. A need for the daily routine of supply/production of news that facilitates the promotional discourse leads to the privileging of decontextualised information, to the emphasis on events, not issues, and to the reliance on organised outside sources. Media coverage of the film thus focused on promotional "one-time" events or a series of one-time events, and on facts, disconnected from interpretation, without providing a structural context as the backdrop against which the film could be interpreted.

CHAPTER FOUR

What Do Female Fans Want?

Blockbusters, *The Return of the King,* and U.S. Audiences

BARBARA KLINGER

In "Are Women Just Bored of the 'Rings'?" Caryn James writes, "I clocked my first yawn at 50 minutes. . . . The final entry in the 'Lord of the Rings' trilogy reveals once more that what the chick flick is to men, this trilogy is to women—or at least to a large secret society of us for whom the series is no more than a geek-fest, a technologically-impressive but soulless endurance contest."[1] For James, *The Return of the King* (as well as the other two films in the *LotR* trilogy) is "primarily a boys' toy." As she argues, "The well-calculated hype and exaggerated praise . . . has obscured what the series really is: an FX extravaganza tailored to an adolescent male's fear of sentiment and love of high-tech wizardry." Given this state of affairs, the female viewer's only real "consolation prize" is Viggo Mortensen, the actor who plays Aragorn.

James's remarks present a common set of beliefs about the gendered nature of today's blockbusters, especially those that rely on special effects and action sequences. Prevailing wisdom has it that such films appeal almost exclusively to male "geeks." Women are thus left cold and left out in the cold by high-tech movie narratives, with their displeasure relieved only by the sight of a handsome male star. Women, it would seem, are neither addressed by nor attracted to one of the media industry's most important products. In fact, according to James's account, they are repelled by the inhuman, overly technological universe offered by the typical blockbuster to the typical audience of adolescent boys.

Certainly, there is some truth to this—no one can deny the strong demographic relationship that exists between male viewers and action blockbusters. When, at times, CGI-heavy films do manage to attract a female following, the nature of their appeal simply seems to confirm truisms about gender: *Titanic* (1997), for example, drew repeat female viewers on the basis of a "swoon-worthy" Leonardo DiCaprio and a Romeo and Juliet–style love story.[2] Ultimately, though, blanket statements about the gendered nature of taste in relation to the blockbuster often obscure as much as they reveal, closing off further inquiry on the basis of apparently self-evident truths. Indeed, two weeks later, the *New York Times* printed indignant responses from women to James's review that suggest both the short-sightedness of her argument and a more complex landscape of reception. One woman wrote, "Dismissing [the films] as something that only has strong appeal to male nerds is simply absurd. The most rabid fans I know are women—and not just because of the Viggo effect (or, better, the Orlando effect). We've got multiple ticket stubs, tattered books, and extended-version DVDs to prove it." Another concurred, offering more clues as to the trilogy's appeal:

> I am neither a geek nor a man and I love these movies and so do nearly all of my female friends. Of course we love Viggo, but it's the epic story beautifully told that keeps us returning to the "Rings." . . . Indeed, it's director Peter Jackson's skill at making such a large subject so, well, human, that makes these movies wonderful and amazing and thrilling—and just right for boys and girls.[3]

As questionnaire responses to *RotK* demonstrate, these sentiments are not unusual. Although world totals show an almost even breakdown, with men comprising 50.1 percent and women 49.9 percent of respondents, in individual nations female participants often outnumbered men. Within the global findings, the United States had the highest percentage of female respondents: of the 4,744 who answered the project questionnaire, over 64 percent were women. High numbers of female survey participants defined other nations as well, including Australia (with more than 59 percent), Slovenia (with almost 57 percent), and China (with more than 53 percent).

The U.S. database, as it features the largest number of female respondents, invites reflection on women's relationship to the blockbuster. Of course, as a survey of only a few thousand of the country's moviegoers, the database does not provide an exhaustive account of the U.S. reception of *RotK* or represent female responses from other nations. It also cannot confirm that women dominated the audience for the film or deny that some women were "bored of the 'Rings.'" The U.S. survey does strongly suggest, however, that women are neither invisible nor unwilling moviegoers in relation to action blockbusters. In fact, they can be avidly invested, using strategies of decipherment that result in deeply pleasurable attachments to movie juggernauts.

To gain a sense of how blockbusters appeal to female audiences, I will investigate certain trends within the U.S. database as they reveal the kinds of enjoyment women found in *RotK*. To this end, I focus on a signature element of many of the media industry's biggest moneymakers: "worldmaking." As David Bordwell explains, cinematic worldmaking involves the creation of a highly detailed, multilayered, and self-enclosed universe that provides a "rich, fully furnished ambience for the action." Previously a province of science-fiction films, the art of worldmaking has increasingly come to preoccupy directors making other types of films, such as gangster-noir *Pulp Fiction* (1994) and fantasy trilogy *LotR* (2001, 2002, 2003). According to Bordwell, the "multi-layer reality" of worldmaking is not simply a matter of mise-en-scène, but has implications for marketing and story comprehension. Worldmaking both lays the foundation for the generation of related products across media platforms (such as movie-related video games and toys) and challenges the viewer to search for "microdata" as he or she watches the richly detailed film. The attempt to fathom a film's densely textured world leads to "a new level of engagement" that lies at the heart of contemporary spectatorial pleasures.[4]

Because worldmaking is frequently presumed to be a draw for male "nerds," little is known about how women relate to this significant aspect of contemporary blockbusters. In what follows, I examine these meaning-making agendas amongst the survey's most dedicated female participants: students under sixteen and between the ages of sixteen and twenty-five, and professionals aged sixteen to thirty-five. Together, these groups comprise nearly 34 percent of all respondents and 53 percent of all women who participated in the survey.[5] My intent is not to make claims about an essential femininity that defines their experience or to argue that this experience defies the mainstream.[6] Rather, I want to chronicle aspects of female fandom, especially "ecstatic" female fans who were rapturously enthusiastic, as vivid manifestations of everyday, gendered viewing of spectacular feature films. Since the *LotR* trilogy has it own special history tied to Tolkien's novels and their legendary place in U.S. culture, it constitutes a particular kind of cross-over blockbuster. As the trilogy demonstrates common characteristics of worldmaking films (such as the creation of unique habitats for denizens), it allows us to explore a case of how visual "otherness" is able to attract a critically unacknowledged audience. As such, responses to the films may provide a view of taste formations that have broader application with respect to what female fans of blockbusters want.

I begin by contextualising the group of participants I have selected.[7] As we shall see, although blockbuster worldmaking is associated with CGI—the "magical" technologies responsible for manufacturing a fantasy universe's realistic look—the survey reveals that blockbusters create multiple worlds that exceed this definition. All films create interior worlds of some kind that attempt to portray a unique milieu for the action; what blockbusters generate with particular facility is a fluid intersection of "outer" and "inner" worlds.[8] Along with the interior world of a film, satellite worlds of moviegoing and fandom not only delineate the blockbuster experience for viewers, but also provide a major source of pleasure. Further, while many women in the study remarked on the impressive verisimilitude achieved by the film's special effects, their responses indicate that other variables in the film's interior world are equally, if not more, important in perceptions of worldmaking. Interpretation and enjoyment of *RotK* relies on the viewers' sense of its ability, as an epic form, to elicit strong emotion and to create characters saturated with morality.

THE U.S. DATABASE AND FEMALE VIEWERS

As Martin Barker has shown, U.S. participants comprise a strikingly enthusiastic group, ranking first amongst nations in the study in regarding the film as extremely important to see and second only to Spain in repeat reading of Tolkien's books (with nearly 70 percent of Spanish and more than 62 percent of U.S. viewers having read the books more than once). U.S. participants demonstrate their zeal in relation to other significant indicators of commitment as well: 82 percent found the film extremely enjoyable, with 13 percent finding it very enjoyable, making those with more qualified opinions a distinct minority. In addition, along with the high percentage who had reread all three Tolkien books (and the 19 percent who read the novels at least once), an impressive 95 percent and 93 percent had watched, respectively, *The Fellowship of the Ring* and *The Two Towers* multiple times.[9] These figures reveal a serious investment in the *Rings* experience, with an especially extensive following for the film adaptations. They also suggest a process of self-selection, in which those with the mightiest passion for the *Rings* and computer access were most likely to go online to answer the questionnaire. While not providing copious insight into moviegoers who were displeased, then, the U.S. data does offer a view of the sentiments of the large fan population that made Jackson's trilogy into a sensation.

In male and female respondents, age and occupation mattered in terms of survey participation. Those fifty-six and older constituted less than 3 percent of respondents. By contrast, those ages sixteen to forty-five comprised 75 percent of respondents, with those under sixteen and forty-six to fifty-five totaling 11 percent each.[10] Although the sixteen-to-twenty-five age group alone represented more than one third of all responses and the twenty-six-to-to thirty-five age group almost one fourth, except for the very oldest category, each age group weighs in with a respectable showing. The tallies for profession are more uneven. At 40 percent of respondents, students clearly dominate, with professionals coming in second at 28 percent. Creative and clerical/administrative individuals comprise 8 percent each of participants, with numbers falling rapidly until unskilled manual laborers weigh in at less than 1 percent.[11]

Among the 3,060 women who answered the online questionnaire, 2,523 (53 percent of all participants; 82 percent of all female respondents) rated the film as extremely important to see, while 2,608 (55 percent of all participants; 85 percent of women respondents) regarded the film as extremely enjoyable. Sixty-two percent of women had read the books more than once, and more than 95 percent had seen both previous films more than once. In terms of age and occupation, of the 1,400 female students of all ages who answered the questionnaire, 1,125 of those under sixteen and between sixteen and twenty-five considered the film to be extremely important to see, while a slightly greater number of this same demographic—1,154—considered it as extremely enjoyable.

With students the most enthusiastic group among survey respondents, statistics for professional women are substantial, but less univocal. Of the 661 female professionals of all ages who answered the questionnaire, approximately 225 or roughly 34 percent found the film extremely important to see and extremely enjoyable. No matter the lower numbers, this professional expressed the urgent sentiments shared by many women when she answered, in response to the question of why she wanted to see *RotK*, "I just had to . . . I wouldn't be able to live with myself if I didn't" (16–25). Such responses demonstrate a kind of avidity associated with dedicated viewers, while also indicating the palpable presence of an already established fan base.

FEMALE GEEKS AND THE SOCIAL EXPERIENCE OF MOVIEGOING

Survey responses demonstrate how intent women are in proclaiming their fandom. These respondents often refer to themselves as "geeks," "die-hard fans," and other labels that indicate the kind of investment in movies often associated with male fans. Many women, especially students and professionals twenty-six to thirty-five years of age, were drawn by the literary antecedent of Tolkien's books. However, for some in the groups I studied, particularly younger women, the films proved to be more powerful in initially attracting their devotion. As one student remarked, "I am a die-hard Tolkien fan . . . [going from] someone who didn't like the books when I first read them [to someone who] now does because of the films" (16–25). Another reported that she "had never read [or been] interested" in Tolkien's work, until her father showed her a DVD of *FotR*. Then, "The first film blew [her] away and made [her] a *LotR* fanatic." Others in the same demographic shifted their loyalties from already established objects of devotion; as one commented, "In the last two years, I've gone from Harry Potter to *LotR*-geek and I'm so happy. I love how the story of the war of the rings has been brought to life." Still others are rooted both in family and fan groups that support their dedication to the trilogy. A student wrote, "I belong to *The International Lord of the Rings Fan Club Magazine;* my whole family is into *LotR*—we have watched it multiple times. I am also part of many fan sites on the Web, which have become like a second family through our shared love of *LotR*."

This viewer's self-identification as a *Rings* geek, then, has origins in various recruitment phenomena, including Tolkien's books, Jackson's films, collateral fandoms (such as that related to Harry Potter), family taste, and/or fan organisations. These phenomena present a matrix of media that create and sustain the fandom, with viewers entering the fan population through one medium and then hotly pursuing the story world in other incarnations as well—a franchise's dream. Additionally, as the enthusiastic recounting of the fandom's origins indicates, some individuals savour their own identity as fans, making the identity itself a source of pleasure. As fan studies have asserted, viewers also gain enjoyment from the social and communal aspects of fandom.[12]

Some viewers, particularly those with a reverent relationship to Tolkien's books, wanted their initial screening of *RotK* to be solo. A professional explained, "I preferred to see the movie alone for the first time. . . . The story has been with me since childhood and watching the movies is a very personal experience for me" (26–35). Another concurred: "the first screening was private, between me, the film, and my memories of the book." In a different vein, while a student and her friends usually attended movies together, they went to *RotK* separately because each "had crushes on different characters" and wanted to "experience the movie" on her own (under 16).

Across the demographics I studied, though, most answered an emphatic "yes" when asked if going to see the film was a social event. Families, friends, fan groups, church groups, and the theatre's anonymous fellowship of fans provided a measure of joy for these viewers. Many women mentioned attending "Trilogy Tuesday," a daylong theatrical showing of Jackson's trilogy (the first two in extended editions) sponsored by New Line Cinema on December 16, 2003, the eve of the December premiere of *RotK*.[13] As one might expect, this forum attracted hard-core fans who were interested not only in an intensive and extensive indulgence in the *Rings* world, but also in basking in an environment that affirmed their own fandom by providing contact with similarly disposed individuals. Here, the theatre was less the atomised assembly of individuals commonly associated with today's multiplex and more the community gathering, reminiscent of circumstances dating back to cinema's origins.

Of "Trilogy Tuesday," two professionals (16–25) wrote, respectively: "I saw this with several friends during Trilogy Tuesday and it was a moving experience. It was incredible to see such a wonderful film with a bunch of like-minded geeks. We all appreciated the movie in the same way and it was terrific to experience that love with 400+ other people"; and "Everyone longs to be part of something bigger than him or herself and these movies really created a safe and valid place to be a *LotR* geek. It has been fun sharing in the geekdom with other lovers of the story for the past three years."

Part of female viewing pleasure is thus tied to the social dimensions of moviegoing, as it enables an expression of fandom and a savouring of the camaraderie around an object of affection, especially perhaps in the context of a larger culture less forgiving of what can be perceived as an excessive attachment to the media. In addition, as other comments in the questionnaire point out, moviegoing fosters sociability before and after the screening event itself: women recount going out to dinner or to parties either as a prelude or postscript to their movie experience or getting online with familiar groups of fellow fans. As one professional remarked, "These movies have a huge social component to them" (16–25). Smaller numbers of viewers treasured the experience of solo viewing, where they could fully immerse themselves in nostalgic recollections of the books and childhood, focus more intently on the film, and/or indulge with less distraction in personal fantasies. Whether moviegoing enabled an individual or collective experience, viewers regarded the theatre as a domain that presented an opportunity for a free and therefore pleasurable expression of geekdom.

The "outer world" represented by the theatre (as well as the Internet) provides a haven for fans that is very much a part of the *Rings* experience. Investigating the "inner world" of the film then allows a further and different perspective on how *RotK* was able to evoke such ecstatic responses from its female fans.

EPICS AND EMOTION

I have heard it said that *The Lord of the Rings* is a boy's book about a boy's life in a boy's world. I don't believe this to be entirely true. . . . It's a book for anyone who has a love of fantasy and epics, for quests and adventure, for entertainment and self-knowledge.

—STUDENT (16–25)

It's not just a man's movie! That's such an amazingly silly thing for people to think—that women won't like it because there's not enough romance. Heck this story is one of the most romantic stories of all times with the heroes' camaraderie and sense of humor. . . . It's romantic (as in values, not male/female relationships).

—PROFESSIONAL (26–35)

These comments about Tolkien's books and Jackson's films indicate that women in the study are quite aware of assumptions about the gendered appeal of *LotR,* as well as about female tastes more generally. As a counter, they suggest that women enjoy genres often associated with men, and don't necessarily look for romance in the stories they consume. Some are attracted, rather, to Romance—a mode of narrative that depicts heroic events in historical or fantastic settings. Beyond the moviegoing experience, female fandom's emotional roots are located in a fascination with the film's re-creation of this kind of larger-than-life world.

At one level, viewers appraise Jackson's adaptation as successful because, through CGI and other devices, he produced a compelling, believable universe that accorded with their experience of the books. A student summed up the nature of this impact, writing that "No more convincing fantasy world has ever been conceived in modern cinema. Middle Earth pulls you in and never lets you go" (under 16). A second expressed the sentiments aroused by this visualisation of Tolkien's books as all encompassing: "My heart, mind, imagination and emotions were wrapped up in the world created by Tolkien and enhanced by the movie creators, cast, and crew. I was enraptured by it" (16–25). Similarly moved, a professional who was a "devoted reader of the books . . . wanted to see Middle Earth come to life in a spectacular way while being true to Tolkien's work" (26–35). Again, especially for those in the twenty-six-to-thirty-five age group, nostalgia fueled the film's affective power: a professional "cried through the end" because it was "extremely emotional to re-live the memories [she] had of reading the book"; for another professional, the film "brought to life all of [her] childhood dreams and [gave] them a real face to look upon." For many viewers, the film brought a "tangible" and "stunningly beautiful" version of the world of Tolkien's books, allowing them to "believe that Middle Earth did exist—even for a little while" (professionals, 16–25 and 26–35).

The alignment of book and film produces pleasurable viewing, eliciting the typical satisfaction viewers experience when their expectations regarding the adaptation of a revered source are met. Thus, fidelity (and the conventions of verisimilitude upon which it rests) is one criterion figuring in female responses to the film's world. At the same time, the comments reflect the importance of spectacle to fidelity's achievement, making believability and spectacle exist in an easy, fluid relationship as pleasurable variables. The viewer is entranced as much by fidelity as she is by the use of CGI to achieve a sense of realism for the fantasy world, her consciousness of magisterial illusionism combined with the immersive lures of classical cinema.[14]

Commentary on the quality of the world's adaptation was substantial, but responses also focused on its emotional rewards and characters. As a student respondent wrote, *RotK* was so memorable because of "the incredibly rich and textured characters and cultures created by the actors and the director." She loved "the films, the world, and the people," finding them "deeply affecting" (16–25).

A sense of the film's epic stature fueled the perception of it as an emotion-inducing vehicle par excellence. When the word *epic* was used to describe the affective impact of the film, viewers deployed the term quite casually, as a means of describing not only the film's impressive range and force, but also its effectiveness at inducing deep and varied emotional responses. Outlining her general response to *RotK,* a student viewer wrote, "It was a great amazing emotional grand ending to a great amazing emotional grand trilogy" (under 16). More keenly suggesting the overwhelming nature of this experience, one professional woman remarked that she was "completely blown away, gobsmacked in awe, full of admiration, and totally ecstatic" (26–35), while another professional wrote that she, "oohed, aahed, cried, cheered, even laughed" (16–25).

What seems to matter most in evaluations of the film is its success in exciting so many different emotions. A professional remarked that the "most memorable thing about the movie is emotion," because it made her "happy, sad, anxious . . . everything that a good film should make you feel!" (26–35). Others in the same demographic wrote of *RotK* in a similar vein: "It was a great emotional finale for the trilogy. . . . This movie was a roller-coaster ride of emotions from happiness, worry, and despair to elation"; "These films are extraordinary and bring about so many emotions in me—towards myself and the world. How often can one say that about a movie?"; and "A visual and emotional masterpiece. Absolutely breathtaking. It takes you through an entire range of emotions in just a few hours."

This last comment, in particular, indicates that the film's epic scale is partly defined and appreciated through its affective range. As the last film in the trilogy and the site of closure, *RotK* is ideally positioned as an affective vehicle. The resolution of plot lines and movement toward the end of this world involves a crescendo of emotion, accumulated as much from this film as from the viewer's experience of the two that preceded it. Far from providing just a verisimilar and spectacular depiction of the Battle of Mordor, the grand scale of this world generates such devotion in these fans because it presents an emotionally charged landscape that they equate with film excellence. The combination epic-emotion-masterpiece defines the ecstatic female fan's taste culture, resulting in the deepest kinds of pleasures for viewers who are as awestruck by Jackson's visualisation of Tolkien's universe as they are by its ability to arouse a panoply of emotions. At the same time, the arousal of emotion helps to give the film's strange world its intelligibility; it literally becomes an emotional landscape characterised by exhilaration, terror, and other such affective registers.

Emotions are also articulated in relation to a more discrete variable of the world as well: characters. Since female appreciation of this milieu tends to be strongly associated with male characters, women's pleasure is mobilised through a series of cross-gender identifications. Still, rather than disturbing the genderised order of things, viewers relate to male characters through desire and/or through their signification of moral verities. By acting as sites of gratification and by representing familiar moral values, characters make the film's milieu legible, meaningful, and comfortable for audiences.

THE MEN OF MIDDLE EARTH

We would always make comments and laugh and (drool) over the Men of Middle-earth. Then sometimes we would be silent and just watch and not say a word. It was awesome.
—STUDENT (16–25)

What leads female audiences to engage passionately with sagas that are dominated by male characters? As the above comment suggests, the tried-and-true formula of casting appealing male actors is successful in attracting female viewers. Indeed, survey responses concerning the male cast's looks are common. Women under sixteen and ages sixteen to twenty-five, for example, described their reasons for seeing the film thus: "there are a lot of hot guys" (student); "the extremely good-looking actors who act well" (professional); "Orlando Bloom and Viggo Mortensen" (student); or, simply, "Orlando Bloom!!!!!" (student). However, female attachment to male characters may begin with the sexually objectifying "female gaze," but it doesn't end with it. As fan studies of science-fiction television series have shown, women's intense investment in male characters dwelling in generic worlds often associated with male tastes runs far deeper than the attractiveness of favourite stars/characters.[15] Further, sexual objectification does not monopolise response or act as a barrier to other modes of appreciation. Indeed, female responses to *RotK* suggest that desire acts as a gateway to the enjoyment of other variables. As one professional woman remarked of her love for the films, "I think honestly in the beginning it was simply because Orlando Bloom and Viggo Mortensen are pleasing on the eyes, but I ended up becoming fascinated with the story" (16–25). Some audience research has treated such claims as veiled attempts to justify the audience member's love of a mass cultural text to a broader culture that disapproves of fannish behaviors[16]; however, female reactions to the film demonstrate, consistently, pleasure in the film's characters that is strongly bolstered by character displays of moral verities—friendship, love, courage, strength, humility, humor, humanity, and perseverance.

Again, as the last film in the trilogy, *RotK* delivers certain things that its predecessors could not; in this case, it allows viewers to take special stock of the moral journeys the characters have taken. The journey for some male characters results in a steady affirmation of their repeatedly tested moral virtues. Sam, a particular favourite in the female cohort I studied, represents the enduring essence of friendship, loyalty, and affection—"the truest best friend anyone could ever have" (professional, 26–35). Others, such as Aragorn or Pippin, are appreciated for the changes they undergo during the *Rings* saga. Here, the classic Hollywood convention that figures character development as a central aspect of narrative form provides the motor for the dynamic changes that define certain characters' attractiveness to viewers across this trilogy.

Thus, a respondent who indicated that she wanted to see the film because of "character depiction and development" identified her favourite character as Aragorn because of his "development [through the] three movies and his ability to persevere against very great odds" (professional, 26–35). Showing something of an edge for morality over sex appeal, another viewer commented, "Well Legolas is definitely the cutest. But Aragorn is my favourite because you get to see him transform from this mysterious dirty wanderer to the stuff that kings are made of" (professional, 26–35). Younger students often pointed to one of the hobbits as a favourite character because they identified with these characters' youthful behavior, as well as their passage from youth to maturity during the course of the story. Remarking that Pippin is her favourite, a student explained that she loved "watching how much he grows up through the course of the books/films. He's also very sweet and makes very human decisions so I can relate to him the most" (under 16).

As this last comment suggests, viewers admire characters not only for their demonstration of virtue, but for their ability to act as role models, adding additional complexity to the cross-gender look. Aragorn, for instance, was one student's favourite character because "He was the reluctant kind who didn't see himself worthy of such a position. He was beyond humble and that is what I aspire to be. He didn't think he could do it alone and he relied greatly on the help of his friends and fellow warriors. He was also eloquently spoken and I need to learn how and when to talk" (16–25). In these cross-gender identifications, male characters can represent almost anything to their female viewers, from their incarnation of a certain humanness and vulnerability to the way they express themselves. The cross-gendered look, then, can be energised by desire, moral assessment, and behavioral observations. These elements, in turn, are linked to certain notions of masculinity and race.

Whether male characters change or continue to portray the same virtues, esteem for them often seems rooted in the idea that they have achieved an ideal form of masculinity and/or race. Of her favourite character Aragorn, a professional wrote that she watches him "experience an inner journey to make peace with his heritage and destiny as a King. He demonstrated loyalty and a willingness to sacrifice himself for the benefit of others. His martial strength was comforting as well" (26–35). As for Gandalf, he brings "morality and ethics to the films. He is so wise and knowledgeable and he really adds the depth to the films that makes them great" (student, under 16). In these and previous cases of admiration I have described, pleasure is found in performances of masculinity that accord with certain traditional images of men at various stages of life: the hobbits as innocent children/adolescents; Aragorn as the humble, reluctant, yet powerful adult warrior-king; Gandalf as the paternal figure who is the repository of erudition and principles. Whereas attraction to Eowyn is manifested through a progressive understanding of her role as a strong woman, appreciation of male characters accords with ideals of masculinity that are more conventional; indeed, their conventionality (such as Aragorn's "martial strength") is a source of their comfort and appeal. For some, these male figures appear as antidotes to the more cynical, less heroic present day, making nostalgia for mythic masculinities a prime ingredient in the pleasure derived from male characters.

The comments about Legolas, a figure who looms large as a favourite across female age groups, reveal in particularly vivid terms the presence of a racial dimension to the selection of favourites. As an elf, Legolas (played by Orlando Bloom) represents what for some viewers is an ideal race. One respondent remarked that "Elves were always my favorite race. Their beauty, their wisdom. I've always seen them as a goal for mankind to ascend to. . . . Legolas is the main elf in the tale. And Orlando Bloom was a brilliant choice as far as I'm concerned. He fits perfectly with the image I've always had of Legolas" (professional, 16–25). Another professional concurred, "I . . . loved Legolas because of his magical powers, pure faultless good looks, and beauty and willingness to befriend people of different races and ethnicities" (16–25). Viewers often see Legolas' relationship with the dwarf Gimli as an exemplar of racial tolerance that demonstrates the elves's special ability to mediate between and accept differences. The elves also appear to embody racial purity; Bloom's "pure faultless good looks" arise as a result not only of bone structure but also of his blond hair and white skin. His racial tolerance is articulated, then, through a heightened relationship to whiteness. Although some respondents complain about the film's literal white and black depiction of good and evil,[17] others are less aware of this problematic, embracing Legolas and his fellow elves as an ideal to be admired and pursued.

FEMALE FANS AND UTOPIA

Questionnaire responses indicate that worldmaking in *RotK* exceeds the boundaries of the film, applying not only to spin-off media or merchandising, but to the sphere of reception, where theatres, the Internet, even individual subjectivities, are reshaped, for a time, into satellite outer worlds. The film thus makes its way from the screen into other spaces dedicated to its intense and pleasurable consumption. The social aspects of moviegoing—that is, the collective experience of watching and discussing the film, from Trilogy Tuesday to gatherings of friends, family, and/or acquaintances attending the movie together to online discussion boards—create a number of adjacent worlds frequented by fans. The movie world and these other worlds are interdependent, creating a wonderland of experience for female viewers that is key to the pleasures they take from the *LotR* trilogy.

While, for Bordwell, worldmaking is linked to the "densely textured world" special effects can create, it is interesting to explore the persistence of more traditional pleasures (like character and emotion) in CGI-heavy blockbusters. In the case of *RotK,* the film's successful visualisation of the book's fantastic features through special effects is critically important to fans, particularly as these effects bolster, in a spectacular way, the book's settings, characters, and set pieces. As we have seen, the awesome nature of the cinematic adaptation of Tolkien also provides an important context for the appreciation of characters' physicality and morality, as well as of the film's affective force.

No matter the specific source of pleasure, the comments of the most enthusiastic female fans are infused with utopian sentiments. As I have mentioned, *RotK* has closure on its side, showing a world where good has finally triumphed over evil and where characters have either returned home or found their destinies elsewhere. It also, importantly, marks the end of the re-creation of the *Rings* stories for the big screen. While big-screen reissues and DVD editions may ensue, *RotK* still marks a signature moment for fans, the cycle's end. In this, the film lays to rest the major dystopian forces of chaos that threatened its world, at the same time as it invests great emotion in resolving the fates of the characters (as signaled by the notorious multiple endings of the film). For fans, the trilogy's end marks a special juncture, where their own fandom and sense of camaraderie with others is experienced in a heightened and poignant manner. In this sense, *RotK* is best able to realise the ideal order that lies at the heart of a utopia for its fans.

Through the depiction of the Shire and other idyllic locations, the worlds represented in the *LotR* trilogy literally invoke the sense of utopia as place—a place of ideal perfection in laws, social conditions, and so on. Certainly, science-fiction and fantasy genres, among others, have the capacity to represent the extremes of dystopian and utopian universes in their settings. But, additionally, as I have mentioned, viewers experience the theatre itself, as well as Internet discussion forums, as utopian spaces in the sense that these venues offer ideal places or states for like-minded communities of fans to express their devotion to the films. This is not to say that no dissent or disagreement is present; only that, by the third film, the *Rings* phenomenon was already such a juggernaut that special event screenings and Web-based exchanges were able, for some, to evoke a kind of euphoric camaraderie that helped to establish and support the viewer's pleasure in both her own fandom and in the film. The accompanying exhilaration produced by characters defined in terms of physical attractiveness, moral virtue, and behaviour, and by the film's epic engagement of diverse emotions, produces yet more pleasures for the committed fan. Yet this exhilaration, as we shall see, is not uncomplicated.

In "Entertainment and Utopia," Richard Dyer discounts the possibility that entertainment can provide "models of utopian worlds"—a contention that fan responses here would seem to disprove. However, Dyer's argument that utopianism is an affective sensation produced by movies (in his example, musicals), "contained in the feelings" movies produce and in their ability to present "head-on, as it were, what utopia would feel like,"[18] helps to define the *Rings'* experience for its most ardent fans. The inner and outer worlds forged by *RotK*, as the apotheosis of the *Rings* trilogy, produce a sensation of "what utopia would feel like." Further, this is an alternate universe, where viewers are provided with "'something better' to escape into, or something that [they] want deeply that [their] day-to-day lives don't provide." As Dyer continues, "Alternatives, hopes, wishes—these are the stuff of utopia, the sense that things could be better, that something other than what is can be imagined and maybe realised."[19] As a viewer commented, "the movie captured well the importance of friendship, perseverance, love and courage . . . qualities that are all too often absent in today's modern movies. It appeals to the optimistic romantic in me" (professional, 16–25).

The compensatory nature of the alternate utopian worlds offered the female fan suggests an awareness of the failings of contemporary entertainment and life. Moreover, the cross-gendered nature of the female gaze, capable of identifying with male characters in a blockbuster setting, goes against the grain of much common wisdom regarding the demographics of action/science-fiction/fantasy blockbuster fandoms. Thus, the elements that compose the utopian affect seem to have a critical edge.

Certainly, the number of utopian sensations elicited by *RotK* is impressive. The film's outer and inner worlds afford the female viewer experiences of ideal fan fellowships, emotional registers, and models of masculinity and race. However, peering further into the utopias related to the film's inner world leaves us with a more complex picture. One of the primary things offered by Tolkien/Jackson's universe is an apparent experience of Otherness—a fantastical setting with fantastical characters and creatures—resolved at trilogy's end through the restoration of an ideal order. This world, involving as it does a "cross-cultural" journey for viewers, must be made both legible and palatable to them. The film's successful articulation of masculinities provides one type of legibility. Further, at the core of the appreciation of male characters is the sense that they represent the possibility of a utopian erotic, moral, and racial landscape. Arguably, female viewers experience the deepest pleasures in the men of Middle-earth because they provide access to this landscape.

No matter how new the world encountered in films, familiar coordinates help to unlock its mysteries for viewers. The virtuous moralities on offer are potent when combined with attractive, white male stars in a setting ultimately defined as an idyllic world order. Epic depictions of masculine moralities, encased in the form of different races and species, from the hobbits to elves, raise the question, then, of how deeply entrenched these depictions are in normative masculine traits and racial ideologies and, hence, how dependent viewing pleasure is on seeing these norms activated in new settings. We have reason to wonder, then, if the form of admiration fueled by utopian affect helps to shore up traditional perceptions of masculinity and race—if, that is, exhilaration arises from seeing vivid confirmation of longstanding cultural convictions about these identities.

This kind of inquiry also leaves us with larger questions about the ensemble of utopian sensations that accompanied screenings of *RotK*. Is utopian affect a corrective to perceived ills and shortcomings, a way to smuggle in confirmation of traditional types, or an amalgamation of both potentials, kept in an invisible and indivisible tension? Women's responses seem to suggest that the utopian sensations that defined their viewing pleasure created an intricate amalgam of progressive and regressive tendencies and, further, that this combination lies at the heart of the almost inexpressible euphoria felt by the most dedicated fans.

CODA

Returning to public coverage of female moviegoers for a moment, it is not hard to find articles that bemoan the lack of films being made for women by major studios.[20] Such films are almost always considered as "women-driven films"—films with coteries of female leads. At the same time, some recent news stories suggest that women's tastes exceed the woman's film, as when it was reported that self-described "big geek" Naomi Novik had recently sold the film rights of her dragon-fantasy series *Temeraire* to Peter Jackson.[21] As I hope to have shown, women are not attracted solely to pictures designated for their market, nor are female film geeks a rarity. While predictable patterns of response for both genders to blockbusters certainly exist, there is still a great deal to be learned about the multifaceted dimensions of taste and pleasure both within and beyond these patterns, as viewers cross daily into the other worlds offered to them by the cinema.

CHAPTER FIVE

The Books, the DVDS, the Extras, and Their Lovers

KATE EGAN AND MARTIN BARKER

I'm kind of in a period of waiting now because we've seen from the first two films that the extended edition is a heck of a lot better and tells the story in a completely different way, the extended version is a far more character-driven rather than just being about what's happened it's more why and the development of characters is far greater in the extended edition . . . so I'm suspending judgement really on the Return of the King until I see the extended edition. Once the extended edition comes out, I'm never gonna watch the shorter one again.

—Jack

I know that when you read the spoilers, it does take away some of the enjoyment, for me, personally—so basically, I made a rule for myself that after about November, because that is when all the big stuff really does start to come out, after the release of the extended edition DVD, I made a rule for myself, if a trailer came up on the cinema, I was not gonna look for any pictures.

—Catherine

I don't know, it sounds really bloodthirsty but there's always the bits where there are big fight scenes going on, and the reason I get the extended edition, the four DVD set, I really, really appreciate what happens when they flesh out the scenes, and add extra bits in, I think it really does add a great deal to the film, there was something that Peter Jackson actually said in one of his commentaries. He said that there were bits of these films that you will only understand if you got the extended editions, because they add an extra dimension to the story, it just seems to give it a little extra kick and it's a good thing to have, to be able to look at a collection of DVDs or videos or books or whatever, and actually know a little bit more about them than say the average person in the street does.

—Bill

It is all still sort of relatively only a couple of months, so it's only just completed in that sense. And I have this feeling that, you know, there'll be the DVD, and then the Extended DVD, and then some other bits they forgot to put in, and then, you know, the Special Edition DVD, and there'll be, y'know, a certain kind of afterlife. A lot of the popularity of the films online is to do with sort of the fact that people—and, y'know, I'm there amongst them—are kind of very interested in how they were made, and how they were made communally, and how they affected the people that were working on them.

—VANESSA

These may seem odd quotations with which to begin an essay on the relations between the books and the films of *The Lord of the Rings*. But we headline them because they point the eye to a curious phenomenon we believe we have discovered through a combined examination of a series of documentary features that came out in association with the film—including a number that address J. R. R. Tolkien and his books—and of our interviews with U.K. questionnaire-completing filmgoers. Notice, for now, the following features in these quotations. In Catherine's response we see that attention to the DVDs is part of a *strategic planning* of her participation in the film—wanting to know much, but not too much. The timing of their release becomes part of her planned preparations. For Bill, the DVDs provide a basis for his feeling *different*, *special*, because he knows that they will give him insider information. For Vanessa, the DVDs are important because of that same insider information, but now for another purpose: to feel that she can understand what it was like to make these films. And finally and most signally for our purposes here, Jack feels that he will not be able to have a *settled view* on the film until he has seen the extended edition. This will be the authentic version, the one in which meanings and achievement can really be measured. Together, what these quotations suggest is that watching the extended DVDs is not simply an addition to the viewing experience, but can be, in different ways, built into people's evolving viewing strategies—their ways of planning how and when they will watch, and what they expect to gain from each experience—and that perhaps the extended edition DVDs do a job that no other can. They allow the crystallisation of the experience, a point at which it is settled and stored, the "value to self" computed.

How are these kinds of points relevant to thinking about the book-film relationship? In order to see that, we need first to consider briefly the state of adaptation theory and research, and the questions they do—and do not—ask.

THE CHANGING FIELD OF ADAPTATION THEORY

There is of course a long tradition of interest in how, and how effectively, books are translated to screen.[1] Perhaps the oldest critical tradition is the "fidelity" tradition. This is a multistranded tradition. At its simplest (and at its closest to reviews and public debates), it can be simply a consideration of which parts get carried over, which lost, and which changed, in particular adaptations. But more complexly, it can be a consideration of the different modes of storytelling in the two media.[2] In popular guise, these kinds of discussion will talk of the "essence" or "spirit" of a book. With greater critical apparatus, they will consider how film can create the equivalents of the internal speech that comes so easily to the novel. Long critiqued[3] (Brian McFarlane wrote one particularly gutsy attack on it in 1996),[4] the fidelity approach still persists. Partly, this has to do with the greater prestige attaching to books compared to films, and also the presence within film studies of many trained in literary traditions.[5] Partly, it derives from a sheer will to decide which are *better* versions (although "better for what purpose" is less often defined). In any event, this fidelity critique manages to live on in places such as the pages of *Literature/Film Quarterly*—where, in particular, screen adaptations of Shakespeare are subjected to withering dismissals.[6] This tradition particularly presumes that the purpose of adaptations is, or ought to be, to "make great literature accessible" to audiences.[7]

But other critical traditions have emerged. It is worth noting three in particular. A scattered body of work has looked at adaptations (and also at remakes) for the ways in which the different versions are *ideologically marked*. How do different versions of a story bear the imprint of the times and contexts in which they were made?[8] A related but less politically charged tradition has considered how new adaptations store up and draw upon references to older versions, and indeed to other apparently unrelated cultural materials—an "intertextuality" critique. Particularly apt for a period in which many films have become increasingly self-conscious and aware of their roots, and in which the history of films has become more accessible through both television screenings and back-catalogue DVD release, this tradition of work connects well with interests in "postmodernism."[9] Meanwhile, other individual studies have broached more "industrial" aspects of adaptations—for instance the longstanding interdependence of novels and films.[10]

ADAPTATIONS AND AUDIENCES

These are valuable traditions. But it is striking just how remarkably absent consideration of actual audiences have been. Audiences do "figure" from time to time in analyses, either as the ill-educated ones who can't cope with "real Shakespeare" or as a "knowing audience" in intertextual discussions.[11] But the lack of address to *actual* audiences means that there has been very little consideration simply of what questions we should be seeking to answer. Beginning this process here, we are interested in unpicking some of the complexities in audiences' ways of relating the books and the films. These are very complicated. We should not assume that everyone reads books before seeing film adaptations. Far from it. Many people knew about Tolkien's books, but never read them (indeed, in some cases avoided reading them) until their enjoyment of the film provoked them to it. Some timed their reading to the films' releases. But even among those who had read, or even reread, *LotR* before seeing the films, there is great variation. Some, a minority as far as we can tell, disliked the films either on general grounds (the books should not be tampered with) or on specific grounds (sections were missed out [the Scouring of the Shire is probably the most frequently mentioned], this character was changed [Arwen and Faramir feature strongly, but others—Aragorn for instance, or Denethor—are also cited]). But many others loved the films *despite* their regrets at particular changes.[12]

But also many others spoke in those other fidelity terms, of the "spirit" or "essence" of Tolkien's work. And here we begin from the realisation that the meanings of these expressions are complicated. They turn on a perception of the *meaning of Tolkien's work as a whole*, a sense of his life and books as a *project of contemporary relevance*. These clearly shape people's judgements on how it is proper to translate and transform Tolkien's books to the screen. Since they do care about being "true" to Tolkien, his life and his purposes in writing matter greatly. But since for many people (other than Tolkien scholars and cognoscenti) their understanding of his life and work came in association with their film viewing, it is vital to look at some of the main circulating sources. There were, of course, many potential sources. There are several biographies of Tolkien in print,[13] and of course plenty of erudite commentary on him and his work. Here, however, we review a series of documentaries about Tolkien's life and work. But we want to argue that those documentaries that came with the imprimatur of the films' makers carried a special power—because those who particularly loved the films came to *trust* the filmmakers. Therefore, in looking at other documentaries, we are mainly interested in bringing into view the differences between these and the accounts given by Peter Jackson, his co-workers, and New Line Cinema.

TOLKIEN COMES TO TELEVISION

We have identified a number of television features of very different kinds, each of which combines a story of Tolkien's life with an account of his work and its importance. Inevitably, they share a great deal of basic information about his life—his early blissful life until his father's death, then industrial Birmingham, his World War I experiences, his deferred marriage to Edith, and his Oxford career. They also differ in significant respects.

1. *The Big Read*, presented by survival expert Ray Mears (BBC Television, November 13, 2003). *The Big Read* was a series across November and December 2003 in which a series of the most popular books in the United Kingdom was presented in turn, and the public invited to vote for their favourite. *LotR* was declared the winner in the final programme.
2. *Beyond the Movie: The Lord of the Rings, the Fellowship of the Ring* and *Beyond the Movie: The Lord of the Rings, the Return of the King*, presented by Rings actor John Rhys-Davies (National Geographic, 2003).
3. *Bilbo and Beyond*, presented by British comedian Rory McGrath (Discovery

Channel, 2001).

4. *J. R. R. Tolkien: Master of the Rings*, presented by Robert di Napoli (Cromwell/Eagle Media Productions, 2003).
5. *J. R. R. Tolkien and the Birth of the Lord of the Rings* (Delta Entertainment, n.d.).
6. A pair of extras in each of the extended editions of the three films, entitled "J. R. R. Tolkien," and "From Book to Script" (2002, 2003, 2004).

These clearly arose from very different contexts, circulated quite differently, and are therefore likely to have very different meanings and value to viewers. At one extreme, for instance, is the Delta DVD. Delta specialises in cheap film-related DVDs sold through American shops such as Wal-Mart. Designed, we suspect, to be an impulse buy near the checkout, this one's main claim to validity is having an English presenter—in fact, the voice of the production company's founder. This DVD offers a stroll through a vast amount of detail on Tolkien's life—much of it predictable, but with some extra details (mentioning his not quite perfect marriage with Edith). All these permit simple parallels between scenes and places that Tolkien encountered and characters and moments in the books (the spider bite in Bloemfontein, the origins of the name Gamgee, the holiday in the Swiss mountains, the possible "two towers" in Birmingham that "fans love to visit," and so on). Throughout, the emphasis is on Tolkien's ordinariness, his "quintessential Englishness," yet still a man with hidden depths perceptible in the twinkle of his eyes. A repetitive set of images comes to life when the narrator tells us just what Tolkien did in a place—and the DVD ends with credits and phone numbers for a series of places you can go and visit. You don't even really need to know the books, only that they are "Adventure with a Capital A—and that's all you need to know to enjoy this film." This is a "potential tourist's guide to Tolkien's life" for those who have just encountered him through the "wonderful Peter Jackson films."

The target audience for the Cromwell/Eagle production is clearly schools. It begins from Tolkien's books' cult status (but never mentions the films). Presented by a quietly authoritative figure (Robert di Napoli), it couples retelling key aspects of Tolkien's life (visualised via illustrations and mock filming) with literary/evaluative questions: Why did he write it? Are the characters just stereotypes? Is it great literature? To answer each of these, a series of expert interviewees (an English teacher, a military historian, a Tolkien artist, a representative of the Tolkien Society, and several rock and pop musicians) answer at length, combining professional with personal responses. Here, we get argued opinions: Aryk Nusbacher, from Sandhurst, argues that World War I was a "pointless war," through which Tolkien realised that wars are a means, not an end in themselves. Pop and rock musicians talk about the books' impact on their work. Helen Kidd, an English teacher, defends Tolkien's writing style, turning aside the question of its literary value: "The question we should ask is why fantasy is regarded as subsidiary to realism, for example, and other things regarded as 'high art.'" And in an extra to the main film, Kidd answers a series of "Tutorial" questions fully inscribed in a literature curriculum. Here, Tolkien is measured against literary traditions, within languages of "pastiche," "difference," "bardic tradition," and "magic realism." Here is documentary as Tolkien-friendly classroom aid.

A little more complicated is *Bilbo and Beyond*, not least because its presenter McGrath—usually laddish joker—here plays it very straight. It too opens with the issue of the extraordinary popularity of the books (and the enduring hostility of the "chattering classes"): "Not in his wildest dreams could he have imagined where it would all lead," says McGrath, pointing to battle reenactors behind him, and proceeds to list the kinds of presence that Tolkien and *LotR* now have (games, websites, chatrooms, and so on). Tolkien is presented as a "bit of a hobbit" himself, into nature, plain food, beer, and conversation. Unlike the other documentaries, it presents the next phase of his life as basically very good (with the blemish of his father's death)—"exciting," "stimulating," and "perhaps nearer to poverty than they would have liked, but rich in literature and language" because of his mother. Raj Persaud, a popular TV psychologist, then discusses Tolkien's preference for men's company and his clubbishness. There is too a strong emphasis on the importance of religion, and on his "idyllic" life in Oxford. Many testimonial interviews tell of his influence on the worlds of role-playing and video games. The overall emphasis in all this is on Tolkien as a cultural phenomenon, and if it is explained at all, it is as a curious combination of "accident" (a several-times-repeated word, exemplified by the process to publication of *The Hobbit*) and cultural opportunity (new movements, new technologies). The nearest this documentary comes to a suggested "theme" is in a closing comment from Persaud, who questions whether Tolkien's work is pure escapism or perhaps rather a means of "mastering difficult aspects of your life." If anything, this documentary poses Tolkien as a "man of his times" who has left behind a trail of strange influences.

With each of these, we would argue that the primary question has to be: what could you *do* with the information and account that they give?

The Big Read is a much more intriguing broadcast and, whereas we would have to search hard to find evidence of the other documentaries' impact, certainly a good number of U.K. respondents did mention this programme. Broadcast by the BBC, *The Big Read* addressed some very British concerns and debates about Tolkien's books. Indeed, the series was marked by a strand of scorn and dislike for *LotR* (attitudes that go back to the books' first publication, declined across the 1970 and '80s, but reemerged with fresh vigour thereafter), and even some attempts to prevent Tolkien winning the audiences' vote for favourite book of the century (one Bath bookshop ran a stunt of giving away copies of Jane Austen, and was duly reported in a subsequent episode of the series). In the section devoted to Tolkien, the programme accompanies Mears through a variety of landscapes that stand in for the world of Middle-earth. Mears calls *LotR* "a work of immense imagination" that creates "a complete world" (this contrasts with the series' presenter Clive Anderson, who calls it a "best-seller," now becoming "blockbuster" films). Mears demonstrates various wilderness skills while recounting and implicitly paralleling the story. For instance, as he walks a boggy area, we are told of the dreadful muddy winters in the trenches of World War I, and of the Dead Marshes in *LotR*—culminating in a comment (now set against beautiful landscape) on this book of Nature bringing "magic back to our literature." Dark landscapes, with furiously moving clouds (cut in with flashes of the Ring, and of an Eye, as in the films) and a sense of desolation accompany the telling of Sauron's threat, while gentle rolling fields, with hedges, cottages, and a church (accompanied by Elgar-like music) indicate the Shire, the hobbits, and everything that is endangered. These visual rhetorics are accompanied by repeated assertions that at the core of *LotR* are values of land, nature, and a slower way of living; the books offer "a tale that champions the values of long-lost ways of living, and totally connects us to the land which surrounds us." The landscapes are "like an extra character." This is helped by the tale itself being like older story forms: "Like the great sagas ... Tolkien intended the story to be heard as much as read." Reading *LotR* is a combination of narrative thrill and personal investment (it may be long and demanding, but "you only get out of life what you put into it"), constituting the reading of it as a kind of moral challenge. We "have the freedom to choose." "Being is more important than having." "There's no reason," says Mears, "progress can't go hand in hand with heritage, culture, and nature." This is a soft ecological reading of Tolkien, promising magic and the emotions of commitment. This is a hard-to-fault unspecific, safe defence of *LotR*—but still keeping that whiff of ethical commitment within the reading. Framing Mears' film, Anderson lightly sneers: "to people like Ray Mears who practically worship it, *LotR* is the best book in the known or even unknown universe. But though there are many who love it, there are plenty who hate it with a passion as well. Do you want it to be voted Britain's best loved book? Or would you rather vote for anything else? It's up to you." Thus did the two faces of official cultural response to Tolkien clash, just as the final film was approaching release.

The *National Geographic* (*NG*) documentaries are another matter altogether. Produced in association with New Line Cinema (they have many interviews with cast and crew and feature much footage from the films), widely broadcast on international channels such as MTV and also available for sale, they prominently proclaim their maker's name. Several authors have recently done important critical work on *NG*, disclosing a complex cultural politics centred on showing images of a "happy developing world" to middle America.[14] To our knowledge, however, no researcher has yet attended to the development, since the millennium, of *NG*'s television and film department, or asked what new strategies and ideological developments this may imply.

The two documentaries are rather different. The first, presented by an unidentified American voice, speaks to us as if we are wholly ignorant of Tolkien and his story world. Only the film's actors are presumed to be known. Its aim is to explain how this "perhaps best loved story of the modern age," which "some have called the story of the century," came to be. It does this by seeking parallels between the fictional world and ours: "At first glance it may seem to be a world completely different from our own. Yet this world is under threat, in a way that is strangely familiar." The story unfolds as a series of virtual parallels (visually reinforced with footage from the film) between the events of Tolkien's life and those in the books, along with repeated statements (for example, from Rayner Unwin) that the book is "rooted in realities." It opens with Tolkien's "love of the land," a motivating force for his books. Specific parallels support this. Orcs are visually paralleled by big machines ripping into the ground, Tolkien's early home Sarehole with the Shire, the troll in Moria with World War I tanks.

Expertise in the documentary is "educational." Professor Martin Carver is carefully introduced as a "mediaeval expert." He takes us through the discoveries at Sutton Hoo, concerning Anglo-Saxon culture and history. This is serious learning for us, and for the filmmakers: "The filmmakers have used Tolkien's imagination as their guide in creating the 4,800 pieces of armour" used in the film. Here, the books have specific importance, in two ways. First, for their *links to the past*. Tolkien offers us a means to reconnect with lost histories—as the Kalevala (which is discussed at length) did for the Finns. One Finn says to camera that he heard in the last man who can sing the Kalevala "the voices of my ancestors." We might think of this as a sort of "lessons for our time"—which is why the books, and the films also, could be important. We need myths and heroes and the like. But second, it notes a difference with Tolkien. Most quest tales focus on *finding* something important. The goal of the heroes in Tolkien, it is said, is to undo a great wrong. The parallel the documentary offers is ecological. We switch to Michael Fry, ecologist with the Wildlife Conservation Society, who went on a quest across the Congo and Gabon to draw attention to the destruction by logging of this unspoilt habitat. The evil that he had to stop was "unrestrained development," and his actions are said to parallel Tolkien's "love of the land" with which the documentary began. So, to watch the films is to be offered role models: "Tolkien's hero is an everyman whom we can admire and emulate, the type we need today."

The second *NG* documentary, associated with the final part of the trilogy, is even more explicit in naming "significances." Narrated by John Rhys-Davies (who acted Gimli and voiced Treebeard in the films), this one offers a series of direct parallels between the "themes" of the film and historical personages: William Wallace (who led resistance to the English occupation of Scotland), Elizabeth I (who "served her country" at her own cost), Theodore Roosevelt (who overcame tragedies and disabilities), Benjamin Franklin (who would not let go of a problem), Rasputin (the living embodiment of Wormtongue's seductive evil), Robert E. Lee (as a man not afraid to be defeated), Winston Churchill (leading his "small nation" against Hitler), Lewis and Clark (brave American explorers), and Edmund Hillary and Sherpa

Tensing (who conquered Everest together, but whom the world sought to divide on grounds of "race"). All these demonstrate that *LotR* is "not a fairytale" but a "relentlessly truthful tale" embodying "profound" and "timeless human values" that are nonetheless rooted in our history and culture. Thus it is way beyond being just filmed entertainment. And its close association with New Line Cinema gives this additional significance.

This documentary was not only broadcast and sold as an independent item, but also appeared as an extra in the vanilla DVD edition of *The Return of the King.* This allows us to note one very striking feature. The same bit of filming is used for quite different purposes in this documentary and in one of the adaptation-related extras on the *Return of the King* extended edition DVD. Both use the scene in which Arwen asks Aragorn why he fears he will behave and fail as Isildur, his forebear, did. In the *NG* documentary, it provides a ground and parallel for an overall rhetoric about reluctant heroes for whom "the question of leadership looms large"—the pivot on which all the positive historical examples turn. In the extended DVD, it is used to illustrate the way in which the films *rescue* the books from a potential error, by turning to the broader myth Tolkien created.[15]

One general point is worth making about all these documentaries: in none of them is there ever any discussion of Tolkien's *politics*. We learn nothing about his party preferences or voting habits (if indeed he did vote), his attitudes to wealth, power, race, colonialism. All these could have been made relevant to his writings.[16] Even his attitudes to women are ducked, although this has been one of the most commonly made criticisms of the books. His Catholicism becomes just a source of moral convictions. In all these documentaries, Tolkien is presented either just as an *adventure* writer or as an *ethical* writer. To be clear: we are not promoting this as a better explanation. We note only how selective and "safe" all these documentaries are. This safeness continues into the final, and most important, group of documentaries we want to consider, those most associated with the film itself.

RETHINKING THE DVDS

On the third disc of each four-disc extended edition DVD for the *LotR* trilogy, there appear those two documentary extras, titled "J. R. R. Tolkien" and "From Book to Script." Rich in information about Tolkien's life and works as a whole, and replete with interviews with a considerable number of experts on these—Rayner Unwin (Tolkien's publisher), Humphrey Carpenter (his biographer), Tom Shippey and Patrick Curry (Tolkien scholars), Brian Sibley (BBC adapter and creator of various film-related books), John Howe (conceptual artist), and many others alongside Peter Jackson, Philippa Boyens, Viggo Mortensen, and other crew members and actors—these extras display a very striking rhetorical organisation. This builds across the three DVDs, and shapes their answers to three key questions that these extras address:

1. Who is J. R. R. Tolkien, and what are the significant events in his life that impacted on the themes of the books? This is the primary focus of each "J. R. R. Tolkien" documentary.
2. Why have certain changes been made between books and films, and certain sequences been left out or included? This is considered in both documentaries on each disk.
3. Who is the true author of the *LotR* films? The trajectory of this argument builds across both documentaries on all three extended DVDs.

The documentaries' answers to these three questions work together to create a coherent argument about Tolkien, the cultural meanings and importance of his books, and the function and status of the films in relation to these.[17]

EXPLAINING THE BOOKS AND "CUSHIONING" CHANGES

Overall, the three "J. R. R. Tolkien" documentaries mount an argument about the status of Tolkien's work: unique in achievement, in being a life's work, and in creating an entire universe (with languages, customs, geography, history, and so on). These extras depict Tolkien's life as one of perpetual return from tragedy and death (the death of his parents, the destruction of places and the way of life that he loved, and the loss of friends in World War I, in particular). The books are a search for meaning in a world gone mad. The story therefore is always *more than* entertainment; it addresses "fundamental themes of human existence" from a very modern and politically virtuous position—"profoundly pluralist," "multicultural and multiracial," "profoundly ecological," offering "hope without guarantees." Tolkien is presented as somehow both a man of his times and a man ahead of his times. And in the first DVD comes a hint of a key rhetorical strategy—the book trilogy is simply "the tip of an iceberg" of a wider mythology that gives *LotR* its meaning.

Mainly, the *Fellowship* documentaries are built around the simple argument that it was impossible to re-create the books on screen, page by page. The filmmakers had to make hard choices whilst trying to remain "true" to the book. But in the *Two Towers* DVD "Tolkien" extra a different strategy emerges, which reaches its culmination in the third. The books are subjected to a *friendly critique*. This begins from the problems posed by the book's separation of Aragorn's and Frodo's stories, then combines this with a retrospective account of the problems posed by the too-talky Council of Elrond, and objects to Tolkien's telling the fall of Isengard in "flashback," after it has happened. Tolkien, the commentators declare, "did things which a professional would not have dared to do"—including not properly developing important characters and giving them a through story, and refusing to allow his publishers to edit his work.

At the simplest level, the "J. R. R. Tolkien" documentary extras are replete with a *sense of the films*. As Jackson, Boyens, and a range of Tolkien scholars and experts guide us through a discussion of Tolkien and the books, the films' music accompanies and comments appropriately on different aspects of Tolkien's life and some of the themes of the book—sad for sad, dramatic for dramatic, upbeat for optimistic. But also, these discussions are visually accompanied by appropriate moments from the films themselves, which visualise the particular Tolkien preoccupation or experience under discussion. Whilst not all these address changes between book and film (for instance, shots of Frodo and Sam smiling at each other underscore the importance of friendship in Tolkien's life and *LotR*), a number of others offer a "collective" interpretation of a theme from the books that thus "cushions" a change between book and film.

In all this, a curious rhetorical device becomes more and more salient. This is the construction of a *single collective voice* telling "the story" of *LotR*. Experts, filmmakers, actors speak one after another in a fashion suggesting that their views completely coincide—there is one, settled, shared view of Tolkien's life—without any evident narration. In the *Return of the King* DVD this reaches a point where one speaker can "complete" a previous person's sentence. So, in a particularly revealing example involving two Tolkien scholars, Bill Weldon offers a broader frame of the Elves' place in Tolkien's mythology, culminating in his saying, "The Elves were put in this world to help fulfil its destiny . . ."—cut to John Garth, who continues without pause, ". . . but failed ultimately because they were too hungry for knowledge." There is, in all this, a singular persona authoring the "Tolkien" documentaries' argument, making individual voices largely irrelevant, except where they testify to their own experiences with the book. But the outcome of this is to permit a justification for the changes made between the books and films.[18] In order to illustrate this, we outline two examples of this rhetorical strategy in action.

THE PALANTIR AND THEODEN: PHILOSOPHICAL READINGS AND CLIPS FROM THE FILM

In the *Return of the King* "Tolkien" documentary, a chain of voices discuss the role of the Palantiri (or Seeing Stones) in the story. Tom Shippey points out that each use of a Palantir causes a character to misread the situation—Saruman misled by Sauron, Sauron misled first accidentally by Pippin then more purposefully by Aragorn, Denethor misled by Sauron—and Sibley then suggests that this "so reflects how modern communications can give people a fraction of something and by so doing influence the way in which they react." This segués into a comparison of Denethor, who is defeated by his partial knowledge and despairs, and Theoden, who also loses a son and distrusts the survivor. But Theoden finds courage and hope in the face of death, and, at the moment that this is said, we are shown the shot of Theoden summoning his troops to charge with the great cry of "Death!" Crucially, this is, of course, one of the film script's transfers. In the book, the charge to this cry happens *after* Theoden has been found fatally injured, as the abandoned "son" Eomer decides it is better to die than to survive in a hopeless world.

In this example, then, a collective, philosophical reading of the use of the Palantiri in Tolkien's story (and its relation to post-Tolkien "modern communications") provides us with a new context for understanding Theoden's character. This is underscored by a clip of a key change from book to film. In this way, an implicit reinterpretation and justification is constructed, a virtuous circuit that offers the films as a *better* rendition than the books.

ARWEN AND THE ISSUE OF REALISING CHARACTERS

We noted above that the *Two Towers* "Tolkien" documentary subjected his books to a friendly critique, arguing among other things that Tolkien failed to develop important characters in his books. Without question, the one character repeatedly connected to this critique is Arwen. Indeed, tellingly, when Sibley makes this comment about character development, his words are punctuated and overlaid by a shot of Arwen from the films (even though Sibley makes no specific mention of her). In the *Return* "Tolkien" documentary, we get much more on Arwen and her importance to the *LotR* story, and an argument is constructed through three key intertextual references/components.

Firstly, we are told that Tolkien wanted to incorporate the Arwen and Aragorn story into the main body of the books, but couldn't find a way to do this. Here, this marks the films as an improvement on the books because of course we know that Jackson and his team *have* been able to incorporate this strand into the main story. But this argument gains added weight in that this change was actually an improvement that Tolkien very much *wanted* to make, but couldn't find a satisfactory way to do so.

We're now told that Arwen is crucial to the story, as she "introduces the theme of death"—a theme presented as central to Tolkien's life experience, creativity, and thematic preoccupations. This takes us beyond "the tip of the iceberg" that is the book trilogy to investigate other, related areas of Tolkien's Middle-earth mythology: namely, the stories of mortal-immortal pairings common in northern European folk tales and very important to Tolkien. To illustrate this, the story of Beren and Luthien from Tolkien's *The Silmarillion* is introduced, along with the links between this story and Tolkien's relationship with his wife (for instance, the dance that Tolkien's wife once did for him "inspired" the image of Luthien dancing for Beren). Finally, in a move that ties these myriad references together, we're told that at the heart of Tolkien's story was the central myth of lost love exemplified by the real-life death of his wife, and that therefore ultimately Arwen and Aragorn, Beren and Luthien, and Ronald and Edith Tolkien are all one and the same.

PUTTING TOLKIEN TO THE RIGHTABOUTS

Here, then, developing across the second and third extended DVDs, is an even more intricate argument of reinterpretation and justification, which, ultimately, warrants the way the relationship between Arwen and Aragorn has been reworked. It is these myriad references, then, that constitute the building blocks of an argument for justifying why Arwen's role has been expanded in Jackson's three films.

These strands of argument repeatedly operate to "explain" the many changes made between book and film. For instance, the argument about neglected character development also lays a basis for explaining the dramatic changes made to Faramir's character, in order to provide him with his own "journey" of discovery in the story (discussed in the *Two Towers* "Book to Script" documentary); the fact that Frodo needed to send Sam away on the stairs of Cirith Ungol in order to complicate his character and make him seem less than angelic; and the need for Frodo to fight with Gollum on Mount Doom because there is no way he would be inactive at this moment (both discussed in the *Return of the King* "Book to Script" documentary).[19]

The general aim of "ironing out" flaws in Tolkien's books is also drawn on twice to justify the moving of Shelob the spider to the third film. For Boyens, while this change avoided Helm's Deep and the Shelob attack "cancel[ling] each other out" in terms of dramatic tension and climax, it also functioned, for Jackson, to make the story truer to Tolkien's timeline of events, because the Shelob encounter ought to have occurred at the same moment as the siege of Minas Tirith. To ensure that this notion of correcting and "ironing out" Tolkien's book is clearly enough marked, these comments are accompanied, in the *Return* "Book to Script" documentary, by their visual iteration. Here, the Shelob chapter titles are shown sliding from their *Two Towers* chapter list into their "rightful" place in the list for *The Return of the King*.

In sum, what these documentaries offer, then, is a particular way of reading the books. The books are *serious* (enthusiastic fannishness is noted at a couple of points, but quietly set aside), but guaranteed also to be great storytelling. They are also *richer in meaning* than you are likely to know on your own. So these documentaries can *enrich* your reading. The books are *incredibly modern*—but only really if you "correct" them in certain ways (either in terms of relating them to modern, post-Tolkien issues or by identifying flaws in Tolkien's character or story development). And so, increasingly across the three, they warrant the changes that the films have made. In this sense, these documentaries constitute the filmmakers' (singular/collective) reinterpretations of the books, which make "inevitable" what they did. By consistently positioning the films as mediator between the books themselves and the extratext that is Tolkien's life, thematic preoccupations, and wider Middle-earth mythology, the films thus become almost an *homage to what Tolkien really meant to do* or should have done if he'd been able to step back and analyse his story from a distance, or at least *might have wanted to do*, if he had only known what we now know.

WHOSE STORY IS IT, ANYWAY?

A further topic accompanies the ones we have just developed, and again unfolds across the three DVDs: how the process of adaptation was managed by the films' three screenwriters (Boyens, Jackson, and Fran Walsh) and how these three attempted to remain true to Tolkien during the process. On one level, the issue of justifying changes is discussed and dealt with in a reasonably consistent way across the three "Book to Script" documentaries. There are certain basic rules of film adaptation: the books, with all their depth and detail, could not be translated, page by page, to the screen. Any film attempting to do this would end up as an incoherent "mishmash." Therefore, the screenwriters had to concentrate on telling what they saw as the main through story—Frodo's journey to destroy the Ring.

This reiterated set of adaptation rules allows the screenwriters and actors to justify why certain key book sequences have been omitted from the film. So, Jackson can ask the rhetorical question "What does Tom Bombadil ultimately really have to do with the Ring?", and argue confidently that the Scouring of the Shire (while an important sequence in the book) is a separate story from that of Frodo and the Ring and would have made the final film "anticlimactic." This combines two common circulating arguments: the notion that Tolkien's books as given were "unfilmable," and that all the changes are just part of what Jackson calls "the normal stuff you have to do to adapt a book."

So why trust the screenwriters' decisions? To make the results more palatable, the DVD extras talk us through the difficult process of adapting this so popular and complex book, from the intimate perspective of those involved. As with other extra documentaries on the sets, props, and costumes, there is continuous emphasis on the time, effort, and hard work put into the adaptation process.[20] The three screenwriters are presented as people who love the book intensely and want to protect and look after it (for instance, in the *Two Towers* "Book to Script" documentary, Boyens refers to herself and Walsh as mothers of the book). These are therefore people we can trust to take care of this story in the best and most respectful ways possible.

At moments where specific changes are discussed, the screenwriters take centre stage to talk us through the process (how to make things cinematic while retaining the story's essence and coherence, how to persuade studio financiers that the project remained commercially feasible). Then there was the hard work that went into adapting certain aspects of the story—the constant rewrites, the years it took to solve such difficult problems as incorporating Arwen into the second film, or staging the final struggle for the Ring on Mount Doom.[21] As with other extended edition documentaries, the cast and crew are presented, here, as a "family," a "fellowship," and very human. And, consequently, we hear about the intricate details of their routines and working rituals, from how Walsh had to manage a family as well as the *LotR* project, to a number of very specific anecdotes about how certain ideas were arrived at in front of the computer screen. Thus, through this, the screenwriters are presented as fallible—but honourable—human beings, and likeable, hardworking ones at that.

This much may seem obvious. However, like the previous rhetorical circuit, this discursive strand then consistently segués into another, concerning the ways in which the screenwriters managed to stay true to Tolkien's spirit. One way in which this is conveyed is through direct associations between the hard work and dedication of Jackson and that of Tolkien. In the *Two Towers* "Book to Script" documentary, for instance, Mortensen notes that Jackson faced problems equivalent to Tolkien's when it came to adapting *The Two Towers*—namely, how to keep people interested in all three story strands within this part of the trilogy. Accompanying such comments are still shots of Jackson thinking and working (one of which is used when Ian McKellen notes that Jackson was always on set in the morning poring over the books), shots that seem to mirror the many still shots we see in the "Tolkien" documentaries of Tolkien in his room at Oxford or under a tree thinking.

The discursive link being made here, then, is that Jackson and his screenwriters worked just as hard as Tolkien did. Just like him, they lived and breathed the world of Middle-earth and its mythology, and, as a consequence, they have interpreted the story rather than just regurgitating it, in a way of which Tolkien would surely have approved. Thus, the overall impression given is that the changes have been made *in the spirit of* Tolkien, with the same care and hard work.

This argument emerges across the documentaries. However, it does also change in one significant way as it travels—in the extent to which these three films can be perceived of as *Tolkien's* films. At the close of the *Fellowship* "Tolkien" documentary, Jackson provides the first of a number of statements on the position of the filmmakers in relation to Tolkien's books. He notes that the filmmakers did not want to bring their own "baggage" to these films, as what was of central importance, for them, was to "take what Tolkien cared about" and put that into the film. Ultimately, *The Fellowship of the Ring* should be seen as "Tolkien's film," and not "ours." This argument is reiterated in the *Fellowship* "Book to Script" documentary. During the process of adaptation, it suggests, the three screenwriters would begin to move further and further away from the books—but would eventually find they had to move back towards the books and Tolkien. This proves that Tolkien was right all along—almost suggesting that the spirit of Tolkien was almost there, behind the scenes, orchestrating the whole thing (that "it was meant to be," in a way that was almost beyond "Peter's control").

In the other two DVDs, however, this position begins to change, with the turning point occurring in the *Two Towers* "Book to Script" documentary. Now we are told by Boyens that it is impossible for the filmmakers and screenwriters to be the guardians of Tolkien's book—that the film is what it is and the books will always exist as a separate entity. This about-turn hinges around, and is meshed within, an alternative line of argument, about the "ownership" of the story.

This line of argument is hinted at, in fact, in the *Fellowship* "Tolkien" documentary, where Patrick Curry argues (with accompanying quotations from Tolkien) that the book was not supposed to be an allegory, but to have "applicability." Its readers would have the imaginative freedom to relate its events to their own experiences. This baton is picked up in the *Return* "Tolkien" documentary by Shippey, who argues that these books are like the great myths: you don't have to have read them to know about them. *LotR* is thus "part of the mental furniture of the culture." Mortensen develops this line of argument. After a discussion of Tolkien carrying "the torch" (of hopes and ambitions) for his school friends who died in World War I, he suggests that this is what Tolkien was doing with his books—handing a story to us, that had been handed to him, so we can see what we can do with it—his suggestion rhetorically accompanied by a shot of Frodo handing Sam his book at the end of *The Return of the King*.

What emerges, then, across the second and third DVDs, is a sea-change in the filmmakers' attitudes about who owns the story of *LotR*. It begins as Tolkien's property, to which the filmmakers pay homage. But by the time of the *Two Towers* extended edition, the filmmakers are more confident because of the positive fan reception for the first film. Within the *Two Towers* "Book to Script" extra, Boyens separates the books from the films. As she says, even the Tolkien purists, the "guardians" of Tolkien's work, have begun to accept the changes made to *The Fellowship of the Ring* and *The Two Towers*. While the arrival of the Elves at Helm's Deep would have been "one of the bizarre things he [Tolkien] would have objected to," Tolkien's guardians cheered at this sequence in the cinema.[22]

Boyens, Jackson, and the many other commentators on these extras are thus able to steer a new course for the *LotR* books *and* films and for their reputation and status on DVD. Making use of the rhetorical benefits of a trilogy unfolding over a four-year period, New Line and the filmmakers are able to reposition their films in light of changing assessments of them and, importantly, through the discursive management of key facts about Tolkien's life, his creative influences, and writing practices. Jackson closes the final *Return* "Book to Script" documentary with the hope that, despite all the changes that have been made to the films, Tolkien would be happy that the myth he created was "now taking on a life separate to him.."

It is clear that a lot of discursive work has gone into these DVD documentaries. Weaving and meshing together Tolkien's life experiences and his writing flaws with ruminations on myths, readers and audiences, and the story's modern cultural applicability, a picture of an important story is created, valid to contemporary life and culture, to be measured against the present rather than the past. With these commentaries, the adaptation has thus bid to become the story-in-itself.

THE EXTENDED DVDS AND AUDIENCE VIEWING STRATEGIES

How might all this relate to the viewing strategies and rituals of dedicated viewers of the films? Following our initial analysis of the DVD extras and our discovery of these discursive patterns, we turned to the open-ended interviews that we conducted, in the United Kingdom, with some of those who had filled in our project questionnaire. It is important to note that, while these 107 interviews didn't represent any kind of statistical or representative sample of *LotR* viewers or the U.K. population, they did represent a cross-section of the different kinds of viewing patterns we identified among committed, and mainly enthusiastic, viewers of *The Return of the King*. They were both male and female and they ranged from young teenagers to the middle-aged. We selected fifty interviews, at random, and went back through the transcripts, looking for two things: firstly, general discussions of viewing strategies and rituals when seeing the third film in the trilogy, and, secondly, general discussions of the role of the extended DVDs within these viewing strategies. Note that while the same set of questions was asked in each interview, our question schedule did not ask specifically about the DVDs. In every case, these discussions were spontaneously initiated by our respondents.

The results were striking. Twenty-five of these viewers described a similar viewing ritual for *The Return of the King*. On first viewing, they would go to be "blown away," to be staggered by the scale and the grandeur of the film (an experience frequently described as "overwhelming," "breathtaking," or "exhausting"). But this (often emotional) first viewing meant that it was impossible to "take it all in," so repeat cinema viewings were necessary to "get a little bit more out of it," to "fill in" the "back bits" of the story, and to focus in on, and appreciate, "the little details" that had been missed first time around.

But then, twenty-four also noted (similar to Jack's comment in the epigraph) that, while repeat theatrical viewings helped them to "get more out of" the films, they were still waiting for the extended versions of the film on DVD before they could arrive at their final, settled judgement on the film as a whole. And, for twenty-one of these viewers, this was because of the extended edition's focus on further character and story development, which, ultimately "flesh[ed] out the scenes," "fill[ed] in so many gaps," and added "richness" to the story, making the extended version, for them, the "more complete" or "full" version of the film. Finally, twenty-seven noted that they had watched the previous extended versions of the films over and over again in the home environment (and planned to do the same with the third extended edition). This is because, as one put it, "every time you see them, you see just *something* else that you didn't notice the first time.." But this is not just an accumulation of more and more detail; it is rather a *search for completeness*, a *complete visualisation* of Tolkien's world that can make it most meaningful.[23]

This strikingly prevalent viewing strategy amongst our interviewees suggests an important thesis. As we've seen, the adaptation extras on the extended DVDs focus, primarily, on (1) the serious nature of the *LotR* books, (2) the richness of their meaning (in terms of their relations to Tolkien's life, the connections with our world, and the intricacies of the world Tolkien created), and (3) related justifications for leaving out moments from the book or shifting their thematic emphasis. What we wish to argue here is that we can best understand them if we see them as addressed to a particular way in which committed audiences are now presumed to watch DVDs of this kind. There are certainly "local" factors—we noted above the filmmakers' acknowledgement of the changing fan reception of each theatrical instalment. But as Pavel Skopal and Craig Hight have argued, extended editions generally are targeted at those dedicated fans willing to pay out extra money for these more expensive, and more extensive, versions.[24]

With this in mind, we propose that the extended DVDs (and their extras) play a distinctive role within a marketing campaign that unfolds over time.[25] They are related to a new use of the story, and to the book lover who has seen the film at the cinema and been blown away, but who now wants to explore the film's intricacies in much more depth, and review its relations with the books. It is an opportunity to reflect on concerns that emerged after the film version had been in circulation for a while.

In one way this account chimes with other recent work on the roles and functions of DVD extras. Barbara Klinger has argued that supplementary extras on DVD have "enabled media companies to extend their reach into the home," shaping viewers' "relationship to specific films."[26] While Pavel Skopal and Craig Hight both argue that specific extras on the *LotR* extended editions work to "re-frame the viewers' experience" of the films,[27] and are promoted for the ability to be "closer to the original narratives constructed within Tolkien's books," and therefore to offer "a more comprehensive viewing experience" to Tolkien fans and film buffs.[28]

But none of the three says much about the role of DVD extras in relation to film *adaptations*. Hight, who directly considers the *LotR* extended DVDs, makes minimal comments on their adaptation extras, instead focusing on their filmmaking extras and the documentaries focused on props, sets, and costumes. All these, for him, work to encourage appreciation of the filmmakers' skills, and to celebrate the general craft of contemporary filmmaking. Meanwhile, for Klinger (who focuses on those who appreciate the technical capabilities of home cinema equipment), "'perfect' DVD movies" are generally action or sci-fi films, or films that foreground spectacular form over content in a way that complements the technical quality of DVD and home cinema technologies.[29] This focus on spectacle cannot account for the more character-driven features and the significance given to just these aspects by so many of our interviewees.

This suggests that film adaptations may thrive within DVD formats and in extended editions for entirely different reasons than provided by Klinger's "hardware aesthetic" thesis. Indeed, a number of our respondents specifically noted the opposite, that the extended DVD experience was more "intimate," while the cinema allowed them to celebrate the films' technical qualities. Hight and Klinger are primarily concerned with exploring how the capabilities of the DVD medium are exploited by film and media companies. At one level, therefore, they are a little suspicious of the pleasures they offer. We see them somewhat differently, at least for those viewers who have a strong investment in a particular story and its adaptation and then circulation on DVD. In this context, DVDs can instead be understood as a *point of reflection* on a film's achievement, the moment when those viewers who have invested most strongly in the experience look for the resources to *sum up what has been achieved*. Could it be that in this way the long-term status and reputation of a film is being secured? That in the case of *LotR*, therefore, the most important feature is the emergent proposal that the books, while still marvellous, have found in the films their contemporary form and meaning?

CONCLUSION

What, then, are we claiming to be the special position of the *LotR* extended DVDs, in consequence of this?

1. They are produced by New Line in implicit acknowledgement that audiences use them to "complete" their experience of a film, and that therefore this can help them to "sum up" for the future the achievement and significance of the films (a future, that at least based on our U.K. interviewees, will involve numerous repeat viewings of the film, giving it an extended "afterlife" on DVD).

2. The DVD extras therefore can function as arguments for the value of the films. They justify its outcomes. This has potential implications for our wider understanding of adaptations generally. For many of those most heavily invested in Tolkien's world, the DVD extended editions with their extras are—and are known by the producing companies to be—used as a way of renewing and *completing* their sense of the story, its salient features, and its ultimate value. The complex movements engendered here, from books to films and back to the books, are going to require a new kind of thinking about literary adaptations of this kind. "Fidelity" matters, but now has a quite different charge, and meaning.

3. For a book-sourced film like *LotR* (and in relation to New Line's implicit acknowledgement of the viewing strategy discussed in point 1 above), adaptation-specific extras can provide reasons to see unity and logic in the results, to do this in relation to changes made between book and film, and, ultimately, to regard the filmmaking achievement as true to the author. More than this, they can make the author relevant to us, to today.

The final implication suggests a new road of theory and research. DVDs of this kind, and in particular the one associated with *The Return of the King*, cannot be accounted for simply as another marketing opportunity. Rather, their contents suggest that they should be understood as *investments in the long-term marketability of the films*. No further purchases are likely to be made, after the first extended edition. But if the most devoted audiences can be persuaded that this, here, now, is the definitive article, and that it rescues and transcends the books, then the value of the films is secured for future re-releases, circulation, and the reputation of company, director, and stars. As one respondent put it, "I'll just constantly watch" the extended DVDs "to remember what Peter Jackson and the directors achieved." If this is right, this new intensive dialogue between studios and committed viewers, and the associated strategic planning of DVD contents, are a new field awaiting our attention.

CHAPTER SIX

Understanding Disappointment

The Australian Book Lovers and Adaptation

SUE TURNBULL

In 1997, well before Peter Jackson's film version of *The Lord of the Rings* had reinvigorated interest in Tolkien's books worldwide, Sian Powell wrote an article in Australia's only national newspaper, *The Australian,* to coincide with the publication of book chain Angus and Robertson's list of the one hundred "favourite books of all time" as nominated by forty thousand customers in Australia.[1] The Angus and Robertson list, Powell noted, had been inspired by U.K. book chain Waterstone's similar list, which was widely considered by Australian publishers and reviewers to be much more "literary" in tone than the Australian one. Despite any perceived difference in terms of the "literary" merit of the respective book lists, what is of interest here is that both the British and the Australian versions placed *LotR* first. As reported by Powell, when asked to comment on these lists, Margaret Harris, professor of English at Sydney University, thought it "odd" that *LotR* still sat so high in the affections of Australians—and Britons: "It was a cult hit 20 years ago, but I don't have a strong sense of it being still in fashion." Had Harris but known, *LotR* was already a cult hit in Australia by the early 1960s, when the first Tolkien Society was established at her own university, although the gathering was initially dedicated to "fun and games" rather than serious Tolkien scholarship.[2]

Given the ongoing cultural connections between the United Kingdom and its former penal colony, the fact that Tolkien's work had clearly found its way to Australia and an avid readership (albeit a predominantly Anglophone and student one) in the 1960s is hardly surprising. However, efforts to determine when the books officially arrived in Australia (as opposed to being carried from the United Kingdom by travellers and immigrants) proved a tad frustrating. Paul Donovan, managing director of Allen and Unwin in Australia, explained that when the company became a completely independent publisher in Australia in 1990, it lost access to all records of sales in Australia prior to that time.[3] Based on his knowledge of the company's practice in the 1950s, Donovan was nevertheless quite certain that the books in their original three-volume format would have come to Australia very quickly after their individual publication dates, as was usually the case. The fact that *The Fellowship of the Ring* was reprinted fifteen times in 1954 tends to support this view. Some seventeen years later, journalist Gordon Farrar of Melbourne's *Age* newspaper was given the U.K. second edition of the Allen and Unwin paperback version (published in the United Kingdom in 1968) in 1971 at the age of nine.[4] This version, with its cover art by Pauline Baynes, he read sixteen times before the back broke, sections went missing, and he was forced to buy a new volume.[5]

Farrar's repeat and dedicated reading from childhood points very usefully towards the pattern of the Australian participants who responded to this project's questionnaire. Within a sample of 551, more than half (59 percent) suggested that they had read all three books more than once, while a smaller number (19 percent) had read them just once. In other words, more than three quarters of the Australian sample came to the film informed by a prior reading of the books. Not unsurprisingly, many people therefore based their assessment of the film in terms of their "fidelity" to the books they loved. The concept of fidelity has a long tradition in theories of film adaptation (see chapter 5 in this volume). Within this tradition, as Robert Stam and Alesandra Raengo point out, discourses around the film adaptation of books often "subtly"—and, one could argue, not so subtly—reinscribe "the axiomatic superiority of literature to film": "Terms like 'infidelity,' 'betrayal,' 'deformation,' 'violation,' 'bastardisation,' 'vulgarization' and 'desecration' proliferate in adaptation discourse, each word carrying its own specific charge of opprobrium."[6] Interestingly, these were not the kinds of terms usually employed by the Australian participants in this study, but then this was hardly surprising since almost three-quarters of them (74 percent) described the film as "extremely enjoyable." In other words, the majority of the Australian sample, who had read the books in advance, also found the film extremely enjoyable, even though they might have some criticisms to make. This finding begs the question "How can one be disappointed in some way with an adaptation—and yet at the same time find the experience 'extremely enjoyable'?"

In order to look more closely at this apparent contradiction, I decided to focus specifically on those respondents who had both found the film extremely enjoyable and had read all three books more than once, indicating a deep attachment to the books. A further sorting of the data thus yielded a smaller sample of 244 people whose responses to the question "What was the most disappointing moment or aspect of the film to you?" were examined in some detail, to determine both the most common criticisms and the kinds of discourses employed. It might be noted here that this smaller sample reflected the profile of the Australian sample as a whole in that the majority were female students aged sixteen to twenty-five, with the next largest grouping being professional women aged twenty-six to thirty-five.[7]

After doing keyword searches within the questionnaire field related to "disappointment," I found that sixty-seven participants (27 percent) made some mention of "the books" in voicing their criticisms, while only seven (2 percent) referred to Tolkien himself. However, many of the expressions of disappointment invoked the authority of the original text and its author's vision without explicitly mentioning either. The primacy of the book was therefore axiomatic, and the authority of Tolkien as its creator frequently asserted, sometimes acerbically: "Tolkien was a stickler for ensuring that everything hung together logistically. The filmmakers left that legacy in tatters" (male, 36–45, professional). Six people referred to Peter Jackson's role in the adaptation of the books to film in relation to changes such as "The Pyre of Denethor sequence. It was just absurd sensationalism, with no logic at all behind it. Jackson would have done best to stick to the books" (male, 16–25, student). But there were also those who were inclined to be more understanding: "I think Peter Jackson did an amazing job considering the expectations so many people had about LOTR" (female, 26–25, creative). Indeed, as will become apparent in many of the ensuing comments, a large number of the Australian book scholars negotiated their major and minor disappointments with the film by suggesting that they "understood" or "accepted"—sometimes begrudgingly—the reasons for the changes. As one older woman noted, "Unfortunately so much of the book had to be left out because of time constraints. This meant that there were things that happened in the movie that had no obvious explanation (e.g., Eowyn being madly in love with Aragorn and then turning up at his coronation with Faramir who was last seen at death's door). Too much chopping" (46–55, clerical/administrative). For one woman, changes to the story line could be justified in terms of the film having to address a "general public," this suggestion thus identifying her as a member of a different audience altogether: a "special" audience who would have willingly sat through a much longer version of the film and who didn't need a conventional romance story to keep them interested:

> I would have liked to have seen the role of Saruman shown more and the book depiction of the Shire when the hobbits return. But this would have made the film too long for the general public. The depiction of Arwen also annoyed me. Even though the relationship between her and Aragorn is important, I don't think her character required such a large role in the films. One reason for this could be that Romance stories also appeal to the general public. (26–35, professional)

Eighteen people negotiated their disappointment with the omissions, changes, and abbreviations in the film by looking forward to the release of the extended DVDs, thus confirming Martin Barker and Kate Egan's suggestion (see chapter 5 in this volume) that for many of the film's cinema audience the extended edition was anticipated as the definitive film text: "Hopefully we [will] get some truer and MORE of the appendices and endings in the extended DVD version" (male, 26–35, self-employed). Although this sentence is clearly missing something, the use of the adjective *truer* without a noun is interesting in that it points definitively to a notion of fidelity based on the "truth" of the original text, and an anticipation that the extended DVDs will come closer to this, whatever it is. Perhaps even more interesting is the use of the collective noun *we*, implying that this respondent also imagines himself to be part of a very particular audience for the film, one with intimate knowledge of the books, for whom the extended versions will constitute a more complete realisation of the books.

In terms of specific criticisms, the most frequently mentioned were:

1. the treatment of Faramir's character and story line, with 8 percent of respondents making reference to the absence of detail about his developing relationship with Eowyn (14 percent);
2. the omission of the Scouring of the Shire, as well as the character of Tom Bombadil (13 percent); and
3. the absence of Saruman from the cinema release of the third film, and the omission of his humiliation and defeat (13 percent).

These and other criticisms relating to the portrayal of particular characters and the absence of specific scenes and moments will be discussed in more detail below.

CHANGES TO CHARACTERS

Expressions of disappointment with the portrayal of Faramir and perceived changes to his story line included the following: "The portrayal of Faramir . . . his character was twisted (e.g. forcing Frodo to take the ring to Gondor since when did that happen??!!) I realise that it is impossible to be completely faithful to the book but I think there was no reason for corrupting his character" (female, 16–25, professional). The use of the verb *corrupting* here is of interest, in that it provides a very clear example of the kinds of negative discourse referred to by Stam and Raengo used to resinscribe the "axiomatic superiority" of the book in relation to the film.[8] Both male and female respondents expressed disappointment at the omission of the Houses of Healing scenes and the treatment of the love story involving Faramir and Eowyn: "Their love story is one of the most delicate and beautiful of all the relationships in the saga and I was VERY disappointed to see it only alluded to—and that very subtly. Also Denethor. Much maligned in the movie. Made me cross" (female, 26–35, creative). Other characters whose portrayal drew criticism included not only Faramir and Denethor, but also Gimli, Gollum, Legolas, and Frodo and the hobbits. In relation to Legolas, it is interesting to note how extradiegetic reasons, the need for the film to appeal to a specific viewership, were again provided:

"Sometimes I didn't like Legolas as a character because it seemed as if his part was very minor [. . .] Legolas/Orlando Bloom shots for the benefit of fan girls" (female, under 16, student). Note that these comments were made by a female student who clearly did not count herself a "fan girl" in this regard. Like the responses above that suggested that the films had to be adapted to appeal to a "general public," this statement once again identifies the participant as someone who considers herself to have a very different relationship with the film from that of the imagined majority.

Of particular note is the following comment, which points to a very precise poetic moment in the book in relation to the portrayal of the character of Legolas: "One of my favourite parts of the book has always been Legolas hearing the wailing of the gulls and feeling the pull of sea longing for the first time. This scene not being included was a bit disappointing but I understood its absence" (male, 16–25, self-employed). Not quite so understanding was a woman who blamed changes to the roles of several of the female characters on a form of political correctness that she regarded as unnecessary: "The book plots were left a little and the female roles were expanded upon. Apparently there has been a bit of press about the story revolving around men. Due to Tolkien's life this is understandable. I don't understand why everything has to be about equal opportunities for women anyway" (female, 25–36, creative).

CHANGES TO THE STORY

The change from the book narrative that occasioned the greatest displeasure was the omission of the Scouring of the Shire, which for a number of people was of vital importance in the portrayal of the hobbits: "[Disappointed with the] fact that the hobbits returned home and everything was fine. In the book they find turmoil in the Shire when they return and I think it shows how far they have come in their journey in the way the handle that, I was disappointed it was left out" (female, 16–25, professional). On the other hand, there were also those who could see good reasons for this omission in terms of film length even while they regretted it not being there: "I had no major disappointment. I would have liked to see the Scouring of the Shire represented where the hobbits realise that at last they are on their own and can't rely on anyone else to save them. But that would have made the film at least half an hour longer" (female, 26–35, professional).

The ending of the film occasioned many comments overall, with equal numbers of people complaining that it was either too long or too short. However, lack of "closure" was clearly a problem for many, not only in relation to the Scouring of the Shire, but also in relation to the character of Saruman, with the extended DVD again holding out the promise of a more "complete" version: "Little bit disappointed that there was no footage of Saruman. Peter Jackson in the commentary of the extended version of the Two Towers mentioned that footage would be included" (male, 26–35, clerical/administrative). Once again, there was an acknowledgement in relation to such an omission that it would have been impossible to realise the books in their totality on the screen: "[Disappointed with the] excision of the humiliation of Saruman by Mithrandir and the cleansing of the Shire but if anything had to be cut these episodes added least to the plot (but not necessarily to the concept of the books)" (male, 46–55, unemployed).

COMMON THEMES

Close analysis of the 244 responses from those who found the film extremely enjoyable and had read the books more than once thus begins to reveal some interesting patterns in terms of how this particular group negotiated their disappointment with the film. For a start, there is evidence that many of the book lovers "know" that the process of adaptation is a difficult one, and, without explicitly stating that the two mediums are completely different, there is an understanding that it would be impossible to convey all of the book on screen. There is, therefore, a degree of graciousness in some of the responses that acknowledge the difficulty of the task facing the filmmakers even as Jackson and his colleagues are criticised for some of the changes that have been made.

Also apparent is the sense that the book lovers regard themselves as a very special audience quite apart from "fans" and the "general public" (as evident, for example, in the negative comment about the filmmakers catering to the tastes of "fan girls" in the treatment of Legolas noted above). This is interesting in relation to Matt Hills' sophisticated formulation of the relationship between fandom and academia, which posits a distinction between the scholar-fan (the academic fan who performs his or her fandom in academic writing) and the fan-scholar (the fan who uses academic theorising within his or her fan writing).[9] Identifying themselves as a special audience rather than as a group of fans, the respondents in this study clearly eschewed the category of fandom, suggesting the need to find other ways of conceiving a particular passion for what might be described as a "cult" text outside the categories of fandom described by Hills.

This particular audience's sense of specialness, it would seem, comes from having read the books first and, in many cases, often. Their relationship with the books, it could be argued, is thus highly individuated in relation to their own personal "stories" and experiences of encountering the books. Knowledge of the prior text (the book), and indeed the emotional impact it has had on them, thus equips the respondents with a yardstick when it comes to making an assessment of the film. Such an assessment then depends upon the practice of what I might call a vernacular form of textual analysis, involving constant comparison between the experience of the book and that of the film.

In describing the practice of such criticism as "vernacular," I am suggesting that it was occurring spontaneously both outside and beyond the formal academic spaces where such textual criticism might occur. And in suggesting that this happened spontaneously, I am suggesting that this special audience could not help but make constant comparisons with the book during the watching of the film, comparisons they were able to articulate *immediately* after the film (as we approached them as they came out of the cinema), or shortly afterwards when completing the online questionnaire.

In terms of the contradiction involved in finding fault with the film *and* finding it extremely enjoyable, it is therefore possible that enjoyment for this particular audience segment comes not only from the realisation on film of the books they know intimately and already love, but also from the performance of a vernacular form of textual analysis in making critical evaluations of the film. In other words, this special audience consider themselves to be in a position of superior knowledge and authority when it comes to making assessments of the film. In asking them to comment on the film on disappointments, we were inviting them to perform this knowledge as an authoritative audience making judgements about how well in their estimation the film measured up to the books.

Ultimately, it would seem, it is the sense of being a special audience in possession of a degree of authority with regards to a reading of *both* texts that explains how the expression of critical judgements (including disappointment) may be an intrinsic part of the profound pleasure to be derived from the film experience. The practice of vernacular criticism may have its own intrinsic and pleasurable rewards, even if the judgements themselves may be negative.

Having started by describing the Australian context of reception for the book and for the film, it seems only fitting to return to this location in order to observe that the geographical location of these respondents hardly seemed to matter at all in terms of the ways in which they accounted for their enjoyment of either the book or the film. In this way, *LotR* proved to be a text capable of transcending national boundaries, uniting its audience in a landscape of the imagination experienced as profoundly real in its emotional and aesthetic effects despite its fantastic and fictional origins.

CHAPTER SEVEN

Involvement in
The Lord of the Rings

Audience Strategies and Orientations

LOTHAR MIKOS, SUSANNE EICHNER, ELIZABETH PROMMER,
AND MICHAEL WEDEL

The film trilogy *The Lord of the Rings* became one of the greatest hits in cinema, reaching an enormous audience, and indeed a great number of different audiences. As a form of the contemporary blockbuster, the trilogy follows the pattern of communicating a multitude of possible meanings and pleasures.[1] The present chapter examines how this special kind of film narrative anticipates different patterns of reception, organises them in a complex aesthetic form, and thus permits spectator involvement on a variety of levels. The indications stem from an analysis of narrative and aesthetic structures, and also from a reception study. First we will present the research design of the investigation, which formed part of the international project on the reception of *LotR*. Then we will discuss the concept of involvement. The last section focuses on the findings of the reception study in relation to forms of involvement. Findings relating to the critical reception of *LotR* in Germany, and its framework of generic presentation (as blockbuster and as fantasy), have been presented in other publications, and though what we present here is connected to those findings (especially in our consideration of the amalgamation of fans' and more general blockbuster clientele's readings of the film), reasons of space do not permit us to elaborate on them.[2]

THE RESEARCH DESIGN OF THE GERMAN
LORD OF THE RINGS STUDY

The German part of the international *LotR* project considered the online questionnaire as part of a multidimensional reception study and of an investigation of the *LotR* phenomenon from multiple perspectives. Based on the "Babelsberg approach," also employed in a study of the television show *Big Brother*, an analysis of the film trilogy was combined with a discourse and context analysis and a reception study.[3] Our approach incorporates both considerations of reception aesthetics and the concepts of contextualisation as developed in cultural studies. The fundamental premise of the approach is that there is a reciprocal relationship between media texts and acts of reception. The structures of media texts can be observed in acts of reception, just as acts of reception can be found in the structures of media texts. The methodology of the Babelsberg approach is oriented towards the systematic triangulation of perspectives used in qualitative social research.[4] As Norman K. Denzin and Yvonna S. Lincoln write, "the use of multiple methods, or triangulation, reflects an attempt to secure an in-depth understanding of the phenomenon in question."[5] Different methods are combined in order to examine media communication in all its complexity from a variety of perspectives.

The *LotR* trilogy is such a complex media phenomenon that it manifests cultural practices in different ways. For this reason, a textual analysis was undertaken of the film trilogy—including the cinema versions of the three films, the "enhanced" DVD versions, and the computer games—as well as a comparison with the literary versions, the novels. This textual analysis was combined with an analysis of the production context that considered the production of blockbusters in general and *LotR* in particular, the marketing of the products, and the importance of the Internet both for marketing and for reception. The third component was an analysis of the public discourse on the trilogy, as reflected in German-language film criticism on the three parts and in public discourse connected with the Academy Awards of March 2004. The research design was rounded out by a multidimensional reception study consisting of four parts:

1. a representative telephone survey before the premiere of *The Fellowship of the Ring*, in three waves of 1,000 respondents, to study the "want-to-see" factor;
2. a standardised questionnaire containing both open and closed questions, answered by 352 *LotR* fans who saw the film on the night of its premiere or in the first week after its release—including some fans who watched the complete trilogy in a triple feature showing on the premiere night;
3. a qualitative survey of fans in five focus groups using the group discussion method; and
4. the evaluation of the 880 German responses to the online survey.

THE "WANT-TO-SEE" FACTOR OF *LOTR*

Before we discuss the findings of the textual analysis and the reception study, we will first present here the results of the investigation of the "want-to-see" factor, which is relevant for the assessment of the film and its reception. The representative telephone surveys were conducted ten weeks, five weeks, and one week before the release of *The Fellowship of the Ring*. First, respondents were asked which films they absolutely wanted to see in the next few weeks, without prompting. Then questions were asked about specific films, including *FotR* and *Matrix Revolutions*. The participants were also asked about their motivation for their moviegoing plans. Ten weeks before the cinema release, 25 percent of the respondents named *The Fellowship of the Ring* without prompting as a film they wanted to see. Five weeks before the launch, 29 percent wanted to see it, and one week before, 31 percent. When asked about the film specifically, the proportions were higher: 44 percent at ten weeks, 42 percent at five, and 43 percent at one week before the premiere.

Evidently, many of the respondents had decided that they wanted to see the film long before it reached the theaters. Furthermore, the influence of short-term marketing was barely detectable, except that the unprompted answers showed greater awareness of the film. There was another exception, however: the values for *FotR* in answers to the unprompted question rose among male respondents aged fourteen to twenty-nine, from 41 percent ten weeks before the launch, to 52 percent at five weeks before, and 60 percent one week before the premiere. At the same time, an effect was observable among respondents who had completed nine years of school: the positive answers rose from 12 percent ten weeks before to 18 percent at five weeks and 17 percent one week before the premiere. Young, less educated men form one of the largest audience groups in cinemas, celebrate a cinema outing as a group experience, and are generally interested in blockbusters and action films. The marketing activities evidently reached them. By contrast, *LotR* fans knew as soon as they had seen the first two parts that they wanted to see the third film. The statement "I'm a 'Lord of the Rings' fan" was the respondents' most frequently named motivation for wanting to see the film. The second most important motivation was the desire to see "how the books were adapted for cinema." The effect of marketing for *FotR* on *LotR* fans was minimal, but it did increase interest among the general cinema audience.

VIEWER INVOLVEMENT AND NARRATIVE MODES IN *LOTR*

A shared characteristic of all interpretations of the term *involvement* is the idea that it refers to participation in processes of reception: "a more or less strong involvement in media reception refers in general to the degree of internal participation with which media users follow a media offering," or the "degree of integration of the recipient in a communicative situation."[6] We can distinguish between high and low degrees of involvement. A viewer who uses a medium perhaps alongside other activities has low involvement; the attitude of reception is aloof. High involvement is characterised by the viewers giving their full attention to the medium, and usually not allowing themselves to be distracted from it. Peter Vorderer has described involved reception as "the attitude of reception in which the recipients are so cognitively and emotionally involved in the fictive events (in this case, the film narrative) that they are no longer aware of the reception situation itself, but 'live' in what they are perceiving, as it were."[7] This strong inner participation is a mental activity on the part of the recipients, but it is brought about by the structure of the film or television texts, and by the reception situation.

The conditions under which involvement occurs have barely been studied up to now. Although Vorderer points out that involvement in parasocial interaction "is created through identification with a film character," this remark is unclear, partly because it mixes two very different patterns under which relationships are created between recipients and film characters: parasocial interaction and identification.[8] A more detailed discussion of the kinds of relationships that can arise between viewers and characters in film and television texts is beyond the scope of this chapter. However, we can note in general that involvement can arise through the relationships to characters. That is, in the case of *LotR* the recipients' relationships to characters such as Aragorn, Arwen, Frodo, Gandalf, Gollum, or Legolas partly determine how fully audiences are absorbed in and "go along with" the film's events: the stronger the bond with one or more characters, the stronger the involvement in the film.

In addition to the relationship to the film characters, however, other textual features of the films also play a part in involving viewers. Decisive factors are the narrative and dramaturgy of the films.[9] The viewer is a structural part of the film narrative, since the collaboration of an interpreting recipient is always necessary for a film to unfold its story. Narratives are generally presented from the point of view of a narrator and his view of the story. At the same time, the narrative is intended for—that is, addressed to—an audience. The narrative causally connects actors, actions, and situations to form a story. The dramaturgy shapes this story in order to make it interesting for viewers, and to integrate them in the story through interpretative processes. Only thus can the narrative bring an audience to experience suspense in a story. The dramaturgy and narrative of a film can—with the support of the aesthetic design—further the process of involvement. Action and special effects, for instance, can draw viewers into the action on the screen, overpowering audiences with visual attractions and increasing visual pleasure: viewers are so spellbound by the visual attractions on the screen that they forget the world around them. In this way, action scenes and special effects are essential elements of film texts, leading the recipients to involvement. The huge battle scenes in *LotR* and the special effects used in them probably contributed greatly to the viewers' involvement. The generic marker of a film (as "fantasy," "event movie," "blockbuster") also affects involvement.

With regard to the blockbuster label, Kristin Thompson suggests that while they target already existing audiences—namely, the fans and consumers of the books, comics, or computer games—"such fans were not enough to support a blockbuster hit, and the filmmakers would have to lure a much larger audience who had never read the books or heard of hobbits."[10] It is necessary to see the potential audience here not only as the existing fan base of the books, comics, or computer games, but also as the sum of cultural knowledges and practices about these products in circulation in society. Hence the film adaptations are guaranteed a certain success, since the characters and stories of the films are already part of the audience's cultural framework. We call this phenomenon *assured reception*.[11] In *LotR* the chances for success are all the greater, since many viewers are already familiar with the narrative from the books. At the same time, however, this fact brings a danger with it, since the film, as an independent narrative, may be based on a different story in the viewers' heads than the books. If the differences between the two narratives are too great, the viewers' involvement will be obstructed rather than facilitated.

The already complex makeup of *LotR* becomes still more complicated when we consider that all three films as a trilogy narrate a continuous story, while at the same time each part of the trilogy narrates a complete story in itself, since all three parts must function as autonomous blockbuster films at the box office. The extended value-added chain—marketing extended DVD versions that contain scenes that are not included in the theatrical versions of the films—creates a complex matrix of narratives and partial narratives from which the complete text of *LotR* arises. Moreover, Tolkien's narrative in book form, as well as numerous film reviews, Internet forums, and countless merchandising products, can function as prefigurative materials for the reception and assimilation of the films in the viewers' respective national and cultural contexts. The urgent question arises: "What exactly is the text of *LotR* in which the recipients are involved?" During a cinema screening, it is certainly the film. Yet the audience is familiar with the other media versions, so the process of assimilation mixes not only the various genre elements of the blockbuster trilogy in the cinema and DVD versions, but also the prefigurative materials. Because the films build on an audience that is familiar with the books, while at the same time trying to gain a much bigger audience, their narrative and informational output must be designed to allow nonreaders to understand the story as well. For this reason the films are obliged to build up interpretative frames as quickly as possible, and through prologue, narration (and the complex network of different stories), emotionalisation (of characters), and montage provide a persistent guide for audiences, taking them by the hand and giving them orientation while at the same time introducing them to the story, without which no involvement would be possible. For viewers who lack prior knowledge, the processes of involvement are probably not as easily realised as for viewers who have read the books. Nonetheless, the films offer sufficient opportunities for involvement through their portrayal of the characters, their various genre frames, and the special effects, which create visual attraction and encourage visual enjoyment.

Finally, to attract as large an audience as possible, Tolkien's books also had to be simplified, and in order to address a young audience other aspects of the story were judged to deserve highlighting.[12] Thus, the film trilogy modernises the fantasy genre by mixing in other genre elements, by giving greater attention to other aspects of the narrative—such as the love story of Arwen and Aragorn—and generally through its visual style. In relation to the narrative and aesthetic structures, the *LotR* trilogy attempts to be attractive to the audience through modernised fantasy genre conventions; through the emotionalisation of love stories, personal development stories, and battle scenes; through editing according to the conventions of horror, splatter, and samurai films; and through the use of extraordinary special effects. In the dominant fantasy framework, there are many other elements that can function as an interpretative frame for the audience, thus forming the basis for processes of involvement.

VIEWERS' EXPERIENCES OF *LOTR*

Involvement takes place at different levels in *LotR:* on the levels of character relationships, narrative and structure, and action and special effects. The importance of the various levels for viewers depends on the recipients' prior knowledge and preferences. After all, viewers of *LotR* are not a homogeneous audience, but a collection of different audiences, characterised by sociocultural determinants such as nationality, gender, age, and ethnicity, or by shared aesthetic cultures: certain preferences, media orientations, and a shared encyclopedia of knowledge, including media knowledge.[13]

The concept of different audiences was integrated in the design of the reception study by positing several different hypothetical audience segments, in the form of focus groups, based on certain premises. Separate focus groups for "Women" and "Men" were established. Three more groups were selected on the basis of shared media experience and orientation: the group of "Computer Gamers," as a hypothetical audience segment with a high affinity to media and media technologies, as well as an increased interest in fantasy; the group "Literary Generation," as a hypothetical audience segment with detailed knowledge about Tolkien's imaginary world; and finally the group "Media Generation," conceived as ordinary moviegoers who are willing to watch the film without knowing the books and without any special preference for the fantasy genre. We postulated that each group would have specific reception strategies and interpretations of the films due to their specific shared experiences, preferences, and values.

The criteria of gender, familiarity with the Tolkien books before and after the films, and other media preferences were also recorded in the other parts of the reception study—the viewer survey and online questionnaire—in order to permit findings about specific audiences in addition to observations about *LotR* fans in general.

EMOTION, EMPATHY, AND IDENTIFICATION IN *LOTR*

As indicated in the product analysis, *LotR* invites involvement at three levels (character relationships, narrative and structure, and action and special effects), and the reception study corroborated this finding.

Viewers' relationships to the characters are an important means of involvement, since the plot is usually driven and empathy built up by means of the characters. *LotR* is unusual in that, instead of the classic (Western) one-hero structure, a group of heroes leads us through the story. Accordingly, the film structure is not simply conducive to identification with and emotional attachment to one principal, psychologically well developed character, but rather offers the recipients a number of stereotypical characters. Depending on the given situation in the film, as well as on the conditions that the recipients bring with them, recipients feel sympathy or admiration, identify with or are repelled by one character or another. Frodo, who as Ring-Bearer is a central figure in the narrative, is perceived by respondents not as the *one* main character, but as one of many, even though his central role is acknowledged. One respondent described the characters in Tolkien's world as follows: "For me *The Lord of the Rings* is the most archetypal fantasy book there is, the one that others have imitated. That's why these are the original characters, which the others have all copied. The dwarf is the prototype of all dwarfs; Gandalf is the prototype of all wizards" (Uke, 27, "Computer Gamers" group). Asked about a favourite character and about the "hero" of the story, respondents gave many different answers. Both in the cinema exit survey and in the online questionnaire, Aragorn, Legolas, Sam, and Gandalf are the four most popular characters. Aragorn was the most frequently named character in both surveys.[14] In spite of his central role, Frodo was chosen as the favourite character by only 6 percent in the cinema audience survey and only 7 percent in the online questionnaire. (See table 7.1.)

Table 7.1: Favourite Characters (all respondents)

Cinema Audience Survey (n=352)	Online Questionnaire (n=880)
Aragorn 20%	Aragorn 29%
Legolas 17%	Sam 23%
Sam 15%	Gandalf 15%
Gandalf 12%	Legolas 11%
Gollum 11%	Frodo 7%
Gimli 9%	Gollum 7%
Frodo 6%	—
Arwen 2%	—

The choice of a favourite character is strongly influenced by age and gender, although Aragorn was favoured by almost all audience segments. The youngest viewers who answered the cinema audience survey (aged sixteen and under) overwhelmingly chose the characters Aragorn and Gimli, but the answers varied increasingly with increasing age of the respondents. The character of Gandalf was chosen significantly more often by those aged twenty-six and over than by younger viewers, attaining second place among older viewers, with 17 percent. Legolas, on the other hand, was more often named as a favourite character by a younger audience segment, that of sixteen-to-twenty-five-year-olds. He was this audience segment's second favourite character, with 22 percent of the votes cast, although he was chosen by only 13 percent of those over twenty-six. Sam is the only character besides Aragorn to achieve a stable rating across all age groups, holding the middle ground at 10 percent to 15 percent of the responses.

Three characters showed clear gender-specific differences in popularity: Gimli, Legolas, and Gollum. Eighty-nine percent of those who named Gimli as a favourite character, and 76 percent of those who named Gollum, were male. Legolas, on the other hand, tended to be chosen as a favourite character by women: 63 percent of those who named him as their favourite character were female. Women also chose female characters among their favourites. As the analysis of the group discussion shows, modern female identification figures are important in the otherwise male-dominated film with traditional gender roles. One respondent argued, "I thought Eowyn was good. But she wasn't the ugly duckling, she was the heroine. So there was something like an emancipated woman" (Rebecca, 22, "Media Generation" group). Women often chose as their favourite characters those to whom they felt to be attracted (Aragorn and Legolas) or those whose roles they could identify with (Eowyn). Men often named characters who transported values that were important to them, such as loyalty or friendship (Sam, Gandalf).

Among the five hypothetical audience segments, few significant differences in the popularity of characters were noted. The exceptions were the "Computer Gamers" and the "Literary Generation" groups. Both of these groups showed more frequent choices of the dark or ambiguous characters (Gollum, Faramir, the Nazgûl captain): "Gollum is the only one who is a little bit good and a little bit bad. All the rest are one or the other. Gollum is both; he's so normal" (Elena, 24, "Computer Gamer"). The "Literary Generation" group also indicated a difference between their favourite film character and their favourite literary character. With regard to the book, most of the answers were limited to Gandalf and Aragorn, but the answers concerning the film were more varied. Although Aragorn was most often named as the favourite character by all age groups and both sexes, and was named in all focus groups, he is no more felt to be the central hero of the story than Frodo is. The results of the group discussion show that viewers either don't perceive any outstanding hero in *LotR* or attribute this role to Sam, as this quotation indicates: "To me, he was actually the hero of the story. I could identify with that. He's the one I admired. He took that friendship so seriously" (Frank, 28, "Media Generation"). Nor are the respondents' choices of favourite characters primarily relevant for the question of emotional and empathetic attachment. Due to the rapid transitions from one character to another, the film trilogy, and especially part 2, makes an emotional bond with the protagonists difficult. This function falls to the ambivalent character Gollum, whom the focus groups felt to be "well resolved" and "touching." The human trait of being not simply good or evil makes Gollum an empathetic figure for many viewers, and one that triggers emotions: "My absolute favorite scene is where Gollum talks to himself. I thought that was amazingly well done; I could have watched that ten times in a row. Where he's always struggling with himself, with his split personality. Terribly emotional" (Katja, 32, "Women" group).

In sum, we can conclude that Aragorn, Gimli, and Gollum are well received by a young, male audience; Legolas is especially liked by women, but also by younger viewers; Gandalf is chosen as a favorite character by older viewers. However, the respondents did not perceive any character as an outstanding hero of the story. For most of the respondents, all of the characters were heroes equally. Only among the focus group "Men" was the tendency observed to see Sam as the real hero of the story and to identify with him. Nor was an empathetic bond with the main characters observable. The rather stereotypical characterisation and the rapid switches between the plot threads held viewers at a distance from the protagonists. Thus an empathetic bond occurs rather with an ambivalent character like Gollum.

NARRATIVE EXPERIENCE AND VISUAL FASCINATION IN *LOTR*

Besides character relationships, we have also identified narrative structure and action and special effects as other levels on which involvement takes place. In this connection we have explained how the blockbuster as a meta-genre, fantasy as the dominant genre frame, and the elements of different genres such as action, love story, splatter, and special effects address different groups of viewers. The multistaged reception study elucidates the way in which viewers actually accept these offered appeals.

The fantasy genre is perceived by viewers as a dominant frame of reference. *LotR* is primarily fantasy, epic and fantasy, a story of good versus evil, or a fantastic legend.[15] It is "fantasy; the best fantasy film yet made" ("Men"). The genre frame supports the inner logic of the *LotR* world, so that its fantastic elements are accepted without question. This also explains why space-time inconsistencies of the trilogy, traditional gender stereotypes, and ethnically stereotypical representations—all typical for the genre—are addressed only as marginal issues: "They [the light-skinned heroes] are inspired by the Vikings. It's only coincidence that they're the good guys, I would suggest. I see that as a kind of design issue, not a malicious background. They just look meaner with all these barbs and the eyes and all that stuff"

(Uke, 27, "Computer Gamer"). In addition to the primary genre frame, viewers accept other communication offerings that the trilogy presents. *LotR* is more than fantasy to its viewers. It is "fantasy, action, but up to now no film has ever been this powerful. Something like a fairy tale, and yet something completely different, something from mythology, a heroic epic. You can find everything in it" ("Women"). Several respondents mentioned the multilayered strategy explicitly: "It was the greatest film project that ever was. It appeals to young people because it's a gigantic fantasy epic, and it appeals to older people who have read the book at one time or another. The whole combination of action, romance and everything—that's suitable for a broad audience" (Henning, 27, "Men"). And: "Yeah, my grandma watches the film for the landscape, and my mother for the war scenes with Eowyn, because she thinks that's so great, and some freaks for the cool special effects—just something for everyone" (Julius, 12, "Men"). The love story of Aragorn and Arwen also plays a part in the film's reception. Thirty-three percent of the respondents in the cinema audience survey indicated that the love story was significant to them. One viewer found the love story to be a point of relevance to her own life, although she saw no other connections with her life-world: "Except that about love and immortality—I thought about that" (Rebecca, 22, "Media Generation").

The respondents had remarkably little to say about the flow of the overall story. Those who did comment on the narrative structure and dramaturgy often mentioned things they found illogical ("I didn't understand the bit about the father who wanted to burn himself with his son" [Manuela, 27, "Media Generation"]) or the ending of the third part, which was perceived as kitsch and too long ("But the happy ending took a long time, and was too long" [Eva, 22, "Women"]).

Thus the viewers' focus was concentrated less on the narrative and dramatic structure of the trilogy than on its spectacular visual power to fascinate: action, special effects, camera and images. A characteristic statement about how viewers experienced the films is that of one respondent: "What I liked about the whole series was its forcefulness. The larger-than-life presentation, plenty of time for a longer look at the elements. The subject matter doesn't especially appeal to me, but it was so well drawn out, I thought that was unique. A great experience" (Rebecca, 22, "Media Generation"). Respondents' agreement with a number of statements in the cinema audience survey also indicates the close connection between involvement in *LotR* and the experience and importance of action elements and special effects. Whereas agreement with statements that concern the narrative structure is rather hesitant (for example, "The love story is important for me"), the battles and the movie experience per se are more important for viewers: 87 percent agreed with the statement "The battles are impressive"; 85 percent shared the opinion "The film was a great cinema experience." (See table 7.2.)

Table 7.2: Agreement with Statements about the Film (cinema audience survey, N=352)

Agreement with the Following Statements	% of All Respondents
The film has grand heroes.	87%
The battles are impressive.	87%
The film was a great cinema experience.	85%
I was carried away by the film.	81%
The film lives up to the hype.	74%
I'm looking forward to talking about the film with my friends.	66%
I found the film moving.	69%
The effects open up a completely different world.	62%
The love story is important for me.	33%
The film is just for boys or men.	9%

An open question about spontaneous associations with the trilogy allowed the respondents to make specific statements about aspects of the movie experience and hence their involvement.[16] The respondents most often mentioned attributes such as "spectacular," "emotional," or "gigantic experience," which refer to the trilogy's character as a cinema experience. The second most frequent kind of answer mentioned characteristics that can be summarised under the rubric of film aesthetics and special effects: common descriptive categories in the viewer responses were "camera work," "great images, landscapes, sets," "great effects," and "never been done before." The respondents also considered the action and splatter elements characteristic of the trilogy. The spontaneous statements mentioned fights, battles, adventures, violence, and heroics (for example, "great battles," "brutal," and so on). References to dramaturgical aspects of *LotR* were only the third most common kind of response ("suspenseful," "boring," "too uneven," and so on).

In the group discussions as well, a strong tendency to emphasise the visual dimension and the special effects was observed. Attributes such as "powerful," "gigantic," and "overwhelming" are typical of the viewers' descriptions of the trilogy: "It seems to be more powerful because all the battles are in it. And it is more powerful!" "Gigantic, intoxicating, it took me three days to realise. Overwhelming." "I've never seen a film with such impressive images." "I was carried away by the images." These are statements that refer to an "overwhelming" effect of the trilogy at the visual level, which relegates all other elements to the background. The special effects are considered an indispensable element, without which the film wouldn't work:

> It's a fantasy film, so it [the special effects] is justified. There are also films where it's just slapped on, it's not necessary. If I look at *Star Wars II* for example, it gets really bad. As if they said, "We've got more on the hard drive, let's put that in," so that it knocks you flat and in the end it doesn't even affect you. [. . .] But here [in *LotR*] that never happens. Except maybe with the Ents, that was stupid. But apart from that it never happens. You want this

larger-than-life fantasy world, you want it that way! And that's exactly what you get. Exactly these emotions that it's supposed to achieve, it achieves them. All these massive battles that look just awesome, or the 5000 orcs, et cetera. (Uke, 27, "Computer Gamers")

The weighted response to the statements suggests that the narrative and dramaturgy play rather subordinate roles in the viewers' film experience and in their evaluation of the film. Visual design and the style of realisation, on the other hand, are important for many viewers. However, we can identify different ways of receiving the film among different audience segments. For example, the experiential nature of the film and the film aesthetics and special effects are more important for fans of *LotR* than for non-fans.[17] Action and splatter, on the other hand, were more important for the non-fans than for fans. The analysis of the group discussion also yielded similar results. Because fan status is closely linked with knowledge of the books, we can observe here a distinct audience segmentation and hence a variety of reception strategies, which are discussed in the following sections.

RECEPTION STRATEGIES: "MEDIA GENERATION" VERSUS "LITERARY GENERATION"

Thus, in addition to the dominant frame of the fantasy genre, the recipients of *LotR* are also susceptible to other addressing strategies that contribute to their involvement. Different viewers accord different degrees of importance to the different strategies of addressing the viewer. What the exact importance of each individual factor is for different audiences can only be determined in a direct comparison of two audience segments. As explained above, people who have read Tolkien's books before seeing the films have clearly different reception strategies from those who haven't. This circumstance was taken into account in the research design by postulating the "Media Generation" and "Literary Generation" focus groups. Knowledge of the books was also asked about in the cinema audience survey.

The "literate viewers"—both in the cinema audience survey and in the group discussion—generally judged the film overall more positively than those who hadn't read Tolkien. They were more positive towards both actors and characters: 68 percent of the readers, but only 57 percent of nonreaders, indicated that the film had good actors. Members of the "Media Generation" (nonreaders) also responded to the characters differently than did members of the "Literary Generation." For one thing, the "Media Generation" viewers appreciated established actors: "I think that one actor [Orlando Bloom] is so cute," one member of the "Media Generation" explained (Rebecca, 22). For another, the nonreaders developed relationships with the film characters. One viewer saw Eowyn as a hero and identified with her through her role. Sam induces empathetic attachment by representing important values for the recipients, such as loyalty and friendship.

A significant specific reception strategy of the "Media Generation" can be observed in their involvement through narrative and structure. More often than the average viewer, the members of this group and the nonreaders in the cinema audience survey mentioned confusing content or the longwinded or kitschy ending of the third part of the trilogy: 12 percent of the nonreaders in the cinema audience survey found the film confusing, but only 5 percent of the readers shared this opinion. Similarly, a larger proportion of nonreaders than of readers had negative comments on the end of the film ("too long," "theatrical, too Hollywood," "a little annoying," "they laid on a little schmaltz there"). The lack of familiarity with the story was a problem for the "Media Generation" at the narrative level. The gaps in the film version, as compared with the books, result in aloofness and even rejection, and hence prevent narrative involvement. Both those who knew the books and those who did not know them commented on the narrative lacunae: "It wasn't well adapted for people who haven't read the book" (Frank, 28, "Media Generation"). Among the "Literary Generation" as well, the problem of narrative lacunae was discussed: "I can hardly imagine seeing the film without knowing the book" (Elmar, 27).

As a solution to the negative experience of narrative reception for the "Media Generation" (and for nonreaders), these viewers shifted the focus of reception to action and special effects. The "overwhelming" effect discussed above played a particularly important role in reception for this audience segment. Accordingly, this group more frequently made statements about the visual presentation (camera, landscapes), about action elements, and about special effects (battles, fights). One member of the "Media Generation" said, "I've never seen a film with such impressive images. 'Star Wars' in its day also had great techniques, and became a cult movie. So I think 'The Lord of the Rings' will also go down in film history" (Rebecca, 22). The shift from the narrative structure towards the visual experience is also expressed in the perception of violence in the film. Only 4 percent of those familiar with the books, but 15 percent of those who had not read them, felt the film trilogy was too brutal.

The "Literary Generation," on the other hand, was found to have a comparative reception strategy. With regard to character relationships, they compared the book and film characters constantly, and devoted great attention to representations that were faithful to the books or deviated from them. They related to the characters less on an emotional, empathetic level than on a cognitive, abstractive level. The more closely a character corresponded to the book version, the greater the enjoyment was for the "literate" viewers. One member of the "Literary Generation" explained his relationship to the characters: "The characters were similar to the way I imagined them. They were very well played. I imagined Aragorn a little differently; he looked so sickly in the movie. In my head, he was a nature boy before" (Uwe, 25). The "literate" viewers tended rather to establish empathetic relationships with ambivalent characters. Some members of this group are moved by Faramir and

Gollum only in the film version, while Gandalf is the clear favorite character in the book.

Because of their familiarity with the books, viewers in the "Literary Generation" had no trouble following the plot. Because they were generally sufficiently familiar with the plot, these recipients derived involvement and enjoyment of reception from their book-specific expertise. Like the characters and their filmic presentation, the narrative structure and dramaturgy of the book and film are dealt with continuously during the process of film reception and appropriation. At the narrative level, scenes dropped or added were especially important (such as the attack of the warg riders, the absence of Saruman in part 3, and so on), as was the addition of new plot threads and addressing offers (such as the love story between Aragorn and Arwen). While correspondences between book and film usually resulted in increased enjoyment, the deviations were controversial: "What doesn't come across as well in the film are the long journeys between the individual stations. In the film, they hike a little, and then they're at the next high point. On the other hand, that's probably hard to realise [in film]," explains Jeannette (27, "Literary Generation"). Other modified situations, such as the ending, which was abridged in comparison to the book, met with approval: "I thought that [the ending] was very logical. That bothered me about the book. Sauron dies and really everything's finished. And then it goes on and on and they have to go to Hobbiton and fight there too. I thought that was useful for the film, and I fully expected him to leave that out" (Lutz, 32, "Literary Generation").

However, the "literate viewers" clearly rejected the addition of the love story element. For 67 percent of the viewers in the cinema audience survey, it was not important, and one member of the "Literary Generation" offered the pragmatic summary: "It [the love story] bothered me too, but it's a Hollywood film. It has to have that."

Action elements and special effects are also an important addressing offering for the "Literary Generation." However, this group contextualises and categorises them in relation to the narrative. Only in the battle scenes do the "literate viewers" go along with the visual spectacle and change their reception strategy: "Where the Riders of Rohan arrive and just march right into the herd of orcs. I never saw that so well dramatised [...] The battle of Helm's Deep was filmed gigantically, but in the third part he really managed to make it even more gigantic" (Lutz, 32, "Literary Generation"). We can conclude that the "Media Generation" audience segment was more strongly oriented towards the dominant genre frame of fantasy than were other groups, and also accepted the genre offering of the love story more positively than the "Literary Generation." Although *LotR* is received and judged positively even by those who did not know the books and the story in advance, the narrative in the films, taken alone, has gaps and logical flaws that make themselves felt as a confusing or long-winded quality. In order to achieve a positive reception experience, members of the "Media Generation" use reception strategies oriented after genre elements (fantasy, romance, and action) and focus on the trilogy's "overwhelming" visual effects.

The reception strategies of the "Literary Generation" audience segment can be described as an "experts' reception": the recipients bring their knowledge, which in some cases is very detailed, of Tolkien's world and its creation to bear on the film trilogy and subject all elements of the films to a constant comparison with the written original version. The continuous comparison of dramatic structure and narrative elements allows the recipients to take a receptive attitude of involvement in the text, and at the same time affords a distanced enjoyment through the process of assimilation by means of expertise. For this group, the importance of action and special effects is subordinate, although these elements of the films are subjected to the same exact scrutiny as all others. Matching and deviating adaptations both add to the viewers' enjoyment of testing their own expert knowledge.

THE BLOCKBUSTER CLIENTELE VERSUS THE FANS: GENERIC HYBRIDITY AND AUDIENCE RESPONSES

Often, fans of *LotR* and its general audiences are pitched against each other. But do they really show, in this case, exclusive patterns of involvement and enjoyment? Off the face of the extraordinary box-office success and the broad popularity the first two parts of the trilogy had already gained in Germany at the time of the release of the final episode, the imaginary division between a community of fantasy fans as direct addressees and a much wider blockbuster clientele, which had figured so prominently as a rhetorical trope in the previous debates, was now seen to be settled, no longer necessarily antagonistic. Despite the many deviations from the novel, one critic dryly remarked, "the sceptical Tolkien-fans love the films as much as those who have never read the books."[18] Only Claudius Seidl believes that those parts of the audience who simply want to watch and understand the films without having read the books were still at a disadvantage, that those parts of the audience would lack the manual to the narrative and the material collection that would add resonance to the inner conflicts of the protagonists into whom the films themselves, as Seidl argues, failed to invest sufficient interest.[19]

Reviewers and critics continued to differentiate various audience segments, regrouping them into the category of the "philologically oriented," the potentially critical fraction of readers of the books, a variety of fantasy fans (ranging from a general preference to hard-core spiritualists), popular-culture consumers, and media users. But all these groups were now embraced and reassembled as mutually constituting the new cross-section of "fans and lovers of the films."[20] The films' integrative power, Sabine Horst argues, was mainly due to a strategy of "infinite diversity in infinite combinations," not least also pursued in terms of generic multiplicity.[21] The trilogy's apparent success in pulling together so many divergent strings and thereby meeting so many different audience expectations all at once put Jackson back at the centre of the critics' attention. Those who had so harshly criticised the director for his lack of fantasy two years (and two releases) ago now once more sang his praises, but this time without any trace of nostalgia for the splatter genius of the past. "This is why these films are so good, this is why their ending is so triumphant," Jens Balzer's verdict read: "Because there is no contradiction between the global public, at which they are targeted, and the personal fantasies of their creator."[22]

The incorporative power of Jackson's *Lord of the Rings* was now taken for granted, but occasionally still characterised as a forceful, even violent strategy of overwhelming the viewer, whose sense perception is taken under fire like an enemy in order to in keep in check any critical impulse: "Of course, one is startled about oneself. [. . .] About how the sheer force of the flood of images which goes down on the viewer and without any resistance washes away even the smallest desire for critical distance and reflection."[23] The sentiment irritating and alienating this particular reviewer the most, however, came creeping up on him from another corner: "It is a strange and peculiar feeling: that a film assembles its audience without a trace of resistance in such an all-encompassing way as a community of believers."

If, indeed, *LotR* offers several possible readings by prestructuring the semantic material narratively, aesthetically, and generically, how do actual audiences demonstrate involvement with and use the often contradictory generic signals they receive? Since the concept of genre, from our pragmatic point of view, serves not only as a descriptive tool for analysing salient textual structures, but also encompasses audience expectations towards a film, it is one aspect that can be tested in empirical audience research studies. Our study shows how audiences recognise generic conventions and use generic cues in order to make meaning of and gain pleasure from the films. As we have pointed out, in *LotR* different strategies of generic address work concurrently to ensure a larger possible audience and therefore a higher box-office success. Our reception research study indicates that there are indeed several audience fractions of *LotR* who are intrigued by different generic strategies. We will use here, again, a basic differentiation of the recipients into "readers" (people who have read Tolkien's books before watching the films) and "viewers" (people who watched the films without any a priori knowledge of the books), taking into account differences concerning gender and age as well as education and profession.

Compared to the "viewers," "readers," of course, perceive themselves more frequently and far more explicitly as fans of *LotR*. Often, readers of the Tolkien books are engaged in, or at least aware of, the ongoing fan discourses on the Internet and in other media before going to watch the movies. As a telephone survey revealed, long before the actual release they have already planned to watch the film, because they are either fans of *LotR* or "want to see how the book is put on the screen." Furthermore, readers of the books seem to have a distinct affinity to the fantasy genre as such. The theatre polls that were conducted in the first week after the release of *RotK* in several first-run cinemas showed that 63 percent of the respondents like fantasy films "very much" or, at least, like them "a lot." Only comedy received a higher rating from the movie attendees. Other genres, such as action, war, thriller, and horror, scored considerably lower on the scale of general preferences. Also the results our focus group interviews clearly indicated that the fantasy genre is a preferred genre of the readers. For them, *LotR* is above all a fantasy film: "It's fantasy," as one of the participants in the focus group "Men" put it, "the best fantasy film ever made, not action." Specific genre conventions are not only quickly identified as such, but also highly appreciated.

However, for readers, the knowledge of the books is of great importance and for most of the forms the basis on which the quality of the films is estimated. The public discourse in the press and on Internet fan sites and forums shows ample evidence of a particular interest taken in the transformation process from text to screen: "Jackson said in advance that he included every single page of the book. That's not entirely true. Most discussions went on about the love story between Aragorn and Arwen, this is only roughly touched on in the book. In the films it always comes back to it. And that they got sent away from Middle earth, that's only in the film" (L., 32, "Literary Generation"). The audience's need to detect if Jackson's cinematic adaptation of Tolkien's world corresponds with their own imagination is a recurrent pattern in the reception. The accuracy of the adaptation is constantly compared and evaluated: "I thought it would be different, but I wasn't disappointed" (J., 27, "Literary Generation"). "I imagined the characters very similar. They were striking!" (U., 25, male, "Literary Generation"). Generally, it can be concluded that the viewing pleasure increases with the grade of thematic and generic knowledge: none of the persons who considered themselves as fans evaluated the film negatively, but 11 percent of the non-fans, interviewed in the theatre polls, thought the film was "bad" or "very bad."

The "viewers," on the other hand, usually had no—or only rudimentary—preknowledge of the story. Their expectations towards the film were more strongly based on the advertising and marketing campaign, on information given and the "narrative image" created in trailers, posters, or newspaper reviews, advocating *LotR* as an epic fantasy adventure, Middle-earth saga, or, simply, the "adaptation of the Tolkien books." M., a twenty-seven-year-old female student ("Media Generation"), explains, "I had no real interest in the movie. I just went to see it because it was on. I didn't know much about it beforehand." Viewers often had problems following the complex course of events, since for them the story had to be constructed in the actual process of viewing the film. The results of the audience research underscore the point frequently raised in critical reviews that persons not familiar with the fantasy genre in general and with the world of Tolkien in particular missed out on story details as well as on some of the pleasures characteristic of the genre. Often, the trilogy was perceived as being "long-winded and boring" (K., 35, "Media Generation") and confusing in parts, as, for example, in the episode involving Denethor, which appeared only in a radically abridged form in the theatrical version of *RotK*. It might be due to this lack of narrative preknowledge that in the theatre polls 12.3 percent of the viewers, but only 4.5 percent of the readers, criticised *LotR* as confusing.

What else, then, had *LotR* to offer an audience that was neither interested in the fantasy genre nor able to comprehend its narrative in all its ramifications? As all parts of our audience research study show, viewers as well as readers put a strong emphasis on emotionalising aspects, such as the romance of Arwen and Aragorn; on elements modernising Tolkien's original narrative design, such as the emancipation of Eowyn from patriarchal conventions of female conduct; on the character development of Frodo and his friendship with Sam; and on aesthetic elements of strong affective impact, such as the battle scenes and special effects as well as the helicopter panorama shots of impressive landscapes. One "viewer" elucidates, "I really liked the vehemence of the serial, its oversized presentation with ample time to observe all the elements. I don't like the subject matter too much, but it was executed so nicely, I think it was unique. What a great experience. If you put all that into a single film, much gets lost" (R., 22, "Media Generation"). In general, the vocabulary used to describe the trilogy draws on superlatives like "oversized," "greatest fantasy ever," "sensational," "spectacular," and "overwhelming." The focus groups often discussed the impressiveness of the images, the astounding landscapes, and the phenomenal battle scenes. In the theatre polls, the interviewees were asked to agree or disagree with a number of given statements about *LotR*. The statements were geared towards giving an indication of the degree to which the films may have succeeded in overwhelming the audience sensually and emotionally (for example, "sensational movie event," "battles are amazing," "the film grabbed me"). The results reveal an exceptionally high degree of agreement in this respect, as the figures in table 7.2 (see above) demonstrate.

Thus, the success of *LotR* lies in its ability to address multiple generic forms, granting pleasure to a wider audience than only the fan community. Our final quote gives a neat encapsulation of such pleasures:

> My grandmother watches it because of the landscapes, my mother because of the battle scenes with Eowyn which she likes and some freaks watch it because of the great special effects—something for everyone. (J, 15).

CONCLUSIONS

The study on the reception of the *LotR* trilogy as exemplified by the third part, *The Return of the King,* yielded insights into the different strategies of assimilation and processes of involvement among different target groups. Involvement was shown not only to arise through textual strategies such as narrative and structure, action and special effects, and the relationships to the film characters, but also to be influenced by factors outside the film itself. The prefigurative knowledge gained from the original literary work, the marketing, the film reviews, the Internet forums, and the merchandising articles plays a part, as does membership in specific fan groups and certain generations. Thus different forms of involvement take place for members of the "Literary Generation" and for members of the "Media Generation." Furthermore, gender and sociocultural contexts in which the various audience groups are integrated also play a significant part in their involvement. The patterns of involvement brought to light in the study also show that further studies are necessary to deal with the modes of involvement in film reception—and to trace their roots not only to the textual structures of the films but also to factors outside the films.

The analysis of the three films in the *LotR* trilogy has shown them to be blockbuster films aimed at optimising the exploitation of potential audiences through a multiple-genre perspective. Although a fantasy framework forms the dominant genre, the films combine elements of numerous other genres, each of which addresses a different audience. The multiple genre perspectives create a complex network of textual structures—in which different genre elements overlap and negotiate their relationships to one another—and audience expectations. The great number of texts that are connected with the *LotR* trilogy, from the original books to the marketing communications, the reviews, the forums, and the DVD editions, which add more scenes to the cinema versions, raises the question as to what *the* text of *LotR* is. The consequences for reception studies are unmistakable: when viewers talk to survey takers about the films, which text are they referring to—just the films, or the other media adaptations of *LotR* as well? Here we are confronted with the mediatisation of everyday life, in which the multitude of media references can hardly be isolated from one another. For this reason, reception studies must in future not only investigate how viewers refer to and deal with textual structures of individual media products, but also ask what knowledge—and not only media knowledge or knowledge generated by prefigurative materials—the viewers use in receiving film and television texts and in integrating them in their life-world outlook.

CHAPTER EIGHT

Global Flows and Local Identifications?

The Lord of the Rings and the Cross-National Reception of Characters and Genres[1]

GISELINDE KUIPERS AND JEROEN DE KLOET

On December 17, 2003, the third part of the film trilogy *The Lord of the Rings* premiered simultaneously in many countries around the world. "The Epic Continues" was the slogan accompanying the launch of *The Return of the King*. In our increasingly globalised world, comparative research has swiftly gained importance in the social sciences.[2] Media and communication studies seems to be lagging behind when it comes to international comparative research projects. A few exceptions possibly counter this observation: a comparative research project on the reception of *Dallas* by Tamar Liebes and Elihu Katz, the Disney project of Janet Wasko and colleagues, a recently published volume on the diverse adaptations of *Big Brother*, and Anne Cooper-Chen's volume on global entertainment media.[3] Still, given the fact that media present people with the most visible manifestations of globalisation, the by and large national orientation of communications and media research is rather surprising.

The launch of the third part of the *LotR* trilogy provided a unique opportunity to study the global reception of a blockbuster movie. The *LotR* project is a timely large-scale international comparative research project. The figures of the study are quite staggering: 24,739 respondents in more than 150 countries (including Antarctica, Vatican City, and several islands in the Southern Sea) took the effort to fill in the online questionnaire. What differences in reception of *LotR* can we trace and how can we explain them? We aim to answer this question by, first, analysing the recognition and appreciation of characters and genres in the quantitative part of the total data-set of the *LotR* project. Differences among audiences are often related to different appreciation of genres.[4] Also the liking and disliking of characters will inform us about the interpretation of the movie. Our quantitative analysis thus takes genre classification and character preference as the basic indicators for its cross-national comparison. The leading question here is whether it is possible to find national patterns in the interpretation of the film. This quantitative analysis of the world data set will be followed by a qualitative analysis of character preferences around the world.

METHODS

In 24 out of the 150 participating countries, over 100 people filled out the survey (see table 8.1). This article will be limited to a comparison of responses from these 24 countries. The first question we want to address is to what extent the appreciation and interpretation of the third part of the *LotR* trilogy is connected to national background. In order to make this comparison, we will look at the appreciation ratings given by respondents, but also at two variables in the data set that we expect to reflect the interpretation of the film: favourite character and ascription of genre (or modality). The latter is the answer respondents chose (from a list of options) to describe the sort of story the film was according to them. Furthermore, we included in the conclusion the number of times that respondents saw the previous parts of the trilogy.

As table 8.1 shows, variations in appreciation of the film—the most obvious factor with which to compare respondents—are relatively small: appreciation was very high in all national samples. Even though cross-national differences are statistically significant, overall appreciation is so high that these differences nevertheless may not be very meaningful. Thus, selection of genre and favourite character are better ways to gauge national differences than are ratings. To establish the relative importance of nationality, we also looked at two independent variables that are very important in studies of media reception: gender and age. For these variables, too, we looked at relations with appreciation, modality choice, and favourite character.

The questionnaire measured the ascription of genre, or "modality," by asking the following question: "What sort of story is *The Lord of the Rings: Return of the King* according to you?" Respondents could choose up to three options from the following list: Allegory, Epic, Fairytale, Fantasy, Game world, Good vs. evil, Myth/legend, Quest, SFX film, Spiritual journey, Threatened homeland, War story. The question about the favourite character was an open question. For further statistical manipulation, this text variable was recoded into a series of dummy variables for each character.[5] To elucidate differences among countries, we have used not only variance analysis but also odds ratios (see below).

Table 8.1: Appreciation of *Lord of the Rings: Return of the King* and Familiarity with Books and Earlier Parts of the Trilogy for Each National Sample, Ranked by Size of National Sample

	Mean Rating*	SD Rating*	Ranking	Seen Part 1 More than Once (%)	Seen Part 2 More than Once (%)	N
U.K.	1.23	.550	2	95	99	4,744
The Netherlands	1.34	.658	9	83	99	3,245
U.S.	1.41	.734	13	85	100	3,064
Denmark	1.49	.685	19	84	78	1,675
Spain	1.37	.688	11	97	94	1,564
Belgium	1.33	.629	7	73	96	1,376
Germany	1.48	.706	18	90	85	1,161
China	1.47	.727	17	56	53	1,083
Slovenia	1.88	1.102	23	62	56	910
France	1.51	.839	20	90	87	649
Australia	1.33	.623	7	91	87	551
Greece	1.71	.927	22	77	67	500
Canada	1.26	.610	5	94	92	485
Italy	2.07	1.062	24	85	75	480
Turkey	1.61	.925	21	79	78	334
Norway	1.25	.537	4	97	94	296
Chile	1.16	.465	1	96	89	224
Colombia	1.44	.801	15	81	73	194
New Zealand	1.29	.645	6	91	90	156
Sweden	1.44	.652	15	93	88	148
Mexico	1.24	.545	3	90	92	142
Argentina	1.37	.897	11	90	83	124
Malaysia	1.35	.618	10	89	81	118
Austria	1.41	.738	13	85	79	114
Other	1.44	.778	-	86	84	1,311
Total	1.40	.728	-	85.5	83	24,648

* 5-point scale, with 1= appreciate very much; 5= do not appreciate at all.

As table 8.1 shows, there are significant differences among between national samples. Actual cultural or national differences, however, ought not only to lead to differences and similarities across countries, but also result in patterns or clusters of similar countries. The notion of interpretable national or cultural differences implies that countries with comparable cultures, or shared histories, show cultural affinities.[6] Thus, we might expect countries that are similar culturally or linguistically to resemble each other in their preferences for specific characters or modality choices. We also might expect certain combinations or characters and genres to be more prominent in countries that are culturally, linguistically, or geographically close. Such recurrent combinations would point to a specific patterning of interpretation of the film.

RESULTS: LOOKING FOR NATIONAL DIFFERENCES

DIFFERENCES IN APPRECIATION

As table 8.1 shows, the appreciation for the film was very high in all national samples. National differences in appreciation were statistically significant—which can be expected with a data set this size—but given the high rating these differences are not very meaningful. It is hard to discern one particular cultural or linguistic region in which the film was appreciated more than average. We could conclude, very provisionally, that the appreciation was even higher in countries belonging to the British Commonwealth and has a tendency to be lower in countries that are culturally relatively remote from British culture, such as Italy, France, Turkey, China, Greece, or Slovenia. But any such generalisation is countered by the fact that Chile and Mexico, definitely not Anglo-Saxon countries, show very high levels of appreciation, whereas appreciation was relatively low in Sweden, Germany, Denmark, and the United States.

The same goes for gender and age differences. These are significant but small, with high overall appreciation. Differences among age groups give no clear picture, although appreciation in the oldest group of informants, over seventy, is relatively low (1.82 on a scale from 1 = highest to 5 = lowest). Average appreciation of men and women (gender representation was almost balanced in the sample) was 1.45 and 1.35, respectively, suggesting that, contrary to the stereotype, women appear to like the film slightly more.

DIFFERENCES IN FAVOURITE CHARACTER

To understand national differences in a population of fans (or enthusiasts), it is more informative to look at variables that say something about the experience or interpretation of the movie. One way to do this is to look at national differences in respondents' favourite characters. There is extensive, mostly psychological, theory and research on the appreciation of fictional characters, for instance on processes of identification and parasocial relations.[7] It may be possible to extend such theories to national or cultural differences.

A first analysis of the relationship between nationality and these two variables (modality and character) indicated a striking difference among countries. Table 8.2 shows so-called odds ratios, with The Netherlands as reference category. These represent the ratio between the chance that a Dutch respondent will make a certain choice (for example, naming Frodo as a favourite character) and the chance that respondents from other countries will choose the same option. If the odds are 1 in The Netherlands, the odds are 1.15 in the United States and .71 in Belgium. In other words, table 8.2 shows that, in comparison with The Netherlands, Frodo was more popular in the United States and less popular in Belgium.

Table 8.2: Odds Ratios of Favourite Character (Reference is The Netherlands. Data for Greece and China are not included because of the different alphabet.)

Country	Aragorn	Gandalf	Frodo	Legolas	Sam	Gimli	Faramir	Boromir	Arwen	Eowyn	Pippin	Merry	Gollum	Mean
U.S.	.98	1.01	1.15	.81	1.51	.63	1.36	.95	.74	.97	.965	2.015	.927	1.09
U.K	.88	.80	1.84	.71	2.45	.37	3.33	1.64	.51	2.5	2.559	2.622	.459	1.69
Denmark	.86	1.10	1.12	.84	1.32	1.00	1.43	1.00	.65	.72	.748	1.432	1.041	1.02
Spain	.93	1.30	1.28	.43	1.94	.36	3.01	2.41	.51	1.41	1.428	.393	.745	1.28
Belgium	1.20	.89	.71	1.32	.74	1.09	1.42	.74	.92	.73	.797	1.223	.784	0.98
Germany	1.11	1.06	1.30	.70	1.80	.68	3.12	1.97	.75	1.82	1.876	1.378	.580	1.46
Slovenia	.82	.97	.99	1.02	.89	.58	.36	.60	.63	.28	.281	.000	.280	0.62
France	1.15	1.19	1.01	.66	1.28	.33	2.64	2.28	1.30	1.27	1.286	1.370	.578	1.31
Australia	1.09	.79	1.32	.75	1.91	.44	1.45	1.33	.72	1.96	1.982	2.786	.824	1.38
Canada	1.12	.61	1.83	.87	2.01	.26	2.99	2.77	.90	2.77	2.808	1.842	.596	1.73
Italy	.76	1.09	.95	1.00	1.16	.54	2.61	2.14	.37	.97	.980	.364	.473	1.08
Turkey	1.43	1.45	.63	1.17	.72	.17	1.33	1.09	1.90	.58	.584	.000	.279	0.92
Norway	1.07	1.58	.84	.62	1.62	.69	3.06	1.23	.86	1.47	1.484	2.744	.871	1.44
Chile	.84	1.49	.95	.92	1.54	.58	3.66	1.98	.48	1.23	1.241	1.591	.379	1.38
Colombia	1.01	1.39	1.37	.96	.90	.15	1.38	.00	.00	1.42	1.440	.000	.492	0.84
New Zealand	1.24	.85	1.31	.61	1.46	.37	2.90	.46	.93	2.33	2.355	2.898	1.106	1.48
Sweden	1.01	1.01	1.26	.46	2.27	.69	3.06	3.03	.98	1.89	1.909	1.199	1.413	1.56
Mexico	.63	1.50	1.18	.72	1.64	.30	1.89	.51	2.68	1.37	1.404	.621	.540	1.21
Argentina	.59	1.04	1.07	.50	1.95	.23	2.92	.00	.88	1.60	1.616	.711	.380	1.09
Malaysia	1.67	1.10	1.56	1.16	1.17	.61	3.87	.61	1.57	1.69	1.702	.748	.317	1.45
Austria	.69	.65	1.09	1.00	2.09	.91	1.56	1.94	.63	1.74	1.764	3.182	.870	1.44
Mean	1.00	1.09	1.17	.82	1.54	.52	2.35	1.37	0.90	1.46	1.486	1.387	.664	—

It turned out to be hard to deduce a clear pattern from these odds ratios. First of all, in their choices the Dutch do not show a clear resemblance with other countries. In their clear preference for the dwarf Gimli, the Dutch resemble the Danes and the Belgians: two nearby countries, which one would expect to resemble the Dutch. However, the hobbit character Sam was mentioned more often by Dutch than by Belgians, but Sam was much more popular in Denmark. The same goes for other culturally and linguistically kindred countries: sometimes there is great overlap, in other cases none at all.

What is most apparent from table 8.2 is the great variation in favourite characters chosen by respondents. Apart from the thirteen characters listed in the table, other less important characters were mentioned too, sometimes even characters who didn't even appear in *The Return of the King,* such as the wizard Saruman, who only appears in parts 1 and 2 of the trilogy, and sometimes characters who do not appear in the film at all, such as Tom Bombadil, who only figures in the books. It was very rare for a character to be mentioned by more than 20 percent of respondents from any country. However, variations among countries are significant too: the British appear to like the loyal son Faramir; Turks are very enthusiastic about Arwen, the elf princess; and Spaniards, Swedes, and Argentinians were relatively unimpressed with the elf Legolas, one of the most popular figures in the film.

A table like this is strikingly evocative, and some of the results ring true in an intuitive way. For instance, for the Dutch it is easy to imagine why our fellow countrymen would fall for the rather blunt jokester Gimli, or that Brits would be charmed by the hobbit characters Merry and Pippin, who in many ways are caricatures of old-fashioned rural British gents. In most cases, however, national preferences seem rather more mysterious: Why don't the Swedes like Legolas as much as others, and why do the Turks like him so much? How to explain the great national variety in the preference for Aragorn, the dark handsome man who ends up becoming the king of the title?

By way of contrast, we briefly discuss some analysis of favourite character and gender and age. The differences were significant here, too, but this analysis shows differences that can be interpreted by means of concepts like identification or attraction. For instance, women mentioned female protagonists Arwen and Eowyn significantly more often than men (respectively 3 and 5 percent of female respondents, against 1 and 2 percent of males), and the two attractive male heroes Aragorn and Legolas (women: 25 percent and 19 percent; men: 16 percent and 9 percent). Men, on the other hand, preferred the heroic wizard Gandalf (18 percent versus 9 percent), the only one among the heroes who never appears to have emotions of any kind; the comic dwarf Gimli (6 versus 2 percent); and the ambiguous creature Gollum, also the most spectacular special effect of the film (9 versus 5 percent). Age differences can be interpreted relatively easily too: age is positively correlated with the mention of Gandalf, who obviously is the least youthful of the main characters, and faithful friend Sam. Young people often mentioned the two candid young hobbits Merry and Pippin, the elf princess Arwen and the people's princess Eowyn, and the heroic young elf Legolas. For both these categories, well-known psychologically oriented explanations seem feasible: identification with people of similar age, gender, or living conditions, and sexual attraction and identification with romantic story lines, presumably mostly for the benefit of the female audience, who apparently had to be compensated for the battle scenes.

The more qualitative data from the *LotR* project, both in the answers to open questions in the survey and in the interviews that have been done in the various countries, might help to understand national "repertoires of evaluation," as Michèle Lamont calls culturally determined patterns of preferences and dislikes. She describes, for instance, how the French generally tend to evaluate things in terms of artistic quality, while Americans judge things rather in terms of morality.[8]

Possibly, character preferences are connected with the ideological, psychological, and social interpretive frameworks as described by Liebes and Katz. On the basis of just the questionnaire, such preferences cannot be interpreted as such. In any case, more psychologically oriented concepts, which are useful for the interpretation of differences in gender and age difference, do not provide much insight into national differences. The idea of a "national psyche" or a "national character" does not, for the time being, appear to be the most useful approach for cross-national differences.

DIFFERENCES IN GENRE ASCRIPTION

The question about the modality, or "type of story," is one of the most original contributions of the initiators of the *LotR* project. Although such a question has not, to our knowledge, been used before in media research, it seems feasible that there would be national specificities in relation with national storytelling traditions. For instance, many Danish respondents chose the "Fairytale" category, which may be connected with the famous Danish writer of fairy tales, Hans Christian Andersen.

As table 8.3 shows, cross-national differences in genre ascriptions (or "modalities") are larger than differences in favourite character. Generally, deviations from the Dutch population (reference category = 1) are higher. In this case, too, it is not always easy to interpret this: What does it mean that the Dutch selected Quest and Spiritual journey more than others? How is one to interpret the fact that Dutch respondents were not particularly inclined to describe the film as "Epic" or "Special effects film"?

The question is, again, whether meaningful patterns can be discerned in national differences. This is complicated: countries that resemble each other in their choice for one modality are quite different in their selection of other modalities. As with character preferences, geographical or cultural closeness does not lead to clear patterns: The Netherlands in some way resembles Belgium, Germany, or Denmark, but not at all in other respects. The most frequent option, Epic, was relatively rare in all these countries, but least so in The Netherlands. The Belgians (mostly

Flemish, so Dutch speaking), and especially the Danes, often referred to *LotR* as "Fairytale," whereas the Germans rarely chose this qualification. "Threatened homeland" was an option often selected in Belgium, but less frequently in The Netherlands, and even less in Germany and Denmark. Neither was it possible to find a pattern for other culturally related countries, like the Mediterranean countries (Italy, France, Spain, possibly Slovenia, Greece, Turkey).

Language difference is likely to be significant in this part of the questionnaire: genre labels can have very different connotations in different countries. Moreover, genres do not always have a proper equivalent in all languages. In Dutch, for instance, for the translation of *fantasy* we had to choose between *fantasie*—that is, "imagination"—and the English word *fantasy*, which only refers to the fictional genre, whereas the English term covers both. In this respect it is interesting to note that the Latin American countries do not show strong resemblances either: the neighbouring countries Argentina and Chile show strong contrasts. A shared language apparently does not automatically lead to similar genre ascriptions.

Responses from English-speaking countries tend to be similar, as table 8.3 illustrates. In almost all cases the odds ratios of the United States, United Kingdom, Canada, Australia, and New Zealand are close. A distinct exception is the label "Threatened homeland"—and it probably is not a coincidence that this is also the most politically charged category. The British were much less likely to select this genre than (especially) Americans, but also than New Zealanders, Canadians, and Australians. In this respect, language may be relevant: English is not only the language spoken in all these countries, but also the language of the book, the film, and all the merchandise. "Epic," the label selected mostly in English-speaking countries, is also the term that was used in the advertising campaign, which was the same around the world: "The Epic Continues."

In contrast with the character choices, correlations between modalities and other background characteristics were not very strong: gender differences were statistically significant at times, but differences were very small: men were somewhat more likely to select "Epic" and "War story," whereas women tended to choose "SFX film" and "Quest." The distribution across age groups shows no patterning at all.

TEXTUAL INVOLVEMENT AND CULTURAL PROXIMITY

On the basis of the descriptive analysis it is difficult to trace clear national differences: insofar as there are differences, these are not very systematic, and, moreover, they are hard to interpret. For this reason we have done cluster analysis to find patterns in groups of variables, in this case patterns of appreciation and interpretation of the film. Attempts to do such an analysis only on the basis of the gender and character variables led to very unstable and not very robust solutions, with about as many clusters as the variables used in the analysis.[9] Nonlinear factor analysis (PRINCALS), another method for analyzing such data, did not yield very robust solutions either.

Table 8.3: Odds Ratios for Modality Choice (Reference = The Netherlands)

	Allegory	Epic	Fairytale	Fantasy	Game world	Good vs. evil	Myth	Quest	SFX film	Spiritual journey	Threatened homeland	War	Mean
U.K	1.85	2.85	.42	.50	.48	.72	.50	.60	2.20	.32	1.43	.77	1.05
U.S.	2.04	4.37	.34	.44	.35	.80	.68	.73	3.18	.25	.96	.73	1.24
Denmark	1.19	1.24	2.06	.47	1.90	.90	.44	.19	1.11	.83	.83	.93	1.01
Spain	1.31	5.38	.27	.67	.98	1.49	.87	.21	1.82	.40	2.04	1.51	1.41
Belgium	3.26	1.07	1.94	.92	3.44	.59	.49	1.75	1.81	.83	2.65	1.22	1.66
Germany	1.02	1.91	.58	.87	.47	.50	.72	.08	.86	.82	.90	.64	0.78
China	1.14	2.17	.41	1.83	3.50	.83	.05	.52	2.87	.57	6.91	.80	1.80
Slovenia	.56	.94	1.04	.50	1.35	1.23	.84	.71	1.16	2.03	.85	.93	1.01
France	1.25	2.93	.59	.93	1.07	.30	1.88	1.25	1.67	1.18	.93	.85	1.24
Australia	2.51	2.93	.35	.60	.81	.62	.66	.72	2.69	.20	1.18	.89	1.18
Greece	3.52	2.92	2.69	.19	1.61	1.04	1.11	.35	2.24	.31	1.43	.60	1.50
Canada	1.91	3.04	.37	.54	.30	.63	.82	.83	2.81	.36	1.27	.93	1.15
Italy	1.99	3.38	.64	.50	1.77	.21	.53	.36	1.41	1.12	.18	.82	1.08
Turkey	.60	2.07	.93	.53	1.04	.75	.88	.15	1.76	.35	.43	1.49	0.92
Norway	.79	1.47	3.17	1.02	1.70	.88	1.12	.30	1.78	.06	1.89	1.10	1.27
Chile	.78	4.92	.11	.70	.44	1.55	.84	.11	3.12	.72	1.52	2.21	1.42
Colombia	.75	2.23	.42	.48	.76	.54	.39	.04	2.02	1.93	.46	2.45	1.04
New Zealand	2.88	3.55	.36	.41	.63	.70	.49	.90	2.87	.54	1.32	.65	1.28
Sweden	1.44	2.22	.87	.85	.33	.70	1.15	.81	2.30	.31	.86	.96	1.07
Mexico	1.39	4.24	.22	.66	.35	.89	.75	.16	3.29	1.03	1.04	1.62	1.30
Argentina	1.47	3.44	.61	.37	1.62	.97	.86	.09	2.81	1.02	1.36	2.30	1.41
Malaysia	.619	1.77	.64	.75	1.27	1.06	.56	.75	3.14	.47	.93	1.74	1.14
Austria	.50	1.64	.74	.92	.00	.78	.56	.16	1.83	.84	.80	.32	0.76
	1.51	2.73	.86	.68	1.14	.81	.75	0.51	2.21	0.72	1.40	1.15	1.05

In the end we chose to do a cluster analysis that also included the number of times that someone had seen the previous two parts of the trilogy, considering that this also is a variable relevant to the experience of the film. This analysis led to a robust and rather simple two-cluster solution, with two clusters of roughly equal size (11,536 and 12,489 respondents). Table 8.4 presents an overview of these clusters, on the basis of the variables underlying this analysis. By far the most important distinguishing variable is the choice for the "Epic" genre. "Epic" was the modality chosen most frequently in the entire data set, selected by more than half of the respondents. The first cluster consists almost entirely of respondents selecting "Epic," while the second cluster is made up almost exclusively from people who chose something other than "Epic." All other modalities were chosen more often by respondents in cluster 2 than cluster 1.

As table 8.4 shows, the first cluster also shows more enthusiastic and devoted fans: the average appreciation is higher; respondents have, on average, seen the previous parts of the trilogy more often and on average also named more favourite characters. There are also some differences in character preferences: Sam, the loyal hobbit friend of the main character Frodo, was mentioned more in the first cluster; Legolas, Gimli, and Arwen were more popular in the second cluster, and there are differences, too, among the less prominent characters. Roughly the differences could be summarised as: respondents in the first cluster appear to prefer people and hobbit characters, and these are also the more "layered," "round," or "complex" characters. In the second cluster, respondents tend to prefer the more fantastic characters: elves and dwarfs.

On the whole, the decisive distinction between the two clusters seems to be the viewing position: the first cluster contains the more involved viewers. They follow the "preferred" reading of the film as "Epic" and this coincides with a more "layered" reading of the characters. In the second cluster we find a variety of readings and interpretation that seem to coincide with, on average, lower levels of involvement— even though the variety is large in this respect. For instance, this cluster also contains the group of respondents who chose the "Spiritual journey" modality, which is the label that comes with the highest degree of involvement and appreciation (compare chapter 9 in this volume).

This is confirmed in table 8.5, which shows that cluster 1 also contains the more dedicated readers. This table also shows the relation between the clusters and the various social background variables. This gives further support to the thought that cluster 1 contains the "standard" reading; the second cluster contains both the older and the very young respondents, and also more women than men—in other words, the audiences that diverge (relatively speaking) from the standard audience for a fantasy blockbuster like *The Return of the King*.[10] In some cases, this divergent reading may be different from the standard reading, yet highly committed.

Table 8.4: Cluster Analyses of Rating, Modality Choice, Favourite Character, and Number of Viewings

	Cluster 1	Cluster 2	% in Cluster 2[a]	All Respondents
Average rating				
(1 to 5, 1 = highest)	1.30	1.51**	—	—
Seen part 1 more				
than once *(in %)*	93.0	79.9	44.2**	86.6
Seen part 2 more				
than once *(in %)*	89.0	75.8	44.0**	82.7
Modality choice				
(% of respondents in				
cluster choosing modality)[b]				
Epic	99.7	2.5	2.3**	52.1
Good vs. evil	29.0	48.7	60.8**	38.2
Fantasy	25.4	44.1	61.6**	34.5
Myth	27.6	35.2	54.1**	30.8
Quest	23.2	36.0	58.9**	29.7
SFX film	19.9	25.3	54.0**	22.3
Allegory	6.8	14.1	65.6**	10.4
Fairytale	4.0	13.6	75.9**	8.9
War story	5.2	9.7	63.2**	7.4
Threatened homeland	4.1	10.7	70.4**	7.3
Spiritual journey	2.7	10.5	78.1**	6.6
Game world	25.4	44.1	61.6**	2.2
Mean number				
modalities named	2.49	2.53	**	
Favourite character				
(% of respondents in				
cluster choosing character[b,c]				
Aragorn	23.3	22.5	47.0	22.9
Sam	22.2	18.9	43.8**	20.6
Frodo	14.5	15.2	49.0	14.9
Gandalf	14.4	12.8	44.9*	13.6
Legolas	11.2	14.1	53.6**	12.6
Gollum/Smeagol	7.7	6.9	45.2	7.3
Gimli	3.8	4.7	53.1*	4.2
Pippin	4.6	3.1	38.5**	3.9
Eowyn	4.4	2.9	37.9**	3.7
Faramir	2.81	2.0	40.0**	2.4
Arwen	1.8	2.4	54.6**	2.1
Boromir	2.3	1.5	37.7**	1.9
Merry	2.3	1.2	33.4**	1.8
Mean number				
of characters named	1.16	1.09**	—	—
N	11.536 (48%)	12.489 (52.0%)		24.747

[a] This column shows the percentage of respondents choosing a value for a specific variable (for example, "Epic" as genre) in cluster 2. The percentage of respondents with this value in cluster 2 therefore is 100 minus this number.

[b] Sum of percentages may be more than 100% because respondents could choose more than one option.

[c] Only shows percentages for countries with Romantic script.

    * p<.01

    ** p<.001

Table 8.5: Clusters and Social Background

	% of Variable in Cluster 2	Deviation of Mean Cluster 2 (in Standardised Values)
U.K.	43.3	-15.2
The Netherlands	68.0	+16.1
U.S.	43.3	-3.8
Denmark	63.2	+9.0
Spain	28.6	-11.1
Belgium	66.1	+8.2
Germany	52.7	+2.3
China	54.8	+3.2
Slovenia	70.5	+9.6
France	42.7	-2.0
Australia	42.3	-1.9
Greece	46.4	-0.5
Canada	41.4	-2.1
Italy	38.8	-2.9
Turkey	52.4	+1.2
Norway	58.1	+2.5
Chile	30.4	-3.8
Colombia	49.5	+0.3
New Zealand	37.2	-2.0
Sweden	49.0	+0.2
Mexico	33.8	-2.4
Argentina	37.9	-1.6
Malaysia	53.4	+0.8
Austria	58.8	+1.7
Other	44.9	-1.6
Men	44.4	-5.5
Women	51.5	+5.5
<16	58.5	+7.6
16–25	47.1	-1.2
26–35	43.9	-4.4
36–45	47.2	-0.5
46–55	51.7	+1.9
56–65	53.4	+1.5
>65	66.0	+2.6
Never read books	67.3	+18.0
Read books partly	53.5	+4.6
Read books once	46.9	-1.0
Read books more than once	40.2	-12.5

The surprise in this table is that the clusters are related to cross-national differences, even though this is a rather rough divide. The first cluster is dominant in all English-language countries, most clearly so in the United Kingdom; in Greece (although not very significantly); and in the countries that can be summarised as "Latin": France, Italy, Spain, and Latin America with the exception of Colombia. The second cluster is dominant in all other countries, from The Netherlands to Slovenia to China. These differences—shown in the table by standardised differences[11] from the mean—are significant, and rather large in some cases. It is important to note that representatives of both clusters are present in all countries. This, too, seems to support the interpretation of the clusters in terms of viewing position. It is hardly surprising that the intended reading of the film is dominant in the countries in which the language of film and book is spoken. More generally, the story as well as the genre are rooted, in many ways, in the Anglo-Saxon tradition: a British story, American production and film conventions, and a New Zealand setting and director. Despite the "Americanisation" of audiences, it is likely that audiences outside this sphere of influence would have a lesser involvement and a larger variety of alternative interpretations.

The dominance of this reading in the "Latin" countries may seem more mysterious. A possible explanation here is the relatively small response in many of these countries: maybe only the more devoted fans participated in these studies. Using the answers to the open questions, and the interview data of the various countries, differences between these clusters will be explored further.

To what extent can these results be interpreted as indicators for the prominence of nationality and the nation-state in media reception? On the one hand, the cluster analysis gives some support for previous studies, showing that shared culture, and specifically shared language, is an important factor in the appreciation of media products.[12] However, this shared frame of reference seems to be a greater area/region than the nation-state: the English-speaking or Anglo-Saxon countries. Moreover, this shared culture seems to result in the following of the intended reading (Martin Barker and colleagues refer to "Epic" as the "modality of least resistance"), rather than the "negotiated" reading.[13]

The second cluster is characterised by pluriformity and deviation from the mean: people, on average, seem less involved, and choose a wider variety of interpretations. This does not point to a very specific effect of the nation-state, but rather to a larger variety that is connected with cultural distance from the "centre" of global media culture. Interestingly, those close to the text seem to rely more on a preferred reading of the text, whereas those with a larger cultural distance from the trilogy employ a more diverse, possibly even resistant, reading.[14] Cultural familiarity apparently does not necessarily feed a more critical, active mode of reception. But caution is needed here, as statistics does not tell us what people actually do with a certain media text. In the last part of this chapter we will therefore zoom in on how international audiences relate to the different characters of LotR.

READING THE CHARACTERS

In the first cluster, consisting of the more involved audiences, the hobbits (in particular the innocent and altruistic Sam), the human characters, and the divine wizard Gandalf are significantly more popular. The first cluster is highly involved in both the books and the film trilogy. In the second cluster, the more fantastic characters, elves and dwarves, characters moreover who are less crucial in the development of the plot, are more popular. The clusters indicate that audiences differ in their reading, but how do audiences read the characters? In other words, what repertoires of evaluation do they employ?[15]

If we look at the first cluster, one striking characteristic in the answers of the respondents (those who opted for "Epic" as the first modality) is that these answers, first, are more elaborate and, second, often concern the trilogy or the film as a whole. Respondents in this cluster tend to choose favourite characters whose story is central to the plot and development of the story line, like Sam or Gandalf.

The popularity of Gandalf in this cluster can be related to his personal growth—the change from Gandalf the Grey into Gandalf the White—that is closely connected with the central plot of the trilogy. One American respondent explains why he likes Gandalf so much: "Gandalf. He had a huge on screen presence and captured my imagination. I often inwardly called on him to put things right for other characters" (male; "Epic," "Quest," "Threatened homeland"). The centrality of Gandalf—the one he inwardly calls upon to help out the other characters—to this man's experience of the film comes particularly to the forefront in his selection of the favourite scene of the movie, when he refers to the impressive change of Gandalf: "Gandalf being defeated in Fellowship of The Ring and falling into the fire below and then returning as Gandalf the White in the Two Towers. Simply because I found it moving—the former upset me and the latter cheered me!" A U.K. respondent refers to the godlike qualities of Gandalf: "Gandalf. He's a figure of godlike power who shows self-restraint wisdom humility endurance courage and love. I suspect he was Tolkien's projection of his ideal self. I remember reading his battle with the Balrog when I was thirteen and being devastated" (male; "Allegory," "Epic," "Myth/legend"). In one of the Dutch interviews, the godlike character of Gandalf is articulated as well; the resurrection of Gandalf is read as a sign of the religious entity that governs Middle-earth: "Somehow, there is kind of basic deity. Gandalf returns back to life and is told that new life is given to him. This is for sure a 'prime power,' a 'deity' that gives him new life. The God of Goodness, so to say" (Vincent). A German respondent, however, points at the humanlike character of Gandalf, which facilitates audience identification with him: "Gandalf. Smart, wise, tranquil and humorous—and yet, still completely human" (female; "Epic"). Both Gandalf's growth during the course of events in the trilogy as well as his humanlike traits help explain his popularity in the first cluster; he is godlike, yet easier to identify with than a more outlandish Elf, and his personal growth mirrors the way the epic evolves.

For quite similar reasons, both the hobbits and some of the human characters, like Faramir and Boromir (but not Aragorn, who can be liked for a whole number of reasons), are significantly more popular in this cluster. One American respondent explains why he prefers Sam: "Sam became a favourite. He starts off so down to earth but by the time he is in Mordor he has become a true hero like Aragorn and Théoden. What's most amazing is that it is his friendship with Frodo that drives him" (male; "Epic," "Myth/legend"). The strong interconnection between the narrative and Sam's personal growth, with which the involved audience of cluster 1 so readily identifies, returns in the following account of a Spanish respondent: "My favourite character is Sam because he is the representation of unconditional friendship (towards Frodo) and because he is a hobbit who passes from innocence about the world into an adult without corrupting himself and while preserving his soul/personality" (male; "Epic," "Fantasy," "SFX film"). Apart from personal growth, it's Sam's perseverance—another human trait—that explains his attractiveness: "Sam because he held the whole thing together he was faithful to the end and literally carried Frodo to Mt.Doom (U.K., male; "Epic," "Quest," "Good vs. evil"). "Sam because he is the ultimate hero who never falters or fails, resists the ring and ultimately is the reason that the quest doesn't fail" (Germany, female; "Epic," "Quest," "Fantasy"). Sam, in these quotes, is often described as "the real hero" of the story, the character around whom the film revolves. Clearly, people who follow the preferred reading of the film would relate most easily to a character that is so central to the development of the story.

Hobbits, with their humanlike character yet devoid of evil, encourage identification too. This becomes clear from the following three respondents: "The hobbits because they are the ones that I most closely relate to. The other characters are the ones you look up to but you see the story through the eyes of Frodo Sam Pippin and Merry. They also make me feel good about myself" (U.K., female; "Epic," "Quest," "Good vs. evil"). "When ROTK came I liked Pippin the best. He reminds me very much about myself and it was good to see that even the smallest and most naïve persons can make a difference" (Norway, female; "Epic," "Fantasy," "Quest"). "While I most identified with Frodo I think at the last my favourite character is Pippin who shows the most growth throughout the film versions and is touchingly portrayed with a great deal of charm and believability by Billy Boyd" (U.K., male; "Epic," "Myth/legend," "SFX film"). A Chinese respondent explains why she likes Sam more than Frodo: "Sam a typical Hobbit, naïve in appearance and firm and persistent in his bone. Compared with Frodo in the film, he is more amiable" (female; "Epic," "Quest," "Good vs. evil"). The same respondent also indicated a liking of Faramir. Even though not all favourite characters can be interpreted in terms of identification,[16] this is the character that seems to invite personal identification more than any other in the film: "Faramir because I can relate to him and his story is one of the most interesting" (U.K., female; "Epic," "Fairytale," "Myth/legend"). "Faramir. His character exhibited strength (letting the Ring go) and weakness (caving to his father's demands) at the same time and that made him very human. In the end he was a brave and good person though" (U.K., female; "Epic," "Fantasy"). "Faramir. His constant search for his father's love and approval was very moving. He was easy to identify with!" (Denmark, female; "Epic," "Good vs. evil," "SFX film").

When we move from the first to the second cluster, the answers of the respondents are both shorter and more divergent. More often people mention the name of the character without any further explanation. Also, many do not name any favourite character at all. In this cluster, respondents refer more often to the name of the actors rather than the characters; they use vague descriptions ("the dwarf cause he's funny") or ones like: "The helper of the one who has the Ring is very loyal and faithful" (The Netherlands, male; "Fantasy," "Quest," "SFX film"). Respondents in this cluster rarely resort to the language of identification. Favourite characters in this cluster are elves and dwarfs, the first being a more fantastic character, the latter mostly a humoristic one. Many praise the humor—for the highly involved audience of cluster 1 less attractive since they are so absorbed in the epic—of Gimli. He is funny, and sometimes he is actually lauded because his character takes you away from the story line. One Dutch respondent explains why she likes Gimli most: "I think his character is just great. He gave some humor to the film. Because the film doesn't have a nice subject (I mean of course the war etc.)" (The Netherlands, female; "Fantasy," "Myth/legend," "Threatened homeland"). Favourite characters of the second cluster, unlike those of the first, are those that remain more or less the same throughout the trilogy. Humor, and beauty and mystique—important traits of dwarfs and Elves, respectively—do not require change, after all.

Whereas Gimli's humor adds fun to the story, the elves add some outlandish beauty to it, in the words of an Italian respondent: "Legolas and the elvish race in general because of the characteristics they have" (Italy, male; "Fantasy," "Spiritual journey"). Legolas is particularly liked, very often because of his looks; many refer to him as Orlando Bloom rather than Legolas. Probably the best summary, focusing on the physical attractiveness of the actor more than the character itself, comes from this female British respondent: "Legolas because he's an elf and really hot" (U.K., female; "Good vs. evil").

Aragorn is one of the characters that is chosen equally by respondents in the first and the second cluster, and that may be because he invites both types of reading: he is a round character, whose story is directly linked with the epic, but he also is a handsome man, and he gets nominated as a favourite character for both types of reasons.

Within the second cluster, there is a wider variety of degrees of commitment to the film and the genre, and even though in general people are less devoted, there are some who show a marked devotion, especially the people who chose "Spiritual journey." In interviews with Dutch viewers, Elves were often referred to by respondents claiming a spiritual reading. Nel, one of the Dutch interviewees, talks about Arwen: "She was mythical in a way, and I felt, divine may not be the right word, but she comes with a certain task, she is sent. She comes to help the good, it is important, and also the way she is visualized is very special, something vague, mythical, dreamlike." For David, another Dutch interviewee, Legolas is the Elf he likes best: "It's almost spiritual, like all elves, their pure character represents . . . they are lighter and more honest, they are not necessarily more or less, but their character is very different, a whole different way of life. [. . .] It gives a feeling there is more in this world than what we see. We actually live in a much larger whole, of which we do not know the boundaries."

To conclude, audiences belonging to the first cluster, those whose first choice of modality was "Epic," show a strong involvement with the trilogy. Their involvement in the narrative structure propels a special liking for characters who, first, are quite like us, human, and, second, whose personal story is central to the narrative and somehow mirrors the plot. The less involved audience from the second cluster are not only less elaborate in their answers, they also show a special liking for the more fantastic Elves, since they are beautiful, and dwarfs, who add humour to the story. This group is more divergent in their reading and are more likely to refer to actors rather than characters and enjoy the special effects of the trilogy. The diversity within this cluster is strong and becomes particularly clear when we look at the audiences who opt for a more spiritual reading of the text. Their identification with the Elves comes from a general interest in spirituality rather than a necessary involvement with the trilogy as such.

CONCLUSION: THE EPIC CONTINUES?

LotR is a profoundly cosmopolitan media text that is increasingly detached from its assumed origin—the United Kingdom—also because of the particular production circumstances in which the United Kingdom, Hollywood, and New Zealand are involved. The text is deliberately detached from national and local contexts, which explains its transnational appeal. Our analysis shows that one can roughly distinguish two groups of viewers: those who are very involved with the standard reading both of the movie and the books, and those who employ a wide variety of readings of the film, which often is connected with less involvement with the film and the books. Interestingly, in particular the fans classify the movie as an "Epic" story, following the marketing rhetoric ("The Epic Continues"). This points to the paramount importance of the marketing of blockbusters like *LotR*.[17]

More involvement with the books and the story surprisingly does not produce more oppositional or negotiated readings of the movie; on the contrary, those less involved seem to resist the dominant reading more. Cultural proximity plays a role here; these viewers are more often (yet not always) located outside the Anglo-Saxon world (for example, in China and Turkey). This finding counters fan studies, which generally show how creative fans employ texts, with which they resist to, rather than comply with, dominant readings.[18] In particular large-scale productions like *LotR* are driven by a carefully orchestrated marketing campaign and media hype, both of which reduce the potential polysemy of the text itself,[19] a reduction that becomes most apparent from the fans' responses to the movie.

The *LotR* trilogy, set in a fictional fantasy world, based on the universal theme of good versus evil, enabled "Hollywood" (a blunt label indeed) to create a global audience on an unprecedented scale. The *LotR* project has enabled us to study the local interpretations and identifications such a global blockbuster generates. The analysis of the world data set has shown that audiences of this film are indeed thoroughly globalised: the film is perceived and liked in many different ways by audiences worldwide. However, even though people vary widely in their appreciation and interpretation of the film, we have found that locality or nationality does not determine how people perceive the film. Only in a very general sense can one say that nationality matters to the liking of *LotR:* our analysis showed that the reading of the film is linked with the audience's "distance from the centre." The further removed from this centre, the more likely people are to diverge from the preferred reading, or "reading of least resistance." However, this "distance from the centre" can be demographic—gender, age—as well as geographical.

CHAPTER NINE

The Functions of Fantasy

A Comparison of Audiences for
The Lord of the Rings
in Twelve Countries[1]

MARTIN BARKER

The *Lord of the Rings* project was designed to discover the functions of film fantasy in the lives of different kinds of audiences; how audiences were prepared for the film by marketing, merchandising, publicity, and media coverage; and how a story like *LotR* plays out in different cultural contexts. In its design, it was intended to permit cross-country, thence cross-cultural, comparisons of responses, and to contribute to the growing body of knowledge on the interplay between global media production and local responses. Our central questionnaire was designed to sort responses by country and language, among other measures. But what does it reveal about the ways in which national contexts frame or shape audiences' understandings of the film? Of the overall total, more than twenty thousand questionnaires were received from just twelve countries. This analysis is based on a comparison of these countries, since the data sets are large enough for these to permit complex investigations without the numbers becoming riskily small:

United States (4,744 responses)
The Netherlands (3,275)
United Kingdom (3,115)
Denmark (1,677)
Spain (1,564)
Belgium (1,378)
Germany (1,161)

China (1,087)
Slovenia (966)
France (649)
Australia (551)
Greece (500)

The various countries did recruit rather different audiences. For instance, while across the world as a whole we achieved an almost exact 50:50 male/female ratio, there were some considerable variations by individual country. The same was true of age and of occupation categories. It was not, however, at these levels that in the end we found data to support a cross-cultural analysis. The key finding this essay considers arose from exploring the relations between several distinct kinds of response in each of the twelve countries: (1) levels of reading of the book, (2) levels of importance and pleasure associated with watching the film, (3) the most commonly made modality choices within each country's population, and (4) within that the most commonly made modality choices by those reporting the highest levels of pleasure and importance. Following a sequence of quantitative searches,[2] in each of which there were some small and interesting tendencies and distinctions, but no overall patterns, the following table emerged (see table 9.1). Its patterning was a complete surprise. This table summarises the ways in which, across the twelve countries, the two kinds of top modality choice (henceforth called the Engaged and the Vernacular choices) relate to the degree of overlap between their respective populations.

Table 9.1: Proportion of Overlap by Country between Overall Populations of Maximum Pleasure/Importance, and That Country's Modality Choice Most Associated with Maximal Pleasure and Importance (in Rank Order)

	Pleasure/ Importance Population	Also Nominating Top Modality Associated with Pleasure/Importance	Proportion	Engaged Modality Choice	Vernacular Modality Choice
China	342	254	74.3	Epic	Fantasy
France	337	208	61.7	Epic	Epic
Belgium	614	369	60.1	Quest	Quest
The Netherlands	1,507	746	49.5	Quest	Fantasy
Slovenia	301	133	44.2	Epic	Good vs. evil
United States	3,313	1,193	36.0	Spiritual journey	Epic
Australia	323	108	33.4	Spiritual journey	Epic
Greece	223	69	30.9	Spiritual journey	Epic
United Kingdom	1,609	480	29.8	Spiritual journey	Epic
Spain	641	148	23.1	Spiritual journey	Epic
Denmark	606	119	19.6	Spiritual journey	Good vs. evil
Germany	624	84	13.5	Spiritual journey	Epic

The meaning of this strong patterning is not transparent. Might it indicate a variation in the degree to which a *specialist* audience, relating to the film differently than the country average, has separated itself off from the rest of the response population? Might it also indicate that the overall levels of expectations varied by country? To put it crudely, if in China the accumulated heritage around Tolkien's story was considerably less than in, say, the United Kingdom, then it was simply much easier to achieve what was felt to be the maximal level. If all the film had to do in France to count as thoroughly enjoyable was to be a good "epic," then it could achieve that without having to be "meaningful" in the ways implied by a notion like "spiritual journey." But then in the other direction, suppose that a longer and stronger sedimentation of the stories into a cultural tradition allowed for the growth of a *specialist* mode of responding—a particularly distinct Engaged mode of response. That could become separated from the dominant Vernacular choice. These notions get some general confirmation by examining the relations across the twelve countries for their rank ordering between levels of repeat reading, levels of importance, the interconnection of these two, the books as prime source of expectations, and modality range. (See table 9.2.) There is a striking overall consistency across the first four columns, with those odd fluctuations involving primarily Spain and Greece.

It was imperative to try to explore the meanings of these key terms. If "Epic" is top Vernacular choice in seven countries, what range of meanings is encompassed in each case? And again, if "Spiritual journey" is top Engaged choice in six countries, and marked off from the Vernacular choice, what range of meanings is encompassed here? What does this tell us about local, stored-up meanings and associations around the books?

Table 9.2: Rank Order of Countries by Levels of Repeat Reading, Importance of Seeing, Repeat Reading, and Books as Prime Source of Expectations

	Repeat Reading	Importance	Repeat Readers within Importance	Books as Source of Expectations
Spain	1	11	1	1
United States	2	1	2	2
Australia	3	3	3	3
Germany	4	2	4	4
France	5	5	6	6
United Kingdom	6	6	5	5
Denmark	7	9	7	7
The Netherlands	8	8	8	8
Belgium	9	7	9	9
Greece	10	4	10	10
Slovenia	11	10	12	12
China	12	12	11	11

METHOD OF ANALYSIS

We needed to analyse the meanings and levels of pleasure associated with the different modality choices, in order to discover how "Epic" and "Spiritual journey" were differentiated for those who chose them. This required a means to analyse the *kinds of language* that people in these different positions used. First, then, random samples of one hundred of two groups were selected: one composed of people who had nominated "Epic" but not "Spiritual journey" (henceforth ESJ) and the other of those who had nominated "Spiritual journey" but not "Epic" (henceforth SJE). For these, I gathered their answers to our initial free-text question, in order to capture the first thing that people wanted to tell us about their responses. Analysing these one hundred would permit a *model* of the two overall modes of responding. The models could acknowledge overlaps as well as distinctions. Since these were volunteered responses, the analysis involved assembling the various speech elements that individuals offered, to examine how far they cohered; thence looking in detail at some articulated cases, to try to discern the larger shape of emergent patterns. With an overall model of the meanings of "Epic" and "Spiritual journey" to hand, this process was repeated for each of the twelve countries, this time random-sampling fifty of each country's Vernacular and Engaged choices, and again exploring their responses to that first free-text question. Finally, research groups in each country were asked to examine my preliminary analysis of their country's sample of responses, and to use their local knowledge to relate these to the history and status of *LotR* in their country, in order to try to make sense of the emergent patterns.

The key was to devise a means of analysing responses in which people declare the kinds of pleasure they gained. For in our choices of expressions, we are already declaring, however minimally, something about the measures we have been applying. Compare five words frequently used to sum up the experience—indeed, with some people, being the whole of their answer to our first question: "astonishing," "satisfying," "enthralling," "enjoyable," and "inspiring." What might we begin to read from people's use of these?

1. "Astonishing" hints at something that outran their expectations, with so strong a charge that the person has a little trouble putting it into words.
2. "Satisfying" suggests that a goal was reached; the experience of the film met some well-formed expectations, and did with reasonable fit match them.
3. "Enthralling" hints at the manner of audience involvement—perhaps, hardly daring to look away from the screen.
4. "Enjoyable" suggests a slightly restrained manner of responding; the bar of expectations was not perhaps set very high, and the film was adequate to the occasion of viewing.
5. "Inspiring" suggests something going beyond entertainment, arousing feelings or ideas that run beyond the film.

Each is made more complex by adding adverbial modifiers: "wholly astonishing," "reasonably satisfying," "just enthralling," "hugely enjoyable," "deeply inspiring." Words of these kinds are a beginning, no more. And other kinds of expression pose quite other problems. What to make of "Wow!!!!" or "Oh. My. God"? These do show that people felt comfortable enough to use informal modes of address. But while expressive, they do even less to declare the *nature* of the experience. To get inside the patterns of people's responses, we developed a system of coding to capture two aspects of people's answers, their "discursive categories" and "moves." The first organises all the different kinds of talk that people deployed. The second examines how they joined them in sequences to make arguments about the film. My procedures were as follows:

1. Following the principle of "repleteness" within Grounded Theory, a coding system was evolved that would embrace all aspects of people's answers. This resulted in ten Discursive Categories, each with a formal definition, as below. All responses were coded under as many headings as were required. The results were entered into a coding table and examined for frequencies, overlaps, and separations.
2. The table also allowed links between ideas (or Discursive Moves). Sometimes these were directly indicated by grammatically linking words such as *because, therefore,* or *so.* On other occasions, the manner of expression pointed to a possible linkage, as in "Made me cry, and realise how important friendship is." More complicatedly, in some cases individual words might hint at a discursive move, as we will see.
3. From these, a model emerged of the key categories used within each group and the commonest moves linking them. With these to hand, it was possible to identify some particularly articulate responses that spelt out more fully what others only partly expressed.

FIRST-LEVEL ANALYSIS: VERNACULAR CATEGORIES

The following ten categories were sufficient to encompass all aspects of the one hundred world samples of S̶J̶E̶, and E̶S̶J̶ respondents:

1. **Self-definitions** (in which respondents gave an account of the kind of person they were, or what experiences they had prior to seeing the film, which constitute the ground of their response to it);
2. **Experiential qualities** (in which people described their experience of the film, and its impact);
3. **Outcomes** from the film (in which people tried to encapsulate themes, or meanings, or lessons they saw the film as presenting);
4. **Envisionings** (in which people described how far, or in what ways, the film

met their prior imaginings or expectations—including from their experience of the books);

5. **Filmic qualities** (in which people discussed the film itself, its plot, particular scenes, cinematic qualities);
6. **The makers** (in which people discussed the contribution of the director, actors, designers, and so on);
7. **Filmic comparisons** (in which people measured *LotR* against other films or film categories, or measured the film's place in history);
8. **Reservations** (in which people named problems, absences, or disappointments in the film);
9. **Recuperations** (in which having nominated problems, people "excused" them in some fashion); and
10. **Significant others** (in which people pointed to real or imagined individuals, or groups who are relevant to their viewing experience).

Most responses, unsurprisingly, required coding under a number of these headings. (Only very abbreviated, sometimes single-word, responses required coding under just one heading.)

ANALYSING THE WORLD AUDIENCE:
SPIRITUAL JOURNEY VS. EPIC

Here are the results of the first-level codings, and the ways in which they began to point forward to the second level:

A. **Self-definitions**. Both groups identify features of themselves as relevant to their responses. Most frequently, this takes the form of reference to prior reading of the books. Seven SJEs and nine ESJs mention reading the books (although two of the latter do this as a negative—calling the books "boring" or "lugubrious"). It is as they go beyond this that we can see a partial differentiation. Among the ESJs there is a scatter of rather mixed references to *how* the books have been read; they include one saying the film "went beyond my imagination," one saying they "hadn't imagined it possible" to film the books, and two saying it was "the way I imagined." But among the SJEs a different tendency shows, with six talking about the importance of "seeing what I had imagined up on the screen." Another three talk directly of being "long term fans." There is a clearer link, for the SJEs, between what they imagined and how the film was envisioned on their behalf.

B. **Ascribed qualities**. Again there are considerable overlaps. A number of words do appear in both groups: "amazing," "awesome," breathtaking," "overwhelming," and "thrilling" are common to both. But again, there are those differences. While ESJs produce twice as many words falling under an *evaluative* heading ("good," "excellent," "fantastic," "beautiful"), SJEs score more than twice as many under an *emotional* heading ("emotional," "moving," "touching"). This, despite identical numbers actually reporting crying during the film. But the most striking differentiation, and the first to point to a discursive move at work, is in relation to what I would call *thematic impact*. In comparison with just one ESJ respondent introducing the idea of the experience being "almost religious," nine SJEs point this way, with expressions such as "inspiring," "religious," "morally and spiritually compelling." This links strikingly with another concept wholly absent from the ESJs, that of *closure*. Eight of the SJEs volunteered expressions implying some kind of completion, as in "summed up everything," "emotional ending," "finalising," and "satisfying." At the level of impact on self, again, while there are overlaps, there are also differences. The shared terms tend to be those of *scale of impact*. Being "bowled over," for instance, is available to both groups. The key difference is that while ESJs are prone to talking of "losing self" in the world of Middle-earth ("world to get lost in," "abducted to a different world") and feeling that the film had almost outrun them ("my imagination is not up to the task"), SJEs tend to talk of being *expanded* by the film ("this fantasy opened up my imagination"), of having their feelings changed about the rest of their lives ("purging negative feelings," "gives me courage and hope," and "lessons about life and self"). A discursive move is surely implied here, one that for SJEs *breaches the boundary* of the film and carries possibilities back into their lives.

C. **Outcomes** are differentiated by their focus on *explicit statements of the status of the story-world*, or *perceived meanings and themes* in the film. Twice as many SJEs as ESJs gave codable responses here. But as important was the variation in the *degree of articulation* of these. While, typically, ESJs would use implicit or imprecise expressions such as "Better values than our world" or "Makes things bigger and better," SJEs would write more overtly such things as "When choices were simple," "true friendship," "a Christian allegory, and morally necessary," and "embedded in my soul." And only the SJEs used any distinctive discursive move to indicate *how* the film achieved these, best caught in this expression: "the themes made me emotional." This implication, that the themes are linked to the emotional experience, recurs elsewhere.

D. There were slightly more **Envisioning** references from SJEs (twenty-one) than from ESJs (sixteen). But there was a clear separation in *kind*. Although there were exceptions to these tendencies, ESJs by and large used expressions that *depersonalised* the vision ("captured the books' grandeur," "did justice to the books," and—interestingly, as we will see—"an adaptation and its own work of art"), SJEs saw the film as embodying *their own* vision ("So like mine I couldn't believe it," "matched mine," "visualised my own fantasies," and "remarkably true to the spirit of Tolkien"). Only on the ~~ESJ~~ side do we find sceptical surprise by reference to the film's origins: "as true to the vision as money could be expected to provide." (This reference returns as a discursive move specific to the ~~ESJs~~.) On the other hand, one could argue that on the ~~SJEs~~' side, the repeated reference to the "essence" and "spirit" of Tolkien's book comes close to constituting a discursive move in itself, since it links the particular facets of the film to a wider explanatory framework.

E. **Filmic qualities:** Both groups described it as a "masterpiece," celebrated the acting, the special effects, the battle scenes (although a few ~~SJEs~~ hinted at a discursive move in saying they were "surprised" at enjoying these). Only in one respect is there a divergence. Four ~~ESJs~~ described the film as a "work of art." The implied measure moves the film away from being primarily experiential into a sphere of artistic quality assessment.

F. **Makers:** A small tendency emerged among the ~~ESJs~~ to refer to people other than Peter Jackson. Here, the names of Alan Lee and John Howe—figures associated strongly with the broader world of fantasy—were named, and praised. These remain isolated additions, unconnected by any visible "moves" to other variables. Any discussion of these would therefore be too speculative.

G. **Filmic comparisons** produced few responses. I simply note that two ~~ESJs~~ but no ~~SJEs~~ name *Star Wars* as a measure for *LotR,* and a further two name "Fantasy" as a related genre. The hint that a fantasy repertoire may be in operation for this group is worth noting. There are no differentiating markers in the ways in which the two groups place the film in history. Both groups, equally, are willing to name the film the "Best ever" or "Best in a long time," to call its making an "Event," and to say that the conclusion of the trilogy now leaves them sad and knowing they will miss it.

H. **Reservations:** Here too it is hard to discern a pattern. Both groups declare regrets at changes and cuts, and there is a reasonable overlap in these. Individual differences could be noted (two ~~ESJs~~ regret the ending being so slow, while none of the other group do so; and vice versa with the loss of the Houses of Healing—but both contain people who regret the loss of the Scouring of the Shire). Two ~~ESJs~~ love the films *in spite of* the books, whereas no ~~SJEs~~ do this—hinting at different roles for the books in the two groups.

I. In the move between *reservations* and *recuperations,* a significant difference emerges, although the numbers are small. Among the ~~SJEs~~, weaknesses in the film are usually explained—and thus excused—by reference to the exigencies of transforming the huge books into films ("I see the necessity," "it's to be expected"). But in two cases, they are blamed on "Hollywood," in its tendency to "syrup." The *opposite* appears among the E~~S~~Js, three of whom praise the film for *surpassing* a "Hollywood" origin.

J. **Significant other** comments were few, and pointed either to some highly individuated circumstance (for example, "these films have been important family occasions for the last three years"), to a note about other responses (for example, "People clapped" at the cinema), or to a generalised "other" that was a reference point against which viewing was measured (for example, "this is true all over the world").

SECOND-LEVEL ANALYSIS: THE DISCURSIVE MOVES

For the first-level analysis, the categorial structure had to be neutral between the two response sets. At the second level, this is neither possible or desirable, for here the "move" categories are generated from the separate patterns of first-level codings. Only one kind of discursive linkage breaks this rule: *listings*. Some respondents simply offered a string of expressions, cumulatively summing up the filmic experience. There is a strong overlap in these. The following could equally come from either group: "Magic, beautiful, awesome, extraordinary," "Impressed, awe-inspired, enchanted, amazed." This should not be surprising, since by listing respondents are saying that their responses were not (yet) unified. Only in one respect are the two groups' listings distinct. Three of the S~~J~~Es, but none of the others, speak in an *active* tense ("I laughed, I cried, I cheered") to sum their responses.

Beyond this, it is possible to identify a set of patterned differences in the kinds of discursive moves used within the two groups. They centre around the role of emotions, and the closed or open nature of the experience of the film. Table 9.3 deliberately emphasises the points at which the two groups veer away from each other. There are partial overlaps, but the analysis of the two hundred-strong cohorts definitely shows a strong area of separation. The table therefore is an analytic construct, since some individuals straddle the two camps.

The responses are not uniform, but there are some distinctions between the two groups that permit a degree of modelling. Tentatively, I would characterise these as follows:

1. *E~~S~~Js* show a tendency to treat *LotR* as a film, to be evaluated as such (for qualities, comparisons, and histories). If it belongs somewhere, it tends to be in its own world, a place to visit (even a "strange" one, as one respondent puts it). It may or may not be continuous with the books, but that does not seem to be a necessary condition for enjoyment.
2. *S~~J~~Es* show a tendency to evaluate the film for its meaning to self, and to make links between experienced emotions and larger themes and meanings. It is a phenomenon in which they personally participate, a place not distant but close (where characters are "friends"), and by journeying there

we are changed. The films become right by dint of achieving the vision that these people have built from their (often long) encounter with the books. Jackson is a guarantor, because he is "like a friend" (or even a "wizard," suggesting Jackson *belongs within* this world).

Table 9.3: Summary Comparison of Epic and Spiritual Journey Responses

"Epic" (Excluding "Spiritual Journey")	"Spiritual Journey" (Excluding "Epic")
Evaluating the film using criteria of *cinematic excellence.*	Evaluating the film using criteria of *being moved and inspired.*
Measuring the film *against other films* and *film history.*	Measuring the film *against other noteworthy experiences.*
The film's key qualities are *scenery, acting, cinematography, special effects.* It is *itself an act of imagination.*	The film's key qualities are *acting, recognition of characters, embodiments of a shared imagination/vision.*
Finding Middle-earth a place to *visit,* and experience as *other. Its distance aids our engagement.*	Finding Middle-earth a place to *journey within,* in order to *come home with moral comparisons.*
Peter Jackson and other makers *contribute to excellence,* with or without the books.	Peter Jackson and the actors *are guarantors of the vision,* permitting some deviations from the books.
Emotions experienced *point to the makers' skills.*	Emotions experienced *emphasise the importance of the lessons.*

This portrait was constructed from sets drawn from across all English-language responses. Thereafter, I explored the relations between the Vernacular and Engaged modality choices in each country, using the same analytic procedures. For space reasons, I move straight to a summary of these.

Table 9.4: Australia
[Engaged = "Spiritual Journey"; Vernacular = "Epic"]

Modal Choice	Self- defs	Experi- ential	Out- come	En- vision	Filmic quals	Makers	Compar- isons	Reser- vations	Recup- eration	Signif. others
SJ	22	96	22	34	20	8	22	32	12	4
E	22	90	12	28	30	2	10	32	16	0

The Australian samples show almost all of the characteristics displayed by the world sample. While both groups include people who cite their reading of the books as a ground for their responses, the consequences are pretty different. To the ESJs, the books are a reason to watch the films, and sometimes to be uneasy about changes and cuts. But these are largely recuperated by the *cinematic skill* of the makers. While a number do describe emotional responses to the film (mostly just as "emotional," which could refer either to themselves or to the characters and events), only in two cases does this lead to a comment about the themes and meanings of the film: one is clearly an overlap with a typical SJE response ("Emotive, conveys well the sacrifices of each character for the good of others"), while the other is a debarring one ("touched the heart-strings, good in this cynical age"). Mostly, the references to emotions lack discursive connections with other aspects, or else they lead to *cinematic judgements* (as in: "Taught me how to adapt a book to the screen," "a triumph of good film-making"). The experiential vocabulary veers towards other kinds of impact: "amazing," "enjoyable," "delight," and "satisfying." Only one person mentions sadness that it is over. The filmic qualities celebrated mention features such as the battles (four times—one negative), the special effects (twice), the scenery (five times), and the cinematography (six times). Two do mention the sense of "reality" achieved, but nothing in either answer suggests that the experience transcends the cinematic ("At no point during the film did I feel that the characters weren't real people who existed in some place out of time"—the inverted negatives in this sentence ward off any imputation of too much "reality").

The SJEs make different discursive connections across codes. The most evident is the move to evaluate the film against the "spirit" or "essence" of the books (five). This is complemented by several saying that the film "brought my imagination to life" (in one striking variant a person says, "A film can clarify confused images and give perspective," a response pointing to the benefits of *developed and shared* interpretations, as well as depriviledging the books as books). They also make connections from emotional response to perceived themes and reality: "tugged my emotions, enlightened my heart and made my spirits soar," from " moved, very real emotions, made me cry" to identifying themes of "pride, sorrow, loss, happiness," "moving tribute to friendship, love and comradeship," and from "sad, happy, bittersweet" to "feels as if Middle-earth really existed." Few SJEs mention cinematic qualities (one mentions the filming of the battles, but only to stress these are "not just" about battles, one mentions Shelob). As opposed to the ESJs, many SJEs record impact on self. These take several forms: from "left speechless" and "left wrung out," to "still in shock days after seeing it," to "felt transported" and "inspired."

Perhaps as importantly, in neither case was it possible to identify *any* "local" references or interests. Nothing relating to the proximity to New Zealand (in fact no mention of the sources of the scenery at all). Nothing indicating a local tradition of responses. The only nongeneral responses were highly individualised ones (one person saying she had been given a name from the books; another reporting on her husband and children's reactions to the film as well as her own). These are two patterns of *generalised* responses.

Table 9.5: Belgium
[Engaged and Vernacular Responses = "Quest"]

Modal Choice	Self- defs	Experi- ential	Out- come	En- vision	Filmic quals	Makers	Compar- isons	Reser- vations	Recup- eration	Signif. others
Q	4	96	8	30	30	8	24	24	8	4

The Belgian responses are best approached by a combination of what they are and what they aren't. In the case of Belgium, the same modality expression topped both Vernacular and Engaged choices: "Quest." But while it is perhaps possible to explain the sameness of the choice, an explanation why it was this one has to be very tentative.

Belgian respondents show a wide range of expressions to capture the strength of their enjoyment of the film: "brilliant," "magnificent," "unbelievable," "fantastic," and "beautiful." Singularly missing are words like "inspiring"—words hinting at consequences for themes. Yet a number of respondents do note the presence of themes, notably the "battle between good and evil." Hardly any self-identify as fans, even though—from other remarks—it is easy to tell that a good proportion knew the books. What is most striking as a presence is the repeated use of the term *adaptation* to describe the book-film relationship. The book, in the ways it is used, functions as an *external measure,* a guide really to what should best be included—but no more than that. There is not one case of what was so strongly seen among the world "Spiritual journey" group; namely, measuring the film version against *personal visualisation or imagination.* One answer only comes a little close to this: "After reading the magical story I had this enormous need to literally SEE the battle between good and evil in this magical world. I wanted to check my ideas about good and evil against those of the film-makers. Succeeded, by the way." Even in this lone answer, there is little sense of this visualisation being something invested in for its own sake. The book does not seem "owned"; rather, the film provides an *alternative* measure, which fortunately happens to coincide, hence the "succeeds, by the way."

Yet a good number of respondents do refer to the film's emotionality—one of the other markers of the "Spiritual journey" folk. But it is as if the emotions are a quality of the *film* rather than a quality of the *responses engendered.* So, we get "emotional, spectacular, simply perfect," and "impressive, beautiful images and colours, emotional, simply fantastic." And these all tend to associate with a mantra that the film(s) are "the best film ever seen," or "worthy close to the trilogy." And there is a strong presence of mentions of the battles, special effects, costumes, acting, and cinematography (several of these often summed up in the word "spectacle"). But this is curiously unauthored. Peter Jackson earns only one mention in the entire set.

This combination indicates a widespread position among Belgian respondents that is *halfway* between "Epic" and "Spiritual journey." Not willing/interested in making the story into a personal vision, therefore rather observing it from a distance, still, it is *more than just a good film*. It becomes a cinematic event, something "never to forget." But there the investment ends.

Table 9.6: China
[Engaged = "Fantasy"; Vernacular = "Epic"]

Modal Choice	Self-defs	Experi-ential	Out-come	En-vision	Filmic quals	Makers	Compar-isons	Reser-vations	Recup-eration	Signif. others
F	2	92	24	22	62	8	18	8	2	2
E	16	88	28	26	34	10	24	6	4	2

Although there is a very high level of enthusiasm among Chinese Engaged respondents, the terms of that enthusiasm seem markedly different from those of other countries. First, there is not one mention of Tolkien. The book is mentioned by just two, in any sense at all. Additionally, there was only one coding under self-definitions, indicating that prior expectations, and a sense of what a "self" going to see the film took with him or her was hardly operating. Instead, what comes across most strongly as an *emergent property* is a sense that the world enacted constitutes an alternative world. The scenery, the special effects, the work of cameras and actors, all constitute a fantasy place to visit. At its most extreme, this takes this form: "This movie is full of the mystery and fantasy of the western world, rich in content, and worth watching." This is, I acknowledge, by far the most overt. But many others appear to point this way. There are mentions of "fantasy." These do vary in the range they appear to imply to the concept. One limits its scope thus: "For myself, I anticipated enjoying the visual impressions translated faithfully from the fantasy text to films. But actually, out of all the elements I enjoyed, the fantasy turned out to be only a very small part. Much more impressive were the great scenes." The distinction implied here between a fantasy world visually reenacted and the "great scenes" implies that something more is added. This answer is unspecific about what this is. But others indicate directly the way the film has *added* something to them, as for instance: "It made me realise the limitations of my imagination. It not only gave me courage, more than anything it expanded my imagination." A fugitive element arises from what the film is compared with. Where in most countries the comparisons for Engaged respondents tend to be unspecific references to "best film ever," there is just one of this kind with the Chinese respondents. Two call it a personal favourite. But what seems to provoke filmic comparisons is the linking of two components: the film's visual "presence" or the quality of the acting, linking with the meanings that arise from this. Here are two examples of this, so the "moves" can be seen: "This film is the classic of all classics! I like it very much indeed! It has deep meanings, and the casting is very good. The characters are portrayed very well, and there is fine attention to detail. Both films from other genres and fantasy films can learn a lot from this film, it is a model of all film making. Very successful!!" "Not only has visual enjoyment, but also cultural value! I think it has meanings as deep as *Titanic*. If only I had a profound understanding of the history and background of the film, I would like it even more!!!" This theme of not having the requisite knowledge is hinted at in other answers, as well. (In just one case, it becomes a problem: "Impressive!! Couldn't get enough!!! The effects are great, but I didn't understand some of the plot.") For those who manage it, it appears that the combination of plot, acting, and effects (a recurrently quoted trio) produces a *sense of a world not previously experienced*.

The Chinese "Epic" sample are substantially more disunited than most other groups. Among them are some who closely approximate to the "Fantasy" group. This one differs only in the use of the word *epic:* "This is the one and only greatest fantasy epic film"—although it does deserve mention that the word *epic* is not used once among the "Fantasy" sample, but here is used five times. Particular answers show an almost exaggerated similarity with the world "Epic" set, as this one, which (almost uniquely) celebrates the commercial potentialities of the film: "My love for LOTR is almost insane! This is the greatest film I have ever seen. I thank J R R Tolkien, Peter Jackson and New Line Cinema for having given me such a beautiful experience, and I wish New Line Cinema would introduce more merchandise from the film into China!!!" A few shows similarities with the world "Spiritual journey" set, as, for instance: "I cried during the film. Not because of the plot or a character, but for a kind of power and spirit in it. It makes me feel moved and excited. This is the best film of the trilogy. It is also the best film I have ever seen," or in "I can't describe it. I only remember that my heart was empty after the film." In one other way this set also reminds us, surprisingly, of the world "Spiritual journey" set, in that it is among this (Vernacular) group that we find the references to the book and Tolkien (seven times). But Tolkien becomes just a maker alongside Jackson, as in the example above, and again in this response: "J R R Tolkien, Peter Jackson and Orlando Bloom are the people I most thank right now." But a series of features here all, more or less overtly, point in the same very curious direction. First, there is the repeated use of "mysterious" and "dreamlike" to characterise the filmic experience. Second, and quite unlike the world "Spiritual journey" set, there is a sense that the end of the film is unequivocally a *victory*. Humans have won, and "a glorious and peaceful era has started." What has happened to the hobbits, and the sad ending? They vanish in most answers, or—in one case—reappear as "hobbit humans." And in a series of quite overt "moves," a number of answers imply that this story marks the *end of an era of legends*. "Beautiful scenery, moving sentiments. An old era has passed and a new era has begun. The courage of mankind has started an era of human proportions." "When the sun rises again, the past is forever lost, and a new era will start." With less forthrightness, others pick up on aspects of this, as in: "The characters have a traditional beauty," and "The fantasy era made everything seem very mysterious." This sensibility I might tentatively characterise as delighting in the film for its *closing into modernity*. Thus, the special effects not only enact magic, but by their very nature *undo* such magic. They are the proof that we are modern, advancing. The film closes the period of legends, and leaves *us*, the "small people," in charge of the world.

Table 9.7: Denmark
[Engaged = "Spiritual Journey"; Vernacular = "Good vs. Evil"]

Modal Choice	Self-defs	Experi-ential	Out-come	En-vision	Filmic quals	Makers	Compar-isons	Reser-vations	Recup-eration	Signif. others
SJ	28	90	6	16	26	4	52	18	10	0
GvE	16	98	10	8	28	6	12	18	16	0

The Danish responses show some very low rates of response among both SJEs and GvEs: to significant others (most strikingly) with not a single reference to others as audiences in either set; but also in references to makers, and in comments on outcomes. For the remainder, the most striking separators are in self-definitions, with twice as many envisioning, and almost twice as many self-, and more than four times as many filmic references among the SJEs than the GvEs. And although it is possible to point to isolated or small numbers of cases where the qualities found in the world set are reproduced (there are somewhat more emotional references among SJEs, for instance, and the filmic references among the GvEs do talk about cinematic qualities slightly more), these are not the predominant patterns. In fact, the SJE choosers make *fewer* outcome references than do the GvEs (and both make very few), which runs counter to the world set.

The pattern is, rather, emphatically towards talking of the film in fantastical terms—although not choosing "Fantasy" as the preferred modality. In both groups, there is a focus on the "otherness" of Tolkien's world, and praise for the film's enactment of this. But while the "Epics" tend to use the terms "fantastic" (seventeen) and "gripped" (nine), SJEs—while occasionally using "fantastic"—prefer the terms "overwhelming" (eight), "absorbing" (five), and "beautiful" (seven). What appears to characterise the SJEs is a sense of the *surprising and overwhelming completeness* of the film. Thus, a good half of those filmic comparisons take the form of assertions that this is the best film ever seen, emphasising its uniqueness. But this lies in the sense of transportation to another whole world. Examples of this sort are: "This was a beautiful topping out of the trilogy, and a complete and perfect film";

"A step into another parallel world"; "This is a film that has struck me deeply. It is enormous in itself as well as very complex. It is hard for me to believe that it isn't reality or that it has never happened. I love it and the other two films. All that universe and a lot of my life, it's inexplicable, but one of the greatest experiences I have had." This sense of finding it beyond one's conceiving is common. ("All my expectations were as nothing once I saw it. Entirely unique and epoch-making. You seldom get the feeling that this is the best film you've ever seen even while you watch it.") It seems that it is the *detail* that makes it so powerful. Conversely, the reservations among the SJEs are more likely than in any other country set to name the absence of some very particular bits as the cause of regret—three unusually mentioning Tom Bombadil, others mentioning Merry and Pippin's decisions on Pelennor Fields, the details of the hobbits' return to the Shire, and Galadriel's gardening gift. In the absence of any discernible strand of ethical appreciation among these, it is no surprise to find that the film is repeatedly celebrated as a fantasy film par excellence: "Delightful to see the book brought to life. A proper fantasy film. Not like many other attempts at fantasy." Others might not use the word *fantasy*, but they enact some of its putative qualities: "It was like being in Middle-earth. The pictures were fantastic, and created an amazing universe."

It is not so much that there is a clear separation or contrast with the GvEs as that these are simply less inclined to attach as much importance to the same experience. The film is "great," "fantastic," "gripping," and "suspenseful"—but that is it. All bar one give an experiential report, but more than a quarter say nothing more at all—and many others have only marginal comments in addition. It is as if here the experience is all—it provokes no further thinking or judgement. Yet it is *only* among these that we find explicit comments on the story's moral values.

Table 9.8: France
[Engaged and Vernacular = "Epic"]

Modal Choice	Self-defs	Experi-ential	Out-come	En-vision	Filmic quals	Makers	Compar-isons	Reser-vations	Recup-eration	Signif. others
E	16	94	8	36	40	12	18	16	8	0

The French responses, as the Belgians, had an identical Vernacular and Engaged modality choice: "Epic." And they share other characteristics with the Belgians. They show strong awareness of film's cinematic aspects, with repeated references to screenplay, scenery, special effects, battles, and music, plus acting. There are a number of references to wider, noncinematic issues. But these take a different form from those found in Belgium. They repeatedly *verge on the philosophical*. So there are references to the film as an "apotheosis," to a range of "mythologies," to the recovery of an "inner child" and "recalling childhood play," to "humanistic visions," to a "waking dream." Curiously, however, while the introduction of these criteria does bring unequivocal praise, it also leads to a *closure* around the event. It is as if people are demonstrating their considerable knowledge, and thus behaving *like film critics*. There are those whose enthusiasm asks nothing more of the film than that it be a good film. ("Extraordinary special effects. Actors' performances perfect! The story's fantastic!" "Splendid crowning of two years' waiting, and completely successful trilogy." "Really good visual and sound quality. Good adaptation of the book. Very, very good performances by the actors.") But those who reference broader themes and criteria do not thereby appear to generate "take-home" meanings. Rather, they simply locate further and deeper dimensions *within the filmic world:* "A lyrical flight into Tolkien's world, an imaginary world, but sufficiently real across its several hours that I was completely stunned on leaving the cinema." (There is a clear implication of it remaining a separate world.) Or: "Tolkien's world and the dream he offered have been perfectly translated." (The film does not transcend being a "dream.") Or: "A great spectacle of a film which created intense emotion while you were in the cinema. Some scenes took your breath away. Music that thrilled. But after nearly three hours, the end was too long." (This experience was bounded by the cinema, as well as being found excessively long.) Just occasionally a response does go further: "A very humanistic film crossing various characters who can each and all rediscover themselves in a story of love and friendship and courage. There are no racial boundaries or barriers between races unless they are based in the war between good and evil. In sum, a mystical film." This answer does, exceptionally, bring together quite an apparatus of external criteria to evaluate the experience, but still ends by placing the film in a category. Entirely missing from the French responses is any hint that *going on a journey* with the characters might constitute the meaning.

Table 9.9: Germany
[Vernacular = "Epic"; Engaged = "Spiritual Journey"[3]]

Modal Choice	Self-defs	Experiential	Out-come	En-vision	Filmic quals	Makers	Compar-isons	Reser-vations	Recup-eration	Signif. others
SJ	22	95	19	19	35	5	14	16	8	0
E	16	94	10	18	40	4	20	34	14	4

The German responses among the SJEs share much with the world set. It is for them a very powerfully emotional experience: the word *overwhelming* is the most widely used. Two typical examples: "It had totally pulled me away emotionally. I was simply sucked into the world and taken over by it. In the end I was totally convinced and won over"; "I was overwhelmed by the sheer power of the impressions and extremely moved (yes, to tears) by the subjects treated, i.e., friendship love courage etc." Worth noting here is, first, the articulated move in the second from emotions to themes—the emotions pull the underlying themes into fuller view. Also interesting is the slight sense that there was an initial *resistance* to such a deep involvement—a suspicion that had to be overcome, and was. This shows in other answers, as well, in the way a number of people acknowledge that they had reservations about the adaptation (scenes lost, or changed), but despite this, they were overwhelmed. In fact, this aside, Tolkien's book as source plays *surprisingly little* role. One of the few to mention it directly half-acknowledges this unusualness: "Genius, but to my taste not close enough to the book!" That qualifier "to my taste" marks it as a *personal* decision. That the film is extraordinary *despite* troubling changes is shown also in this simple counterposition: "I was overwhelmed. A masterpiece! Since I am a longstanding fan of Tolkien's book I am a bit disappointed that important scenes are missing." The missing parts do not lead to any qualification on the judgement on the film; it is still a masterpiece. The regrets about the book stay separate enough in this to permit the film to be experienced as overwhelming. What is striking about the SJE group is that they are small (the reduced figure of thirty-five testifies to this) and strikingly unified.

The ESJs do not sit in some easy contrast with the SJEs. They share a very high level of emotional engagement—although the word *overwhelming* is still frequently used (SJEs = twenty-four; ESJs = sixteen), and of course other expressions can do much the same work. The prime difference is in stepping beyond its filmicness. While a considerable proportion (27 percent) of the SJEs talked either of Middle-earth as a fantasy world they wanted to go to and stay in, or talked about the themes addressed through the film (love, courage, friendship), just two (4 percent) of the ESJs made this move. There are two other curious differences. There are many more references among the ESJs than among the SJEs to "sadness that the trilogy has ended"—it is for many a complex part of their emotions (best captured in this answer: "Excited and melancholic because now I have seen the last part and the Elf ship will not return to make it continue"). This might hint at a journeylike relation, typical of particularly Engaged book lovers. And indeed the ESJs do give *more* attention to the fact and processes of adaptation. Unlike the SJEs, there are several unrecuperated reservations, where changes or absences lead to qualification on the praise. There are also occasional others using criteria hinting at its weaknesses as a film—two calling it "bombastic," two finding the film (and especially the ending) "kitschy" and sentimental. These are not found at all among the SJEs.

Overall, then, it seems that insofar as we might paint a broader portrait from these samples, there appears to be in Germany a relatively small and enclosed body of fans whose relation with the books did not preclude passionate involvement in the films—it was not a *literary* fascination, but a fascination with the otherness of Tolkien's world.

Table 9.10: Greece
[Engaged = "Spiritual Journey"; Vernacular = "Epic"]

Modal Choice	Self-defs	Experiential	Outcome	Envision	Filmic quals	Makers	Comparisons	Reservations	Recuperation	Signif. others
SJ	20	93	16	29	38	9	16	24	18	9
E	12	88	12	16	29	14	20	8	2	10

The Greek SJEs and ESJs both share similarities with their respective world sets. The SJEs share the ways of envisioning, and the tendency to find broader meanings and associations. In envisioning, the book never functions simply as a source, but works either via a notion of the "spirit" of Tolkien, or via respondents' picturing the world of the books. This contrasts with the ESJs, whose envisioning references are without exception general comments on fidelity of adaptation. Typical SJE examples are references to the "substance and spirit" of the books, and statements that the film "visualised exactly what I had read in the book and what I had in my imagination." The broader meanings are given as the movie "symbolising the uppermost meaning of loyalty, friendship and of course love," and "projecting timeless values, right morals, and bravery nowadays." That last word hints at something not found in other sets, of some kind of direct association with contemporary events and feelings. This recurs more overtly in this complete answer: "Exceptional because it took us to the fairytale world of Middle-earth, where there are not so many political and economic interests, and good reigns." In another complete answer, an unusual element appears—a reference to some kind of collective whom the film addresses: "It reminds all of us of fundamental values which have lost their meaning today: comradeship—devotion—the good of all above personal interest—unity—love!" That sense of a "we" to whom the film speaks is unusual, but interestingly does recur in the ESJs, where five respondents talked of a generalised "we/spectator" who are drawn into the film. It also makes the film itself "exceptional" (a word used repeatedly), because it is "one of the very few" projecting such values today, and lifts the film above the ordinary. What is interesting is a matching *relative absence* of references to emotions, and this is true on both sides. There are just three, in all, among the SJEs, and here, rather than providing routes into the values (as in the world set), they appear to link with an emphatic reference to "epic." (All bar one emotion references among ESJs are in listings.) Here is the clearest case: "I was deeply moved and swept away by it, both by the beautiful scenery, action-packed scenes and most importantly by its heroic epic feeling that remained true to the books without the director using any cheap Hollywoodish tricks to evoke emotions." In this answer, the emotions are part of a feeling of the film's *authenticity* (the non-Hollywood aspect), but hardly hint at anything extrafilmic. And "truth to the books" is measured through imagination. Also, in the Greek case, the "we" that is hinted at welcomes in non–book readers ("attracting a wider audience than just fans"), and there are some for whom the books are not any kind of measure who still describe the film in terms of its wider "values." For instance: "I was waiting for this film since I watched the second part of the trilogy. But the last part was the best, it was worth waiting for! I can say that it is the best ending that an adult tale can have, even though it made me think a lot." There is more than a hint in here that this respondent did not know the story except through the film, but still found it extending beyond the cinematic ("made me think a lot"). This is a more *inclusive* and *politicised* enthusiasm than in some other cases. The ESJs, on the other hand, combine a strong strand of celebration of the movie's filmicness (the strongest case: "I love it because it had very good special effects, music, costumes, acting, photography, and plot") with a recurrent sense of Tolkien's world as at a remove. This is conveyed in words like "magical," "enchanting," and "phantasmagorical" in references to the film's "dream-like" nature ("It lets you escape from everyday routines. You enter a dream seeing the film, and feel strange feelings"), in accounts of the strength of the film's ability to capture its audiences ("Splendid, with amazing effects and roles irreproachably executed by the actors. They brought the film's atmosphere into the cinema, so that we spectators felt we were almost participating"), and sometimes quite explicitly (with references such as "the spectator is transported to another fantastical world," and "it takes you on a journey far away"). If the SJEs show signs of an emergent political assessment of the film, there is no trace of this among the ESJs. Here, there are hardly any volunteered references to themes or lessons from the film. And the most explicit among the few puts it as an *extra* to filmic qualities that transport us elsewhere: "Magnificent, phantasmagoric, epic, but also including teachings about friendship and love." If there is anything "local" about these responses, it lies not in the one reference (among the ESJs) to an analogy with Sophoclean drama, but rather in the sense that this is a vision *potentially shareable with everyone.* "Tolkien" is not the private property of a hermetic group of enthusiasts, but available to all who wish to participate.

Table 9.11: The Netherlands
[Engaged = "Quest"; Vernacular = "Fantasy"]

Modal Choice	Self-defs	Experi-ential	Out-come	En-vision	Filmic quals	Makers	Compar-isons	Reser-vations	Recup-eration	Signif. others
Q	10	100	2	16	26	6	18	20	6	6
F	18	98	4	26	24	4	26	14	12	2

The Netherlands Engaged responses are quite unlike the world "Spiritual journey" set. First, there are only two mentions of anything suggesting an ethical or broader cultural dimension to the story—and they are both, as we will see, slight oddities. Second, there are absolutely no references to Peter Jackson or any other makers of the film—only two very general mentions of "they" who made it; yet there is great attention to the cinematic qualities of the film (special effects, music, cinematography, settings, acting, and so on). Third, there are few emotional references, and these are passing mentions, unlinked to any "moves." On the other hand, there are five direct references to fantasy as a category, along with other terms pointing in that direction: "enchanting," "magical," "fantastical," and (more complicatedly) "draws you into their world." That something complex is at work here is suggested by this full answer: "Super good fantasy film, but very believable, there is a lot of reality in it, it seems like it really happened, real history, a beautiful world, a super beautiful story, the connection of helping each other is also very beautiful." Here, the story's fantastical nature hints that this might be a cutoff world. But the answer recuperates this with the emphasis on its "reality," that it feels as if it really happened. But the hint at broader cultural themes at the end is an *add-on,* an "also." What unites them is the notion of their "beauty"—a recurrent term. The other hint at a broader meaning comes in this answer: "Tremendous to imagine yourself in another world time sphere. Good and evil people, greed, camaraderie, and closeness." The first sentence transfers the film firmly into another world; only once there do we meet the broader themes. This is fantasy in the sense of a posited elsewhere, which we visit, and in which we become caught up ("sucked in," "fully engaged"). There is very little sense of *respondents' imaginations* as something already active, and making demands, except a few references to being a Tolkien reader or an existing fan. Rather, the book seems like a thing-in-itself, awaiting "adaptation." At their most articulate, respondents appear to emphasise the *filmic* over the literary, as in this answer: "Breath-taking! I was already a big fan of Tolkien's books. But the way in which his words were transformed into images, and then the magnificent music ... simply unbelievable." The "words" here retain no rights over the transformation.

A number of the above elements are reproduced in the Netherlands Vernacular modality choice: "Fantasy." Here, the set displays the same attraction to the word beautiful, and the book claims no rights over the film. Indeed in a couple of cases there is an explicit statement of the separateness, as here: "It is a sort of supersensorial mythological show of what goes on in the world. It is a terrific film and you have to accept that the medium of film is totally different from the book. You should not compare them to each other. The book is just not transferable (adaptable) into film. Still, it is carefully done and now and then I got goosebumps." Where the book is mentioned by others, it is purely as adaptation—occasionally respondents regret "some scenes" having been lost, but never as a complaint—it is just that films are different. In no case at all does the story produce an imaginative realisation or visualisation against which the film is measured. The above full answer is worth quoting on another ground, as it is the only case of a possible noncinematic account of the film. There is not one single reference to wider cultural or ethical meanings in the film. There is one open mention that the film takes the viewer "for a short time out of this gruesome world and makes you desire another world." There is hardly a generic placement of the film (there is one naming of "fantasy," and one of "epic"). Other than these, the film is entirely measured in its own terms, for the strength of the immediate experience it generates. This is indicated by the number of codings (eighteen) that are effectively contained only within the experiential qualities category, and how many also are listings (typically "Magnificent, simply very impressive, a very beautiful film," "Tremendous. Fantastic," or "Phenomenal, unforgettable, fascinating"). It is also striking how few emotional references there are—two refer to crying for the last segment of the film, and one other simply calls it "emotional." No "moves" arise thereby to other claims about the film. Overwhelmingly, this set evaluates the film as film, commenting (if at all) on special effects, battles, music, acting, and settings. The makers hardly function at all within the talk, and the film is evaluated either in relation to the first two parts or just generally as "the best I've ever seen." This set has the narrowest range and reach of all the sets. Possibly, what prompted the choice of "Fantasy," which unifies them, is a lowest common denominator, somehow indicating intensity of experience without committing to any particular further meanings.

Table 9.12: Slovenia
[Vernacular = "Good vs. Evil"; Engaged = "Epic"]

Modal Choice	Self-defs	Experiential	Out-come	En-vision	Filmic quals	Makers	Compar-isons	Reser-vations	Recup-eration	Signif. others
E	4	90	10	4	16	4	22	10	2	2
GvE	10	78	8	8	18	4	30	8	2	6

The Slovenian responses display a gulf between the responses of those who have read and invested in Tolkien's world and those who have not. The immediately most obvious feature of the two sets is that there is a considerable number of both sets whose answers are very short (just counting those only one or two words long, GvE = sixteen; E = ten). But in the other direction there are a quite small number of rather long answers in both sets. This becomes more interesting when we realise that there are explicit or implicit comments within the longer answers on the situation that has produced the welter of shorter ones: "The film is the most beautiful thing I've ever seen. It's about friendship and trust. About virtues that are dying out in the civilisation of today. And it's exactly what makes it special. It's not important that the film is a fantasy, or however you say it. It's presented in a way that feels like it is really happening" ("Epic"). This answer counterpoints its own feelings to another, rejected account. Typically, this example not only distinguishes itself from others around it, but also imputes a clear message to the film. This small group of long, committed answers is equally divided between the Engaged and Vernacular groups. They are a very small group who are likely to talk of their commitment to *LotR* as a "way of life," or as "a second Bible." There are other kinds of evidence that *LotR* was relatively unknown to many viewers. A number (especially among the Vernaculars) declare their delight in finding out the fate of characters, leading to a level of involvement that depends to some extent on revealed plot details: "I liked it very much. The filming and acting were very good. It gave you the impression that you were there. I am sorry though that the film is over and that the heroes in the film split up." (Other partial answers said on this score: "the plot was very interesting," and "Extremely interesting story, full of unexpected turns.") In other cases, people report rushing to the books after seeing the films, as though this is something special. Where the book is mentioned as a source of expectations, this is often a very casual reference, as, for instance: "I liked the film, just as I liked the book." Even those who, unusually, mark themselves as longtime book readers do so in a way that suggests that the book has not become embedded into a *cultural response:* "Phenomenal. All my expectations came true and I got the chance to see an extraordinary ending to an unbelievable saga, the book of which I read long ago." In another direction, there is sometimes a real force to uses of filmic traditions as a measure of this one's success. Alongside the several in each set that simply say something like "Best film I've ever seen," there are some for whom knowledge of film clearly counts strongly: "A highlight of the film industry. All other films could only be used to advertise the LORD trilogy, or perhaps they'd better not, because the films really would be too 'long.' This is where the seventh art begins and ends." The strong film literacy (the reference to film as the "seventh art") is not peculiar to this answer but resonates in milder ways in a number of other answers. What the Engaged and the Vernacular responses have in common is the predominantly short answers, the weak levels of envisioning, and the overall lack of "moves" constructing categorial languages into *arguments* about the film. And the relative lack of such "moves" means that, such as there are, tend to be pretty unpatterned, which in its turn supports the notion that this story is unembedded within Slovenian culture.

Table 9.13: Spain
[Engaged = "Spiritual Journey"; Vernacular = "Epic"]

Modal Choice	Self-defs	Experi-ential	Out-come	En-vision	Filmic quals	Makers	Compar-isons	Reser-vations	Recup-eration	Signif. others
SJ	34	88	12	42	20	10	34	6	10	12
E	28	94	4	32	36	4	36	8	10	2

The Spanish responses display, in both sets, very high and wide expectations along with acceptance of achievement. They are the most enthusiastic group. Indeed, the Spanish E~~SJ~~ group share some characteristics with the U.S. SJ~~E~~ group, for example—an indicator, surely, that the bar was set high. Both groups include a number whose response to the film is clearly mediated through their own prior imagining of this story-world ("I have seen with my eyes everything that I imagined when I read the books"—this could easily come from either group). ESJs and SJEs share a strong sense of the film's emotionality (twelve SJEs and thirteen ESJs directly naming this). This answer (in fact from an ESJ respondent) could have come from either camp: "This is a film, and a trilogy, that I have lived with so intensely with my own feelings appearing on screen." If there is a difference, it is perhaps that in some of the ESJs the emotion is an extra to the other film's qualities, as in this answer: "It is wonderful, grandiose, but at the same time it makes you cry." A significant number of both, but especially the SJEs, define themselves as fans—and some of the latter particularly tell stories about themselves. To quote one in full: "I got to know the world of *The Lord of the Rings* some years ago through my cousin. It taught us to play a new game where the only things we needed were imagination, pencil, paper and dice. From that moment I was hooked so I read the books and since then I have amassed a great collection of books, including some about the movie, and some little figurines as well." First, that the film is seen as *continuous* with other involvements. It is a *world* that this person likes to inhabit. The film needs no special measure; it just adds and fits. This agrees closely with others who only discuss their love of the book, as if this tells all that needs saying about the film. It also comports with the several who talk of the film as the "fulfilment of a dream," or who talk of visiting Middle-earth via the film. There is in both camps intense awareness of the film as adaptation. But whereas with the ESJs attention to envisioning is matched by that to the film's qualities, this is not the case with the SJEs. While the ESJs will frequently mention the battles, the special effects, the acting, and the music, these appear largely taken for granted by the SJEs (several times simply referring to it having "come to life" and being "on the screen")—who instead talk more about the completeness of Tolkien's world, and about it being the "best story" ever told and now the "best film ever seen." The one surprising thing in the two Spanish sets is how *few* reference any thematic outcomes. This was one of the features that differentiated the SJEs from the ESJs in the world sample. Here, there are just two in the ESJ set, and six in the SJE set. The strongest is indeed very strong: "This is a myth that thanks to Peter Jackson has now been shown to millions of people who never knew Tolkien's books. This trilogy must be shown to future generations because not only is it a world of fantasy, it also depicts a better world for us, with everybody united under the same motto: freedom." But this rare politicised comment should be compared with the following: "It has been a very emotional story that makes you dream about another world far away from the audience." That sense of distanced otherness is more typical of the Spanish responses. But the two do share one association: that sense of a generalised audience. The Spanish SJEs make a larger, if still small, number of references to wider audiences than do most other groups.

Table 9.14: United Kingdom
[Engaged = "Spiritual Journey"; Vernacular = "Epic"]

Modal Choice	Self- defs	Experi- ential	Out- come	En- vision	Filmic quals	Makers	Compar- isons	Reser- vations	Recup- eration	Signif. others
SJ	22	96	16	34	32	12	22	20	14	10
E	22	96	14	26	34	14	18	28	10	2

British respondents share strongly in the overall tendencies found between the SJE and ESJ groups. But there are some local tendencies exemplified. The SJEs show a tendency not only to emotional responses, but to moving from these to broader understandings of its meaning and significance. Examples of such moves are to: awareness of the "deep scars the hobbits will bear," "parallels to ordinary life," "I feel stronger because of it," "if I could, I would enter it right now and have an adventure of my own." But as important is the strand that emphasises the relationship between personal and filmic imagination. "As I imagined," "from my imagination," "coheres with my own," "matched my own," and "amazed at how the 3rd continued to translate what I have in my own mind's eye." There is some overlap with the ESJs in phrases such as "brought the book to life," but not one of the ESJs uses this highly personalised account of their imaginations.

In their film evaluations, ESJs once again refer to the battles (three), the special effects (five), and the music (three), coupling this with references to "adrenaline rush" and "edge of the seat" experiences. They make more reference to Peter Jackson, thanking him or offering praise. The SJEs talk rather about characters and acting, and praise the "reality" of the film. While both groups will say in large rhetorical terms that this is the "best ever," when they become more specific the groups pull apart. The ESJs insistently judge it as a *film* (one comparing it with *Star Wars*, three calling it a fantasy, others more generally naming it a "milestone in filmmaking," the "best film ever"); the SJEs, while a few do mention special effects and battles, tend rather to use expressions suggesting an evaluation of particular scenes: "the stirring speeches," "Pippin's song," "oh my god Gollum."

The SJEs appear to take ownership of the books, though Tolkien gets fewer mentions than with the ESJs and not one refers to the "spirit" or "essence" of his works. It is as if while Tolkien may have *written* the books, they now belong more widely. In only one case does an SJE see the changes from the book as unrecoverable. In all other cases of reservations, things like the closeness to their own imaginings recuperate. The nearest one of the ESJs comes to this is a very telling answer, since it reveals a distinctive strategy; one complete answer read: "I loved it. As a fan of the books I was disappointed at some of the missing parts and changed ending but as a cinema fan I found it breathtaking." This tactical split, allowing separate criteria of judgement, is not possible for those for whom emotional engagement is a journey into meanings. Among the ESJs we find one response where the relation with the book causes a critical distance. Here is the complete response: "It brought one of the greatest stories in literature to a conclusion as well as could possibly be done within the confines of a film." Here, a clear preference is shown for the *literary* mode of expression without outright rejection of the cinematic.

"Spiritual journey" here associates with finding meanings in the film that transcend the cinematic, go beyond fantasy, achieving emotional intensity and a close relationship to respondents' personal sense of self and the world. This is *not* escapism or a distant world. To quote one answer in full that has no analogue among the ESJs, but accentuates tendencies found among many other SJEs: "It portrays a world long gone in which your choices are simple. Hard work, pleasure in the small things of life, good and evil in obvious measure. It shows a world cultures that are both simplistic [*sic*] and more sophisticated than the world we live in today. It is a world I would like to live in." There is here a clear sense of what Middle-earth amounts to, a clear relation with our own world, and a *reaching* for it as an alternative.

Table 9.15: United States
[Engaged = "Spiritual Journey"; Vernacular = "Epic"]

Modal Choice	Self-defs	Experi-ential	Out-come	En-vision	Filmic quals	Makers	Compar-isons	Reser-vations	Recup-eration	Signif. others
SJ	26	100	20	34	34	16	6	42	26	6
E	12	90	10	36	3	16	18	28	16	8

The U.S. responses strongly match the overall world samples for SJE and ESJ. But there are some suggestive variations. The first comparison, as ever, is over envisioning. While SJEs tend to talk either of the "spirit" of the books or of seeing the books "come to life," ESJs rather talk of "fidelity" to the books, or of their "grandeur." But even in this most common differentiator, there are signs of variation. Not one SJE in the sample, for instance, speaks of seeing his or her imagination come to life; and several ESJs, significantly, remark on the book's inadequacies: its "lugubrious" or "boring" nature. The other strong differentiator is the issue of broader values. While the key criteria for ESJs are the film's cinematic features (with repeated references to "technology," "effects," "scenery" and "views," "costumes," and "cinematography"), for the SJEs mention is more likely to be made of "acting and performances," and of "completing" the films and "summing up everything." Contrary to the world sets, *both* groups equally reference emotions as a key part of their experience of the film. It is interesting to see that this "listing"—"We laughed, we cried, we kicked ass"—occurs almost identically in *both* groups. It is as if emotion is more expected, more readily achieved, and amounts to and means less. It is not a basis for a move into "values." Rather, it is just what you expect of any reasonable movie. The bar has been set low, as caught in these examples: "Overwhelmed by the spectacle and emotion, cried for the last hour. It was better than I expected." Taken on its own, this sounds strong. Seen in context of the pattern I have identified, it suggests that it *didn't take that much to become overwhelming.* Another indicator of the same tendency is in the minimal talk about the makers. In each set there are just five mentions, and absolutely identically they simply say "Peter Jackson" did a great job. "Hollywood" is a silent presence, only possibly coming into view in comments explaining away reservations without "naming" a reason: "given overall restraints," "that's to be expected" (a repeated phrase) "nowadays."

EVALUATING THE FINDINGS

There appears to be a generalised tendency, across our world set, but also within particular country sets, towards a distinction and separation. Where Tolkien's books have been long known and have attained a determinate cultural presence, the films attract a distinctive following who love them as a form of nonreligious spirituality. To read the books, and thence to watch the films, is to accompany the characters on a journey whose point is ethical self-discovery. Being set in a "far place" assists in this. It removes the complications of *particular* personal and political affiliations, and instead allows people to focus on the properties that go with making moral choices in general, combining with others and having the will and courage to see a task through—even at great cost. Organisations such as national Tolkien Societies can help, by linking people and providing opportunities for in-depth conversations, to sustain this orientation. But you don't need to be a member for this to occur— simply to have had the books around, available and alive within a culture's currency over time, can enable many individuals to experience the story's "call" to this manner of participation.

Responding much more to the way the film is marketed (its Blockbuster feel, the "eventness" of the movies' releases, the hue and cry of publicity), the public presence of Tolkien enables others to respond to the scale of the film, and the effort of making it: thence, its "epicness." These two orientations are interconnected. To have had the book "around" for a long time, to have had it accrete general meanings within a country *both* enables the serious commitment of the "Spiritual journeyers" *and* double-digs the cultural soil to permit the enthusiastic, but more temporary, engagements of the "Epics."

The longer and stronger the Tolkien-reading tradition in a country, the more likely it is that that country will have returned a pattern based on the separation-and-connection of "Spiritual journey" and "Epic" orientations. But as we move away from this, we see other patterns emerge. This is, I would argue, is caused by two processes. Either the books have not been well known and therefore have not sedimented into the local culture, or something in the local culture, and perhaps particularly the local filmic culture, cuts across the absorption of Tolkien's story in these modes. Where the first of these is the case, the story bears a mark of being "foreign," perhaps of exoticness, and is therefore strongly measured against other locally established criteria. This is what I believe is happening in, for example, the case of China. Where the second is the case, as I believe has been the case in France, another commitment intermingles with the responses to the story, and makes it become "local" in distinctive ways.

This strong statement of the outcomes of my cross-cultural analysis requires several cautions. The first is to recognise the risk that the patterns disclosed in table 9.1 are an artefact of the analytic process. A considerable chain of quantitative and qualitative steps was required before this pattern emerged. It is not, however, the result of design-demand characteristics. And the fact that it was possible to reproduce *and* conduct a different *kind* of investigation, using randomly sampled qualitative responses, is surely a ground for some confidence. Our questionnaire recruited opportunistically, with the aim of attracting a sufficiently large number of responses to allow us to look for complex internal differentiations, and thus locate patterns. But if the original population was heavily skewed, and this carried over into the sample sets, biases would be imported even into the qualitative analyses. It is necessary therefore to be cautious.

But for all this, it is worthwhile to ponder the seemingly distinct country patterns because it takes us to the crux of the issue of cross-cultural comparisons. What does it mean to "belong" to a "national culture"? People do not "belong" in some unitary sense to a "culture." Only either extreme nationalism or extreme cultural relativism of a kind that models cultures from isolated "primitive" societies can sustain such a notion.[4] All kinds of factors will interrupt some singular "membership" of a national community. Diasporic movements of people, travel, international news, transnational media products, cultural and political beliefs—all these and many more make difficult the idea that people are constituted in some simple sense by membership of their "national community."

Yet at the same time we have to recognise that in complex ways nations *are* important. This is most evidently so where nation and language broadly coincide. It means that conversations, debates, and flows of ideas are largely (but of course never entirely) contained within a country's borders. Even without language, we know that the historical formation of "nations" has included forming a "sense of a national self." Benedict Anderson's work on the rise of the "imagined community," while criticised, still importantly draws attention to the ways in which a "common language" of laws, taxes, geography and day-to-day rules and practices generates a sense of "us," which transcends personal experience.[5] And other researchers have added to this—for instance, Michael Billig, who did important work on the constant reinforcement of "vernacular nationalism" by ordinary uses of "we" and "they" in media talk.[6] But if nations are formed in the imagination, other nations constitute points of both repulsion *and* attraction. It is only necessary to mention the ways in which "America" has been found, by many researchers, to be an ambivalent imaginary node for many non-American people, to see the force but complexity of this.[7]

In other directions altogether, sociological work on gendering, on generations, and on life careers all point to processes that cross cultural borders. Women's experience of life, many feminist scholars have argued, shares features across all societies—and that is likely to play a role in their response to something like a film, irrespective of country. Karl Mannheim's classic 1928 work on the formation of generations has drawn attention to the ways traumatic moments in history (wars, revolutions, or sudden cultural shifts) can produce a cross-country sense of distinctness[8]—the "1960s" being a classic example of this, and one that is particularly relevant to the laying down of a set of meanings around Tolkien.[9] And finally, life-career researchers have begun to explore the ways in which, in the circumstances of modern life, there may be typifying patterns to the stages in which many people, in different countries, live, experience, hope for, plan, and fantasise their lives.

FINAL THOUGHTS AND WIDER CONTEXTS

All these considerations make very complicated the idea that there might be country-specific responses to a film like *LotR*. But not impossible. In this final part, then, I record some possible insights and explanations that emerged when information exterior to the project, on countries' national, local, regional sensibilities and sensitivities, is entered into the equation. The gathering of these materials is manifold. First, there is the sizeable body of scholarship and criticism on Tolkien and *LotR* we sketched in the introduction. Second, there is the large body of materials on the presence of Tolkien and *LotR* in regional cultures collected alongside the project. Third, there is what sociologists and anthropologists call "local, embodied knowledge"—knowledge, quite simply, readily available because of one's affiliation with a local culture. For the purpose of researching how Tolkien and *LotR* are embedded within a national culture, three elements are crucial: the point of entry into the culture (the *first* publication of the books, and their sedimentation within readerships); the reputation of the works (the *summary* of opinions and interpretations); and its affiliation (the *range* of meanings and ideas associated with Tolkien and *LotR*). Putting these together, one can arrive at speculative but insightful overviews of how well (or not) the books and films have resonated within certain national cultures, and to what extent they have challenged them.

To some extent, the answers to this question have been suggested by previous chapters, on audience responses in individual countries (Australia, Belgium, Germany, The Netherlands, Slovenia, Spain, the United Kingdom, the United States, and Canada), prefigurations and receptions, and book-reading implications. Rather than prescribing judgements, I invite readers to cross-check my findings with the ones offered there.

But here, I would like to conclude by offering an honestly speculative, personal view. Various colleagues have debated this vigorously. But I am left even so with possibilities sufficiently intriguing that I can't simply pass them by. I am not trying to go systematically, and country by country, back through the patterns, to offer an interpretation of each set of results. I have instead focused just on those where I *might* be able to make sense of them.

My final thoughts address the three groupings: (1) those countries where Tolkien has a long history, and that reproduce strongly the general separation of Engageds and Vernaculars; (2) those countries that appear to have deviated from the world tendency because of some local characteristics; and (3) those countries where Tolkien has only recently arrived, and where, as a result, the take-up of the story is strongly framed through local cultural experiences. Six countries particularly share the world tendency: Australia, Germany, Greece, Spain, the United Kingdom, and the United States. In all six cases Tolkien has had a longstanding presence. We know most, by a large amount, about Tolkien's presence in the United States. The early history of the books' reception, via its official Houghton-Mifflin import in the mid-1950s to the much more widely received 1965 Ace Books pirated edition, has been very fully documented,[10] as has the books' subsequent influence on the hippie movement, and on the rise of Dungeons and Dragons and gaming and fantasy cultures generally.[11] But this leaves unexplored the residues of these "captures" of Tolkien by particular groups and interests. My analysis suggests that these residual influences might have combined into a rather gamelike engagement. There are enough snippets and supportive anecdotes to speculate that Tolkien and *LotR* may have become a generalised cultural presence, linked closely with many others ("hippies" for the West Coast, "geeks" for the Midwest and East Coast). It tallies with the fact that the U.S. "official organisation" for Tolkien fans is the more wide-ranging Mythopoeic Society, which exists "for the study, discussion and enjoyment of fantastic and mythic literature." Tolkien takes his place—an honoured one, without question—among a range of other contributing authors.

The situation is less fully known in the other five countries. But there are general characteristics, each with its own "key terms." Australia shows great similarity with the United Kingdom and United States: the books really took off in the 1960s, with a strong university base. By 1975, they were popular enough that a Braille edition had been published. In 1997, a survey of forty thousand readers found *LotR* to be the country's most popular book. This seems to have been something of an underground popularity, surprising commentators. One long-term Australian Tolkien fan encapsulates this attitude by saying,

> The attitudes and sensibilities of those who loved it, is a hard one. They are all intelligent, with a love of language, and mostly broad minded. They came from the right and the left, the poor and the rich, the religious and the atheist (I can't think of any agnostics in the mix

though). They tend to like punning, and have a good, but gentle sense of humour. Some exceptions there. Mostly the thing that stands out about my friends who like LOTR are that they are ALL very intelligent, with a love of language.[12]

Tolkien in Australia entered a rich mix of debates about "Englishness" and "Australian identity." As such, *LotR* shows an embeddedness in Australian culture that is akin to what popular-culture scholars often describe as a "cult"—it demonstrates a deep grounding with certain hard-core followers, fanning out across wider cultural fields at the occasion of heightened visibility.

Spain and Greece show a distinctive kind of embeddedness. In Spain, the books first appeared in translation in the late 1970s, from a very small publisher, Ediciones Minotauro (taken over by a much larger publishing house, Editorial Planeta, in 2002). While it is unclear how this might have impacted on its reception, there has been a long and steady growth of awareness of Tolkien's work, and an absence of any substantial controversies (Tolkien's work was not associated with either the pro- or anti-democratic movements, for instance). The story became part of a more generalised secularisation, in which the unitary authority of the Catholic Church became at least supplemented by other cultural resources. In that context, it did, perhaps, not so much "connect" to, as exist "alongside" other cultural forces.

In Greece, the books were first translated during the 1980s, and have been republished regularly ever since. In fact, they can be found everywhere, sold together with literary work of reputation, as well as odd works on mysticism, esoteric teachings, and the like. In Greece, Tolkien is also well known through the English original (the website of the Greek Tolkien Society, "The Prancing Pony," is offered in both English and Greek). Perhaps the most important connection is a particularly strong ethical dimension to responses to the story in Greece, a position I sense (and our Greek colleague confirmed this) it shares with literature and high art in general, which is considered in Greece as an ethical resource, and movements to restore or maintain the true spirit of something past are always present and militant (the Olympic ideal as it were). Thus, "heritage" has a strong impact upon Greek identity.[13]

In France and Germany, too, Tolkien has a long history of public presence. Yet cultural settlement is less easy to distinguish. In both cases, "disturbances" seem to obstruct readers' and audiences' attempts to display their deep relationship with the films and books (either that, or there simply is none). In France, the modality choices do not at all follow the world pattern. There appears to be a *measuring* of responses against wider philosophical criteria that I have not seen elsewhere (I am left to wonder if the long tradition of treating film with a philosophical seriousness has shifted the ground of the films' reception). In Germany, too, Tolkien has a long history, but any deep "embedding" is obscured by topical concerns around the timing of the release of the films. In 2004, the British *Guardian* newspaper reported the results of a national poll in which "the German public placed *The Lord of the Rings* at the top of their most loved literature." Commentators explained the surprise success of this and some other books set either in the Middle Ages or in fantasy worlds by reference to a current "low and pessimistic mood."[14] Concurrent with this, and also related to the timing of the films' releases, is the noted reference to *LotR* as a film linked to "war." (As evidenced in the chapter in this volume on the German reception and genre, this could mean different kinds of war, including World War II and the war against Iraq). In any case, topical concerns seemed to run side by side with Germany's reception of Tolkien. One could speculate that this prevalence of topical concerns means there is no overarching "embedded" cultural trope that glues German readers and audiences to *LotR*. Although popular in France and Germany, *LotR* isn't a cult in either country.

Finally, in China, Tolkien has a short and marginal history. As our Chinese colleague Liu Jun pointed out, the books were published at the occasion of the films' release, at the end of 2002. Using the opportunity, the Yilin Press, one of the best presses in China, with a high reputation for translating good foreign literature books, published all three parts of the book, releasing them all over the country, and all in hardcover. The sale of the books went so well that they had to be reprinted within one month. At the same time, pirate editions also appeared. Up to 2006, over 300,000 copies of the trilogy had been sold. This late but rapid take-up suggests an emergent wave of enthusiasm—but with no time for a pattern of discourses to settle. Under such circumstances, a sense that Tolkien's story—filtered through Hollywood—might constitute part of the arriving "Western imaginary" is surely plausible.

Much as these speculations appear to shed light on the cultures the films arrive in, it is necessary to remind ourselves that they only bear relevance for the *relationships* between groups of people sharing a nationality and a group of films. Key terms like *cult, subculture, heritage,* and *spiritual journey* point to the degrees and characteristics of those relationships. Awaiting more comparative study, the present research allows me to say that "fantasy," when it is embedded within a culture, and when it is not obstructed by topical/local concerns, functions as a facilitator that allows audiences to look beyond the film, into imagined, and imaginary, views shared across and within cultures.

CHAPTER TEN

Beyond Words

The Return of the King
and the Pleasures of the Text

SUE TURNBULL

It's Boxing Day 2003, and the Multiverse Science Fiction and Fantasy Group based in Melbourne has booked out two cinema screens for their own private evening screenings of *The Return of the King*. In Australia, viewing the latest instalment of *The Lord of the Rings* has already become what many attendees describe as a Boxing Day ritual: a ritual observed not only by the Multiverse group, but by people all over Australia. I am in the foyer by arrangement with the cinema manager and the convenors of the group, ready with questionnaires about the project. I am warmly welcomed, and invited to place leaflets (directing members to the online questionnaire) on all seats in the theatre. Looking round the foyer, I note that about twenty of the group have come in costume—there are a variety of Aragorns and Arwens, and at least one obvious Gandalf. Why are they here? And why are they dressed up?

The literature on fandom has frequently pointed to the ways in which fans seek to interact with a cult object through a variety of strategies, partly as an act of homage but also as a way of creating their own interface with the text.[1] Such an interface, in this case an embodied masquerade, enables the fans to immerse themselves imaginatively in the text, blurring the boundaries between the "real" world in which they "actually" live and the "fantasy world" they inhabit in their imaginations.[2] The performance of embodied fandom may therefore be an index of a much larger emotional investment in *RotK*.

It is through such a performance interface that fans not only seek immersion within a fantasy world, but also find a way to join a "community of the imagination" as opposed to the imagined community posited by Benedict Anderson.[3] In this way, as Kurt Lancaster insists, the desire for immersion is not so much about losing contact with this world (as is frequently asserted in negative depictions of fandom) as it is about finding and extending a community through "play."[4] As a consequence of such "play," the fan then "returns" to the real world enriched with a greater sense of connection to others through the fantasy experience. As one older (forty-six to fifty-five) female from Sydney noted about *RotK*, "We saw the first session screened in the company of a theatre full of people like ourselves, people who were passionate about the story/film and were not afraid to express that passion. There was cheering sobbing applause—a powerful sense of camaraderie. It felt like a huge fellowship."

Whilst this is a vivid description of how seeing *RotK* in a cinema with likeminded others was one of the major "pleasures" to be derived from the film, I will argue here that there are other forms of embodied engagement in a text that are much harder to locate, and that this may be an inevitable consequence of employing research tools that are reliant on the written or spoken word. Indeed, what fans say about a text is always going to be limited by the questions they are asked and the kinds of discourse that are available in which to talk about the experience, not to mention perceptions of who is doing the asking and why.

As Matt Hills points out, what is *not* said may well be just as, if not more, important than what *is* said.[5] In other words, it is the gaps in the various accounts offered by both academics and fans about the nature of their engagement that may be most revealing. For example, the sensuous pleasure of wearing a long velvet dress with a tight bodice that moves sinuously with your every movement, whilst reimagining oneself as Arwen/Liv Tyler, are not the kinds of embodied pleasures about which a fan is often invited to speak, although the wearing of such a dress whilst watching the film may be an exquisite dimension of the pleasure of the text. There are also, of course, inherent dangers in Hill's suggestion (and my own speculation), since it invites the researcher to invent his or her own creative solutions to fill in the gaps. Indeed, whose fantasy I am expressing here, mine or the fan's? As audience researchers, we need to hang on to at least some connection with empirical evidence.

The empirical evidence I want to hang on to is the 551 questionnaires completed by the Australian participants in the worldwide study who were willing to try to report on their engagement with the film. As interesting as they were, the Multiverse group were not our only respondents, and indeed were well nigh impossible to locate amongst the questionnaire responses, as they were not asked to identify themselves as such. Whilst it would have been possible to contact the group more directly, this would have led to the study of a particular kind of fandom. Instead, my focus was the value criteria used by Australian respondents as a whole to account for their engagement with the film.

In looking at these criteria, I want to explore (following Hills) the apparent "dialectic" of value at work between the intensely subjective and personalised statements with which some fans wrote about their experience and the ways in which these were counterbalanced (not uncommonly by the same person) by the perceived need to provide more objective statements of aesthetic value that signalled the construction of a critical distance (not necessarily negative) between the viewer and the film.[6] I am, therefore, trying to map a network of responses to the film that involve familiar issues of "affect," "emotion," and "aesthetics"—all of which were evident in the questionnaire responses.

In terms of method, I began by reading the first 125 Australian questionnaire responses in their entirety, underlining key words and phrases that related to questions about pleasure and enjoyment, noting the recurrence of specific terms and patterns of response. It was then possible to use the Access database to search the Australian data set as a whole, in order to assess the frequency with which such terms as *emotion* were used, along with related terms such as *awe, cry, tears, feel/felt* and to cross-reference these for gender, age, and other factors, including how many times the respondent had read the books. Not surprisingly, given the skewing of the Australian data towards women, I found that it was mostly the female respondents who responded emotionally. However, this was not always the case, as is apparent in the following table:

Table 10.1: Emotional Languages

Search Term	Male	Female	Total
Emotion	18	40	58
Awe	15	14	29
Felt	10	15	25
Feel	9	13	22
Cry	0	9	9
Tears	2	4	6

Of particular interest here is the use of the term *awe* by the male participants, from one young self-employed male's one-word answer "awe" to the question "How did you respond to the film?" to the use of the term by a male student who had read all three books more than once and who located his "awe-ful" response in relation to the cinematic feat involved in translating book to film. As he writes, "I was in awe of the scale of what was created, both the work of the film-makers and their special effect/computer graphics and of the size of the world Tolkien created."

Six male and six female respondents used the slang variation *awesome,* and whilst all the females who used this adjective were in the sixteen-to-twenty-five age group, it is interesting to note that the males ranged from one under sixteen to two in the forty-five-to-fifty-five age group. Those who wrote "awesome" tended not to write very much else, allowing this one word to sum up the totality of an "awe-ful" response. However, in general, variants of the term *awe* were used in relation to the aesthetic, affective, and emotional dimensions of the respondents' experience.

As Sue Harper and Vincent Porter discovered in their analysis of the data derived from the postwar Mass-Observation studies of U.K. cinema audiences, none of the men admitted to "crying," possibly because of the social opprobrium associ-ated with men weeping.[7] However, in this sample, two men did admit to being "moved to tears," and a number of male participants were prepared to admit being emotionally moved in more general terms, describing the film experience as: "Very emotional and satisfying. Left me in awe of how well they had brought the best book ever to life."

Three thematic clusters began to emerge from my searches, which I labelled as the "felt connection," "emotional impact," and "aesthetic rationales." At this point I began to speculate about how such labels might be theorised, in relation to the con-cepts of affect, emotion, and aesthetics.

FROM AFFECT TO AESTHETICS

The question of "affect" was of particular interest, since many respondents strug-gled to describe how deeply they were moved. In choosing to use the term *affect* here, I am deliberately avoiding the term *effect*, with its negative connotations of "effect studies" that attempt to measure the (usually negative) impact of the text, often in relation to "violence."[8] In a recent intervention in philosophical debates about the media and questions of affect, Brian Massumi suggests that affect constitutes an autonomic bodily response to some form of external stimuli, such as a film, and insists that it is quite separate from "emotion," which comes afterwards.[9] Here, we might note that the desire to measure such embodied responses to film goes back at least as far as the Payne Fund Studies, published in the United States between 1933 and 1935. These studies were largely motivated by contemporary social anx-ieties about the effects of moviegoing on audiences, such effects largely being imag-ined as "bad." One study, by Wendell Dysinger and Christian Ruckmick, used heart monitors and other devices to gauge accelerated heartbeats, rising blood pressure, and sweaty palms.[10]

According to Massumi's reading of more recent scientific literature on the subject of autonomic affect and its relationship to emotional response, the brain actu-ally processes the physical stimulus about a half a second later, leaving an intrigu-ing "gap" when anything might happen. This is the moment, he argues, that separates the autonomic visceral affect from the subjective emotional response.[11] However, Dysinger and Ruckmick, in the 1930s, did not make this distinction, which is indeed hard to sustain except in theory.[12] They were therefore interested in how the physical signs they measured were related to emotional responses such as excitement, arousal, and fear. For them, emotional responses were regarded primarily in a negative light, even though it might be argued that such emotions might be extremely pleasurable within a specific context. Indeed, as many of the participants in this study revealed, feeling terror and sadness, supposedly negative emotions, were part of their very real enjoyment of *RotK*.

Which brings me to the definition of *emotion*, still a "notorious problem" in the scientific literature.[13] Apparently, things haven't improved much since the philosopher William James asked the question "What is an emotion?" in the nineteenth century when he really meant "feeling," and the debate is still raging. According to a synopsis of the most recent literature,[14] the latest proposition is that "emotion" precedes "feeling," with the latter being a kind of cognitive appraisal of the former: a suggestion that can be interpreted as "that 'thing' has made me cry" (let's say a moment such as the lighting of the beacons in *RotK*). "Now how do I feel about that?"

At which point, another set of cognitive criteria supposedly comes into play that seeks to locate the beacon moment within various kinds of cultural and aesthetic frameworks. For example, "How do I *think* about what I feel thus far? How will I *judge* it? How will I respond to being moved in this way?" In other words, what kinds of aesthetic judgement can I or will I bring to bear in an assessment of the value of this experience? And how will I account for it? Whilst each of these questions deserves its own commentary, most pertinent to my discussion here is how the "pleasurable" experience of a film, which may incorporate affective, emotional, and aesthetic responses, will always be conditional on what one brings to the encounter.

This proposition is of particular significance here, because of the high levels of expectation and preparation that preceded many people's viewing of *RotK*. Almost 70 percent of the Australian respondents considered it extremely important to see the film, whilst 59 percent had read all three of Tolkien's books more than once. And, as for having seen the previous two films, just over 90 percent had seen *FotR* more than once, whilst almost 87 percent had seen *The Two Towers* more than once. In fact, only 6 people out of 551 had never seen either film before, and only 10 percent had not read the books at all. Not surprisingly, then, almost 60 percent of the respondents suggested that their expectations of *RotK* were based on the books, whilst about 30 percent suggested it was the two previous films that had shaped their expectations.

BEYOND WORDS

I want to begin with those who paradoxically described the affective experience of watching the film as being "beyond words." In other words, those who were rendered "speechless" by the film and who claimed to find it hard to express the intensity of their experience. Describing oneself as "beyond words" is, of course, a rhetorical strategy, which nevertheless points towards the perceived gap between what is experienced *at the time* and what can be said *afterwards.* As one person wrote, "I am at a loss to describe my feelings."

This latter comment comes from a thirty-six-to-forty-five-year-old profession-al woman who had prepared for the viewing in a variety of ways. She had read the books five times, and had joined a *LotR* chat room and message board, where she had spent "many happy hours discussing both the films and the books with friends I have made on the internet." In this regard, this respondent also adheres to Lancaster's notion of the performative fan, someone who has sought an interface with the fantasy world where new communities of the imagination have been forged.

However, despite finding the film "an intensely emotional experience," she is not entirely uncritical, and seeks to demonstrate her fan scholarship in a move that takes her from an acknowledgement of a deeply felt experience to a position of crit-ical distance: "One part disappointed me a little—Frodo's character was changed somewhat in a few places from how he was portrayed in the book and this jarred with me a little even though I can understand why Peter Jackson did this."

This is important. It demonstrates that it is quite possible to be a committed fan seeking immersion in a fantasy world in which one has a powerful emotional investment, and yet metaphorically keeps "one foot on the floor"—or at least to describe one's reaction in terms that suggest this to be the case. Thus, this viewer willingly confesses to being immensely moved, and yet, at the same time, implies that she was able to maintain a critical awareness of how Jackson was manipulat-ing Tolkien's original text. Here, she is using a set of criteria common to adaptation theory, in terms of the concept of the "fidelity" of the copy to the original.[15] Which brings us to yet another possible source of pleasure, the performance of fan schol-arship.

THE FELT CONNECTION

Whilst some respondents sought to characterise the affective experience of the film in terms of their inability to find words, others attempted to describe the impact of the film by recounting their physical reactions. Such reactions included actual bod-ily sensations (goosebumps, laughter, tears) to more metaphorical descriptions of affect registered in and through the body ("mind-blowing," "heartbreaking"). Clearly, for many viewers *RotK* produced an excess of feeling, resulting in a range of embodied responses that were offered by the respondents as testimony of their deeply felt emotion. As a female respondent commented, "I cried buckets"; she chose as her most memorable moment in the film the example used above, "the lighting of the beacons that started chills up and down the spine."

So powerful were these felt/emotional experiences that a number of participants made claims to the effect that "this was a film you didn't watch so much as experi-ence," suggesting that they felt as though they had "lived through the journey" with the characters. Here, I want to suggest that this "lived" experience might derive from a number of different sources, including, most obviously, the actual duration of the film. As one female viewer, who felt as if she had been on "an epic journey with the characters," suggested, "This was probably the result of a number of factors, combin[ing] the sheer length of the film, the fact that it was released in three parts over three years, the scale of the production and the nature of the story itself."

Another factor in this experience was clearly the range of emotions experienced whilst watching it: from "terror to sadness to pity to humour," as one respondent described it. The responses of "Sara,"[16] a professional woman in the twenty-six-to-thirty-five age range, are of particular interest here since she uses the concept of "real" a number of times in a number of different contexts. What follows is an annotated version of some of her qualitative responses to the questionnaire as a whole:

> The anticipation was justified and the emotion very *real*. At no time during the film did I feel that the characters weren't *real* people who existed in some place out of time. [Where is Middle Earth?] I've always thought of it as a kind of alternate *reality* and time line. [Favourite character?] I'm torn between Frodo and Gandalf. Both characters evolved through the journey and I felt as if I lived through the journey with them. The emotion felt *very true*. The characterisations felt *real*. (My emphasis)

Here, Sara first uses the term *real* to describe her own emotions whilst watching the film. Next, she uses it to assert the "reality" of the characters, before placing them carefully in an "alternate reality." At one level this is all very confusing; at another it makes perfect sense, especially if we understand that she is attempting to rationalise her reactions to the experience she is describing. What these comments therefore demonstrate is that whilst whatever happened between herself and the movie on screen felt *real*, there is a perceived problem in accounting for this in all its complexity: a problem she herself acknowledges and to some extent wants to avoid, at least for a time anyway. As she goes on to note, "I prefer to see this sort of movie on my own. I don't want to be distracted by people around me and I don't want to have to immediately discuss the movies with companions. *I want the experience to sink in first—absorb it before I can discuss it intelligently not emotionally*" (my emphasis).

Here, Sara makes a distinction between the perceived value of discussing her personal response to the film "emotionally" as distinct from "intelligently," thus implying a hierarchy beginning with an embodied response and culminating in rationalisation. This is precisely the hierarchy implied in the move from questions of affect to questions of aesthetics, and is by no means unusual, especially in relation to film spectatorship, where the dialectic of value, as described by Hills, is routinely enacted.

As Vivian Sobchack points out, whilst popular film reviewers often comment on the visceral pleasures of film, film theory has had a great deal more trouble coming to terms with the sensory pleasures of the cinema and how to account for these, except in relation to either pornography or horror.[17] Using her own experience of watching Jane Campion's *The Piano* as an example of "our common sensuous experience of the movies," Sobchack suggests that this involves "The way we are in some carnal modality able to touch and be touched by the substance and texture of images, to feel a visual atmosphere envelop us, to experience weight, suffocation, and the need for air; to take flight in kinetic exhilaration and freedom even as we are relatively bound to our theater seats; to be knocked backwards by a sound; to sometimes even smell and taste the world we see on screen."[18] If we accept Sobchack's account as "true," then there are indeed ways in which we actually *live through* a film, experiencing it in and through our bodies, especially when those bodies are yearning towards the screen for the fulfilment of an already anticipated experience. In this way, fantasy worlds do indeed become "real" landscapes inhabited by "real" people, whose experiences we share both viscerally and emotionally even as we are ultimately bound to our theatre seats.

For some viewers, then, the inevitable conclusion of their lived experience of *RotK* was imbued with a deep sense of loss. As one respondent writes, "Waiting for the trilogy to come out has taken three years and now that it is over you feel as if part of your life is missing." Or, as another lamented, "It was the single most emotional powerful thrilling awe inspiring human fantastical heart wrenching experience of my life—I don't know what I'm going to do now that it's over. It's the end. There is no more *LotR,* nothing else to pour my heart and my time into—there's nothing to wait for and it breaks my heart."

Whilst both of these respondents were female and under sixteen, I want to take their dramatic expressions of loss as indicative of the ways in which the *LotR* films could indeed become part of the lived experience of the audience, an embodied, deeply felt, and emotional event they tried to honour and account for in words that often seemed inadequate to the task.

"RESPONDING INTELLIGENTLY NOT EMOTIONALLY"

As Sara's comments suggest, many people preferred—and probably found it much easier—to talk about the film after the event "intelligently" rather than "emotionally," either by using the more conventional discourse of popular film appreciation or by comparing the film adaptation with the book. Thus the film was described as "visually stunning," the cinematography was applauded, the music design appreciated. Indeed, for one sixteen-to-twenty-five-year-old male student, the experience was epiphanic in that it was the first time he "recognised that cinema was comparable to the greatest classical art." Hills suggests that the language of aesthetic appreciation is often employed as "a way of holding the emotion at a distance whilst still acknowledging that you are touched or moved by the text, but not in a pathologising way."[19] Thus this young man goes on to describe his favourite moment in the film, the charge of the Rohirrim: "it was so emotionally charged, I felt like joining in the war cry!"

However, as many of the questionnaire responses demonstrated, far from being used as a distancing technique, the language of film aesthetics was regularly used to validate and even explain an emotional response. Thus "Hannah," a young woman also under sixteen, has no hesitation in acknowledging the intensity of her felt connection with her favourite character, Pippin: "I felt his emotions more strongly than anyone's. I laughed when he did and when he was sad, I felt sad too." At the same time, she also recognises that this intensity of feeling was a direct result of "the subtle moments of truly skilful filming, where something about a particular shot was breathtakingly beautiful and emotional."

Here, the language of aesthetic appreciation is used to account for the intensity of her emotional response. In other words, she is acutely aware of how the film, as film, worked on and through her to produce the emotional affects she found so intensely pleasurable. This was a significant finding, in that it pointed to an awareness of the affect of cinematic effects expressed by a broad range of respondents, who were clearly watching the film with what might be described as "one foot in" and "one foot out," maintaining a critical awareness even as they registered, and indeed welcomed, the emotional force of the experience.

THE DIALECTIC OF VALUE

What a close reading of these responses thus reveals is the ways in which respondents endeavoured to explain the nature of their engagement with the film by providing subjective statements of affect, *as well as* objective assessments of how these affects might have been achieved via a range of filmic strategies. The dialectic of value proposed by Hills is thus fully operational here, although, as has been demonstrated, it is rarely a case of any one individual being either entirely subjective or entirely objective, but of oscillating between the two poles of the continuum in an endeavour to locate the source of their pleasure.

Called to account for an experience so many claimed to be "extremely enjoyable," their attempt to put this into words can thus be read as a kind of rationalisation, but also as an attempt to express the sheer complexity of an embodied and emotional experience that is now over: the experience of "living through" *RotK*, an experience already and always beyond words.

CHAPTER ELEVEN

Heroism in
The Return of the King

JOSÉ JAVIER SÁNCHEZ ARANDA, JOSEBA BONAUT, AND
MARÍA DEL MAR GRANDÍO

> Of all the universal themes that form the superstructure of Tolkien's mythology, heroes and heroism is the most widely written about, discussed, and dissected. A quick scan of any comprehensive Tolkien bibliography bears this out. If there is so much material on Tolkien and heroes, where in the world does one begin?
>
> —ANN C. PETTY

We wondered the same after analysing the topic of heroism in the film of *The Return of the King*. More precisely, the intriguing question for us was the audience responses to this issue. At first glance, it appears easy to answer the question "Who is your favourite character?" because both the book and the movie mentioned Aragorn in the title. Indeed, the official poster showed Viggo Mortensen carrying the symbolic sword Anduril. The development of the plot pointed up the key role of this character in the chain of events.

However, other issues then called into question this initial conviction. The first element was the story's complexity, with its parallel plots and a core group of characters who could be on the same level as the cinematic Aragorn. With these competitors, we can then think of other possible characters and their special connotations for specific publics, such as women's relation to the enhanced Eowyn. On the other hand, as happened with *The Fellowship of the Ring*, the hobbits' centrality to the script, and the popularity of the actor who plays Frodo, could influence responses. In addition, there were also some doubts as a result of the changes from Tolkien's book. In light of these, our original expectations about the answer to our original question needed some reconsideration.

This essay focuses on the audience and explores how viewers respond to Peter Jackson's third movie. For this purpose, we have drawn upon material gathered through the project's online survey. Specifically, we explore responses to the question concerning people's favourite character. Being an open question, those who answered could freely express their opinions. Although they might not use the word "hero," the vast majority of participants clearly answered the question with this concept in mind. Obviously, it was not the same in all cases. Characters like Treebeard and Galadriel were selected because of their distinctive peculiarities. However, apart from this circumstance, we noticed that the concept of heroism was at work.

In the following discussion, our first section addresses the concept of the hero in Tolkien's books and then presents the results of the survey. Thereafter, we study each of the two main characters to show their perceived qualities. We finish with some comments about the film version and the public's reaction to the changes from the original text.

A GENERAL APPROACH TO THE CONCEPT OF THE HERO

It is well known that Tolkien was trying to write an epic story in order to create a mythical world for the English reader.[1] His story shows the difficulty of finding a suitable classification for a book written in the twentieth century but with characteristics more like the famous legends known to Tolkien, who was an expert professor of philology.

It is very difficult to explain and classify some elements in his books. One of most singular aspects is the nature of Tolkien's main characters, his heroes. It has been said that Tolkien's books were essential to restoring the representation of the hero in modern fiction,[2] and that their characterisation was one of the books' major contributions to literature.[3] But in order to understand the nature of that contribution, the concept of heroism needs to be set within a wider and more complex frame of study.

As other authors have suggested, the attraction of *LotR* lies in the strength of its depicted characters, who have been well accepted by the audience.[4] The process of identification may have something to do with offering solutions to problems that *LotR*'s audience could face in daily life. Thus, it could be a sort of connexion between fiction and the real world.[5] As Ann Petty suggests, "In spite of the reign of the anti-hero in modern literature, the media-consuming public has never lost its taste for the heroic, especially if those heroes are exciting, a bit dangerous, endearing, and ultimately uplifting. Tolkien's characters still fill that need, and have become part of a voracious public appetite for mythic empowerment."[6]

Tolkien deals with heroism from a position of knowing a great deal about literary fiction. He was no amateur who created stories without paying attention to the topics he wrote about. He knew very well the discussions and debates about the nature of the literary, and he writes from within twentieth-century perspectives on literature. Therefore, it is not so weird that a story with so many battles is defending the use of pacific means to attain victory.[7]

To create a convincing mythical world, an author must present heroes who develop within the action. According to some critics, the strength of Tolkien's story is that it offers a variety of characters to whom the audience can be attracted.[8] As Petty says, "This is part of the explanation for the longevity of Tolkien's stories. There is a variety of hero types in his books—a little something for everyone. Although you certainly can't say that cyberpunk heroes or their ilk can be found in Tolkien's fiction, what you can say is that certain elements in each of Tolkien's heroes can also be found in these modern versions, which is why fans of Middle-earth are still willing to embrace the slogan 'Frodo Lives.'"[9]

As already noted above, the definition of heroism can be underlined as a key role in Tolkien's literature. On the other hand, according to Martin Barker's recent argument, it may be necessary to retheorise how the processes of "identification" are supposed to work. The following findings are intended to shed light to this complex topic.[10]

TWO HEROES FACE TO FACE

Choices of favourite character by Spanish respondents show some striking patterns in that the two most popular characters are very different kinds of heroes. With almost the same number of "votes," Sam and Aragorn were picked as favourite characters, but for different reasons. The quantitative data show that respondents choosing Sam and Aragorn share similar profiles. Only by turning to the qualitative analysis can we identify two different attitudes in our public.

Table 11.1 presents the figures for favourite character choices among the Spanish audience. In what follows, we analyse the audience's attitude towards these two heroes in the movie. Here, we explore first whether the decision to choose one of the characters was related to the viewers' sociodemographic characteristics (age, sex, occupation, and so on) or to their special and personal engagement with the movie.

Table 11.1: About Favourite Characters

Favourite Characters	%
Sam	20.4
Aragorn	19.3
Gandalf	15.9
Frodo	7.9
Arwen	7.3
Legolas	6.3
Eowyn	3.8
Other characters	19.1
Total	100

We find almost no difference between those choosing Sam or Aragorn in terms of their sex, age, or occupation. The two profiles are very alike: mostly men, between sixteen and twenty-five, and students. In this, they are similar to the rest of the participants in the survey, except that there are more women, and there is a slight increase in the twenty-six-to-thirty-five-year-old age group among those who picked Aragorn and Sam as favourite character.

As a whole, these figures do not show big differences, and we can say that these factors are not decisive for the audience in making their choices. If we compare these figures with the overall sample, we do not see any variations either. However, there are some for those who have chosen other characters, such as Frodo, as the following tables illustrate.

Table 11.2: Sex and Favourite Character

Sex/Favourite Character	Aragorn	Sam	Frodo	Average
Male	70.3	70.5	58.2	72.9
Female	29.7	29.5	41.8	27.1
Total	100	100	100	100

Table 11.3: Age and Favourite Character

Age/Favourite Character	Aragorn	Sam	Frodo	Average
Under 16	6.1	5.3	5.7	6
16–25	56.1	58.6	59.0	58.2
26–35	31.8	30.1	20.5	29.7
36–45	5.1	5.3	10.7	5.1
Over 45	0.9	0.7	4.1	1.1
Total	100	100	100	100

Table 11.4: Occupation and Favourite Character

Occupation/Favourite Character	Aragorn	Sam	Frodo	Average
Student	50.7	52.7	5. .6	53.6
Home/child care	14.5	11.3	10.7	12.2
Skilled manual	9.5	7.2	10.7	9.6
Self-employed	7.8	7.5	12.3	7.5
Creative	6.8	7.8	4.9	6.4
Others	10.7	13.5	2.8	10.7
Total	100	100	100	100

Table 11.5: Kind of Story

Kind of Story	Aragorn	Sam	Frodo	Average
Epic	25.7	24.7	24.4	25.4
Good vs. evil	22.5	20.8	17.0	20.3
Myth/legend	12.2	13.9	14.0	13.8
Fantasy	12.0	13.6	9.5	13.3
SFX film	7.1	7.6	14.0	7.3
War story	5.2	2.4	1.7	4.1
Threatened homeland	3.5	4.2	7.5	3.9
Allegory	7.8	4.6	4.5	3.1
Quest	5.6	4.7	4.8	5.0
Spiritual journey	1.9	1.3	0.9	1.6
Game world	0.8	0.4	0.3	0.6
Fairytale	0.7	1.4	1.4	1.3
Total	100	100	100	100

Table 11.6: Most Memorable Moment

Most Memorable Moment	Aragorn	Sam	Frodo	Average
Battle of Pelennor Fields	21.6	15.4	6.6	18.5
Destruction of the Ring	8.9	12.3	18.0	11.4
Aragorn's speech (Gates of Mordor)	14.7	9.4	3.3	8.8
Grey Havens	4.8	8.2	13.1	7.4
Sam carries Frodo	5.1	12.9	7.4	6.5
Aragorn kneels to the hobbits	5.1	5.7	4.1	4.8
Eowyn's fight with Witch King	2.1	2.8	1.6	3.3
Aragorn's coronation	7.2	0.3	0.8	3.1
Other moments	30.5	33.0	45.7	36.2
Total	100	100	100	100

In terms of engagement with the movie, we do not find any substantial differences in the way two audiences define the story. As we could expect, the choice of the favourite character is related to the audience's most memorable moments. Neither Aragorn nor Sam is the main character in the most preferred scene (the Battle of Pelennor Fields) or the fight between Eowyn and the Witch King. We must underline that the number of responses is higher when the chosen character is in attendance. We must also point to other moments where Sam is the main character because they too show above-average percentages, even though the figures are smaller. For instance, when Sam and Frodo are about to destroy the Ring (chosen by 4.1 percent of those who picked Sam as favourite character) and the scene in Shelob's Lair (3.8 percent). Thus far, the results have allowed us to profile the two groups. We have learnt in detail the characteristics of these two groups but we cannot yet explain their different attitudes. To go further, we need to look into the reasons why audiences prefer one character over another, since it seems evident that the reasons must be different. We next set up a comparison to check how distant they are from each other.

INTRODUCTION TO A MYTHICAL HERO: ARAGORN

Generally speaking, viewers like Aragorn because he is "the hero *par excellence* of the story" (survey, female, 26–35, self-employed). Although he is not recognised as the king of Gondor in the movie until late on, Spanish viewers highlighted that Aragorn is "a king," something that defined him as a man of great magnitude.[11] In fact, of course, Aragorn is Isildur's heir, and his destiny is to reestablish the lost throne of his lineage. Therefore, he performs actions that only great men can undertake. For instance, he is a warrior who has to command his troops and formulate military strategies. As this participant suggests, in these ways Aragorn is a traditional epic hero: "I like Aragorn because he is the typical hero of the movies. From the very beginning you see that he is the leading character. Besides, he is so cute! He has all the hero's virtues: he encourages everybody and always exhorts the troops. I like his past as an adventurous wanderer knowing that he is the chosen one" (focus group, female, 26, student).

For the Spanish audience, there is no doubt that this character is full of classical features. To mention a few, Aragorn's virtues are courage, strength, charisma, honour, and justice. As one viewer said, Aragorn is "a king without a throne but he is the symbol of a hero with his nobility, loyalty and deep values. A prototype everybody can think highly of" (survey, male, 16–25, skilled manual). In this sense, it is quite interesting to underline the process of identification that viewers establish with a kind of hero such as Aragorn. Above all, the audience admires his extraordinary personality. As the following spectators suggest, "he represents the good virtues that I admire in a person" (survey, female, 16–25, student), "he inspires heroism, bravery and a wish to carry out big deeds" (survey, female, 16–25, student). However, Aragorn is not simply the typical hero per se. Some features differentiate him from other brave men in the movies. It is really interesting how Aragorn combines these great virtues with other characteristics that are closer to the Spanish audience. Viewers mention his modesty and patience. They underlined that it is not easy for Aragorn to be a superhero. In fact, for the audience, "Aragorn is not perfect" (survey, male, 35–45, self-employed). Among other human qualities, Aragorn is also a weak man who needs to make huge efforts to overcome his fears and doubts: "Aragorn embodies weakness and doubts, but also willpower. He knows he must do something big and he stays put till the end" (focus group, male, 22, student).

THE CLOSENESS OF THE MIMETIC HERO: SAM

Unlike such extraordinary figures as Aragorn, Sam is a brave man from an ordinary background who is chosen by his supporters because of his closeness to daily life. He is a small, unknown hobbit who embarks on an adventure without being warned of its significance. He just cares about doing what he always does: taking care of his friend. Sam's virtues are more concrete and focus on goals of less magnitude. Because of this, his bravest actions are not done out of his sense of duty; rather, Sam is a hero because "he represents what a person can do just for love or friendship" and "symbolises the victory of the personal and daily effort" (survey, male, 16–25, student). As some of our participants declared, "Sam embodies friendship and loyalty and the sense of responsibility" (survey, male, 16–25, student). As one participant says, "Sam is the authentic hero for me. He is my ideal man. He is such a good guy! And, at the end, he is the one who fixes everything" (focus group, male, 22, student). It is striking how the audience thinks that Sam's heroic role is less visible. Viewers like Sam because he is an "unusual" and a "hidden" great man (survey, female, 26–35, self-employed). Connecting with this, among the most mentioned of Sam's virtues are "humility" and "sacrifice" (survey, male, 16–25, service work). As happened with Aragorn, we find strong connexions between this character and his supporters. Overall, "he is the friend everybody would like to have" (survey, male, 16–25, creative). What makes Sam a hero is carrying out his mission in a perfect way. However, it is this marvellous aspect of everyday life that is closest to the audience's sense of their own possibilities.

From analysing our data, we can say that viewers may dream about being a powerful person and embarking on an enormous quest, but what also appeals to them is the idea of an ideal life full of good and close-at-hand virtues.

THE HERO OF THE BOOK VS. THE HERO OF THE MOVIE

This study of *RotK* reveals how the audience's attitude changes, and we can verify that the process of identification corresponds to different motivations. In our case, in order to define Sam and Aragorn, the respondents have used concepts poles apart but coherent with the roles of these characters. It does not mean one character is better that the other. The key issue is that the connections are based on specific peculiarities. From this basis, we are also able to address one of the most debated topics about the adaptation of the book into a movie. A number of critics, with a more hostile attitude towards some of the changes from Tolkien's books, have complained about the ways some of the heroes have been altered. For example, they have complained about the treatment of Aragorn, among others.[12] For many, the manner of his arrival at the Pelennor Fields diminished his strength, and the figure of the future king of Gondor was not emphasised enough. Another negative reference was his kiss with Arwen after the coronation. Curiously, those researchers who have analysed the cinematographic adaptation have been more critical of Peter Jackson's work. There is no agreement between the critics and the respondents, and the opinion of the audience shows how viewers have accepted the director's opinion. Kayla McKinney Wiggins, for example, says, "Throughout the films, Aragorn is conflicted about his role as king and protector of his people. He doubts himself and his ability to fill such a role. In dream sequences and face-to-face meetings, Arwen must constantly reassure him that he will be king and that he is worthy of her love. This reading of Aragorn's character is at odds with his characterisation in the novel and with his role as epic hero."[13]

It seems the films' director has tried to present a hero who is closer to the audience, a more credible one. And, because of that, some critics have pointed to the loss of the mythical hero such as Tolkien made of Aragorn. "Peter Jackson, in contrast, offers the conflicted, modern protagonist, smaller in scope and lesser in nature. Curiously, the effect is not to bring us closer to these characters but to shove us further away. We can't know them with the fundamental recognition that is a part or our primal consciousness, the part of ourselves that reaches out to myth, and folklore, and legend as essential truth, as absolute identity."[14] Aragorn's trajectory in the movie is full of personal doubts.

But the Spanish public does not appear to care about these changes in the cinematographic adaptation, and there are even some who say that Aragorn's merit lies in his overcoming his doubts. This is the reason why he is a hero. On the other hand, in Sam, Tolkien introduces a closer hero, far away from the high mimetic; we can define it as low mimetic.[15] Lynnette Porter defines him as an "every-person hero."[16] He presents everyday features for the public. Sam embodies this kind of hero because he lives a situation closer to that of the audiences.[17] To a certain extent, Jackson does not change the essence of Tolkien's character of Sam, but he underlines several aspects that make empathy with him more profound, in particular Frodo's rejection of him, and the beautiful scene where Sam takes Frodo in his arms. The audience probably accepts these changes because they are presaged in the book.

Judging by the public's responses, it could be said that changes introduced in the characters of the movies, especially Aragorn, have in the main been well received by the audience. The introduction of closer heroes, such as Sam, is accepted even though it implies a modification from the book. Emotional elements that define the characters are important in creating an appeal to the audience.

CHAPTER TWELVE

The Fantasy of Reading

Moments of Reception of *The Lord of the Rings: The Return of the King*

DANIEL BILTEREYST AND SOFIE VAN BAUWEL[1]

Like most other films, *The Lord of the Rings* is part of a rich cultural history that goes well beyond the realm of cinema. Not only is the trilogy an excessive post–classical Hollywood adaptation of J. R. R. Tolkien's work and worldview, Peter Jackson's *LotR* also extends into the world of the epic, mythology, fairytales, and folk tales, with references to Biblical and other legends. In generic terms, the series has most often been labelled as a piece of adventure and fantasy, as it imaginatively constructs alternative worlds and tells stories that go well beyond the real world's natural laws, introducing imaginary creatures, spectacular monsters, and humanlike superheroes.

In her work on the fantastic, Vivian Sobchack distinguishes three types of film that contemporary audiences readily identify with the fantasy (meta)genre. Besides horror and science fiction, Sobchack identifies the genre of the fantasy adventure, which extensively draws "upon fairy-tales and folk-tales filled with quests, transformations and magic spells, Greek and Nordic myths, legends about spirits, ghosts, and mermaids." Although fantasy genres make the invisible visible and escape the constraints of empirical knowledge and the limits of rational thought, Sobchack underlines that fantasy adventure is basically about human effort and action, about "tests of character and action that transcend the division of experience into physical and spiritual."[2] Fantasy adventure tries to make visible "intangible desires and transformations of character" and literalises "the desire for eternal life, love, and power."[3] The key element is that fantasy represents the realm beyond reality, outside verisimilitude.

Although *LotR* contains references to other genres (for example, western, horror) and is far from being generically stable, it is clear that the cycle strongly exploits fantasy adventure elements in its narrative drive, thematic concerns, and overall aesthetic project. This chapter, however, does not intend to define once again *LotR* generically, but rather is interested in how audiences make sense of *LotR* as a piece of fantasy. More specifically, we are interested in how audiences react to *LotR* as a powerful piece of cinematographic fantasy, which was overwhelmingly marketed as an inescapable event.[4] Inspired by literary reader-response theories, as well as by reception studies and other qualitative audience approaches within media and film studies,[5] we are interested in audiences' engagements with, and their signifying practices in, receiving *LotR*, more specifically the third movie in the cycle, *The Return of the King*.

We draw here upon two combined audience studies, an online survey and a more qualitative study using focus group interviews.[6] The survey produced data from 1,296 respondents in Belgium,[7] while the interviews involved 80 participants.[8] During the group interviews, four central issues were explored. First, the respondents talked about the *film-as-event* (press attention, media hype, and so on), followed by the concrete *viewing context* (the experience of cinema-going, film consumption as a social event, and so on) and a discussion of respondents' engagement with the *film text* (genre, narration, appreciation, characters, and so on). Finally, we also invited talk about their personal *viewing experience* during the screening of *RotK* (identification, empathy, role taking, discussion, and so on).

Going through this overwhelming set of data and insights coming out of these, we were struck by how the respondents underlined that *LotR* and *RotK* definitely had been an important event in the "career" of (for most of them) clearly engaged film fans. Also, all responses dealing with the level of enjoyment indicated that the *LotR* movies were unique, even within the blockbuster and event movie tradition. Here we cannot fully explore all veins of these rich materials. Rather, we have tried to summarise some of the key findings of these combined audience researches, with a special attention to reception as a dialectical process—an idea that was so dear to proponents of reader-response theories. We present the analysed materials via some "moments of reception."[9] Referring to the German tradition of reception aesthetics, and in particular the work of Hans Robert Jauss,[10] we open with *horizon of expectations*, which we consider to be a first structuring "moment." This concept deals with the aesthetic, cultural, and social expectations with which audiences encountered *RotK*. Thereafter, we are interested in the *viewing context*, followed by some findings in relation to how the spectators/readers "read" or give meaning to the *text* and are engaged with it in their personal *viewing experiences*.

Although the boundaries of these moments of reception are of course extremely permeable, we think this concept can help in understanding various aspects of the reception of *RotK*. While most reception studies within the fields of media and communication fail to look at reception as a complex process, entailing various sorts of activities, engagements, and influences, we need to perceive some additional structure in respondents' signification process in regard to the *LotR* films and other circulating texts.

VIEWING EXPECTATIONS AND THE CONTEXT OF VIEWING

The reading or signifying process is not a singular isolated practice, but a discursive process surrounding a particular text. Therefore it is important to take this broader context into consideration in analysing a film's reception. First, it was important to gain information about the movie and how through this the process of signification began. So we asked our respondents to mark their major sources of information about the movie. Our survey data indicated three major sources as core elements in the creation of respondents' horizon of expectations. First of all, of course, there were the first two parts of the *LotR* trilogy itself, which for most respondents (76 percent) opened a whole spectrum of expectations. Then there were the trailer (63.9 percent) and the books (59.4 percent). The Internet (45.6 percent) and the peer group of friends (45.1 percent) were identified as major elements in driving the spectators' expectations. This does not mean that the promotional campaign was not critically assessed, as the following quotation from a female respondent illustrates:

> The first time I saw a trailer from the first movie with a large group of Uruk-hais and dwarfs who came from the mountains downhill, I was sitting in front of my computer and I thought: "That's something I've never seen. This has to be incredibly impressive." I got a cold shiver and it had a huge impact on my first impression of the movie. But at the same time, you get overwhelmed by trailers, billboards, posters . . . with the feeling: Yes, I have to see this, but I would also have this feeling without seeing the trailers and billboards.

A key factor in the construction of the hype around *RotK* was the media. Respondents had mixed feelings about the role played by film criticism and other media outlets. Their attitude ranged from a satisfaction with the media coverage to statements criticising the media's excessive attention to *RotK*, as illustrated by following quotation: "It is like they invented hot water again. Of course it was a large project, but you have to see it in *its* context, it is only a film." Three major peaks of overwhelming media attention were related to: the premiere of *RotK* (December 2003), the Golden Globes (January 2004), and the Oscars ceremony (March 2004), where the movie won eleven Academy Awards. The opinions of participants on these awards differ, but again critical remarks were made. Some respondents even pointed out that the high number of awards was not deserved and that *RotK*'s success was inspired by the academy's wish to reward the whole trilogy rather than the individual film as such.

The reasons participants went to see *RotK* seemed to be very individual. Some claimed they were fantasy fans. Others went because they had read all the books, or because they had seen the first two films and wanted to know how the story ended. Others referred to Howard Shore's musical score, while still others indicated a wish to escape reality, to relax, or even a response to social pressure:

> If I hadn't gone to see the film, I would have had the feeling of missing something because there was a lot of to-do about the film and people are preoccupied by it whether they wanted it or not. People talked about it and if you wanted to be part of it, you did have to see it. The books were of course fantastic, like the first films, which was also an extra stimulus. I found it important to watch the ending. That was something to look forward to.

> I went to the pre-launch screening of the first movie. I could not imagine missing it. I had read the book for the first time when I was thirteen years old; from then on I reread it, every other year. To some degree, the book changed my life. I'm really into the fantasy/science fiction world, all of my friends are. During my time at the university, I was part of a sort of subculture which was right into this. I also played role taking games and so on. That is the central theme of my life.

People's individual experiences are clearly affected by their viewing context—that is, by the place and time of viewing, company, and so on. But a key element in understanding the viewing experience of *LotR* as a spectacular fantasy tale is related to the "big-screen" experience. Interviewees continuously underlined that it was important for them to watch the film in a huge movie theatre, and this was part of the viewing experience as an event. A twenty-year-old male claimed,

> I feel I've been part of something important. This film is really a milestone. You join the event and talk about it. I think it is an important event. My motivation to go and watch the movie was quite obvious. I had seen the first two, each time in the same company. It was a sort of tradition. That was something special. The films are not to be underestimated. Compared to this movie, others seem grey and mainstream. That is not the case at the moment. Really, I think that I have been part of something important which will be discussed for years.

READING THE TEXT

Thinking about *LotR*'s relation to the fantasy genre, respondents had their own interpretations. While the international survey indicated that respondents across the world commonly referred to the movies as "Epic," as "Spiritual journey," or as "Quest," Belgian respondents saw it somewhat differently. They often referred to *LotR* as a "Legend/myth," describing it as "a story about good and evil" and basically "a story about friendship." During our interviews, many respondents also compared *LotR* to a fantasy story or fairytale.[11] A twenty-year-old woman and seventeen-year-old boy claimed that *LotR* was a fairytale that was linked to reality in different ways. They described it as a "mirror of reality." Others may not entirely agree, but still wonder to what degree *LotR* is a fairytale or a mirror of reality. A twenty-year-old female, for instance, queried the low level of reality of the trilogy when saying, "I think the *Lord of the Rings* films are not fairytales at all, but rather they're fantasy stories. There are protagonists who relate to the genre of the fairytale, but if you look at the background of Tolkien then you see a lot of references towards reality. The story is very detailed and extended, the costumes, language, the weapons; it is a whole culture which could have existed. For me it is history." The feedback to the real world is strongly present in different ways. As one participant says, "I can perfectly understand the fact that Frodo wanted to keep the Ring. That's something human." As indicated by Elihu Katz and by other Tolkien analysts, morality is an important element as a key to the real world.[12] This was present in the interviews. A thirty-six-year-old man, for instance, observed that the *LotR* trilogy was not made for children, but rather consumed by adults, so it could "absolutely not be a fairytale." It was rather a sort of a morality play, a playground for good and evil, a story about friendship.

Analysing the scenes most strongly remembered by participants, two types of answers can be distinguished. On the one hand, specific scenes were remembered because of their positive reference to friendship and affection, as here, where a male participant refers to his identification with Frodo: "The saddest moment in the film is in my opinion the scene where Frodo asks Sam to leave him because he can't trust him. Sam does everything for Frodo and I knew that he was not going to leave him. If anybody could be my friend, it would be Sam. I don't think that Sam is depicted negatively. Maybe I can compare myself to Frodo because I also wouldn't resist the temptation." On the other hand, scenes were remembered because of their negative connotations: "Then there was the ending and what we saw was a load of rubbish. I found this just rubbish. In the book when I read it, it was a good piece. But the previous scene ended in such a strong way and then they quickly added on some other parts." Even when participants were not familiar with Peter Jackson's earlier work, the overall tendency was to feel that he had done an incredible job. A few even suggested that Jackson had made a masterpiece, one that moreover did not lose "the soul" of the books. This included his ability to make flesh-and-blood characters. When asked about favourite or disliked or disfavoured protagonists, participants often referred to the movie's characters as if they were real people. A forty-two-year-old male, for instance, described who was for him the most human: "Sam is a small man who is always prepared to help. Sam as a protagonist is based on batman, the personal assistant of the officer, and Sam paid 'homage' to these people. These people look after everything and everybody. This is very spectacular and emotional. Sam who dedicates himself to getting Frodo to Mount Doom—this is a small part in the movie, but takes much longer in the book."

FILM EXPERIENCE AND EVALUATION

Character preference is strongly related, of course, to the identification and recognition of particular aspects of a character. The reflection on one's own life was something that was present in several statements, such as those made by a thirty-four-year-old woman, an eighteen-year-old girl and a nineteen-year-old boy: "Sometimes I do also see myself as less than others, but this does not mean that you are less. The live experience and the friendship between travel mates can be compared to a job situation. I also try to give my children some wisdom." "I would prefer to be like Legolas more than to identify myself with him. I'm very impulsive and would sometimes rather be more thoughtful. I also can't identify with other characters. They all have something that attracts me and would fit me, but none of them lights up." "Sometimes I feel like a dwarf. I can't identify myself with the elves, rather with the dwarves." Identification and empathy were strongly related to the so-called message of the films. It was amazing how most participants saw the film text as an articulation of a specific discourse or message. Nearly all respondents tried to interpret the fantasy surface of the movies, and delved into a deeper meaning and into basic themes. Many participants, for instance, argued that this "message" was about friendship, while others basically stressed the idea of the good-versus-evil story. Other respondents referred to determinism as the basic theme of the film, while for some *LotR* was about the dichotomy between arrogance and modesty. In a couple of focus group interviews, respondents drove the discussion of this to a higher level, and concluded that many themes are present in the cycle. These participants stressed the fact that the "message" of the film is different for everyone.

A minority of ten participants was also familiar with role-playing games. Here, three groups can be distinguished: (1) participants who were familiar with role playing and took part in it ("I also play an elf in the game,") (2) those participants who were not actively involved in them but did not have a negative attitude towards those who are ("If others want to simulate the scenes, let them do it, it is important that they are having fun"), and (3) those who were familiar with role-playing but would never take part in it and have a rather negative attitude towards it ("I'm not that crazy").

A few participants, like two forty-year-old males, stressed the fact that you have to take part in role playing "to be a fan" of *LotR*. But everyone interpreted the idea of fandom in his or her own way. For most of the fans, the identity of "being a fan" was linked to merchandise, indicated, for example, in this quotation: "I have all the books and my room is full of posters. The statues are also very pretty, but I can't afford them." Watching a movie like *RotK* could relate or even "create" an identity of fandom similar to taking part in role-playing games or consuming merchandise. Like the articulation of the fandom of *Star Wars*, *LotR* fans take part in the participatory fandom established on the Internet.[13]

SOME CONCLUSIONS

The *LotR* trilogy was a major event in contemporary popular culture and film history. It has been described as a milestone in the blockbuster tradition, boosting both popular and serious interest in the fantasy genre. The cycle was also marketed as a major cultural event and an unprecedented artistic performance, while it was discursively supported and constructed as a movie that would break all commercial, technical, and production value records.

This publicity and marketing campaign is only part of the explanation of the overwhelming success of and the critics' and audiences' fascination with the trilogy. This chapter has tried to understand audiences' engagement with *RotK*, understood as a social event, as a meaningful text of fantasy and as the provider of a rich viewing experience. We were also interested in viewers' horizon of expectations, which might have been structured to some degree by the discourses spread around by the marketing and publicity campaign. This publicity discourse frequently referred to the fantasy genre. Our analysis suggests that, from the beginning, audiences did not rely only upon the publicity campaigns. Certainly, the dream world represented in the trailers and marketing around *LotR* were important in triggering the interest to go and see this fantasy movie. But audiences also heavily relied upon their own knowledge of the fantasy genre and Tolkien's work in particular. The interviews also revealed that the experience of watching the movie in a theatre was important in relation to the fantasy genre. Respondents often articulated the need to see such a spectacular adventure on a big screen. For audiences, this spectacle resides in the narrative, in characters, as well as in the impressive battery of special effects related to *LotR* as a fantasy film and as a big-screen event.

While the prefigurative materials set the general tone in regard to the fantasy elements, it is clear that for our audiences it was the film itself that most established the spectacular character of the story. This is illustrated by the bold references to the *LotR* as a legend, a myth, or a fairytale. Although verisimilitude was left behind, people still linked it to reality. For audiences, fantasy as a genre is able to reflect or comment upon reality, and it was even seen as a "mirror." This reflection of reality was understood in different ways, not at least in arguments claiming that *RotK* was a sort of a morality play with a concrete worldview.

For some Belgian respondents (for example, fantasy fans), these identifications can be considered as part of the creation of an identity in dialogue with fandom. Although the prefiguration set some boundaries around the interpretation of the film text, respondents were reading it in different ways. *LotR* can thus be seen as a fantasy, but people's imaginings around the film texts still widely differed.

CHAPTER THIRTEEN

Understanding Text as Cultural Practice and as Dynamic Process of Making

LOTHAR MIKOS

The concept of "text" is a central category in film studies, media studies, and cultural studies. Individual films and television programs, individual books and comics, individual pop songs and web pages are conceived as texts. Moreover, culture as a whole is generally assumed to have a textual nature, so that the beach, for example, is treated as a text, just as a high-rise building or an English garden is. The central notion is that a text is, from a semiotic point of view, "a combination of signs,"[1] and at the same time an identifiable whole, a work that is susceptible to academic analysis or interpretation. Film and television analysis in media studies and text analysis in cultural studies are concerned with the study of such discrete texts that are distinguishable from other texts.[2] The premise of such analyses is that a potential for meaning is inherent in the texts. The realisation of this potential is performed by readers or viewers in their reception and appropriation of the text. The approaches characterised as reception aesthetics, such as those in Wolfgang Iser's approach to literature, assume a dialectical relationship between the text and the reader, and their interaction.[3] The text is realised only in the reader; only in the reader can it take on meaning. The reader with a text "performs meaning," and this "performance of meaning always takes place in a context."[4] The context illuminates and stabilises the meaning of the text. As this implies, texts in themselves are very unstable structures. Only by being embedded in a context, or, more exactly, in contexts, do they become useful and usable for social processes of communication aimed at understanding. A text is a potential until it is used by a reader or viewer, when it enters into the circulation of meanings in the society.

With the development of communication and media technologies in the past hundred years, not only has the number of texts been multiplied many times over, but their quality in the social process of communication has been transformed. Whereas at one time we could assume that a text was unmistakably unique, and bore a relationship to only a small number of other texts, a text today must position itself in a textual universe that is populated by countless texts that exist in numerous media manifestations. The cultural and media phenomenon of *The Lord of the Rings* exists in several material versions: as a book, as an animated film, as a film trilogy, as a computer game, and as a comic. The film trilogy by Peter Jackson positions itself in a textual universe that is already populated not only by other *LotR* texts, but also by numerous texts that refer in some way to *LotR*. This is yet another illustration of what John Fiske observed about our culture: "Each narrative is a rewriting of these already written 'knowledges' of the culture, and each text makes sense only insofar as it rewrites and re-presents them for us."[5] Thus texts are entangled in a complex net of intertextuality, and the users move in a cultural field in which all these mutually enmeshed texts are inscribed. The film trilogy of *LotR* is inscribed in different ways in different cultural contexts, since the reception history of the books by J. R. R. Tolkien also varied in the various cultural contexts. Thus it is permissible to ask what we mean when we speak of *LotR* as a text. Do we mean Professor Tolkien's books? Or the three films by Jackson? Or the cultural knowledge of *LotR* that has arisen through the use of its various textual materialisations?

Furthermore, the question as to the status of the text arises even if we are dealing only with the films. First of all, we are dealing with three individual films that together form a trilogy. Since they were released in cinemas at one-year intervals, each one must function as a complete narrative in itself, and they must also function as a coherent narrative all together. Moreover, the trilogy consists not only of individual films (*The Fellowship of the Ring, The Two Towers,* and *The Return of the King*), but also of different versions of each film that have been published on DVD. These versions, containing additional scenes, are longer than the cinema versions. In the booklet accompanying the "extended edition" of the first part, we read, "This special Extended Edition of *The Fellowship of the Ring* is a unique version of the film, specially created for this DVD. With no constraints on the film's running time, director Peter Jackson extended the movie by more than 30 minutes with more character development, more humour, more story, more of J. R. R. Tolkien's world."[6] The second part, *The Two Towers,* is forty-two minutes longer with the supplementary scenes than the cinema version, and the third part, *The Return of the King,* goes beyond added scenes. The accompanying booklet says, "For the extended version of the film, Jackson and his cutters have not simply pasted in scenes that were not used in the original version. Instead they started from scratch, editing this special edition as if they were making a whole new film." The chapter index therefore distinguishes between new scenes and extended scenes. For the DVD, the third part is divided into seventy-eight chapters, of which fifteen are "new" and twenty-four are "extended" in comparison with the cinema version. In addition, copious supplementary material is available to the DVD users, including the documentaries on the making of the film, interviews with Jackson, maps of Middle-earth, and so on. "Within the *Lord of the Rings* special edition DVDs, each part of the supplementary materials serves a different function. Accessed individually, these extras offer distinct but overlapping forms of experience for users."[7] On the third DVD of *RotK,* the user can select a map of Middle-earth and then choose among the routes of certain heroes: (1) Frodo and Sam, (2) Merry, (3) Aragorn, Legolas, and Gimli, (4) Gandalf and Pippin. Once the user has chosen a route, he can select various settings along the route and see the heroes in action there. "A crucial difference from the film is that, when you have selected a route, you can follow the adventures of the protagonists without the interruption of other characters' sequences in parallel montage."[8] To a certain extent, the viewer can thus compose his own film. However, he will only want to do this after having seen the cinema version and/or the extended DVD version. DVDs invite repeated viewing, especially since each of the supplementary materials offers access to a specific perspective on the story and the composition of the film.

The special extended DVD editions of the films illustrate how their presentation has changed through the introduction of the DVD. By now the sales revenue of DVDs and videos has left box office earnings far behind: "DVDs had become the leading source of theatrical revenue, with box office accounting for 22%, television accounting for 27%, and DVD/videotape accounting for 51%, according to Kagan Associates."[9] For the *LotR* trilogy, this proportion has progressed still further in favor of DVDs. For the DVD editions of *FotR* in the United States, "the proportion of the total DVD sales income to the total domestic theatrical box office was 82.1%."[10] This shows that the television set has become the preferred medium for the consumption of films. At the same time, this fact has changed the way audiences use films. Using the supplementary materials on the DVDs affords viewers other ways to generate a narrative that would not be possible if they only watched the films. Depending on the scope of the bonus material, the films are accessible by multiple strategies. "The *LOTR* special editions, for example, require multiple viewings simply through their sheer size, with extra materials that are more than twice as long as the (extended) films themselves."[11] This also influences the process of making meaning, since every new feature opens up new paths of interpretation, or in a sense provides a new frame for interpretation. The way in which an individual user assigns meaning to the film depends on the specific functions of the supplementary material that he uses, and at the same time on the complex network of interpretation frames that he generates in the process. The film as a text is altered by the paratexts[12] or secondary texts[13] present on the DVD: it is extended, but also restricted.

The question "What is the text of *The Lord of the Rings?*" is raised not only by the relationship between individual films and the narrative of the trilogy as a whole, nor simply by the relationship between the cinema versions and the special extended DVDs of the individual films, nor yet by the influence of the bonus material on the DVDs—but also by the computer games, the film reviews, the many web sites, and the merchandising items, not to mention Tolkien's books on which the film adaptation was based. In view of the dialectical relationship between the text and the reader and their interaction, and in view of the fact that a text is only realised in the reader's response, we must assume that all the secondary texts mentioned here have an influence on the viewers' realisation of the films. They influence the primary text's interaction with the audience. Furthermore, different audiences are prepared or put in the mood for the films by different secondary texts: the "normal" moviegoer is prepared by the trailers and posters; the cineaste by film reviews and his knowledge of other films by Jackson; the *LotR* fan by having read Tolkien's books, and by the countless web sites that dealt with the films before their release. Especially on the Internet, the films were discussed before their cinema release, and long before they were available on DVD. As Bertha Chin and Jonathan Gray put it, "'pre-viewers' are discussing a 'pre-text.'"[14]

The Internet offers new opportunities for precommunicative communication, which also influences perceptions and the formation of meaning in the subsequent interaction between the film text and the viewers.

> After all, we rarely find people meeting for coffee to discuss a film in detail *before* watching it. But, opening up new spaces for textual becoming, the Internet discussion groups of the *LotR* films challenge common-sense notions of textuality and of the relationship between text and audience. The existence of such groups asks of us how pre-viewer discussion creates a framework for interpretation of the *LotR* films post-release, and what it can tell us about textual meaning.[15]

After having discussed this question, Chin and Gray draw the assessment: "In the tale of textuality, solitary textuality's part has ended, and it is time to usher in pre-textuality and intertextuality."[16] Is that the case?

When we examine the three films in the trilogy, we are still dealing with solitary texts. They have beginnings and ends, they each have over two hours' duration, and viewers can receive them as texts. The end of singular textuality, as Chin and Gray invoke it, is a result of the shift in perspective from the text itself to its reception and appropriation and the audience's use of the text in everyday life. An essay by Gray illustrates how strongly this change in perspective determines the conclusion that solitary textuality is at an end. In this essay, Gray discusses fans and anti-fans under the title "New Audiences, New Textualities."[17] Gray joins Nick Couldry in pleading for an audience-oriented perspective on textuality, because the viewer's way of dealing with the text can oscillate between a "close reading" and a "distant reading," and indeed the distanced viewer need not even have seen the primary text. What is apparent here is not the end of the solitary text, but rather a shift away from an understanding of text rooted in literature and/or film studies towards an understanding rooted in media and cultural studies. The question is no longer "What is a text as the work of an artist?" but rather, "What is a text, when considered as a social object?"[18] From this perspective, text always has a double definition, because a text always contains the conditions of its reception and appropriation. In this sense, the text is "at once a closed aesthetic space, with lines of force radiating inwards from the framing conditions that establish its closure, and a space of opening which begins to merge with its edges, its borders with the nontextual or the heterotextual."[19] Because texts as closed aesthetic spaces are situated not only in a textual and inter-textual universe but also in social and cultural practice and hence in a social and cultural universe, they can evoke different interpretations and ways of reading them. As a result, our attention is drawn to the "reading formations" that influence ways of dealing with film texts. A person's way of reading aesthetically closed texts is "the product of definite social and ideological relations of reading composed, in the main, of those apparatuses—schools, the press, critical reviews, fanzines—within and between which the socially dominant forms for the superintendence of reading are both constructed and contested."[20]

These formations enter into a mutual relationship with the text as an aesthet-ic object, one that, in the case of a film such as *RotK,* for example, has a narrative order. For this reason the meaning that the audience produces in its interaction with the discrete aesthetic text cannot be deduced from the text alone. The question that arises is therefore not "What is the text?" so much as "What can the object of tex-tual analysis be?" Couldry proposes the following working definition: "we can call a 'text' a complex of interrelated meanings which its readers tend to interpret as a discrete, unified whole."[21] The shift in perspective is apparent: text is now what the viewers interpret as a text, and not the object that incites them to interpret. Even Tony Bennett and Janet Woollacott had talked about "text and reader conceived as being co-produced within a reading formation,"[22] since text and viewer can be seen as cultural and social roles that are concretely realised in social reality only when an aesthetic product, together in cozy co-production with a reader or viewer, brings forth meaning as a text in the context of (inter)textual, cultural, and social univers-es, the "reading formations." This is how texts and their readers or viewers take their places in the circulation of meanings. In this perspective, text and textuality must be understood as a cultural and social practice, and as a category of the dynamic process of generating meaning in cultural and social processes.

The new information and communication technologies and the processes of digitalisation have not exactly changed text, since texts continue to exist as discrete aesthetic products. Certainly the three films in the *LotR* trilogy can be seen as dis-crete, aesthetic products. Yet they exist in different variations, as films in cinemas, as cinema films on DVD, as individual films and as a trilogy, and as extended and reedited versions on the special extended DVDs. Moreover, the number of secondary texts that accompany these primary texts has increased exponentially, especially through the Internet. The new technologies do not change texts so much as the social and cultural contexts, the "reading formations" that influence the creation of meaning in co-production between text and reader or viewer. Text analysis of discrete, aesthetic products such as films remains possible; however, we must always specify which textual materialisation the analysis refers to (the cinema film, the extended DVD version, and so on). Furthermore, future analysis has the task of bringing to light the relationships of the different textual materialisations to one another, and to the narrative, the dramaturgy, and the aesthetic presentation. The consequences for audience studies are graver, since "under these contemporary conditions of media culture it has therefore arguably become impossible to clearly isolate out what the meaning of a single, specific, bounded text would be."[23]

Consequently, audience studies are no longer concerned simply with investigating the meaning of a film such as *RotK* for different audiences, but with investigating the processes that have contributed to making it a part of the circulation of meanings in cultural and social contexts. For this purpose, audience studies must make use of a variety of methods in order to be able to examine *RotK* as a cultural and social phenomenon. Classic text analysis is one such method, because only it can expose how the dramatic, narrative, and aesthetic structures of the film involve the viewers in the co-production of meanings. Yet it must be combined with methods of audience studies in order to focus on the audience's side of this co-production.[24] Moreover, it must also focus on the institutional conditions, the intertextual frames, the social and cultural conditions of the viewers' life-world and their everyday lives, as well as on the social discourses with which the co-production of meanings shares a mutual relationship. Ultimately the goal is to discover what meanings are generated under what social and cultural conditions between discrete, aesthetic products and varied, socially structured and culturally socialised audiences. The example of *The Lord of the Rings* as a film trilogy adaptation of the books by J. R. R. Tolkien, composed of the individual films *The Fellowship of the Ring, The Two Towers,* and *The Return of the King,* their various DVD versions, the other primary texts such as the computer game, and secondary texts such as film reviews and the Internet forums, has illustrated what challenges audience studies face in the world of digitised media. As both texts and society become more differentiated, the importance of audience studies will continue to increase, and text analysis will be just one part of them.

CHAPTER FOURTEEN

Our Methodological Challenges and Solutions

MARTIN BARKER, ERNEST MATHIJS, AND ALBERTO TROBIA

Because of the scale of its ambitions, the *Lord of the Rings* project was always going to face some tough methodological challenges. The project was to be big—combining a sweeping search of marketing and ancillary materials around the film with a worldwide audience survey and follow-up in-depth interviews. The questions we were posing were also ones that, by and large, had been addressed only speculatively up to this point. So the work of making them operational—just how *do* you make the topic of "fantasy" researchable, just for one?—was itself a task. The research was international, with research groups in twenty countries. We wanted to examine how the film's reception was shaped by the cultural conditions in different countries— another big question. We needed to explore these processes across time—people's history with this story, from book, through rumours and predictions, to their experience in the cinema, and how they thought about the film afterwards. Perhaps most importantly, we wanted the project to go beyond certain barriers that we felt our field of research was hitting. It is fine to show *variety* and *complexity* in the responses to things such as films, but it isn't enough. We wanted to be able to disclose *patterns* and *connections*. And we wanted to do all these in ways that ensured that other academics, and those fascinated by Tolkien's story, would feel they could be confident in our findings.

These are the jobs that methodology does. Methodology is, if you will, the accumulated wisdom of researchers about how to travel sure-footedly from having interesting general questions to developing structured means of gathering, organising, and analysing materials that can answer those questions. Methodology is not a mechanical toolbox. Any serious research project has to weigh a whole series of things. From available resources, what can be attempted? Given that choices must be made, what are the most urgent questions? What can be learnt from the best of existing research? Where has it not yet gone? We would argue that a great deal of methodology comes down, less to right and wrong procedures, although these are important, than to bold choices among possibilities. Along the way come the points where researchers can dip into the available "rule books" on how to do various bits as reliably as possible.

How we met out methodological challenges is the topic of this final chapter. A good number of those challenges were foreseen, and our solutions—as good as we could make them, after long rounds of debate—were built into our research design. In some cases, we had to solve difficulties "on the fly." But methodology is also about opportunities. If a project is designed to answer only one question, that is as far as it can take you. Sometimes it is possible to design research that might contribute to an indefinite number of questions. This is what we tried.

Of course no researcher begins with a blank slate. Every good piece of research begins by estimating the state of the field(s) on which it draws and learns from the strengths and weaknesses of what has already been done. In our case, that was particularly the broad field of audience research.

THE CURRENT STATE OF AUDIENCE RESEARCH

Our sense is that media audience research is on the cusp of a set of changes. And we hope to be among the influences that help mould where it goes. It would be hard, even without space restrictions, to characterise fairly the many diverse currents that are at present flowing within audience research, let alone discuss them all fairly. In this short section we cannot get near this. With an apology to all the kinds of work here missed or marginalised, our aim is to paint a working portrait of the main current traditions and paradigms of audience research, which says something about the available concatenations of theories and concepts (how to think about "the audience"), questions (what the primary interests and concerns are), methods (typical ways of investigating), and objects (what *kinds* of audience most interest researchers).

In many countries, despite its theoretical poverty, moralistic conceptualisations, and methodological narrowness, the mass communications tradition still stands strong, examining those "masses" that are currently provoking "public concern." This is the strand of work still widely beloved of governments, policy bodies, and public commentators, and that gets much funded as a result. Its influence has undoubtedly declined—but without really being replaced. Its main sociological "alternative" (the quotation marks signal our hesitations), the uses and gratifications approach, still has adherents, but hardly constitutes a force now. In and around these, influential figures like George Gerbner have cast long shadows.

Elsewhere, the European tradition of reception theory has generated important concepts such as "interpretive community," but long stayed firmly textual. Only quite recently has it, primarily in the United States (and in film studies), moved from textual elaboration to empirical research, through the work of such people as Janet Staiger and Barbara Klinger. But beyond these, with perhaps two exceptions, the picture is one of variety (which is good) but less elaboration and conversation (which is bad). The two exceptions have to be the contributions of Pierre Bourdieu and of Stuart Hall.

Bourdieu's conceptualisations of culture have had a wide impact, albeit sometimes in oversimplified forms.[1] In France, for some years, he was a signal force. But his methods—broad cultural surveys coupled with close qualitative analyses—have been less followed.[2] Perhaps more than anything, it is his notion of the links between class and cultural taste systems that continues to resonate. And this has linked quite well with the tradition of cultural studies considerably led by Stuart Hall's encoding/decoding model. From the 1980s, a substantial body of work and ideas emerged, especially from the United Kingdom. Typically oppositional, its primary address was to the uneasy lines connecting mass media and popular culture and knowledge. When it moved abroad, and especially to the United States, its focus shifted. Fan studies took and celebrated the notion of the "active audience," making of this a substantial specialist field—although one that to outsiders seems often inflated and to be making exaggerated political claims. But perhaps just as important has been cultural studies' "textualism." The powerful refocusing on culture as "textual" (semiotically rich and charged, a major medium through which contemporary political life is formed and conveyed) has nagged at the edges of audience research, telling it what to look for and what it must find.

All these traditions have mainly looked at what we might call "mainstream" audiences for objects like television.[3] Outside such spheres, the picture is patchy. Theatre researchers, for instance, briefly turned to their audiences, but an international research association formed for this purpose was short-lived.[4] Instead, the main strengths here have been in the historical study of audiences—yet this is something only now being attempted in fields such as film.[5] In the literary field, there has been a strong growth of historical studies in reading practices.[6] Methodologically, these have involved a combination of interpretive work and archival mining. But there has been little contemporary work, except where, locally, as in Scandinavia, groups of researchers come together. Art audiences are hardly touched, other than through Bourdieu's work and occasional rich historical accounts (Michael Baxandall, for instance[7]). Museum studies has grown its own professionally driven traditions. The study of music audiences is a partial exception, with the added bonus that researches in this field both draw fruitfully on Bourdieu's conceptualisations and attend to the social processes of music listening.[8] In parallel fields, the study of sports fans has become a substantial subset of an essentially sociological approach. In short, a good deal going on, but with little by way of shared theories, questions, or methods.

It is important to note, however, that the term *audience* has become increasingly questioned. Not an innocent term, it seems to picture people as recipient end points for cultural processes.[9] A number of developments have led to challenges to this. In roundabout ways, Jürgen Habermas' influence led to an interest in audiences as *publics*—people *using* media and cultural forms as the bases for their involvement or noninvolvement in democratic domains.[10] This has found resonances in studies of children, and in the ways they may learn to be citizens.[11] In quite another field, the emergence of the various forms of digital media (games, the web, mobile phones, and so on) has pushed notions of "interactivity" to the fore—again, directly challenging the implicit metaphors within the term *audience*. In an almost reverse direction, fields such as tourism studies have seized (albeit with intense debates around the work of people such as John Urry[12]) upon the idea of people "gazing" upon Other Cultures, and erected wholesale models of a new international political/cultural economy. This has been much influenced by the work of Michel Foucault on the power-knowledge nexus. Meanwhile, quite outside our fields, others have been quietly borrowing some ideas from us, and turning them to unexpected uses. The field of consumer research, for instance, has been transforming itself.[13] The idea of the "consumer" is getting a history and a (theoretical and methodological) makeover. Given all these, it is not surprising that when a journal for our field began to be debated in the late 1990s, its title was debated hard—those involved eventually settled on *Participations* as a relatively neutral, but indicative, term.[14]

A summation of where we are is therefore hard. A surprising amount of work is going on, in many countries and within different research paradigms. In some countries the impulses to and backgrounds of research are primarily sociological (and the influence of Jesus Martin-Barbero in Latin America is one signal example of a "local" force); in some the drivers are more cultural/humanistic. But outside mass communications (with its continuing stilted dedication to variable-manipulating laboratory studies[15]) and uses and gratifications (with its needs-oriented questionnaires), there are few agreements on questions, concepts, or methods. And in different regions of the world, and indeed in different language communities, the main working models and exemplars for studying reception processes just do vary greatly—far too much to make any substantial international collaboration easy.

A common thread in much "new audience research" is a recognition that audience engagements are deeply interwoven with wider cultural memberships. This is a major achievement in itself. It challenges the decontextualised "individual" of mass communication theory, and puts audiences back into society and history. But in so doing, it lands us in the heart of other debates. If watching films is necessarily part of "culture," what is the relationship between culture, work, and politics? How does the *business* of entertainment relate to its pleasures? Might not the very separation of culture as "leisure" (this is "just for fun," "escapism," and so on) itself mark an ideological process? When corporations make films, maybe they also make ideologies. All such questions—and there are many of them—challenge the sufficiency of audience research to tell us what we might need to know about the signifi-cance of a film such as *The Lord of the Rings.*

Another strain of argument takes up the complexities raised by that idea of "cul-tural memberships." Cultural studies early on challenged the notion of unified "cultures," with agreed tastes and scales of values. To this was soon added a ques-tioning of the idea of singular "selves" who respond as one kind of person and from one position. Real people think and respond at different times by age, sex, ethnic-ity, class, politics, family, and many other memberships. But global population shifts (and the associated idea of "hybrid" nationalities) and the rise in global knowledge systems make who "we" are ever more complex. This had strong impli-cations for cross-cultural research. The danger would be that we might take some-one responding from, say, Denmark, to be in some simple sense responding as "Danish." It made it vital that we think about how to draw out people's sense of the communities (real, virtual, imagined, wished for) they belonged to, whose values and ways of responding they shared.

In this messy, fragmented, but exciting set of contexts, we formed and attempt-ed our world project.

OUR PROJECT'S PARTICULAR REQUIREMENTS

As this book makes clear, our project had three, interlinked stages: gathering and analysing prefigurative materials, recruiting and analysing responses to a question-naire, then selecting individuals for detailed interviews—and analysing those. Each of these stages makes its own tough methodological demands. The challenge mul-tiplies inasmuch as we wanted to link them. Here, we focus in on some of our most important decisions.

But ahead of any of these detailed discussions, we must remember that the very idea of studying "the audience" has been a topic of debate, because of arguments that the "thing" being studied may only come into existence through the act of research-ing it. "Audiences" may only exist because researchers constitute them. This is a prob-lem that a number of researchers have addressed. Kim Schrøder and colleagues, for instance, write, "All audience research is intrusive. We cannot study audiences empirically without at the same time interfering with the very phenomenon we wish to study—the everyday practices through which people use and make sense of the media—or interrupting people's lives for the duration of the research encounter."[16] But while this is an inevitable feature of audience research (as of course of many other kinds of social research), it neither invalidates the idea nor undermines the importance of asking, How can we make sure that we do the research as well as is possible? It does of course mean that among our considerations has to be an assess-ment of the ways in which our very processes of generating evidence may have shaped what we gathered. More specifically, there is the difficult question of the ways in which the *implements* (questionnaires, interviews) might privilege certain understandings and might predetermine the kinds of answers we could come to. The only solution we see to this is simply a regular dose of honest self-examination. Otherwise, such concerns simply freeze research.

It may help to divide this discussion into two sections: one addressing the gathering and organising our research materials, the other dealing with processes of analysis. Our goal was to gather very large bodies of data and materials in forms that could thus allow us to pose questions, and to look for patterns, separations, connections, or simply puzzling features.

An example may clarify what we mean here. Our research was addressed to the functions of film fantasy in the lives of different kinds of audiences. Of course, the concept of "fantasy" has been widely discussed for a long time. It is not just an academic concept; it is also, if you will, a *public concept*. That is to say, it is used by cultural commentators to pass judgement on people's tastes and preferences—frequently, to find them wanting. In 2005, the British *Guardian* newspaper featured author Natasha Walter commenting on the popularity of Tolkien, and the Harry Potter novels and films. Walters warns against "patronising" these audiences, and quotes others calling fantasy "infantile" and "regressive." Yet she then herself proceeds to describe them as "providing comfort," as filling "god-shaped holes," and as "making no demands on us."[17] Many of our audiences would simply disagree strongly with these judgements about them. But it is not only cultural critics who make these judgements—they are very frequently embedded within academic discussions as well. Audiences get categorised and judged in these processes. Our research questions could not ignore these. Those very debates about "fantasy" might influence people's expectations, their sense of the value of this film, and their sense of self when they watched it.

The term *fantasy* marks out, if you like, a fought-over territory—and words are weapons of the war to control it. This means that we would have to try to do three difficult things at the same time:

1. We had to gather large bodies of those "debating" materials—press, magazine, television, radio, Internet—to see what sorts of views of the film were being circulated in different places and spaces. But we could not thereby assume they had an influence, or what that influence might be.
2. We had to gather large samples of audiences' talk about the films and the books, so that we could hear *in their own words* what they meant to them. This meant both having very large numbers of people responding, and having them tell us a lot about their responses. This volume of materials was itself going to be a real challenge.
3. But we could not solve that challenge by imposing our own definitions on them in advance. If we did, we might well be imposing just another version of those public categories. Nor could we predetermine some "sample" of those people we needed to hear from, and thus limit the amount we

gathered. Instead, we had to recruit as widely as we could, and find ways to let the meanings and patterns emerge.

These were the general requirements that drove a great number of our methodological decisions. More than anything, it drove our decision to combine quantitative with qualitative approaches.

CROSSING THE QUALIQUANT

There is a wide range of writing about the issues involved in trying to combine quantitative and qualitative modes of investigation. Two tendencies stand out from this literature. First, there is more writing about the likely virtues of the combination than actual working examples of the practice; second, those researchers who have attempted it have on a number of occasions seen the two stages as *serial* rather than *integral*. They do *some of each* and hope that the results will be mutually informing.[18] It may help for a moment to think of this as like a river, the Qualiquant, up which we are trying to take a body of cargo. Research is hard work, so it is definitely against the current. Our cargo has to be towed from the banks. But the residents of each side—the Qualis and the Quanters—are pretty suspicious of each other. They live different lives, speak different languages. They have very different beliefs about the right way to tow a boat effectively. Therefore, in the main, it is just easier to work from one bank at a time—even if it means our boat tends to drift sideways. If only they could be got to work together, large volumes of cargo could be handled much more easily!

We had no choice but to try to build a bridge, and get the two parties talking to each other. This was most particularly true because, with our central implement, the questionnaire, we planned to collect thousands of responses. Without a solution, these would be useless. The questionnaire's design was a major preoccupation. There are many good books on questionnaire design, offering helpful advice and examples on a wide range of topics such as question order, problems of ambiguity, the kinds of language to use, differences between open and closed questions, and overall length. But no questionnaire can be devised simply by reference to these sorts of cautionary rules. Rather, these lists of features are best seen as quality checks, brought into the equation near the end of the design process. Our design process was the result of an interplay between three overarching challenges:

1. *What did we want to find out?* We could not directly ask people our Big Questions. We had to find ways to translate them into smaller ones that would be meaningful to anyone answering us. For example, since we were centrally interested in investigating the ways different audiences related to fantasy, a lot of our thinking went into how we could get audiences talking about the *idea* of "fantasy" without presuming its meaning. And remem-

ber that this had to comprehensible, in translation, to people from Guatemala to Germany, Los Angeles to Laos.

2. *What were we going to do with the answers?* Perhaps the hardest message to convey to students of research methods is that at the beginning of any research project, the most important questions they need to address is what they will do at the end. It is no use gathering materials or data in forms, in quantities, and of kinds that you cannot use. The kinds of analysis you plan to do have to drive the design. For example, we wanted to explore how group memberships might influence people's responses to the film. So we needed to get people to give us information about themselves. That is quite easy with sex and age—but what about occupation? Designing a way to get usable information about people's occupations anywhere in the world (Mumbai to Mexico, or London to Lagos) is not easy—because the worlds of work are so differently constituted. Our solution was bold but effective, as we hope to show.

3. *Why would anyone complete our questionnaire?* We live in a world where most people know about questionnaires. Governments require us to complete some. Commercial bodies often try to get them done. Others are done for fun—magazines inviting us to rate ourselves, for instance. We frequently see them (and ourselves, thereby) discussed and pontificated upon. Why should they do ours? The issue of how our questionnaire should look, read, and be publicised, preoccupied us. We needed it to become, ideally, part of the experience of watching and talking about the film. It had to be *fun to fill in.* We could reasonably hope to capture people who were enthusiastic about the film—even perhaps those whose enthusiasm took the form of *anger* at the film—but what about those whose main reaction was that the film was "Alright—for a night out"?

It was out of imaginative juggling between these three that our questionnaire emerged. As we outlined in the introduction, the key move was the coupling of quantitative and qualitative questions. We asked people to allocate themselves on several multiple-choice lists (enjoyment, importance, kind of story), and then immediately to explain their answers in their own words. So we could potentially explore not just how many said they really enjoyed the film, but also what kinds of people most enjoyed the film, and how their ways of stating their enjoyment related to that of people who did not enjoy it so much. We could explore their relations with the books, and how (through, for instance, their expressions of disappointments) their relations with the books overlapped with or were different from those of other groups. And of course there is no reason to suppose that only one kind of person enjoyed the film. So, potentially, we could *build portraits* of the viewing strategies and responses of different groups. All these possibilities were consciously built into our research design.

But as we've said, a good design often yields more than is originally thought of. For example, one idea not originally planned, but which proved productive, was to explore the relations between responses to questions about favourite characters and most memorable moments or aspects. This allowed us to extract data relevant to debates about "identification." Combined with the reasons for choosing different characters, it allowed a detailed study of different relations with the film.[19] This was simply not planned for.

Take the debate over the question about occupation. The U.K. team proposed that we should not ask people to name their occupation—we believed that this would result in an unmanageable list of answers. Instead we suggested producing a short list of *kinds* of occupation, and that we should embrace the notion that people might partly choose their answer by how they *felt* about their work. A person working in advertising, for instance, might see themselves as creative, or as a professional, or as an executive. A person working in farming might see themselves as either unskilled or skilled manual, or even as a service worker. Since we were interested in attitudes to "fantasy," this could be valuable. After much debate, this tack was agreed upon—although it does run counter to more standard sociological researches. Early signs are that this has paid off—a number of distinctive groups emerged from our analysis, and are being explored.[20] But of course a decision the other way could well have produced other, equally interesting findings. This is once again a case of methodology being less about right or wrong, more about decisions with consequences.

We tell these stories to show that committing ourselves to a Qualiquant approach did not solve all our problems—it simply moved and changed them.

OUR SAMPLING STRATEGY

Sampling is a key issue in social research designs, and was one we had to face. The advantages of sampling are well known: low costs, economy of time, and a better organisation of research.

There are two main types of sampling methods: probability (random) sampling and nonprobability sampling, respectively typical of (but not exclusive to) quantitative and qualitative research. In *probability sampling*, definitively codified in the 1930s by the Polish statistician Jerzy Neyman,[21] all units of the target population have an equal, calculable, non-zero probability of being included in the sample.[22] Many researchers believe that probabilistic samples are better, because they are *representative* of reality. In brief, they maintain, what we can say about the sample can be extended to the reality sampled (by statistical inference). Another advantage is that we can calculate the sampling error, which is a crucial datum in order to assess the validity of a sample. The main problem, with this kind of sample, is that we need the complete list of the target population to extract it, and very often this is impossible to obtain. This is no small issue. We can't say whether a sample is representative or not, because we generally sample precisely in order to find out something about a reality we don't yet know. This is called the *sampling paradox,* and it applied with great force to audiences for *LotR. Nonprobability samples* are generally "purposive" or "theory-driven."[23] This means that they are gathered following a criterion that the researcher believes to be satisfying, in order to achieve typological representativeness. Being purposive, these kinds of samples are rather heterogeneous. Miles and Huberman, for example, listed sixteen different qualitative sampling strategies.[24] The difficulty with nonprobability samples it that we have only loose criteria for assessing their validity.

The strategy chosen for the *LotR* project involved a new mix of quali-quantitative solutions, in order to be consistent with the general "philosophy" of the project, which aimed at interweaving different methods and techniques. This hybrid direction is gradually getting a footing in the social researchers community, as the success of mixed strategies as respondent-driven sampling (RDS) clearly shows.[25] We could not possibly extract a probability sample, simply because we couldn't know the complete film audience. In fact, we weren't searching for statistical representativeness; rather, we were more interested in *typological representativeness.* That is, we needed as many *types* of respondent as possible and as many *forms* of argumentation as possible. Does everyone who sees a film equally count as "the audience"? For some purposes, yes—but not if you want to explore influence and meaning. Someone who falls asleep, or leaves halfway through—or perhaps rejects and forgets the whole experience the moment they leave the cinema—may not be an "audience" in the same sense as someone who returns again and again to it. We needed a research design that would allow us to build a picture of *as many kinds of viewers* as possible. In a case like this, the best choice is a "qualitative," nonprobability sampling.

The best way to reach quickly the huge target population needed for our research, cheaply and manageably, was to use *Internet sampling*.

> Internet sampling is a procedure that is administered, partly or fully, through the Internet. This entails procedures which enable the researcher to bring questionnaires to the attention of prospective respondents, by either directly forwarding them the questionnaire, or informing them of the availability of the survey and asking them to participate. This is facilitated through email or web pages.[26]

Of course, Internet sampling still has problems. For example, the number of Internet users is significantly lower among older people. For this reason we supported the web questionnaire with a paper version of the questionnaire administered to audiences at cinemas.

Ultimately, of our 24,739 respondents, 22,486 completed the questionnaire online, with the remaining 2,253 completing the paper version. Only some countries were in a position to use the paper questionnaire (with Italy having the highest proportion, at 29 percent of the total). A comparison of the two sources did reveal some clear differences. Internet completers were younger, with higher representation of students and professionals. They had higher levels of knowledge of Tolkien's books, and were more committed to the films. So, having the two sources could alert us to the biases in our main sample.

We can't therefore say that our sample and its subsamples are representative of some broader population, because we chose the nonprobability alternative. But we believe we can be rather confident, considering our success in gathering almost 25,000 responses, that we achieved a very good *typological* representativeness—that is, we have sufficient members of all our main categories to be able to describe with confidence their patterned similarities and differences.

MAKING SOME KEY CONCEPTS RESEARCHABLE

This project was concerned with some tricky concepts. We touched on this earlier in relation to the concept of "fantasy." Another difficult concept for us was "pleasure." They are difficult for several reasons. First, both of them, at one level, seem very *obvious*. Richard Dyer has explored equivalent problems with the concept of "entertainment," showing how the term is often used to block discussion and investigation—it is too obvious to be worth pursuing.[27] In the same way, people will say "it's only fantasy" or "I just enjoy it," as if that ends the discussion. But both "fantasy" and "pleasure" have been the topic of heavy theorisation. *Fantasy* is already a term with many meanings. It can mean generally the human capacity to imagine wildly, without many formal constraints—to invent, to daydream, to construct amazing scenarios. It can mean a genre of literature, which has in the last forty years become a publishing phenomenon. It can, for some people, be a term within a formidable array of other concepts, which constitute the broad psychoanalytic tradition—here "fantasy" supposedly arises from repressed desires, frequently rooted in childhood experience. But in addition to these, some more specialised understandings have been developed, as in the strong tradition of work that views fantasies as culturally loaded vehicles through which we live our membership of our societies, and conceive our relations to Others. The problem is not simply that these approaches do not tidily coincide, or that evidence for one or another is more or less persuasive. It is more that what counts as evidence on one approach simply would not be acknowledged on another.

The cultural studies tradition is awash with writings about both fantasy and pleasure, and with claims about their implications and consequences. In film studies, perhaps no work has been individually more influential than Laura Mulvey's essay on "visual pleasure."[28] Mulvey claimed to identify the pleasures that men and women *must* respectively feel, in light of the textual organisation of mainstream Hollywood films. Hers is among many others that arrive at very negative accounts of the cultural meanings and implications of popular culture, through theoretically based assertions about the kinds of pleasure films afford and the apparent costs to self of such enjoyments. But at another extreme, other scholars and theoreticians have been charged with simply celebrating whatever "the people" enjoy. The accusation of "populism," levelled by among others Jim McGuigan,[29] has once again more to do with the supposed consequences of pleasures than with the nature of those pleasures.

The level of theorisation has not been matched by the quantity of researches into *actual* pleasures—who has them, what they feel like, what they do to get them, and what they do with them once they have them.[30] But in the last twenty years, a small number of studies—often quite exploratory—have begun to unpack these complexities. Ien Ang, in her study of *Dallas* viewers, begins to unpick the complex components of people's pleasures and dislikes.[31] She shows, for instance, that pleasure can be perverse, deriving from finding the programme poor and feeling superior to it and its "ordinary audiences." Martin Barker and Kate Brooks attempt to characterise the logic of different kinds of pleasures (what you have to be and do to get them, what viewing conditions best promote them, and so on) in action-adventure films.[32] Thomas Austin has explored the character of men's responses to a film such as *Basic Instinct*.[33] More recently, Aphra Kerr and others have explored audience pleasures in video games—and once again immediately point to unexpected complexities.[34] But for all these valuable pieces of research, theories of pleasure and fantasy have largely marched on, regardless.

In this sense, we began with a commitment. This research was pitched and designed within what is generally known as the cultural studies tradition. If nothing else, this involves a belief that a cultural "text" like *LotR* cannot be signed off as "just fantasy" or "just entertainment." The story itself, in book and film forms, has to be seen as a complex vehicle for both pleasures and meanings. Its narrative organisation, its kinds of characters, the manner of its telling, its past and present reputation, and its social circulation—all these make any possible audience response far more than a matter of "entertainment" or "effects." The film comes out of and resonates in all kinds of ways with this point in history. Therefore, any enquiry into audiences for *LotR* would have to enter into the complicated ways in which people understand their part in all this, and the ways in which the film plays a role within people's wider sense of their world.

That meant getting people to talk to us about how their responses to the film engaged with other aspects of their lives. And not just as individuals. As people talk about things like films, they draw upon shared languages, and they address themselves to others in groups—and this sociality is a core part of people's responses. Such communities can be very local (a lot of young people's language operates to share understandings, to the exclusion of adults), or very wide (shared international languages in antiglobalisation campaigns). And they can be fought over.[35] The use of words can be very positive (the history of the term *cool* as a summation of a cultural stance, including ways of using one's body, would be a case in point). They can be negative (the history of derogatory terms for women has been a substantial case study in itself). They can change over time—the capture of the term *gay* and thence the reclaiming of the word *queer* by homosexual activists are good examples. The study of these, it has been argued, enables researchers to bring into view many of the practices through which people build and maintain their social lives, and the ways people understand the world and each other. All this is part of what has been widely termed the "turn to language" in much recent social theory.

EXPLORING AUDIENCE CATEGORIES

These are indeed exciting times when it comes to the development of ways of handling and analysing people's everyday talk. The "cultural turn" or "linguistic turn," as it has sometimes been called, within social, historical, and literary theory generally came out of the realisation that social processes could not be understood without proper attention to the ways in which people understand the social (and indeed physical) world they inhabit.[36] Ways of understanding the world are developed and communicated, oftentimes by powerful means. These are not simply rational constructs, but involve elements of imagination and fantasy, senses of self and others, stories, pictures, hopes and fears. These are to be found not so much within organised bodies of words and images such as books, speeches, laws, films, or poems, but within people's ordinary talk.

There are a number of very different traditions for how to think about, and how to deal in research with, words. At the back of our project were two particular bodies of work: discourse theory and vernacular theory.

The field of discourse theory and analysis has mushroomed mightily in the last twenty years, as researchers have developed theories and methods for examining language in action and argued over its role in the production and maintenance of forms of political power and domination. Every commentator on the field has noted the variety of emergent conceptualisations and associated methodologies within this field.[37] A substantial array of detailed concepts and methods has been developed and deployed, to enquire into everything from "excuses" used by smokers for not quitting, police interrogation techniques,[38] Bill Clinton's management of the Monica Lewinsky affair,[39] and the "banal" practices of newspapers in defining who "we" are as a nation.[40]

But until recently, these approaches have not been much used in audience research—perhaps for two reasons.[41] Discourse analysis, in almost all its varieties,[42] has tended to focus on very small samples, chosen by the analyst because she or he sees it as particularly indicative. We could not limit ourselves to this, although it is evident that each interview on its own could be a rich source. But also, discourse analysis shares with wider approaches to texts and textual analysis and shares with them a belief that language is a mode of power. So, typically, discourse analysts will analyse "texts" such as films, and then deduce likely impacts on viewers. Audience research has to start at the other end and ask, How do different audiences engage with our film, and what pleasures and meanings do they gain from it? Ultimately, it might even be possible to reconstruct different versions of "the film"—how the various parts and facets of it bind together to become a meaningful whole—via the detailed accounts of particular audience groups.

From another direction, ethnographers have examined the ways in which local cultures can be formed around shared modes of talk.[43] The early work of the "ethno-scientists" has recently been revisited and redeveloped by Thomas McLaughlin, who, among other case studies, explores the ways in which informal communities around fanzines debate and construct working accounts of the world and what they want to achieve.[44] This sort of work has been made relevant to film studies in a range of ways. Rick Altman, emphasising the *historical* development of genre ideas, explores many cases where genre labels evolved over time, and at the behest of very partic-ular groups.[45]

Just recently, a few researchers have begun to develop ways of redressing this gap. Barker and colleagues, in their study of the U.K. *Crash* controversy, showed how some audiences had sufficiently soaked up the local category "sex and violence" that they had gone to see the film with front-loaded expectations as to what it must be.[46] Very recently, Klinger has shown how an expression such as "chick flick" can enable people to think and plan their (repeated) encounters with films, readying themselves to experience appropriate emotions.[47]

Our goal, then, was to take the best from discourse and vernacular theories and develop ways of applying these to our very large datasets. This was not easy, and there were hazards. Words do not come with flashing lights attached, to say "this is a key term, with many implications." To an extent, you need people close enough to a cul-ture to know that certain words are doing substantial cultural work. In the design of our core questionnaire, this constituted a problem particularly for our key ques-tion, in which we asked people to say what *kind of story* it was for them. But even once identified, we needed to be careful about differences in uses and implications. Below we give the example of how the U.K. team explored the complex meanings of the term *epic*.

A further problem is knowing how to move from identifying ways of talking to saying something about the *kind of community* (its membership, their shared val-ues, ways of operating, and so on) to which those ways of talking belong. Here, we think, we reach the boundaries of our research and have been very cautious about crossing it. One instance, to illustrate this. Analysis of our database showed us that there was a quite sharp separation between those who told us that among their key sources for knowing about the film were the web and the Internet, and those for whom this was not the case. Users of new media used much more *emotional* lan-guages for discussing the film than users of traditional media did. This is without question an interesting finding, and certainly runs counter to the claims of some new media theorists that interactivity signals the death of narrative enthrallment. But because of the ways in which we had chosen to gather information, we cannot go much further to say *how* people are feeling that they belong to web communities. That will require other kinds of research.

Aware that this is an emerging area, we have devoted a lot of our time to trying out new analytic procedures that can take full advantage of our having a very large and highly organised body of responses. Chapters 8 and 9 are attempts at such a cross-cultural analysis of responses.

FINDING PATTERNS WITHIN THE DATA SET: APPROACHES, PRACTICES, SOFTWARE

The main task of analysis is to find significant patterns or distinctive groupings within a body of materials or a dataset. There is a payoff among the size and complexity of these, the difficulty of the task of analysis, and the potential value of what can be learnt. The larger and more complex the body of materials gathered (where, for instance, it involves qualitative materials), the more that can be learnt but the harder analysis becomes. For this reason, if for no other, computers and research software have become indispensable to contemporary social research. In this section, we explain two rather different approaches to this used in this research.

A quali-quantitative research design needs a particular approach. In order that the two aspects can relate to each other, it is necessary to adopt one (or more than one) of the following solutions:

1. It may be possible to formulate questions in both multiple-choice and open-ended forms, in order to verify similarities and differences, which was one solution adopted in our project. The tricky issues are, first, not to irritate your audience by appearing to ask the same thing twice; and, second, to have thought in advance about how the quantitative and qualitative answers are going to inform and interrogate each other.

2. Researchers can carry out a post-coding of qualitative responses, in order to prepare them for subsequent statistical treatment—a standard option in many researches, and one used in a number of the analyses in our project. This becomes most effective if the overall research design produces the means to choose limited samples for specific purposes. Generally, this approach can be very effective, but it is *very* time-consuming.

3. Techniques have been developed to effect a form of automatic coding of the responses to the open-ended questions, to explore the main topics and isotopies[48] in the data as well as their axial orientation, with the possibility then of seeing how they are correlated with quantitative variables.

4. Finally, there are ways to search for some ideal types of respondent, using quantitative variables and cluster analyses, which can then be further "read" in the light of qualitative responses.

Each of these strategies has been used at some stage in the project, often by different participant groups who come from different research backgrounds. We explain here two broad strategies—each using computers and software in distinctive ways.

At the close of the project, the almost 25,000 questionnaire responses were assembled into one database and made available to all research teams in one of two formats: either Microsoft Access or the Statistical Package for the Social Sciences (SPSS). These software systems operate differently, and invited different kinds of analysis.

The U.K. team, among others, worked with Access. Access as a relational database permits searches by individual field or by increasingly complex cross-field searches. In principle, therefore, it makes possible two routes of searching. Either a researcher can move from identifying patterns in multiple-choice responses to locating and then analysing associated qualitative materials, in order to see how they too are patterned. Or he or she may progress from identifying interesting tendencies in the qualitative responses to a consideration of what, if any, associated quantitative patterns emerge. The weakness of Access is that it will not perform statistical operations.

An example to show how this worked. Field 5 contained responses to our modality question: "What kind of a story is *Lord of the Rings* for you?" People had been asked to nominate up to three from our list of twelve, or to nominate their own. We began with simple counts—how many people had chosen each? We then looked at combinations—which of the twelve were most and least frequently paired? From these searches alone, we were able to develop a very informative map of the semantic connections and oppositions in people's responses.

We were able, then, to begin to link each modality choice with those in other fields. If across the world the most common choice was "Epic," was this true in all main countries?[49] It wasn't. We were also interested in the relations between modality and enjoyment and importance. Here, we made a major discovery; while "Epic" was the most *common* choice among world respondents, another choice—"Spiritual journey"—was more strongly chosen by those reporting the highest levels on enjoyment and importance. The meanings of these modality terms, remember, could not be assumed. Therefore we began a series of complex semantic investigations, from two quite distinct directions. First, we sorted all responses from people[50] who had not only chosen "Epic" from our list but had spontaneously used the term in earlier answers. We examined the uses of the word, to see what kinds of judgement on the film they suggested or implied. Eleven meanings emerged. We then scaled these (on three levels) for the extent to which they appeared to celebrate, simply describe, or criticise the film. Finally, we looked at who had made these attributions, and found that the celebratory uses were most likely to be used by those also nominating "Spiritual journey." Second, we isolated the two sets of responses—people nominating "Epic" but not "Spiritual journey," and vice versa—randomised them in Access, and sampled one hundred for their responses to our first free-text question: "What did you think of the film?" A coding system was developed, to the point where all components of the answers were covered, and portraits of the two sets elaborated. There were, of course, some overlaps, but we found that the "Spiritual journey" choices showed much higher levels of *emotionality*, less interest in the *cinematic* aspects of the film, and a much greater tendency to *discuss the moral meanings and implications* of the story.

This was not the end of our exploration even of field 5. But we hope it illustrates the ways in which Access allowed the U.K. team to delve deep into our data and their meanings. It was painstaking and at times very slow.

Several teams—the Italian, German, and Dutch especially—worked with SPSS. Data analysis here can be carried out with respect to three main objects: (1) variables, (2) cases, and (3) words.

The analysis of *variables* typically characterises quantitative research, with three main kinds of analysis. *Monovariate* analysis is based on one variable, and its aim is *descriptive* (how is reality?). *Bivariate* analysis is based on two variables and its aim is *explicative* (why is reality thus?). In our project, all the questionnaire responses were subjected to monovariate and to bivariate analysis (mainly cross-tabulations of responses to pairs of answers). These in themselves provided an array of broad patterns, from which the various national teams then developed their further preferred methods of analysis. *Multivariate* analysis is based on more than two variables. It is less common, generally, and was not widely used by us because of the particular nature of our sample, which would not support some inferential techniques typical of multivariate techniques.

The techniques for the analysis of *cases* are relatively few. The most important is *cluster analysis*. Cluster analysis is actually a "family" of techniques (hierarchical, partitioning, local density, and neural).[51] It is particularly useful when the researcher aims at building a typology of objects—that is, when she or he wants to classify them. In our research it was used to catalogue the types of audience. The purpose of cluster analysis is to detect groups of respondents who show similarity to each other when compared to respondents who belong to other clusters. In addition to identifying the clusters, of course, we have to determine how the clusters are different—that is, to determine the specific variables or dimensions that vary. Cluster analysis yields very robust results, and does not require a probability sample, because it classifies objects in a typology, irrespective of their number.

Using this approach, the Italian team detected four ideal types of spectators: the *enthusiastic fan*, the *disappointed fan*, the *critic reader*, and the *mass spectator*.[52] These types, interestingly very similar to the ones emerging from the German research, came from interpreting the results shown in graph 1, which indicates, for each cluster, the means (shown on the y-axis) of the variables considered in the analysis (x-axis). These were: global evaluation, importance of the film, having seen the other two films, and having read the book. We can see, for instance, that cluster 3 (the path outlined by the graph's little rhombus) is characterised by high values of the

Figure 14.1: Ideal Types of Spectators

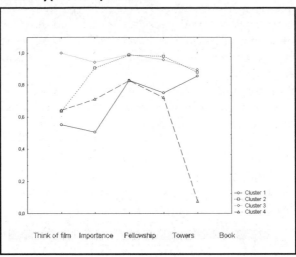

means with respect to every variable: hence the name *enthusiastic fan.* Following the same approach, we could reconstruct the other types of audience. The "name" of the cluster, of course, is not given by the computer. This is a task for the researcher, who, reading carefully a graph such as this, interprets and labels the clusters.

The *statistical* picture, then, was rather clear, but we wanted to go *beyond* this picture, having the big opportunity to look at the responses to the open-ended questions. We wanted the most "representative" cases of each group, but how could we find them? Fortunately, the output of a cluster analysis can assist in answering this kind of question. Each cluster, in fact, has a statistical centre, called the "centroid." Calculating the distance of each case from the centroid (SPSS, Statistica, and SAS does this job very easily), we could locate the cases closer to a certain ideal type. This allowed us to understand the meaning of the groups emerging from the data, transcending the raw statistical figures. From this, the Italian researchers realised that the four clusters coming out of the analysis could be reduced to three, because the qualitative responses of cluster 1 (the disappointed fan) and cluster 2 (the critic reader) were almost identical (some expressions were in fact identical). The research could benefit from the fact that there was a difference between the responses to the open questions and to the closed questions. In short, people expressed different (and paradoxically less detailed!) thoughts through words. This is a clear example of a methodological "loop"—that is, a form of triangulation *within* the same research design, as explained below, in which the findings from both the qualitative and quantitative approaches are *mutually informing,* and shows that triangulation is achievable even at a cheap price.

Unlike cases and variables, *words* can also be analysed apart from the matrix. In our research, words could be found in: (1) open-ended questionnaire responses,

(2) transcripts from interviews and focus groups, and (3) public texts of various natures (for instance, press materials).

To consider words as data, we have to face numerous problems, the most important of which is that their meaning is not the same for everyone. This is a problem that, of course, in a world research project becomes huge. It begins with the translation of our tool for gathering data (the questionnaire) into different languages, and with the disambiguation of certain key concepts. That alone required arriving at shared definitions among the different research teams at the beginning of the research. It further required us to find virtual synonyms for key terms in the questions (for example, *myth* and *quest*). Having solved these problems and gathered responses, people's answers need to be analysed.

WORDS IN OPEN-ENDED QUESTIONS

Open-ended responses have to be post-coded for two main reasons: to cut down and summarise the complexity of words and speeches, and to allow further statistical treatment. Traditional post-coding procedures involve the development of categories and the subsequent assignment of words and speeches to a value label corresponding to a given category. This is a hard and time-consuming task, but generally it guarantees a good reliability.

In recent years, following the French school of *Analyse des données*, many researchers have turned to Lexical Correspondence Analysis (LCA), an evolution of factor analysis for qualitative data.[53] The main idea of this new approach is that words alone (the focus of classic content analysis) have no meaning. They make sense only in association and/or in opposition with other words or groups of words, and as typical of certain kind of people. LCA is not interested in similarities, but instead in *differences*. Even words with a low occurrence, then, could be significant, providing that they are *typical* of certain people or group of people. LCA has two main goals: (1) to find regularities in the data and (2) to find only those few dimensions of meaning that explain these regularities, employing factorial techniques. To accomplish this, data are organised in a word-by-text matrix: the words are placed in rows, while the answers (that is, the texts) are placed in columns, as in table 14.1. The number in each cell indicates how many times a certain word has been said by a given case.

Table 14.1: Lexical Correspondence Analysis

Words	Case 1's Answer	Case 2's Answer	Case 3's Answer
DVD	0	2	1
Fantastic	5	0	1
Magic	4	1	0
Peter Jackson	0	3	2

Given such tables, a computer is able to run the LCA algorithms.[54] The procedure is fast (SPAD and T-Lab are the main programs[55]) and yields a sort of autocoding of open-ended questions. The main output of LCA, in fact, is a factorial space (basically a Cartesian coordinate system) that shows the semantic orientation of significant words on opposite axes, thus contributing to their disambiguation. Words and meaningful groups of words (that is, isotopies) are considered significant if they are distant from the origin of the factorial space. "Understanding a factorial axis means finding what is similar, firstly all that is on the right of the origin (barycentre), and secondly all that is on the left of it, and then expressing concisely and exactly the opposition between the two extremes."[56] Each axis allows the researcher to reconstruct an *ideal syntagm*—that is, a *theoretical model of a latent proposition* in the corpus.

LCA was used by both the Dutch and the Italian research teams. The Italian responses, for instance, are characterised by two different semantic axes, interpreted reading the words located on the left and on the right (for the x-axis) and at the top and the bottom (for the y-axis) of the factorial space. These axes are: (1) *boring vs. amusing* (with respect to the film) (x-axis) and (2) *"aesthetic" book adaptation vs. "technical" book adaptation* (y-axis).[57] As an example, the group of words (or "isotopy") that permitted us to interpret the "boring" semiaxis were: "abnormal," "deadly dull," "horrible," "long," and so forth. These words, which characterise the "boring" isotopy, were located at the extreme left (negative x-semiaxis) of the factorial space.

WORDS IN INTERVIEWS AND FOCUS GROUPS

The analysis of the words contained in interviews and focus groups is different, and can take three main directions: quantitative, qualitative, and computer-assisted (typically quali-quantitative). In the first case, a post-coding is required; then the data are tabulated and/or cross-tabulated, and finally the researcher interprets the results. There are two drawbacks in this approach: firstly, as above, post-coding is onerous; secondly, a lot of interesting data get lost. The main advantage is that the researcher has the possibility of employing some statistical techniques. Nevertheless, considering the small size of the samples generally utilised in researches based on interviews and focus groups, the statistical option is often an avoidable luxury, unless both the qualitative and quantitative approaches are used in a "loop" strategy, as happened in our research.

The second direction is often called an *ethnographic* or *narrative* approach. The analyst first tries to identify the main *topics* within the transcriptions. Then he or she chooses the *quotations* he or she thinks are more significant (considering also the *context* in which they are situated) or the chunks of data, for each theme, that show some commonalities. Some sort of coding procedure could be adopted at this point. The researcher could also build a classification and/or a typology. Finally, he or she tries to interpret the findings. However, this is a general scheme.[58] For example, within Glaser and Strauss' *grounded theory* the analysis should be done during data collection, until a "theoretical saturation" has been achieved.

In the case of qualitative analysis, in fact, many different practices (for instance, fixed, iterative, and subjectivist),[59] paradigms (even within qualitative sociology itself: constructivism, ethnomethodology, interactionism, interpretivism, cultural studies, postmodern sociology, and so forth), and also disciplines can be adopted. This plurality of paradigms and methods, far from being a drawback, contributes instead to enrich the analysis. This is not accepted by some orthodox methodologists,[60] but it is the approach that from the beginning characterised our project. Accepting the idea of triangulation (or the idea of the *loop*, which is our more specific interpretation of triangulation), we implicitly accept, and actually encourage, the *cohabitation* of different paradigms.

WORDS IN THE PRESS

Traditionally, press materials on cinema, like the critical reception of a film, are studied qualitatively. This approach stems from a combination of a film studies and cultural studies perspective on cinema. The film studies approach focuses on the activity of interpretation, and is concerned with which meanings *inherent* to the film are communicated in criticism. Robin Wood, David Bordwell, and Rick Altman have studied how ideology, narrative, and genre are treated in film criticism.[61] The cultural studies approach is more concerned with how interpretations are *created* by criticism. Janet Staiger, Barbara Klinger, and Ernest Mathijs have emphasised how ideology, style, and rhetorics are evoked by critics.[62] But qualitative studies of reception have never managed to convincingly prove that their observations are also representative for an entire reception. Staiger's discussion of gender and sexuality in the critical reception of *The Silence of the Lambs* (Demme, 1991), for instance, may well refer to a very marginal discourse, one that hardly touches the film's mainstream reception. Studying the press materials circulating around the release of *RotK* thus required an integrated approach, combining the attention to detail of a qualitative analysis with the representativeness of a quantitative one. To that aim we employed an advanced form of content analysis.

Content analysis is basically a technique for quantifying the qualitative. Its main applications and better results have always been in the field of mass communications and political speeches since the 1950s, when Harold Lasswell and Bernard Berelson first introduced the method. The key question that content analysis tries to answer is well known: Who says what to whom and with what effect?

Nevertheless, it is not clear yet whether content analysis can deal with the *latent* content of a text or only with its *manifest* content, as Berelson's classic definition claims.[63] Of course, the manifest-latent distinction is not neutral, because it is strongly linked with the tricky issue of "hidden persuasion." The success of Berelson's definition made content analysis compatible with the functional approach to mass-media research, while this very fact made it suspect to most critical currents.[64] This must be kept in mind when using content analysis. Increasingly, researchers have sought to separate content analysis as a theory (distinguishing manifest from latent contents, and implying cumulative effects) from its usefulness as a family of techniques.[65] Since the 1960s, interest has grown in the possibilities of transcending its reductionist tendencies, by developing forms of qualitative content analysis that can discern patterns and relationships within materials.

In this research, content analysis was utilised, for example, to see how the press followed the launch of the *RotK*. Using T-Lab, the Italian team carried out a study of the Italian press (newspapers and magazines), in order to know on which topics it focused its attention. Five topics emerged from the analysis: the premiere of the film, the night of the Academy Awards, the adaptation of the book, Hollywood and the showbiz, Tolkien's world. The topics were detected simply by building some baskets of keywords and then counting the frequency of each basket in the corpus, in order to evaluate their weights. For example, the "premiere of the film" topic was characterised by the following words (next to the word is shown the number of phrases in which it occurs): *Italy* (26), *day* (25), *January* (24), *cinema* (20), *to release* (17), *premiere* (16), *town* (15), *marathon* (11), *Bologna* (10), *to screen* (8), *Thursday* (8), *place* (7), *wait* (6), *ticket* (6).

Using the co-occurrence tool provided by T-Lab, we could investigate also some significant relationships between words. This showed, for instance, the first fifteen strongest associations with the phrase *Peter Jackson* used in the Italian press (the corpus considered consist of thirty-nine articles, published both in magazines and newspapers), based on the *cosine coefficient*.[66] Many associations are quite predictable. But one of the most interesting is between *Peter Jackson* and *fantasy*. This means that, when an Italian journalist wrote about Peter Jackson, it was highly probable that she or he used also the word *fantasy* in close proximity.

But proximity is not everything. The U.K. team wanted to know how, when, and by whom terms and remarks, references and words, were introduced into the discourses surrounding the release of *RotK*. Therefore we developed an advanced coding method for the content analysis of press materials that would also identify the time and place of the public presence of the words concerned. The method is derived from Karl Erik Rosengren's study of the Swedish literary frame of reference, Marcus Hudec and Brigitte Lederer's study of theatre reviews, and Wesley Shrum's analysis of performing arts reviews.[67] At its base lies the "mention": a term or word within the print message that contains meaning, in the form of its references, allusions, opinions, indications, or implications. According to Rosengren,

A mention may be regarded as an expression of an association made by the reviewer, and . . . can be used as an indicator of topicality. . . . All the mentions made in all reviews of the press in a region during a given time period (or in a representative sample thereof) may be regarded as an expression of the lexicon . . . available to the reviewers and constituting a central element of [their] frame of reference.[68]

In this case, all mentions of *RotK* or Tolkien in all British media were coded. The coding system consisted of eight dimensions:

1. **Date/time:** (as appropriate)
2. **Source** (name of publication or broadcast channel and programme)
3. **Scale** (a five-point scale from more than a full page/more than thirty-minute feature, to less than a quarter of a page/under-one-minute mention or feature)
4. **Emphasis** (feature, lead item, significant attention, filler, mention)
5. **Kind of report** (preview or review of the film itself; related release review [for example, of DVDs, rereleases, and so on]; interview; news report; gossip/trivia, advertisements for the film, merchandise, or tie-ins; unrelated report referencing *LotR;* reader's letter.
6. **Key expressions**
7. **Key references**
8. **Notes**

This method was employed most rigorously by the teams from Belgium, Germany, and the United Kingdom (which had the largest set of pre- and postrelease press materials; see table 14.2).

Combining content analysis with a strong focus on source and timing allowed for the analysis of topical references and for detection of when certain remarks, phrases, and words entered into the discourses accompanying the release of the film. (See chapter 4 for some of the results of this.)

Table 14.2: Prefigurative Items
(United Kingdom Only, October 1 –December 31, 2003)

Marketing	193
Merchandise (info/samples)	147
National newspapers	946
National magazines	542
National radio	22
National TV (freeview)	64
Internet	647
TOTAL ITEMS	2,512

OTHER APPROACHES WITHIN THE PROJECT

Besides these two broad approaches, a number of teams and individuals within the project worked in other ways with its assembled materials, and we see it as one of the project's major strengths that this was possible. Each of these further approaches drew upon particular traditions to examine in detail some particular aspect or component. Here we discuss just one of these: the political economy approach.

In order to paint a picture of the global conglomerate(s) involved in the production, distribution, and marketing of the prefiguration materials, researchers within the American team drew upon political economy traditions. This allowed for the classifications and descriptions of merchandising and its range and functions. There are strong traditions of critical enquiry into these sorts of materials, their economic and strategic importance to studio finances, and the ways in which films themselves may be shaped by the pressures to produce these ancillary materials. According to Janet Wasko, who headed this effort in our project, a political economy approach to film is, in essence, an institutional approach—it sees the actors in the communication process as agents of organisations, put in the public domain first and foremost to serve the interests of those organisations with the accumulation of "wealth" or the allocation of resources.[69] So it is that the first interest of a Hollywood studio like Warner Bros., or even a smaller subsidiary like New Line Cinema, is in maximising its own profits, either purely financially or in indirect ways (through creating a reputation, a market share, or a portfolio, for instance). *RotK* offered an excellent case study for this approach.

Within our project, Wasko and other teams (for instance, the Belgian team of Daniel Biltereyst and Philippe Meers, but also the French team of Divina Frau-Meigs) have widened the scope of research beyond material goods to include less tangible goals and ways in which the institutions in charge of producing and releasing *RotK* used diverse means and agents to guard their interests and maximise their profits. The key concepts that were put at the centre of the political economical approach in our project were:

1. the ties between existing popularity (an existing fan base) and maximising profit (this meant collecting materials evidencing how New Line approached *LotR* fans);
2. property/copyright (tracing the ownership);
3. the merchandise (collecting evidence of all rights, tie-ins, and revenues from sellable products related to the films); these were divided into: books, typical merchandise (toys, T-shirts, action figures), high-end merchandise (collectibles of higher value, such as jewelry, furniture, and so on), games, merchandise promos, and events (including the sites were these were announced); and
4. promotion and publicity (evidence of straightforward publicity for the release of the films).

This categorisation not only enabled a thorough view of the ranges and density of publicity efforts, but also contributed to a better understanding of techniques used to create interest, such as media hyping, blanket coverage, piggybacking, synergies of ownership and interest, and the conflation between supposedly independent agencies (like the press, fans, or reviewers) and the institutions promoting the films.

THE IDEA OF "TRIANGULATION"

From its inception, as we've explained, this was an ambitious project. But we wanted to conduct it in ways that could give some *measure of assurance* in our resultant claims. Trustworthiness of outcomes mattered to us—we didn't want to offer "just interpretations." Given these ambitions, it should not surprise that we were led towards the idea of "triangulation." "Triangulation" proposes that findings can be more trusted if they are arrived at and supported by more than one method, and based upon more than one body of materials. Mutually supporting outcomes are stronger, on this argument, than the singly supported. The idea of "triangulation" emerged and developed in the United States in the 1960s.[70] It came at a time when "old certainties" were being shaken. This was the period when qualitative research began to come into its own, with the rise of Grounded Theory. It was also the period in which qualitative researchers sought to assure themselves and others that their results could be trusted as much as the old-guard quantitative researchers, with their triad of "validity, reliability, generalisability."

Major work was done on the concept of "triangulation" in the 1970s by Norman Denzin.[71] Denzin importantly distinguished four kinds of triangulation: data, investigator, theoretical, and methodological. But from other people's developments of these, it is possible to see that a number of rather separate issues are being—perhaps unhelpfully—contained under one term.[72]

The central problem with "triangulation" was soon perceived, and argued most forcefully by one of Denzin's own colleagues, Yvonna Lincoln.[73] This was that research does not simply *reflect* the world it investigates; it *constructs* the materials differently according to its methods and assumptions. Therefore, the more precise and genuinely independent each of the contributory components, the less they will be *able* to support each other, because they will be formulated in incommensurable ways. So, imagine two researches into how audiences might "identify" with characters in a film, one using quantitative, the other using qualitative, methods. The quantitative analysis will typically theorise the implications of "identification" (for example, how can we measure the differences between high and low "identifiers"?) and operationalise these into questions. Responses to these will then be the *evidence* for or against the preconstituted idea of "identification." The qualitative research will typically stage situations of talk, in which people will be asked to say how they feel about the characters, and any use of the term *identification* (or near-synonyms) will be analysed. The analyst will then construct an account from this evidence. The problem is that in the first case the term *identification* has become a *specialist* concept, while the second seeks to gather *vernacular* concepts. The two do not mean the same thing, and cannot assist each other.[74] The price is, thus, that the *better in their own terms the individual researches, the less easily they can be measured against each other.* Only "loose" researches can be mutually supporting, if they are constructed independently of each other.

We tried something different. We endeavoured to incorporate means of triangulation *within* our research design, so that the form in which quantitative results were generated immediately pointed towards the qualitative stages of our investigations. Our codings and analyses of the prefigurative materials were designed to be tested by the second and third stages. Each part was designed to generate preliminary propositions for the next to take further. Upon consideration, we chose to give this a new name: the *methodological loop.* This "loop" derives from a complex way of conceiving the classic "circuit of culture—that is, the ways in which the production, distribution, and reception of cultural forms and meanings are interwoven.[75] Following are two rather different illustrations of how we believe that this has benefited our research. The first relates to the connections between our analysis of prefigurative materials and the ways in which our respondents drew upon these. In analysing audience responses, as already discussed, we had found that "Epic" was the most commonly chosen modality term, both across the world and within the United Kingdom. Our coding of media coverage allowed us, then, to ask which media source in the United Kingdom most used and emphasised this term. This turned out to be, unequivocally, the right-wing *Daily Mail,* which indeed issued a special edition to celebrate the film. That provokes interesting questions about the influence of this widely read newspaper. And certainly we could point to definite instances of its influence (quotations found only in its pages turned up in interview responses, for instance). However, we were also able to conduct a qualitative examination of the range of meanings of *epic* used within the *Mail* and among audiences. This revealed significant differences. Whilst the *Mail* presented an account of the film as about an *embattled society,* among audiences a different emphasis on *hope* indicated a rather different direction. This required looping back and forth between the two bodies of materials in order to disclose their relations.

The second was quite different. In our investigation of book-film relations, we realised early that people who were highly committed to the books could still greatly enjoy the films, whilst recognising many kinds of deviation from the original. We therefore turned our attention to the ways in which New Line Cinema *sought to explain and justify* its handling of the books. A prime resource for this turned out to be the extended DVDs of the films. Our analysis of these threw up a paradox. Our audiences clearly demonstrated in very many cases that they were waiting until they had the final extended edition before finalising their judgements on the films. We therefore examined that by comparison with the previous two—and found (as shown in chapter 5) that this offered a *new justification* of the changes. We could best make sense of this if we conceived New Line Cinema as working with a distinct model of audience behaviours—a "figure" of the audience—within which the DVDs provide the *point of sedimentation* of people's responses. This was therefore not simply a loop in our methods—moving back and forth between different parts of our research material—but a discovery of a *strategic recognition in the producers* of the same kind.

In both cases, we believe something very complicated is involved, and more than simply a *method*. It involved a way of conceiving the relations between the production, marketing, circulation, and reception of the film in which the *producers themselves* held and worked with conceptions of these kinds.

CLOSING REMARKS

In very many ways, including in its methodologies, the *LotR* project was an experiment. We took chances, and tried things to see what happened—both in gathering data and materials and in their analysis. To a considerable extent, we wanted to find out how far we could go, and to see what could be learnt if we asked new questions in new ways. It might have gone horribly wrong—but it didn't. We have tried to indicate clearly where we are sure of our findings and where we have to be much more tentative. We know that we have walked tightropes in some of our methodological moves, but again we have tried to declare and show these so that they can be examined critically. Methodology, to us, is a two-way path. It is vitally important that all processes and claims should stand up to critical scrutiny, and that means that there have to be many kinds of shared checks on validity and trustworthiness. But methodology is also about enabling—developing and sharing new means of formulating questions, gathering data and materials, and analysing them.

A big and ambitious project, then, designed from the start, through its methods of gathering, to allow a wide range of theoretical and methodological approaches to work on its data and materials. In this book you will have found a *core set* of our findings, but these will be only a small proportion of what has already emerged, and will continue to emerge, from this project. Henceforth the judgements on the quality of the achievements will not be ours, and that is as it should be.

The World Data Set

The following tables present the raw data from the project's world questionnaire. Any researchers interested in exploring the dataset for themselves may do so by approaching the UK Economic and Social Data Services.

What did you think of the film?

Extremely enjoyable	17,449	70.8%
Very enjoyable	5,148	20.9%
Reasonably enjoyable	1,578	6.4%
Hardly enjoyable	262	1.1%
Not enjoyable at all	201	0.8%
No answer	109	

How important was it to see the film?

Extremely important	14,732	59.7%
Very important	5,987	24.2%
Reasonably important	3,043	12.3%
Hardly important	639	2.6%
Not important at all	284	1.2%
No answer	62	

What kind of story is *The Lord of the Rings* for you? Please choose up to three.

Allegory	2,586	3.8%
Epic	13,044	19.2%
Fairytale	2,808	4.1%
Fantasy	9,885	14.5%
Game-world	531	0.7%
Good vs evil	10,734	15.8%
Myth/legend	8,897	13.1%
Quest	8,288	12.2%
SFX film	5,572	8.2%
Spiritual journey	1,877	2.8%
Threatened homeland	1,688	2.5%
War story	2,174	3.2%

What was the main source of your expectations?

The books	13,343	59.6%
The director	326	1.5%
One of the stars	434	1.9%
The first two parts of the film	7,334	32.8%
A game associated with the film	150	0.6%
Nothing in particular	803	3.6%
Other answers	2,357	

Sex

Male	12,174	(50.1%)
Female	12,108	(49.9%)

Age

Under 16	2,486	10.2%
16–25	11,722	47.9%
26–35	5,938	24.3%
36–45	2,563	10.4%
46–55	1,305	5.3%
56–65	364	1.5%
Over 65	103	0.4%

How often have you seen *Fellowship of the Ring*?

Once	3,321
More than once	20,948
Not at all	219

How often have you seen *Two Towers*?

Once	3,851
More than once	19,882
Not at all	341

How many times have you read the books of *The Lord of the Rings*?

Read all three books once	5,195	21.2%
Read all three more than once	11,614	47.4%
Read some of the books	1,625	6.6%
Still reading for the first time	1,603	6.5%
Haven't read them at all	4,469	18.2%

Where do you live? (top twenty response levels)

United States	4,744
Netherlands	3,275
United Kingdom	3,057
Denmark	1,677
Spain	1,584
Belgium	1,378
Germany	1,161
China	1,087
Slovenia	966
France	649
Australia	551
Greece	500
Canada	485
Italy	483
Turkey	334
Norway	296
Chile	224
Colombia	194
New Zealand	156
Sweden	148
Other countries	1,790

Notes

INTRODUCTION. RESEARCHING *THE LORD OF THE RINGS*: AUDIENCES AND CONTEXTS

1. Pierre Bourdieu, *Distinction: A Social Critique of Judgement of Taste* (London: Routledge, 1986), 32, 271–272.
2. Janet Staiger, *Interpreting Films: Studies in the Historical Reception of American Cinema* (Princeton, NJ: Princeton University Press, 1992).
3. Thomas Austin, *Hollywood, Hype and Audiences: Selling and Watching Popular Film in the 1990s* (Manchester: Manchester University Press, 2002), 1.
4. Kim Schrøder, Kirsten Drotner, Stephen Kline, and Catherine Murray, *Researching Audiences* (London: Arnold, 2003); Janet Staiger, *Media Reception Studies* (New York: New York University Press, 2005), 17–94; Robert Holub, *Reception Theory: A Critical Introduction* (New York: Methuen, 1984); Arild Fetveit, "Anti-Essentialism and Reception Studies," *International Journal of Cultural Studies* 4, no. 2 (2001): 173–199.
5. See Laura Mulvey, "Visual Pleasure and Narrative Cinema," *Screen* 16, no. 3 (1975); republished in Tony Bennett, S. Boyd-Bowman, C. Mercer, and Joan Woollacott, eds., *Popular Television and Film* (London: BFI, 1981), 206–215; David Bordwell, *Making Meaning: Inference and Rhetoric in the Interpretation of Cinema* (Cambridge, MA: Harvard University Press, 1989).
6. Recent overviews of such interest are to be found in the work of Henry Jenkins, Matt Hills, Martin Barker, and Ernest Mathijs, but some discussions of these concerns go back way further. See Henry Jenkins, "Reception Theory and Audience Research: The Mystery of the Vampire's Kiss," in Christine Gledhill and Linda Williams, eds., *Reinventing Film Studies* (London: Arnold, 2000), 165–182; Matt Hills, *Fan Cultures* (London: Routledge, 2002); Robert Wyatt and David Badger, "What Newspaper Critics Value in Film and Film Criticism," in Bruce Austin, ed., *Current Research in Film: Audience, Economics, and Law* (Norwood, NJ: Ablex

Publishing Corporation, 1985), 54–72; Greg Taylor, *Artists in the Audience: Cult, Camp and American Film Criticism* (Princeton, NJ: Princeton University Press, 1999); Ernest Mathijs, "Bad Reputations: The Reception of Trash Cinema," *Screen* 46, no. 4 (2005): 451–472 ; Bruce Austin, "Portrait of a Cult Film Audience," *Journal of Communication* 31 (1980): 43–54; Bruce Austin, "Critics' and Consumers' Evaluation of Motion Pictures: A Longitudinal Test of the Taste Culture and Elite Hypotheses," *Journal of Popular Film* 10, no. 4 (1983): 156–167; Barbara Wilinsky, *Sure Seaters: The Emergence of Art House Cinema* (Minneapolis: University of Minnesota Press, 2000); Martin Barker, Jane Arthurs, and Ramaswami Harindranath, *The Crash Controversy: Censorship Campaigns and Film Reception* (London: Wallflower Press, 2001); Annette Hill, *Shocking Entertainment: Responses to Violent Movies* (Luton: University of Luton Press, 1997).

7. Such an integrated approach is advocated by Barbara Klinger, "Film History Terminable and Interminable: Recovering the Past in Reception Studies," *Screen* 38, no. 2 (1997): 107–128.

8. For a bibliography of different prints and editions of Tolkien's writings, including translations, see Wayne Hammond, ed., with Douglas A. Anderson, *J.R.R. Tolkien: A Descriptive Bibliography* (Winchester: St. Paul's Bibliographies, 1993).

9. Neil Isaacs and Rose Zimbardo, eds., *Tolkien and the Critics* (Notre Dame, IN: University of Notre Dame Press, 1968); also see Neil Isaacs and Rose Zimbardo, eds., *Understanding the Lord of the Rings: The Best of Tolkien Criticism* (London: Houghton Mifflin Company, 2005); Richard C. West, *Tolkien Criticism: An Annotated Check List* (Kent, OH: Kent State University Press, 1981).

10. For a selection of work along these lines over the years (with some emphasis on early examples), see Lin Carter, *Tolkien: A Look behind the Lord of the Rings* (New York: Ballantine Books, 1969); Gunnar Urang, *Shadows of Heaven: Religion and Fantasy in the Writings of C.S. Lewis, Charles Williams, and J.R.R. Tolkien* (London: United Church Press, 1971); Lee D. Rossi, *The Politics of Fantasy: C.S. Lewis and J.R.R. Tolkien* (Ann Arbor, MI: UMI Press, 1971); Randel Helms, *Tolkien's Worlds* (London: Thames and Hudson, 1974); Tom Shippey, *The Road to Middle Earth* (London: Grafton, 1982); David Harvey, *The Song of Middle Earth* (London: Allen and Unwin, 1985); Marli Schütze, *Neue Wege nach Narnia und Mitelerde: Handlungskonstituenten in der Fantasy-Literatur von C.S. Lewis and J.R.R. Tolkien* (Berlin: Lang, 1986); Jane Chance, *The Lord of the Rings: The Mythology of Power* (Lexington: University of Kentucky Press, 1992–2001); Jared Lobdell, ed., *A Tolkien Compass* (New York: Open Court, 2002); Wayne G. Hammond and Christina Scull, *The Lord of the Rings: A Reader's Companion* (London: HarperCollins, 2005).

11. In a defence against indignations, Terry Pratchett sums up some criticisms of *The Lord of the Rings* as a "cult classic" that is "inexplicably popular but unworthy." See Terry Pratchett, "Cult Classic," in Karen Haber, ed., *Meditations on Middle-Earth* (London: Simon and Schuster, 2001), 75.

12. Isaacs and Zimbardo, *Tolkien and the Critics*, 1.

13. David Glover, "Utopia and Fantasy in the Late 1960s: Burroughs, Moorcock, Tolkien," in Chris Pawling, ed., *Popular Fiction and Social Change* (Basingstoke: Macmillan, 1984): 185–211; Brian Rosebury, *Tolkien: A Cultural Phenomenon* (Basingstoke: Palgrave Macmillan, 2003); Anne C. Petty, *One Ring to Bind Them All: Tolkien's Mythology* (Tuscaloosa: University of Alabama Press, 2002); Gregory Bassham and Eric Bronsson, eds., *The Lord of the Rings and Philosophy: One Book to Rule Them All* (New York: Open Court, 2003); Peter Kreeft, *The Philosophy of Tolkien: The Worldview behind the Lord of the Rings* (New York: Ignatius Press, 2005); Mark Eddy Smith, *Tolkien's Ordinary Virtues: Discovering the Spiritual Themes of the Lord of the Rings* (Downers Grove, IL: Inter-Varsity Press, 2002); Ean Begg, *Lord of the Rings and the Signs of the Times* (London: Guild of Pastoral Psychology, 1975); Patrick Curry, *Defending Middle-Earth: Tolkien—Myth and Modernity* (Great Barrington, MA: Floris Books, 1997); Hal Colebatch, *Return of the Heroes: The Lord of the Rings, Star Wars, and Contemporary Culture* (Canberra: Australian Institute for Public Policy, 1990).

14. For a bibliography of these fan criticisms, see *http://www.uni-klu.ac.at/~jkoeberl/Courses/ Tolkien/biblio.pdf* (accessed May 15, 2006).
15. Probably the earliest studies from this perspective are John S. Ryan, *Tolkien, Cult or Culture?* (Armidale, New South Wales: University Press of New England, 1969); and Bruce A. Beatie, "The Tolkien Phenomenon: 1954–1968," *Journal of Popular Culture* 3, no. 4 (1970): 689–703. Others include Nigel Walmsley, "Tolkien and the '60s," in Robert Giddings, ed., *J. R. R. Tolkien, This Far Land* (London and Totawa, NJ: Barnes & Noble Books, 1984): 73–85; Martin Barker, "On Being a 1960s Tolkien Reader," in Ernest Mathijs and Murray Pomerance, eds., *From Hobbits to Hollywood: Essays on Peter Jackson's The Lord of the Rings* (New York: Rodopi, 2006), 81–100; Tracie S. Speake, "The Power of the Ring: J R R Tolkien and American Popular Culture," *The Sextant* 1 (Summer 2003): 71–86.
16. Rosebury, 1–3.
17. The sheer quantity of its producers' archived materials, deposited with the New Zealand Film Archive, attests to this and is a resource still awaiting research.
18. See Vivian Sobchack: "Most Hollywood historical epics not only repeat the narrative within the film through a doubling narration but also repeat that narrative outside of the film—within its cinematic discourse." "'Surge and Splendour': A Phenomenology of the Hollywood Historical Epic," in Barry Keith Grant, ed., *Film Genre Reader II* (Austin: University of Texas Press, 1995), 280–307, this quotation 293.
19. Talk given to the Department of Screen and Media, University of Waikato, Hamilton, New Zealand, May 9, 2002. Botes has produced his own three-DVD documentary version, which New Line would not allow him to issue but which the company itself edited down into yet another *LotR* boxed set for issue in August 2006. The trilogy's texts are recycling still further with probable Blu-Ray and HD DVD issues. See "Short Ends," *Onfilm* 2 (2006): 13. After global success, the exhibition of properties from the project has returned to the nation's museum, Te Papa, and has attracted remarkable numbers again.
20. Richard A. Petersen and Narasimhan Anand, "The Production of Cultural Perspective," *Annual Review of Sociology* 30 (2004): 311.
21. Michael Dorland, "Policy Rhetorics of an Imaginary Cinema," in Albert Moran, ed., *Film Policy* (London: Routledge, 1996), 125.
22. David Hesmondhalgh, *The Cultural Industries* (London: Sage, 2002), 50.
23. G. Campbell, "Planet Middle Earth," *New Zealand Listener* (December 15, 2001), 18–24.
24. See Sandy George, "Gunning for a Bigger Stage," *Screen International* (November 12, 2004). See also the *Year 2005 Production Report* from the U.S. Center for Entertainment Industry Data and Research, which cites a 531 percent increase in film production in Australasia from 1998 to 2005, available at http://www.ceidr.org/2005CEIDRReport.pdf (accessed August 4, 2006).
25. See P. J. Huffstutter, "Not Just a Tolkien Amount: 'The Lord of the Rings' Movie Trilogy Boosts Tourism and Brings Other Benefits to New Zealand; Locals Call It the 'Frodo Economy,'" available at http://www.newsday.com/entertainment/news (accessed September 16, 2005).
26. Geoff Lealand and Helen Martin, "Aotearea/New Zealand," *Australian Screen Education* 39 (2004): 15.
27. Bertha Chin and Jonathan Gray, "'One Ring to Rule Them All': Pre-viewers and Pre-Texts of the *Lord of the Rings* Films," *Intensities: Journal of Cult Media* 2 (2001) (accessed May 11, 2006).
28. Rumour in fact has it that the trilogy may have made back its entire negative costs from licensing agreements before even the first film was released. "No quaint cottage industry anymore, marketing Middle-earth has assumed a world-girdling corporate form, a behemoth encompassing publishers, merchandisers, law firms, webmasters, not to mention countless hordes of opportunistic hangers-on. For sheer commerciality, *Rings* has arguably become the most profitable fictional work of all time. . . . New Line Cinema's 300-plus international licensing agreements alone recouped the movie trilogy's $300 million price tag months before the first film even hit the mul-

tiplex." Ethan Gilsdorf, "Lord of the Gold Ring," *Boston Globe* (November 16, 2003). Couple that with the New Zealand tax advantages, and we have another of Hollywood's famous auditing miracles.

29. See, for instance, the official insider's guide to the films, the location guidebook, and stories from actors: Brian Sibley, *The Lord of the Rings: The Fellowship of the Ring Insider's Guide* (Boston: Houghton Mifflin, 2001); Andy Serkis and Gary Russell, *Gollum: How We Made Movie Magic* (Boston: Houghton Mifflin, 2003); Ian Brodie, *The Lord of the Rings Location Guidebook* (London: Harper Collins, 2003); Sean Astin and Joe Layden, *There and Back Again, an Actor's Tale: A Behind the Scenes Look at The Lord of the Rings* (London: Virgin Books, 2005).

30. See Warren Buckland and Chris Long, "Following the Money: *The Lord of the Rings* and the Culture of Box Office Figures," and Janet Wasko and Govind Shanadi, "More Than Just Rings: Merchandise for Them All," in Ernest Mathijs, ed., *The Lord of the Rings: Popular Culture in Global Context* (London: Wallflower Press, 2006).

31. See, for instance, Jane Chance, "Is There a Text in This Hobbit? Peter Jackson's *Fellowship of the Ring*," *Literature/Film Quarterly* 30, no. 2 (2002): 79–85; Jim Smith and J. Clive Matthews, *The 'Lord of the Rings': The Films, the Books, the Radio Series* (London: Virgin Books, 2004); Janet Brennan Croft, ed., *Tolkien on Film: Essays on Peter Jackson's The Lord of the Rings* (London: Mythopoeic Press, 2005); Lynnette R. Porter, *Unsung Heroes of 'The Lord of the Rings': From Page to Screen* (Westport, CT: Greenwood Press, 2005); Robert Eaglestone, *Reading The Lord of the Rings: New Writings on Tolkien's Trilogy* (London: Continuum, 2005). More recent developments in adaptation research have shifted to exploring the variety of ideological meanings that different adaptations achieve, along with a broader attention to the role of intertextual referencing within them. For good illustrations of both, see Robert Stam and Alessandra Raengo, eds., *Literature and Film* (Oxford: Blackwell, 2004).

32. Barry Keith Grant, *A Cultural Assault: The New Zealand Films of Peter Jackson* (Nottingham: Kakapo Books, 1999); Ron Magid, "Imagining Middle Earth," *American Cinematographer* 82, no. 12 (December 2001): 60–69; Iain Lowson, Keith Marshall, and Daniel O'Brien. *The World of the Rings* (Richmond, Surrey: Reynolds and Hearn, 2002); Harmony Wu, "Trading in Horror, Cult and Matricide: Peter Jackson's Phenomenal Bad Taste and New Zealand Fantasies of Inter/National Cinematic Success," in Mark Jancovich, Antonio Lazaro-Reboll, Julian Stringer, and Andrew Willis, eds., *Defining Cult Movies: The Cultural Politics of Oppositional Taste* (Manchester: Manchester University Press, 2003), 84–108; Ian Pryor, *Peter Jackson: From Prince of Splatter to Lord of the Rings* (New York: St. Martin's Press, 2004); Greg Wright, *Peter Jackson in Perspective: The Power behind Cinema's The Lord of the Rings: A Look at Hollywood's Take on Tolkien's Epic Tale* (Los Angeles, CA: Hollywood Jesus Books, 2004); Alec Worley, *Empires of the Imagination: A Critical Survey of Fantasy Cinema from Georges Méliès to The Lord of the Rings* (New York: McFarland & Company, 2005).

33. Michael N. Stanton, *Hobbits, Elves and Wizards* (New York: St. Martin's Press , 2002); Hal G. P. Colebatch, *Return of the Heroes: The Lord of the Rings, Star Wars, Harry Potter and Social Conflict* (Perth: Cyber Editions Corporation, 2003); Russell W. Dalton, *Faith Journey through Fantasy Lands: A Christian Dialogue with Harry Potter, Star Wars and The Lord of the Rings* (Minneapolis, MN: Augsburg Fortress, 2004); Anna Dawson, *Studying The Lord of the Rings* (London: Auteur Publishing, 2006).

34. See the chapters by Douglas Kellner, Sean Cubitt, Ken Gelder (on the cultural significance of *The Lord of the Rings'* themes), and Ian Conrich and Jennifer Brayton (on merchandising and fandoms) in Mathijs and Pomerance. Also see the chapters by Jenny Lawn and Bronwyn Beatty and Davinia Thornley (on the New Zealand reception), and Matt Hills, Kirsten Pullen, and Judith Rosenbaum (on fandoms) in Mathijs, *The Lord of the Rings: Popular Culture*. Also see Elana Shefrin, "Lord of the Rings, Star Wars, and Participatory Fandom: Mapping New Congruencies between the Internet and Media Entertainment Culture," *Critical Studies in*

Media Communication 2, no. 3 (2004): 261–281; Suman Basuroy, Subimal Chatterjee, and S. Abraham Ravid, "How Critical Are Critical Reviews? The Box Office Effects of Film Critics, Star Power, and Budgets," *Journal of Marketing* 67, no. 4 (2003): 103–117.

35. See the chapters by Erik Hedling ("Framing Tolkien: Trailers, High Concept, and the Ring"), Jonathan Gray ("Bonus Material: The DVD Layering of *The Lord of the Rings*"), Jon Dovey and Helen Kennedy ("Playing the Ring: Intermediality and Ludic Narratives in the *Lord of the Rings* Games"), K. J. Donnelly ("Musical Middle-Earth"), and I. Q. Hunter ("Tolkien Dirty") in Mathijs, *The Lord of the Rings: Popular Culture.*

36. A substantial account of this can be found in Kate Egan and Martin Barker, "*Rings* around the World: Notes on the Challenges, Problems and Possibilities of International Audience Projects," *Participations: Online Journal of Audience & Reception Studies* 3, no. 2 (2006).

37. This project simply would not have been possible without the funding from the U.K. Economic and Social Research Council. We also acknowledge the additional funding from the University of Wales, Aberystwyth, which allowed us to extend the project by five months, enabling a much fuller achievement. Colleagues in some other countries also received funding to support their work, and acknowledgements of these are to be found in specific chapters. A full list of participants and contributors is given in the acknowledgements. We also want to extend our special thanks to Janet Jones, now of the University of the West of England, Bristol, who was originally part of the U.K. team, but who had to withdraw for health reasons. Her early contribution was enormously valuable.

38. The countries were Australia, Austria, Belgium, Canada, China, Colombia, Denmark, France, Germany, Greece, Italy, The Netherlands, New Zealand, Norway, Russia, Slovenia, Spain, Turkey, the United Kingdom, and the United States.

39. See Ariel Dorfman and Armand Mattelart, *How to Read Donald Duck: Imperialist Ideology in the Disney Comic* (New York: International General, 1973); Harold A. Innis, *Empire and Communications* (Oxford: Oxford University Press, 1950). For an excellent introduction to both stances, see Marita Sturken and Lisa Cartwright, *Practices of Looking: An Introduction to Visual Culture* (Oxford: Oxford University Press, 2001).

40. Sonia Livingstone, "On the Challenges of Cross-national Comparative Media Research," *European Journal of Communication* 18, no. 4 (2003): 477–500; Annabelle Sreberny, "The Global and the Local in International Communications," in James Curran and Michael Gurevitch, eds., *Mass Media and Society* (London: Arnold, 2000), 93–119.

41. Tamar Liebes and Elihu Katz, *The Export of Meaning: Cross Cultural Readings of Dallas* (Cambridge: Polity Press, 1993); Ernest Mathijs and Janet Jones, eds., *Big Brother International: Critics, Formats and Publics* (London: Wallflower Press, 2004); Janet Wasko, Mark Phillips, and Eileen R Meehan, eds., *Dazzled by Disney? The Global Disney Audiences Project* (Leicester: Leicester University Press, 2001).

42. See Joshua David Bellin, *Framing Monsters: Fantasy Film and Social Alienation* (Carbondale: Southern Illinois University Press, 2005); Richard Dyer, *Only Entertainment* (London: Routledge, 2002); Andrew Gordon, "Science-Fiction and Fantasy Film Criticism: The Case of Lucas and Spielberg," *Journal of the Fantastic in the Arts* 2, no. 2 (1989): 81–94; James Donald, *Fantasy and the Cinema* (London: British Film Institute, 1989); Dorfman and Mattelart.

43. Among the best studies of this kind that we know, we would mention Máire Messenger Davies, *Fake, Fact, and Fantasy: Children's Interpretations of Television Reality* (Mahwah, NJ: Erlbaum, 1997); Maya Götz et al., *Media and the Make-Believe Worlds of Children: When Harry Potter Meets Pokémon in Disneyland* (Mahwah, NJ: Lawrence Erlbaum, 2005).

44. See Mathijs, "Bad Reputations"; Janet Staiger, "Hitchcock in Texas: Intertextuality in the Face of Blood and Gore," in her *Perverse Spectators: The Practices of Film Reception* (New York: New York University Press, 2000), 179–187; Cynthia Erb, *Tracking King Kong: A Hollywood Icon in World Culture* (Detroit, MI: Wayne State University Press, 1998).

45. Justin Lewis has commented on this summary dismissal, pointing out that, aside from the problematic work we talk of here, there is a more valuable tradition of work arising from the American mass communications tradition exemplified by people such as Andrea Press. And Andy Ruddock (*Understanding Audiences* [London: Sage, 2001]), among others, has argued for abiding benefits of the uses and gratifications approach. We are happy to acknowledge these other strands, but maintain our view that the *dominant* position is as we have described it. A look at the pattern of research presentations at any year's International Communication Association Conference, we think, will indicate its continuing force.

46. A very recent example. In a book summarising the current "state of the art," one essay by Rhodes and Hamilton discusses the Third Person effect. This well-attested phenomenon records that very many people believe that they are not influenced by, for instance, violence on television, but are worried about their impact on others. David Buckingham (*Public Secrets: 'EastEnders' and Its Audience* (London: British Film Institute, 1987), for instance, has noted this, and argued that parents—who know their own from close proximity—may worry about their children being *frightened,* but do not believe that they are *made violent.* In mass communications/media psychology, however, this translates into a *conviction that we as researchers know better than the parents can,* and that our job is to "educate" them to believe that they *are* harmed, even if they deny it (see Nancy Rhodes and James C. Hamilton, "Attribution and Entertainment: It's Not Whodunit but Why," in Jennings Bryant and Peter Vorderer, eds., *The Psychology of Entertainment* [Mahwah, NJ: Lawrence Erlbaum, 2006], esp. 121).

47. For discussion and debate on these issues, see *Communication Review* 9, no. 2 (2006).

48. Sonia Livingstone and Moira Bovill, eds., *Children and Their Changing Media Environment: A European Comparative Study* (Mahwah, NJ: Lawrence Erlbaum, 2001).

49. Barker et al.; Martin Barker, "Loving and Hating *Straw Dogs:* The Meanings of Audience Responses to a Controversial Film," *Participations: Online Journal of Audience & Reception Studies* 2, no. 2 (2005), and 3, no. 1 (2006); Martin Barker and Ernest Mathijs, "Understanding Vernacular Experiences of Film in an Academic Environment," *Art, Design and Communication in Higher Education* 4, no. 1 (2005): 49–71.

50. One particularly apt example is J. P. Telotte, "The Blair Witch Project Project: Film and the Internet," *Film Quarterly* 54, no. 3 (2001): 32–39.

51. See Fernand Braudel, *On History* (Chicago: University of Chicago Press, 1982); Klinger.

52. See Jean Baudrillard, *For a Critique of the Political Economy of the Sign* (St. Louis, MO: Telos Press, 1973). For a critical assessment, see Douglas Kellner, "Boundaries and Borderlines: Reflections on Jean Baudrillard and Critical Theory," in *Illuminations, the Critical Theory Website,* available at http://www.uta.edu/huma/illuminations/ke112.htm.

53. Martin Barker, "News, Reviews, Clues, Interviews, and Other Ancillary Materials: A Critique and Research Proposal," *Scope, an Online Journal of Film Studies* (February 2004), available at http://www.nottingham.ac.uk/film/scopearchive/articles/news-reviews.htm (accessed May 2006).

54. Even this research project will have added to the "noise" around the film. Several media reported on the project, and its existence made "newsworthy" "talk" in itself. Most reports were positive or neutral; some were hostile. We are still proud to have been called names by the English tabloid paper the *Sun* (there is honestly no better route to credibility than that). An error in currency conversion led one American newspaper (*USA Today*) to believe we were going to pay our research assistant an exorbitant salary, which generated even more talk, and hundreds of applications for the post (much to the desperation of our personnel office). See "Fraud of the Rings," *Sun* (December 20, 2003); Martin Wainwright, "Worldwide Quest for the Magic of Middle Earth," *Guardian* (December 20, 2003).

55. For an exploration and application of this, see Mathijs, "Bad Reputations"; Ernest Mathijs, "Reviews, Previews, and Premieres: The Critical Reception of *The Lord of the Rings* in the United

Kingdom," in Mathijs, *The Lord of the Rings: Popular Culture.*

56. See Rick Altman, *Film/Genre* (London: British Film Institute, 1999); Bordwell; Kendall Walton, "How Remote Are Fictional Worlds from the Real World?", *Journal of Aesthetics and Art Criticism* 37, no. 1 (1978): 11–23; Kendall Walton, *Mimesis as Make-Believe* (Cambridge, MA: Harvard University Press, 1995); "Fearing Fictions," *Journal of Philosophy* 75, no. 1 (1978): 5–27; David Lewis, "Possible Worlds," in Michael M. Loux, ed., *The Possible and the Actual: Readings in the Metaphysics of Modality* (Ithaca, NY: Cornell University Press, 1979), 182–189; Nicholas Rescher, *A Theory of Possibility* (Oxford: Blackwell, 1975). For an examination of how Lewis and Rescher can be applied to film analysis, see Thomas Elsaesser and Warren Buckland, *Studying Contemporary American Film: A Guide to Movie Analysis* (London: Arnold, 2002), 212.

57. See, for instance, Gunther Kress and Theo van Leeuwen, *Multimodal Discourse: The Modes and Media of Contemporary Communication* (London: Arnold, 2001).

58. The four books that arose from two London conferences on Hollywood and its audiences all contain materials of relevance here: Melvyn Stokes and Richard Maltby, eds., *American Movie Audiences: From the Turn of the Century to the Early Sound Era* (London: British Film Institute, 1999), *Identifying Hollywood's Audiences: Cultural Identity and the Movies* (1999), *Hollywood Spectatorship: Changing Perceptions of Cinema Audiences* (2001), *Hollywood Abroad: Audiences and Cultural Exchange* (2004). In addition, it is worth considering among other things Tom Stempel, *American Audiences on Movies and Moviegoing* (Lexington: University Press of Kentucky 2001); Jeffrey Richards and Dorothy Sheridan, eds., *Mass-Observation at the Movies* (London: Routledge & Kegan Paul, 1987). Vivian Sobchack opened up a relevant theoretical line of enquiry in her *The Address of the Eye: A Phenomenology of Film Experience* (Princeton, NJ: Princeton University Press, 1992).

59. This is the outcome of a great deal of research on fans, for instance. See in particular Henry Jenkins, *Textual Poachers* (London: Routledge, 1992). See also, in connection with film audiences, Barker and Brooks, *Knowing Audiences: Judge Dredd, Its Friends, Fans and Foes* (Luton: University of Luton Press, 1998).

60. An essay exploring some of these problems is forthcoming—see Martin Barker, "Discourse Analysis and the Problem of Researching 'Impossible Objects,'" in Mike Pickering, ed., *Cultural Studies Methods* (Edinburgh: Edinburgh University Press, 2008).

61. We are still analysing this aspect of the research. One striking finding already to have emerged is that there is a surprising, highly structured difference between those whose answers indicate use of digital sources (the Internet and World Wide Web) versus those using only conventional (press, television, and so on). The former show a more *emotionally committed* response with a stronger sense of *belonging to a community.*

62. The details of that project were published in Barker, Arthurs, and Harindranath.

63. Chinese, Danish, Dutch, English, French, German, Greek, Italian, Norwegian, Russian, Slovenian, Spanish, Turkish, and Welsh.

64. A minimal amount of data cleaning was necessary. In a small number of cases, double-clicking the "submit" button caused two entries in the database. We found just one simply abusive response, and deleted it as pointless.

65. We will not list all conference papers members of the teams made in relation to the project, but we would like to highlight a few occasions where different teams of the project made presentations: Lothar Mikos, Susanne Eichner, Elizabeth Prommer, and Michael Wedel of the Hochschule für Film und Fernsehen organised a conference/workshop on the methodology of the project, in Potsdam (April 30–May 1, 2004); Martin Barker, Kate Egan, and Ernest Mathijs organised the closing conference of the project in Gregynog, Aberystwyth (December 10–12, 2004); team presentations were made at the ESA Research Network for the Sociology of the Arts conference (Rotterdam, November 3–5, 2004), the Society for Cinema and Media Studies conference (London, March 30–April 1, 2005), and the International Communications

Association conference (New York, May 26–30, 2005). Martin Barker also presented findings from the project at the Tolkien Society annual conferences in 2004 and 2005. Details of the papers and participants can be found at the websites of the respective organising societies.

Publications directly stemming from the project include: Martin Barker, "*The Lord of the Rings* and 'Identification': A Critical Encounter," *European Journal of Communication* 20, no. 3 (2005): 353–378; Daniel Biltereyst and Giselinde Kuipers, eds., *Tijdschrift voor Communicatiewetenschap en Mediacultuur* 34, no. 1; Wasko and Shanadi; Daniel Biltereyst and Philippe Meers, "Blockbusters and/as Event: Distributing and Launching *The Lord of the Rings*"; Mathijs, "Reviews, Previews and Premieres"; Susanne Eichner, Lothar Mikos, and Michael Wedel, "'*Apocalypse Now* in Middle-Earth': 'Genre' in the Critical Reception of *The Lord of the Rings* in Germany"; Anne Jerslev, "Sacred Viewing: Emotional Responses to *The Lord of the Rings*"; Mariano Longo, "Cooperation versus Violence: An Ethnographical Analysis of *The Return of the King* Video Game"; Stan Jones, "Fixing a Heritage: Inscribing Middle Earth onto New Zealand," in Mathijs, ed., *The Lord of the Rings: Popular Culture;* Martin Barker and Ernest Mathijs, "Seeing the Promised Land from Afar: Perceptions of New Zealand by Overseas *Lord of the Rings* Audiences," in Adam Lam and Nataliya Oryshchuk, eds., *How We Became Middle-Earth: A Collection of Essays on The Lord of the Rings* (London: Walking Tree Publishers, 2007).

ONE. *THE LORD OF THE RINGS:* SELLING THE FRANCHISE

1. This chapter draws on material presented in Janet Wasko and Govind Shanadi, "More Than Just Rings: Merchandise for Them All," in Mathijs, ed., *The Lord of the Rings: Popular Culture*, 23–42.
2. New Line Entertainment, "About Us," available at http://www.newline.com/about/index.shtml (accessed January 28, 2004).
3. Jonathan Bing and Cathy Dunkley, "Kiddy Litter Rules H'wood," *Variety* (January 8, 2002), 1.
4. David Rooney, "Not of This Earth," *Variety* (January 4, 2004), 1.
5. "Toy Biz Granted Master Toy License for One of the Most Highly-Anticipated Film Franchises of All-Time," *Business Wire* (June 12, 2000), available at http://www.licensingmedia.com/news/html/ddhistory2000.html (accessed April 30, 2004).
6. Michael White, *The Life and Work of J. R. R. Tolkien* (Indianapolis, IN: Alpha Publishers, 2002).
7. White, *Life.*
8. There is a discrepancy in the reporting of ownerships rights at this point in time. Lowson et al. say that UA maintained some rights, but the National Arbitration Forum states that Zaentz has held the rights since 1976. See Iain Lowson, Keith Marshall, and Daniel O'Brien, *World of the Rings: The Unauthorized Guide to the World of J.R.R. Tolkien* (London: Reynolds and Hearn, 2002); National Arbitration Forum, "Start-up Trademark Opposition Policy Decision: The Saul Zaentz Company v. Gandalf R.r.1.," Claim Number: FA0112000103063 (February 19, 2002).
9. Miramax actually began development of the first film, but let it go into turnaround to New Line because they couldn't commit to financing three films at one time. Thus, Miramax also receives a piece of the "backend" of the films (Adam Dawtrey, "Will 'Lord' Ring New Line's Bell?" *Variety* (May 21–27, 2001).
10. See National Arbitration Forum.
11. White, 252.
12. Hugh Davies, "Lord of the Rings Royalties Owner Issues Pounds 11m Writ," *London Daily Telegraph* (August 20, 2004), 7.
13. See Vanessa Juarez and Misty Schwartz, "Hell on Middle-Earth," *Entertainment Weekly* (December 15, 2006), 17–18. This suit plus other copyright issues are currently complicating

plans for the production of *The Hobbit*. Also, in 2003, Viggo Mortensen led a group of actors in their demands for more compensation, and received undisclosed bonuses from New Line.

14. Nina Munk, *Fools Rush In* (New York: HarperCollins, 2004), 256.
15. John Lewis, "Following the Money in America's Sunniest Company Town," in Julian Stringer, ed., *Movie Blockbusters* (London: Routledge, 2003), 61–71.
16. Biltereyst and Meers, "Blockbusters."
17. See MPAA, "Research and Statistics," available at http://www.mpaa.org/researchStatistics.asp (accessed November 1, 2006).
18. See www.boxofficemojo.movies; see also John Horn, "Crossed Swords, Cold Cash," *Newsweek* (December 10, 2001), 78.
19. Stephen Galloway, "Movies and the Media: Marketing Expenditures Spiral Ever Upward . . . ," *Hollywood Reporter* (July 1, 2006), available at http://www.hollywoodreporter.com/hr/search/article_display.jsp?vnu_content_id=1003254883 (accessed November 17, 2006).
20. Toby Miller, Nitin Govil, John McMurria, and Richard Maxwell, *Global Hollywood* (London: British Film Institute, 2001).
21. Dawtrey, "Will 'Lord' Ring New Line's Bell?" *Variety* (May 21–27, 2001).
22. Biltereyst and Meers, "Blockbusters," 81.
23. Dawtrey, 1.
24. "The Fellowship of New Line," *Primedia* (September 2001): 1.
25. Dawtrey.
26. "'The Lord of the Rings' Generates More Than 350 Million Hits on Website as New Line Prepares to Unveil Footage in Cannes," *PR Newswire* (April 10, 2001).
27. Nigel Reynolds, "Stars Given Early Viewing of the First Hobbit Film," *Daily Telegraph* (May 11, 2001), 7.
28. Ibid.
29. Maris Matzer Rose, "NL 'Rings' in New Strategy," *Hollywood Reporter* (December 5, 2002), 1.
30. "26 million Lord of the Rings Bookmarks Help Deliver Youth Audience," *PR Web* (December 24, 2003), available at http://www.prweb.com/releases/2003/12/prweb95721.htm (accessed December 1, 2004).
31. Bill Higgins, "Outwellington'ed," *Variety* (December 8, 2003), 79.
32. Claude Brodesser and Paul Sweeting, "Longer Two Towers Headed to Theaters . . . ," *Video Business* (August 25, 2003), 7.
33. Andy Seiler, "The Line for 'Return of the King' Tickets Goes around the World," *USA Today* (November 28, 2003), 6E.
34. Pat O'Brien, "Tickets to 'Lord of the Rings' Trilogy up for Bid on eBay," *Press-Enterprise* (December 7, 2003), F10.
35. Dawtrey. See Eric Hedling, "Framing Tolkien: Trailers, High Concept and the Ring," in Mathijs, ed., 225–237, for more detailed discussion of the *LotR* trailers.
36. See Jonathan Gray, "Bonus Material: The DVD Layering of *The Lord of the Rings*," in Mathijs, ed., 238–253.
37. VNU, "The Rings' Lord over the Entertainment Industry" (December 19, 2003), available at http://www.nielsenmedika.com/newsrelease/2003/LOTR.htm (accessed November 17, 2006).
38. Aliya Sternstein, "Web Strategy Treads the Cutting Edge of High Tech," *Variety* (August 23–29, 2004), 41.
39. Ty Braswell, "In Search of QEIB: Gordon Paddison Interview," *imedia connection* (May 8, 2003), available at http://www.imediaconnection.com/content/1179.asp (accessed December 2, 2006).
40. Shefrin, 262.
41. Shefrin, 267.
42. Joseph Szadkowski, "All Things Middle Earth in Site about Film Trilogy," *Washington Times*

(December 27, 2003), B1.

43. "'The Lord of the Rings' Generates."
44. VNU; Sternstein.
45. Sternstein reports that there were 400 *LotR* sites when New Line opened its site, and 300,000 sites after the first film opened in December 2001.
46. Erik Davis, "The Fellowship of the Ring," *Wired Magazine* (October 2001): 120–132; Braswell; Sternstein.
47. Gillian Flynn, "*Lord of the Rings:* Ringmasters," *Entertainment Weekly* (November 16, 2001), 44.
48. Sternstein.
49. "'The Lord of the Rings' Generates."
50. Braswell.
51. Dawtrey, 1.
52. "The Fellowship."
53. Rose.
54. "The Fellowship."
55. "Airline to Middle-earth Scores a Flying Hat-Trick with New 'Lord of the Rings' 747," *Business Wire* (November 17, 2003).
56. New Line Entertainment, "New Line Home Entertainment Breaks New Ground with the Lord of the Rings: The Two Towers Adventure Card," Press Release (August 13, 2003).
57. Dawtrey.
58. Brodesser and Sweeting.
59. Doug Desjardins, "Hot Ad Campaigns Pump Up Video Release of Hit Films," *DSN Retailing Today* (June 10, 2002).
60. Janet Wasko, *How Hollywood Works* (London: Sage, 2003), 170.
61. Time Warner, *Factbook* (New York: Time Warner, Inc., 2003), 4.
62. "Who's Afraid of AOL Time Warner?" *The Economist* (January 24, 2002), available at http://www.economist.com/agenda/displayStory.cfm?Story_ID=952225 (accessed December 1, 2004).
63. Jill Goldsmith, "With Billions at Stake, Toy Biz Is No Longer Child's Play," *Variety* (June 9, 2002), 1.
64. Ian Markham-Smith, "Lord of the Rings Films and Products Set to Out-Magic Even Harry Potter," *TDC Trade* (December 28, 2001), available at http://www.tdctrade.com/imn/01122804/films05.htm# (accessed December 1, 2006).
65. "Movie's Merchandise Proving a Big Hit," *The Sentinel* (Stoke) (December 19, 2003), 6.
66. Teresa Howard, "Now Playing at a Toy Store Near You," *USA Today* (December 8, 2003), 10B.
67. "Rings Merchandise Hits $1.2 Billion," *Dominion Post* (April 30, 2004), 1.
68. A. W. Mathews, "Companies in Licensing Face-Off over 'Rings,'" *San Diego Union-Tribune* (December 21, 2001), E-7.
69. "Movie's Merchandise," 6.
70. Gail Schiller, "News: Marketing," *Hollywood Reporter* (June 10, 2004), 2.
71. Schiller.
72. Mark Rahner, "Lords of Merchandising Churn Out Tchotchkes," *Seattle Times* (December 14, 2003), K4.
73. Mark Monahan, "A Magic Formula to Print Cash," *Daily Telegraph* (September 29, 2001), available at http://www.telegraph.co.uk/arts/main.jhtml?xml=/arts/2001/09/29/bfpott29.xml (accessed December 1, 2006).
74. "New Line Cinema's 'Lord of the Rings: The Fellowship of the Rings' Ignites Marketplace," *PR Newswire* (January 15, 2002).
75. apple-style-span>L. M. Holson, "apple-style-span>A Franchise Fantasy,"apple-style-span> *New York Times* (November 9, 2003), Section 6, 28.

76. B apple-style-span>Ward, "37 Things about Lord of the Rings," *The Ottawa Citizen* (December 13, 2003), I-8.
77. See Wasko and Shanadi for a more detailed discussion of *LotR* merchandising.
78. Rahner.
79. Biltereyst and Meers, 84–85.
80. See Stephanie Schorow, "Beloved Tolkien Trilogy Sets Cash Registers Ringing," *Boston Herald* (October 23, 2004), 25.
81. Ethan Gilsdorf, "Lord of the Gold Ring," *Boston Globe* (November 16, 2003), 12.

TWO. AN AVALANCHE OF ATTENTION: THE PREFIGURATION AND RECEPTION OF *THE LORD OF THE RINGS*

1. Michael Atkinson, *Village Voice* (June 6, 2001).
2. Jürgen Habermas, *Strukturwandel der Öffentlichkeit* (Frankfurt: Suhrkamp Verlag, 1962).
3. For an elaboration of this approach, see Mathijs, *The Lord of the Rings: Popular Culture*, 6–9.
4. See selected chapters in Mathijs, *The Lord of the Rings: Popular Culture;* Mathijs and Pomerance, *From Hobbits to Hollywood.* As a symptomatic anecdote we would like to cite one story: in January 2007, New Line executive Robert Shaye announced he would not consider offering the direction of the in-development project *The Hobbit* to Peter Jackson as long as Jackson would not drop his lawsuit for arrears in royalties of *LotR* ("Jackson Barred from Filming Hobbit," *Vancouver Sun* [January 12, 2007], C11; "The Breaking of the Fellowship," *Empire* 212 [February 2007]: 24–25). This convolution of the aesthetic and the legal is indicative of how, as John Fiske has it, "the role of the insurance assessor becomes indistinguishable from that of the critic," and it demonstrates, once more, how the public presence of a film at its production level is never just about its textual or aesthetic properties. See John Fiske, "The Cultural Economy of Fandom," in Lisa A. Lewis, ed., *Adoring Audiences* (London: Routledge, 1992), 44.
5. We would like to acknowledge several archives that have made information on the prefiguration and reception of *LotR* available. The Belgian Royal Film Archive has been of tremendous assistance in providing press clippings from around the world, and the British Film Institute offered valuable assistance in collecting U.K.-based press materials. The Aberystwyth-based project enabled us to collect literally all the press materials relating to *The Return of the King* between October 2003 and January 2004, and gave access to invaluable information about 24,739 viewers' preferred use of prefigurative materials in their preparation for *The Return of the King.* Staff of the Koerner Library at the University of British Columbia assisted us in accessing virtually all North American press materials between 2001 and 2004. Online archives and numerous other sites have been helpful in completing an overall view of *LotR*'s public presence. We would also like to thank the teams and researchers in Australia, Belgium, China, France, Germany, Greece, Italy, The Netherlands, New Zealand, Russia, Slovenia, Spain, South Korea, the United Kingdom, and the United States for providing materials they collected from their own local press. The full total of materials used lies around 6,500.
6. See Davinia Thornley, "Wellywood and Peter Jackson: the Local Reception of *The Lord of the Rings* in Wellington New Zealand," in Mathijs, *The Lord of the Rings: Popular Culture,* 101.
7. See "Peter Jackson's Lord of the Rings at New Line" (posted August 23, 1998), available at www.aintitcool.com/node/1948.
8. See "Where My Faith in Peter Jackson and Lord of the Rings Comes From" (posted August 25, 1998), available at www.aintitcool.com/node/1970.
9. We use the term *hype* here in the meaning attributed to it by Biltereyst and Meers, 2006.
10. For a wider exploration of these developments, see Jennifer Lawn and Bronwyn Beatty, "On the Brink of a New Threshold of Opportunity: The Lord of the Rings and New Zealand Cultural

Policy," in Mathijs, *The Lord of the Rings: Popular Culture*, 43–60; and Barker and Mathijs, "Seeing the Promised Land from Afar."

11. Jamie Wilson, "The Lord of the Web Causes Chaos," *Globe and Mail* (June 23, 2000), R7; Fox News website via nzedge.com (July 7, 2000).

12. Mark Burman, "Hobbit Wanted," *Guardian* (July 30, 1999).

13. See Ernest Mathijs, "Reviews, Previews, and Premieres: The Critical Reception of *The Lord of the Rings* in the United Kingdom," in Mathijs, *The Lord of the Rings: Popular Culture*, 119–142. By far the weirdest connection to local British—or in this case Scottish—concerns and speculations about the impact of *The Lord of the Rings* is one short article in the *Scotsman*, in which the author expresses fears that a successful reception of the films might lead to a deterioration in personal hygiene among Britain's youth culture, inciting youngsters to be filthy. According to the writer, "Tolkien fanaticism has long been a barometer of idiocy and poor personal hygiene," and she is clearly scared that the films' popularity might encourage "dippy, unwashed" appearances (Hannah McGill, "Youth Culture Risks Picking Up a Filthy Hobbit," *Scotsman* [November 3, 2000], 5).

14. In some very early reports Sean Connery was also frequently mentioned, as a contender for the part of Gandalf; see "New Line Cinema," *Screen Finance* (September 7, 2000).

15. Jerry Mosher, "Morphing Sean Astin: Playing 'Fat' in the Age of Digital Animation," in Mathijs and Pomerance, 301–318.

16. Philip Kemp, "Gone to Earth," *Sight and Sound* 11, no.1 (January 2001): 23.

17. And it did not stop at national media. Regional media used similar tactics. *Wales on Sunday* reported on the move from shooting to postproduction of *The Lord of the Rings* on the back of the assumption that Tolkien's Welsh connection (he spent time as a youth in Mid Wales) would make the story of interest to readers.

18. It is indicative of the local penetration that even papers as local as the *Bristol Evening Post* (January 25, 2001) considered reporting on this part of their remit.

19. A typical example is the report in the Italian *Corriere Della Serra* (May 12, 2001), which highlights the prices and amounts of money at stake.

20. Erik Hedling, "Framing Tolkien: Trailers, High Concept, and the Ring," in Mathijs, *The Lord of the Rings: Popular Culture*, 225–237.

21. Julian Dibell, "Lord of the Geeks," *Village Voice* (June 6, 2001).

22. Specific case studies of the box office figures (from the opening weekend as well as the subsequent weeks and months), and the reception of the trailers, DVDs, soundtrack, spin-off spoofs (which of course also contribute to the presence of their subject of ridicule), distribution, the location industry (including museums, pilgrimages, and visits), and critical reception in New Zealand, Germany, Belgium, the United States, the United Kingdom, The Netherlands, and Denmark are available in Mathijs, *The Lord of the Rings: Popular Culture*; Mathijs and Pomerance; and Biltereyst and Kuipers, *Tijdschrift*.

23. Suman Basuroy, Subimal Chatterjee, and S. Abraham-Ravid, "How Critical Are Critical Reviews? The Box Office Effects of Film Critics, Star Power and Budgets," *Journal of Marketing* 67, no. 4 (2003): 103–117; Chin and Gray.

24. Roman Jakobson, *Essais de Linguistique Générale* (Paris: Editions du Minuit, 1963).

25. Shefrin.

26. For a more detailed overview of *LotR* fan activity we refer to selected chapters in Mathijs, *The Lord of the Rings: Popular Culture*, in particular the case studies by Kirsten Pullen and by Jennifer Brayton. Two remarkable characteristics of the *Lord of the Rings* fandom are its high degree of media literacy (see the chapter by Judith Rosenbaum), and its sense of an imagined community—a feeling of shared thought. See also Mathijs and Pomerance.

27. *Houston Chronicle* (December 14, 2003). Similar considerations are also at the front of Jennifer Brayton, "Fic Frodo Slash Frodo: Fandoms and *The Lord of the Rings*," in Mathijs and Pomerance,

137–153.

28. For reasons of space, we are leaving out a more detailed discussion of the use of "television."

29. The *Times* affiliated itself strongly with the immediate run-up to the releases, as did the *New York Times* in the United States. New Line considered both as "privileged partners" who could count on extra materials (fold-outs, free posters, website materials, photos, and so on) to woo readers. Their mentions seem to confirm New Line's strategy of attempting to control the hype by proffering preferential media treatment. See Mathijs, "Reviews, Previews, and Premieres."

30. Philip French, "Are the Critics Able to Stop a Turkey in Its Tracks?" *Observer* (May 21, 2006); Jay Stone, "Why We Movie Critics Are Feeling a Little Insecure," *Vancouver Sun* (December 2, 2006), F17.

31. See, among others, Daniel Biltereyst and Philippe Meers, 'Blockbusters and/as Events: Distributing and Launching *The Lord of the Rings*, in Mathijs, *The Lord of the Rings: Popular Culture*, 71–87.

32. As reported in *Publishers Weekly* (December 23, 2003).

THREE. PROMOTIONAL FRAME MAKERS AND THE MEANING OF THE TEXT: THE CASE OF *THE LORD OF THE RINGS*

1. Throughout this chapter I will make reference to the group effort of this project. I wish to thank to Dejan Jontes and Tanja Oblak for their excellent contributions to this paper.

2. The film premiered in Slovenia on January 17, 2004; the world premiere took place on the weekend before Christmas, or four weeks in advance of the first showing in Slovenia.

3. D. Stephen Reese's definition says that frames are "organizing principles that are socially shared and persistent over time, that work symbolically to meaningfully structure the social world." D. Stephen Reese, "Prologue: Framing Public Life: A Bridging Model for Media Research," in D. Stephen Reese et al., eds., *Framing Public Life* (Mahwah, NJ: Lawrence Erlbaum, 2003), 11.

4. Additionally, 91.5 percent of the Slovene respondents/viewers were under thirty-five years old and 98.1 percent were under forty-five years old. The demographic composition of *Lord of the Rings* audience reflects the cinema-going demographics in Slovenia, where more than 90 percent of cinema-goers are younger than forty-nine, and confirms that the viewers of *LotR* were casual audience—that is, the regular cinema-goers or a bit younger—and not the committed readers of Tolkien's books who would have some preknowledge of the Tolkien's trilogy. On cinema attendance in Slovenia, see Mediana TGI, Institute for Market and Media Research, Mediana, Ljubljana, 2006, "Obiskovalci Kinematografov po Starosti in Izobrazbi [Cinema Visitors According to Age and Education], 2003, 2004, 2005," in *Statistical Yearbook of the Republic of Slovenia*, available at http://www.stat.si/letopis/index_letopis.asp (accessed February 5, 2007).

5. Nicholas Abercrombie and Brian Longhurst, *Audiences* (London: Sage, 1998), 121.

6. John Fiske, "The Cultural Economy of Fandom," in Lisa A. Lewis, ed., *The Adoring Audience: Fan Culture and Popular Media* (London: Routledge, 1992), 30–49.

7. Cornel Sandvoss, *Fans* (Cambridge: Polity Press, 2005), 29.

8. From December 1, 2003, to February 1, 2004, we monitored all major Slovene media: all five Slovene daily newspapers (*Delo, Slovenske novice, Finance, Večer, Dnevnik*); ten weeklies (six general-interest weekly magazines, two women's weeklies, two teen magazines: *Dru ina, Mag, Lady, Jana, Nedeljski Dnevnik, Stop, Smrklja, Pil Plus, Mladina, 7D*); the monthly *Premiera*, devoted solely to film; one magazine devoted to popular culture in general; and two national television stations (national public service TV and commercial POP TV).

9. For a discussion of a reception of *LotR* and of domestification of global culture in Slovenia, see Breda Luthar, "Kulturna Globalizacija, Film in Promocijski Re im" [Cultural Globalisation,

Film, and Promotional Regime: The Case of Lord of the Rings]," *Teorija in Praksa* 43, nos. 1–2 (2006): 5–24.

10. Nick Couldry, *Inside Culture: Re-imagining the Method of Cultural Studies* (London: Sage, 2000), 86.

11. For a different understanding of the text as an event that places the emphasis on the aesthetic background at the expense of social, cultural, and economic context, see Hans Robert Jauss, "The Identity of the Poetic Text in the Changing Horizon of Understanding," in James L. Machor and Philip Goldstein, eds., *Reception Study: From Literary Theory to Cultural Studies* (London: Routledge, 2001), 7–28 (originally published 1978).

12. Janet Staiger, *Interpreting Films: Studies in the Historical Reception of American Cinema* (Princeton, NJ: Princeton University Press, 1992), 36.

13. Ibid., 46.

14. Similarly, Janice Radway argues that changes in textual features or generic popularity should not be considered as the direct evidence of ideological shifts in the culture. What she calls the "institutional matrix" of the cultural industry should be taken into consideration (publishing and marketing of romance novels in her case). The institutional matrix is the necessary context in which we can understand their textual form (*Reading the Romance* [London: Verso, 1984], 19–45). The buying of books and the reading of books are thus not merely the result of the interaction between book and reader. They are also influenced by publishing as an organised culture and the technology of production, distribution, advertising, and other promotional techniques.

15. See Justin Wyatt, *High Concept: Movies and Marketing in Hollywood* (Austin: University of Texas Press, 1994), 25.

16. See Robert Sklar, *Movie-Made America: A Cultural History of American Movies* (New York: Vintage Books, 1994), 323, on the changed distributional strategies in the film industry of the 1970s. According to Wyatt (23), high-concept films are differentiated within the marketplace through an emphasis on style and an integration with their marketing.

17. See Janet Wasko, *How Hollywood Works* (London: Sage, 2003), 194.

18. This is reflected in their answers to the question of the kind of story *The Lord of the Rings* was for them. The largest proportion of "casual"/unskilled viewers defined it as a fight of good versus evil.

19. *Dnevnik,* December 2, 2003, on the world premiere.

20. *Dnevnik,* January 9, 2004.

21. An author's byline is not necessarily an assurance of an independently authored text. Usually it merely designates the person who compiled information from the promotional material or someone who used promotional press releases, Internet sources, or foreign press sources to put together an article that is mainly promotional in style and content and reproduces the framing of the film offered by promotional discourse.

22. See Karen S. Johnson-Certee, *News Narratives and News Framing* (Lanham, MD: Rowman & Littlefield, 2005), 133, on the strategic ritual of factism in journalism.

23. P. David Marshall, "Intimately Intertwined in the Most Public Way: Celebrity and Journalism," in Stuart Allan, ed., *Journalism: Critical Issues* (Maidenhead: Open University Press, 2005), 19.

24. See Angela McRobbie, "*Jackie* Magazine: Romantic Individualism and the Teenage Girl," in McRobbie, ed., *Feminism and Youth Culture* (Basingstoke: Macmillan, 2000), 86.

25. Ibid., 84.

26. The difference between the film role and the private celebrity persona is usually completely erased in magazines aimed at young women. The male stars of *The Lord of the Rings,* Mortensen, Wood, Bloom, and Astin are represented as the embodiment of some of the features of their fictional film personalities and portray the values of the fictional characters they play in the film.

27. Short news reports on her weight problems and her supposed resistance to Hollywood beauty standards were also part of the publicity for the first and second parts of the trilogy: "Dieting,

No Thanks," *Pil Plus* (January 16, 2004); "Happy and Fat" *Lady* (December 17, 2004); "Liv Has Gained Weight," *Slovenske Novice* (January 3, 2004).

28. Graeme Turner, *Fame Games* (Cambridge: Cambridge University Press, 2000), 158.

29. I don't want to engage in a deeper discussion of the cultural aspects of the phenomenon. Very briefly, the overall expansion of the phenomenon of celebrity is, according to P. David Marshall (*Celebrity and Power: Fame in Contemporary Culture* [Minneapolis: University of Minnesota Press, 1997], 26), an effective means for the commodification of the self. At the same time, however, the phenomenon is an embodiment of the egalitarian nature of modern culture and is thus associated with capitalism as well as with democracy. David Chaney (*Cultural Change and Everyday Life* [Basingstoke: Palgrave, 2002]) defines the modern types of fame as an articulation of the transformation of the concept of authority and prestige in mass societies, where the traditional foundations of authority have been eroded. Authority no longer rests on role/position, which would confer authority independent of the actor occupying a given position.

30. The classification of forms of reading/reception of *Dallas* in different cultural/national contexts is made by Tamar Liebes and Elihu Katz, *The Export of Meaning: Cross-Cultural Readings of Dallas* (Cambridge: Polity Press, 1993).

31. Cultural domination is tied not to a lack of information, but to the "exclusion from the power of naming."

32. *ND*, January 25, 2004.

33. See Colin Campbell, "The Desire for the New," in Roger Silverstone and E. Hirsch, eds., *Consuming Technologies: Media and Information in Domestic Spaces* (London: Routledge, 1992), 56.

34. See H. White, *Figural Realism* (Baltimore, MD: Johns Hopkins University Press, 2000), 70. See also Allan's argument on gendered nature and masculinist epistemology of objectivist discourse.

FOUR. WHAT DO FEMALE FANS WANT?
BLOCKBUSTERS, *THE RETURN OF THE KING,* AND U.S. AUDIENCES

1. *New York Times* (December 21, 2003).

2. Melanie Nash and Martti Lahti, "'Almost Ashamed to Say I Am One of Those Girls': Titanic, Leonardo DiCaprio, and the Paradoxes of Girls' Fandom," in Kevin S. Sandler and Gaylyn Studlar, eds., *Titanic: Anatomy of a Blockbuster* (New Brunswick, NJ: Rutgers University Press, 1999), 64–88.

3. Letter, *New York Times* (January 4, 2004).

4. David Bordwell, *The Way Hollywood Tells It: Story and Style in Modern Movies* (Berkeley: University of California Press, 2006), 58, 59, 60.

5. The exact figures for female participants are: 431 students under sixteen; 900 students, sixteen to twenty-five; 48 professionals, sixteen to twenty-five; and 237 professionals, twenty-five to thirty-five years of age.

6. Along the same lines, the information doesn't warrant categorical statements about how female responses differ from male responses. Random sampling of the data does suggest, however, that women express the importance of the emotions raised by the epical filmmaking of *RotK* more explicitly and in much more detail than male viewers.

7. To analyze individual responses from the groups that form the basis of my study, I examined a random sample of approximately thirty questionnaires for each group by age and occupation. I want to thank Katarzyna Chmielewska, my research assistant, for her substantial help in quantifying the U.S. database. I also want to thank Bjorn Ingvoldstad for his research assistance in the project's early stages.

8. As Annette Kuhn argues, the theatre has often constituted a memorable world for moviegoers.

See *Dreaming of Fred and Ginger: Cinema and Cultural Memory* (New York: New York University Press, 2002). The blockbuster does not monopolise the creation of this outer world, then; it stands as a particularly visible instance of the meaningfulness of this world to fans. Further, the "inner" and "outer" worlds blockbusters generate for their fans are part of larger processes involving other kinds of films and other kinds of moviegoers. For more on this see Kuhn's "Heterotopia, Heterochronia: Place and Time in Cinema Memory," *Screen* 45, no. 2 (2004): 106–114.

9. See chapter 12 in this volume.
10. Exact figures for age were: sixteen to twenty-five, 36 percent; twenty-six to thirty-five, 23 percent; and thirty-six to forty-five, 16 percent.
11. Figures for other professions are: 3 percent each for self-employed, executive, and service; 2 percent each for home/child care, unemployed, and skilled manual; and 1 percent for retired.
12. The ability of fandoms to create communities among women and others is a familiar formulation in fan studies and has emerged in discussions of fandom in relation to many media, from literature to the Internet. See, for example, Janice Radway, *Reading the Romance: Women, Patriarchy, and Popular Literature* (Chapel Hill: University of North Carolina Press, 1984); Henry Jenkins, *Textual Poachers: Television and Participatory Culture* (New York: Routledge, 1992); Nancy Baym, *Tune In, Log On: Soaps, Fandom, and Online Community* (Thousand Oaks, CA: Sage Publications, 2000).
13. For more on Trilogy Tuesday, see theonering.net/features/newsroom/files/.
14. As Tom Gunning writes, "The realism of the image is at the service of a dramatically unfolding spectator experience, vacillating between belief and incredulity" ("An Aesthetic of Astonishment: Early Film and the (In)Credulous Spectator," in Leo Braudy and Marshall Cohen, eds., *Film Theory and Criticism* [New York: Oxford University Press, 2004], 865). Gunning's work on the early "cinema of attractions" has been widely used in relation to special-effects cinema. Not all points of his argument apply here, but they provide a framework not only for thinking about the contrasting potentials of effects within classical cinema, but also the role of contemporary epic CGI adaptations in heightening the play between realism and illusion in the viewing experience.
15. On this point, see, for example, Jenkins; Constance Penley, *NASA/Trek: Popular Science and Sex in America* (New York: Verso, 1997).
16. On this point, for example, see Ien Ang, *Watching Dallas: Soap Opera and the Melodramatic Imagination,* trans. Della Couling (London: Methuen, 1985).
17. For example, a professional identifying herself as a political science student wrote, "I had to very consciously ignore the Europeanness of the good guys and the otherness of the bad guys (especially the Southrons and the Haradrim). I also admit to wondering if white nationalist types like the movie and hoping that they don't" (26–35).
18. Richard Dyer, *Only Entertainment* (London and New York: Routledge, 1992), 18.
19. Ibid.
20. For example, "Hollywood vs. Women," *Entertainment Weekly* (October 6, 2006).
21. *New York Times* (October 11, 2006).

FIVE. THE BOOKS, THE DVDS, THE EXTRAS, AND THEIR LOVERS

1. Various writers identify the first major exploration in this area as George Bluestone, *Novels into Films: The Metamorphosis of Fiction into Cinema* (Baltimore, MD: Johns Hopkins University Press, 1957).
2. See, for instance, the arguments of Seymour Chatman, "What Novels Can Do That Films Can't (and Vice Versa)," in Gerald Mast, Marshall Cohen, and Leo Braudy, eds., *Film Theory and Criticism* (New York: Oxford University Press, 1992), 445–60.

3. See, for instance, the tart comments on "adaptation-as-betrayal" in Andrew S. Horton and Joan Magretta, eds., *Modern European Filmmakers and the Art of Adaptation* (New York: Frederick Ungar, 1981)—a book that proposes an alternative account via the concept of "twice-told tales."

4. Brian McFarlane, *Novel to Film: An Introduction to the Theory of Adaptation* (Clarendon: Oxford, 1996). "Fidelity critiques" do not go away so easily. Robert Giddings and Erica Sheen responded in their (edited) *The Classic Novel: From Page to Screen* (Manchester: Manchester University Press, 2000).

5. See the comments on the "jejune" state of adaptation theory as a result of the dominance of literary-connected film programmes in the United States, in James Naremore, ed., *Film Adaptation* (London: Athlone Press, 2000).

6. See also, for example, the sardonic commentary in Lynda E. Boose and Richard Burt, eds., *Shakespeare the Movie: Popularising the Plays on Film, TV, and Video* (London: Routledge, 1997).

7. A clear statement of this notion can be found in Neil Sinyard, *Filming Literature: The Art of Screen Adaptation* (London: Croom Helm, 1986), this quote p. ix.

8. See, for instance, two essays on *Cape Fear* in McFarlane, 171–193; Kirsten Thompson, "*Cape Fear* and Trembling: Familial Dread," in Robert Stam and Alessandra Raengo, eds., *Literature through Film: A Guide to the Theory and Practice of Film Adaptation* (Oxford: Blackwell 2005), 126–147.

9. See especially recent work on remakes (the renaming is a good signal, in fact), for instance Andrew S. Horton and Stuart Y. MacDougall, eds., *Play It Again, Sam: Retakes on Remakes* (Berkeley: University of California Press, 1998); Constantine Verevis, *Film Remakes* (Edinburgh: Edinburgh University Press, 2006).

10. This is broached, for instance, in John Orr and Colin Nicholson, eds., *Cinema and Fiction: New Modes of Adapting, 1950–1990* (Edinburgh: Edinburgh University Press, 1992).

11. For a clear example of the former kind, see Carol N. Dole, "Austen, Classics and the American Market," in Linda Troost and Sayre Greenfield, eds., *Jane Austen in Hollywood* (Lexington: University of Kentucky Press, 2001), 58–78; for an extraordinarily lazy set of declarations about the "knowing audience," see the chapter "Audiences" in Verevis.

12. In a separate essay we are exploring some fascinating patterns our questionnaire data and materials revealed concerning the distribution of *kinds of disappointment* across generations of readers.

13. Most notably, Humphrey Carpenter, *J R R Tolkien: A Biography* (London: Allen & Unwin, 1977).

14. See, in particular, Catherine A. Lutz and Jane L. Collins, *Reading National Geographic* (Chicago: University of Chicago Press, 1993); Zhang Chengzhi, "The Eyes You Find Will Make You Shiver," *Inter-Asia Cultural Studies* 5, no. 3 (2004): 486–490.

15. We do not wish to overplay this example. There are clearly other processes at work. Bearing in mind that this documentary was first available before the release of *The Return of the King*, it had to avoid "spoilers." This might throw light on another oddity. During the comparison with Agincourt, the voiceover suggests that King Henry's rousing speech at Agincourt can be equated with the appearance of the Elves at Helm's Deep. No mention is made of the fact that this was a key change between book and film—nor is there any reference to what would have been the more obvious analogy: namely, Aragorn's direct invocation of Henry's speech in the final battle before the Gates of Mordor (also not present in the books). Keeping this high-drama moment back was surely a marketing decision, whereas the Elves' arrival needed justifying to suspicious fans.

16. This glossing over of potentially problematic aspects of Tolkien's work is further evidenced in both the *National Geographic* and extended edition documentaries, where Jackson and Boyens appear to elide the class dimensions of Sam and Frodo's relationship in the book, and stress pure friendship rather than the notion of upper-class gentleman and lower-class gardener or "batman."

17. As we will go on to argue, we see these documentaries as complementary, with each building

on and complementing the argument of the last. For us, this seems justifiable, in the sense that these two documentaries are located together, one after another, on the same menu page of each extended DVD (and, indeed, and as Craig Hight has also noted, if the viewer selects the "play all" function on this page, these extras will always play in the order given on the menu). For us, our aim here is to consider, as Hight does, how "possible combinations" of extras on particular DVDs can function "as part of trajectories, shaped by the disc's interface." Craig Hight, "Making-of Documentaries on DVD: *The Lord of the Rings* Trilogy and Special Editions," *Velvet Light Trap* 56 (2005): 11.

18. Arguably, this "collective voice" strategy could also be seen to serve two other, related purposes. Firstly, to demonstrate that the experts on Tolkien have given the filmmakers their seal of approval—that they are aligned with the views and interpretations of the filmmakers, and that, therefore, lovers of Tolkien's books can trust these filmmakers to do appropriate service to the books. Secondly, this strategy also seems to highlight to viewers that the cast and crew working on the films all know and understand Tolkien's books and, equally, understand how and why Jackson is adapting the books in the way that he is.

19. Interestingly, this "correction" argument is given a further seal of approval by key Tolkien "guardian" Christopher Lee, in the *Fellowship of the Ring* "Book to Script" documentary. There, Lee notes that many of the changes made to the first film were not only necessary but also, in many cases, improvements on the book. Lee's assertion of the necessity of omitting Tom Bombadil from the first film would surely have derived force, for devotees, from his well-known status as a lifelong fan of the books. Notably, Lee's contribution lessens in the extras on the *Return of the King* DVD, no doubt because of his heavily publicised discontent at being cut from the theatrical version of the *Return of the King* film.

20. See Hight, 13, for further discussion of these discursive strategies in other *LotR* extended extras.

21. The success of this discursive strategy was acknowledged by many of our U.K. project interviewees, with, for instance, one respondent noting that "if you *do have* any criticism of it, it kind of makes you forget them . . . because of the fact that so much work went in to it" (including "the amount of time they had to edit down the *script*"), another noting that "Philippa Boyens has got a clear understanding of what some of the messages are in the book," and another commenting that "it's quite interesting when you buy the DVDs and you watch how Jackson's *done* it, he's quite *frank* about it, he's got to portray a *story*" and "he can't put everything in."

22. This, coupled with Boyens's discussion of the need to balance the focus on fidelity to the book with the commercial concerns of the studio (cited earlier in the chapter), runs counter to Hight's argument (13) that the *LotR* extended extras make no reference to the economics of the film production or to the reactions and views of the Tolkien fan base. This suggests, firstly, that the adaptation extras may serve a different discursive function to the more filmmaking-specific extras on the extended DVDs, and, secondly, that Hight's argument may be rather driven by a residual ideological commitment to "prove" that filmmakers work to conceal their material interests.

23. For a more elaborated consideration of this notion of "completeness" among our respondents, see Martin Barker, "Envisaging 'Visualisation': Some Challenges from the International *Lord of the Rings* Audience Project," *Film-Philosophy* 10, no. 3 (2006): 1–25.

24. Pavel Skopal, for instance, notes that 25 percent of the 20 million copies of the *Fellowship of the Ring* DVD sold on the North American market were extended DVD copies, and that, clearly, these were aimed at "high-value customers" willing to pay out the higher price for another, more extended version of the film. Pavel Skopal, "The Adventure Continues on DVD: Franchise Movies as Home Video," *Convergence* 13, no. 2 (2007): 185–198, this quote 186.

25. This sense of a long-term marketing campaign extends much wider than just the extended edition DVDs. At the outset, *LotR* was seen as a risky proposition, not at all guaranteed to be a

success. This meant, among other things, that merchandisers were initially hard to recruit. Following the dramatic success of the first film, all this changed. For one good source on this, see Buzz McClain, "The Lord of the Marketers," *DVD Exclusive* (May 2004), 20, 23.

26. Barbara Klinger, *Beyond the Multiplex: Cinema, New Technologies, and the Home* (Berkeley: University of California Press, 2006), 61.
27. Skopal, 6.
28. Hight, 6.
29. Klinger, 61 and 78–85.

SIX. UNDERSTANDING DISAPPOINTMENT: THE AUSTRALIAN BOOK LOVERS AND ADAPTATION

1. Sian Powell, "Readers Choice," *The Australian* (October 15, 1997).
2. Michael Kennedy, email message to author (July 26, 2006). As manager of the Australian Tol Harndor list, Kennedy suggested that it was a literal toss-up as to whether the founders would establish a Monty Python Society or a *LotR* society. Tolkien won the toss.
3. Personal telephone call with author (July 26, 2006).
4. Gordon Farrar, email message to author (August 7, 2006).
5. Curious but true. The first Australian publication of *LotR* was a Braille edition, put out in 1975 by the Queensland Braille Writing Association.
6. Stam and Raengo, 3.
7. The Australian sample constituted 551 respondents the majority of whom (74 percent) found the third film "extremely enjoyable." The second largest group (20 percent), found it "very enjoyable." The majority also considered it "extremely important" to see the film (70 percent) and suggested that it was the books that largely formed their expectations of the films (60 percent), although the next largest grouping (30 percent) suggested that it was the two prior films. By far the majority of the Australian respondents were students (41 percent) in the sixteen-to-twenty-five age range and female (59 percent), with the next largest grouping being twenty-six-to-thirty-five-year-olds (24 percent) and professional (30 percent).
8. Stam and Raengo, 3.
9. Hills, *Fan Cultures*, 2.

SEVEN. INVOLVEMENT IN *THE LORD OF THE RINGS:* AUDIENCE STRATEGIES AND ORIENTATIONS

1. For an approach to *The Lord of the Rings* as a blockbuster and genre film, see Susanne Eichner, Lothar Mikos, and Michael Wedel, "*Apocalypse Now* in Middle Earth: Genre in the Critical Reception of *The Lord of the Rings* in Germany," in Mathijs, *The Lord of the Rings: Popular Culture,* 143–159.
2. The research team in Babelsberg consisted of Dr. Lothar Mikos (project leader), Dr. Elizabeth Prommer, Dr. Michael Wedel, Susanne Eichner, and Sabrina Schäfer, and the students Ulrike Aigte, Nadine Baethke, Angela Burghagen, Patrick Jantke, Jesko Jockenhövel, Jörn Krug, and Cornelia Robe. The project, titled "Production, Marketing, and Reception of 'The Lord of the Rings' in Germany," was carried out from September 2003 through March 2005, in the degree course on audiovisual media studies at the University of Film and Television, Babelsberg. The findings are to be published in 2007.
3. Lothar Mikos and Elizabeth Prommer, "Das Babelsberger Modell, " in Lothar Mikos and

Claudia Wegener, eds., *Qualitative Medienforschung: Ein Handbuch* (Konstanz: UVK, 2005), 162–169; Lothar Mikos et al., *Im Auge der Kamera: Das Fernsehereignis "Big Brother"* (Berlin: Vistas, 2000); Lothar Mikos, "Big Brother as Television Text: Frames of Interpretation and Reception in Germany," in Mathijs and Jones, *Big Brother International,* 93–104.

4. Lothar Mikos, *Fern-Sehen: Bausteine zu einer Rezeptionsästhetik des Fernsehens* (Berlin: Vistas, 2001); Ien Ang, "Ethnography and Radical Contextualism in Audience Studies," in her *Living Room Wars: Rethinking Media Audiences for a Postmodern World* (London: Routledge), 66–81; Lawrence Grossberg, "Introduction: Birmingham in America?" in his *Bringing It All Back Home: Essays on Cultural Studies* (Durham, NC: Duke University Press, 1997), 1–32; Lothar Mikos, *Film- und Fernsehanalyse* (Konstanz: UVK, 2003); Uwe Flick, "Triangulation in Qualitative Research," in Uwe Flick, Ernst von Kardorff, and Ines Steinke, eds., *A Companion to Qualitative Research* (London: Sage, 2004), 178–183; Uwe Flick, *An Introduction to Qualitative Research* (London: Sage, 2006).

5. Norman K. Denzin and Yvonna S. Lincoln, "Introduction: Entering the Field of Qualitative Research," in Norman K. Denzin and Yvonna S. Lincoln, eds., *The Landscape of Qualitative Research: Theories and Issues* (Thousand Oaks, CA: Sage, 1998), 4.

6. Uwe Hasebrink, "Nutzungsforschung," in Günter Bentele, Hans-Bernd Brosius, and Otfried Jarren, eds., *Öffentliche Kommunikation: Handbuch Kommunikations- und Medienwissenschaft* (Wiesbaden: VS Verlag, 2003), 117; Andreas Fahr, "Involvement," in Günter Bentele, Hans-Bernd Brosius, and Otfried Jarren, eds., *Lexikon Kommunikations- und Medienwissenschaft* (Wiesbaden: VS Verlag, 2006), 113.

7. Peter Vorderer, *Fernsehen als Handlung: Fernsehfilmrezeption aus Motivationspsychologischer Perspektive* (Berlin: Edition Sigma, 1992), 83.

8. Ibid., 84; Donald Horton and R. Richard Wohl, "Mass Communication and Para-Social Interaction: Observations on Intimacy at a Distance," *Psychiatry* 19 (1956): 215–229; Christian Metz, *Psychoanalysis and Cinema: The Imaginary Signifier* (Basingstoke: Macmillan, 1990); Murray Smith, *Engaging Characters: Fiction, Emotion, and the Cinema* (Oxford: Oxford University Press, 1995).

9. Mikos, *Film- und Fernsehanalyse.*

10. Thompson, "Fantasy, Franchises, and Frodo Baggins," 46.

11. A term coined by Michael Wedel in a project group discussion.

12. Thompson.

13. Pierre Bourdieu, *Distinction: A Social Critique of the Judgement of Taste* (Cambridge, MA: Harvard University Press, 2002); Herbert Gans, *Popular Culture and High Culture: An Analysis and Evaluation of Taste* (New York: Basic Books, 1974).

14. The following evaluation is based only on the 880 German-language responses to the online survey.

15. Online questionnaire, question 5: "What kind of story is 'The Lord of the Rings' to you?"

16. Question 3 in the cinema audience survey: "What are your spontaneous thoughts about the film?"

17. In addition to demographic data, the cinema audience survey also asked about fan status (question 4, "Would you describe yourself as a 'Lord of the Rings' fan?") and knowledge of the books (question 7, "Have you read the 'Lord of the Rings' books?").

18. J. Distelmeyer, "Zuhaus in Mittelerde: Das Fantasy-Genre und seine Fans," *epd film* 12 (2002): 18–23.

19. Claudius Seidl, "Hinter tausend Kriegern keine Welt," *Frankfurter Allgemeine Zeitung* (December 17, 2003).

20. S. Horst, "Willkommen in Bruchtal!," *Freitag* (December 19, 2003), 52.

21. Ibid.

22. Jens Balzer, "Erlöst," *Berliner Zeitung* (December 17, 2003).

23. Ibid.

EIGHT. GLOBAL FLOWS AND LOCAL IDENTIFICATIONS?
THE LORD OF THE RINGS AND THE CROSS-NATIONAL
RECEPTION OF CHARACTERS AND GENRES

1. The Dutch research was done in conjunction with a group of students of communication science at the University of Amsterdam. We want to thank Monique van Bracht, Tisha Eetgerink, Sabrine Engländer, Arlette de Haas, and Pauline van Romondt van Vis for their enthusiastic participation in this project. Moreover, we want to thank Daniel Biltereyst, Philippe Meers, Martin Barker, and Ernest Mathijs for their helpful comments.

2. See, for instance, Ulrich Beck, "The Cosmopolitan Society and Its Enemies," *Theory, Culture & Society* 19, nos. 1–2 (2002): 17–44; Michèle Lamont and Laurent Thévenot, *Rethinking Comparative Cultural Sociology: Repertoires of Evaluation in France and the United States* (Cambridge: Cambridge University Press, 2000).

3. Liebes and Katz, *The Export of Meaning;* Wasko et al., *Dazzled by Disney;* Mathijs and Jones, *Big Brother;* Anne Cooper-Chen, *Global Entertainment Media: Content, Audiences, Issues* (Mahwah, NJ: Lawrence Erlbaum, 2005).

4. Sonia Livingstone, *Making Sense of Television: The Psychology of Audience Interpretation* (London: Routledge, 1998).

5. Because of the large number of respondents, we had to resort here to a rather crude recoding: every answer that contained a specific name was seen as an answer where this character was named as a favourite. This means that recoding sometimes didn't completely represent the respondent's answer, for instance with answers like "In the book I preferred Frodo, but in the film my favourite was Aragorn" (favourites: Frodo and Aragorn); or "My favourite is Sam because of his loyalty to Frodo (Sam, Frodo). However, this is only a problem in a very small number of cases. Also, it was not possible to include languages with a non-Romantic language (Chinese, Russian, Greek) in this analysis.

6. See G. Hofstede, *Culture's Consequences: Comparing Values, Behaviors, Institutions, and Organizations across Nations* (Thousand Oaks, CA: Sage, 2001); G. Hofstede and G. J. Hofstede, *Cultures and Organizations: Software of the Mind* (New York: McGraw-Hill, 2005).

7. C. Hoffner, "Children's Wishful Identification and Parasocial Interaction with Favourite Television Characters," *Journal of Broadcasting & Electronic Media* 40 (1996): 389–402; Jonathan Cohen, "Parasocial Break-up from Favourite Television Characters: The Role of Attachment Styles and Relationship Intensity," *Journal of Social and Personal Relationships* 21, no. 2 (2004): 187–202; A. M. Rubin and M. M. Step, "Impact of Motivation, Attraction, and Parasocial Interaction on Talk-Radio Listening," *Journal of Broadcasting & Electronic Media* 44 (2000): 635–654; for a critical discussion, see also Barker, "The *Lord of the Rings* and 'Identification.'"

8. Michèle Lamont, *Money, Morals, and Manners: The Culture of the French and American Upper-Middle Class* (Chicago: University of Chicago Press, 1992); M. Lamont, *The Dignity of Working Men: Morality and the Boundaries of Race, Class, and Immigration* (New York: Russell Sage Foundation, 2000); Lamont and Thévenot.

9. The reason for this is that we didn't find clear relations between the various modality choices or favourite characters, but also there weren't very strong correlations between particular character preferences and modalities. Neither personality choice nor character preference, moreover, was strongly linked with appreciation. However, see chapter 9 in this volume.

10. See Biltereyst, "Blockbusters"; Meers, "Fandom."

11. This means that differences from the average are converted into standard deviations. A differ-

ence of 1 means that the score is 1 standard deviation higher than the average; -1 means that the score is 1 standard deviation lower than the average.

12. See Daniel Biltereyst and Philippe Meers, "The International Telenovela Debate and the Contra-flow Argument: A Reappraisal," *Media, Culture & Society* 22, no. 4 (2000): 393–413; J. D. Straubhaar, "Beyond Media Imperialism: Asymmetrical Interdependence and Cultural Proximity," *Critical Studies in Mass Communication* 8, no. 1 (1991) 39–59.

13. See Stuart Hall, "Encoding/Decoding," in Centre for Contemporary Cultural Studies, ed., *Culture, Media, Language: Working Papers in Cultural Studies, 1972–79* (London: Hutchinson, 1980), 128–138; David Morley and Charlotte Brunsdon, *The Nationwide Television Studies* (London: Routledge, 1999).

14. See Hall.

15. Lamont, *Dignity*.

16. See Barker, "The *Lord of the Rings* and 'Identification.'"

17. See also Biltereyst.

18. Jenkins, *Textual Poachers;* John Fiske, *Reading the Popular* (New York: Routledge, 1991); *Understanding Popular Culture* (New York: Routledge, 1994).

19. See Biltereyst; Thomas Elsaesser, *Hollywood op Straat: Film en Televisie in de Hedendaagse Mediacultuur [Hollywood on the Street: Film and Television in Today's Media Culture]* (Amsterdam: Amsterdam University Press, 2000); Julian Stringer, ed., *Movie Blockbusters* (London: Routledge, 2003).

NINE. THE FUNCTIONS OF FANTASY: A COMPARISON OF AUDIENCES FOR *THE LORD OF THE RINGS* IN TWELVE COUNTRIES

1. This owes a great deal to comments, often critical, from colleagues in the *LotR* network around the world. Many thanks to all of you.

2. For reasons of space, this essay cannot explain every procedure followed, each methodological decision made, or how the key findings were located. For anyone who has a particular interest in examining these, a much fuller version of this essay is available on request from the author.

3. Based on thirty-eight responses, which was the full set of "Spiritual journey" mentions excluding "Epic."

4. In the 1960 and '70s, a substantial debate took place within the social sciences over this. Triggered in part by the Sapir-Whorf hypothesis (see, for instance, P. Kay and W. Kempton, "What Is the Sapir-Whorf Hypothesis?" *American Anthropologist* 86, no. 1 [1984]: 65–79) that languages embody and thus enforce separate cultural understandings of the world, and then carried into the philosophy of the social sciences by Peter Winch's influential *The Idea of a Social Science and Its Relation to Philosophy* (London: Routledge and Kegan Paul, 1958), this kind of extreme cultural relativism underwent stringent criticism. For one particularly astute challenge, which criticises Winch at both epistemological and political levels, see David Lamb, "Preserving a Primitive Society," *Sociological Review* 25, no. 4 (1977): 689–719.

5. Benedict Anderson, *Imagined Communities: Reflections on the Origin and Spread of Nationalism* (London: Verso, 1991).

6. Michael Billig, *Banal Nationalism* (London: Sage, 1995).

7. See, for instance, Dominic Strinati and Stephen Wagge, eds., *Come on Down? Popular Media Culture in Post-War Britain* (London: Routledge, 1992); Philip Davies, ed., *Imagining and Representing America* (Stafford: Keele University Press, 1996).

8. Karl Mannheim, "The Sociology of Generations," in his *Essays on the Sociology of Knowledge* (London: Routledge and Kegan Paul, 1952), 276–320.

9. On 1960s readers of Tolkien, see, in particular, Martin Barker, "On Being a 1960s Tolkien

Reader."

10. See, in particular, Joseph Ripp, "Middle America Meets Middle-earth: American Discussion and Readership of J R R Tolkien's *The Lord of the Rings, 1965–69,*" *Book History* 8 (2005): 245–286.
11. See, for instance, Speake, "The Power of the Ring."
12. Personal message to Sue Turnbull.
13. Yannis Skarpelos, email to the author, June 2006.
14. Krysla Diver, "Troubled Germans Turn to *Lord of the Rings,*" *Guardian* (October 4, 2004).

TEN. BEYOND WORDS: *THE RETURN OF THE KING* AND THE PLEASURES OF THE TEXT

1. Jenkins, *Textual Poachers;* Will Brooker, *Using the Force: Creativity, Community and Star Wars Fans* (New York and London: Continuum, 2002); Hills, *Fan Cultures.*
2. Kurt Lancaster, *Interacting with Babylon Five: Fan Performances in a Media Universe* (Austin: University of Texas Press, 2001).
3. Hills, 180.
4. Lancaster, 155
5. Hills, 71.
6. Hills, 129.
7. Sue Harper and Vincent Porter, "Moved to Tears: Weeping in the Cinema in Postwar Britain," *Screen* 37, no. 2 (Summer 1995): 152–173.
8. See Martin Barker and Julian Petley, *Ill Effects: The Media Violence Debate,* 2nd ed. (London: Routledge, 2002).
9. Brian Massumi, *Parables for the Virtual: Movement, Affect, Sensation* (Durham, NC, and London: Duke University Press, 2002).
10. Garth Jowett et al., *Children and Movies: Media Influence and the Payne Fund Controversy* (Cambridge: Cambridge University Press, 1996), 69.
11. Massumi, 28.
12. Wendell S Dysinger and Christian Rucknick, *The Emotional Reactions of Children to the Motion Picture Situation* (New York: Macmillan, 1933).
13. Klaus Scherer, "What Are Emotions? And How Can They Be Measured?" *Social Science Information* 44, no. 4 (2005): 695–729.
14. Ibid.
15. Stam and Raengo.
16. Pseudonyms have been used to ensure confidentiality.
17. Vivian Sobchack, *Carnal Thoughts: Embodiment and Moving Image Culture* (Berkeley and Los Angeles: University of California Press, 2004).
18. Sobchack, 2004, 65.
19. Hills, 28.

ELEVEN. HEROISM IN *THE RETURN OF THE KING*

1. "Tolkien's 'basic passion' was for 'myth (not allegory!) and for fairy-story, and above all for heroic legend on the brink of history' [letter, no. 131 to Milton Waldman, 1951]. This passion was dramatically expressed in a body of work unique in the history of English-language literature. So unique, in fact, as to lead us to consider with incredulity the reading *The Lord of the Rings* as nothing more than a ripping good yarn." Wright, *Tolkien in Perspective,* 33.
2. " . . . in fact, that *The Lord of the Rings* is at least partly an attempt to restore the hero to mod-

ern fiction" (Wright, 60).

3. "Roger Sale, one of the sages under whom I studied at the University of Washington, went so far as to claim, 'In any study of modern heroism, if J.R.R. Tolkien's *The Lord of the Rings* did not exist it would have to be invented Why? Precisely because of the Stultifying effects of modernism."("Tolkien and the Fairy Story," in Isaacs and Zimbardo, *Tolkien and the Critics*, 247). Oddly enough, Reilly sees Tolkien's work as "a major contribution to modern literature" (Wright, 61).

4. "One reason *The Lord of the Rings* works for so many contemporary readers is that it provides a world in which we can glimpse an authentic and powerful truth, one that we know is correct even though great powers of evil and error threaten to overwhelm it. His heroes seem like authentic heroes because doubt and despair—the great threats of modern world—are legitimate enough threats that they claim would-be heroes such as Saruman and Denethor" (Joe Kraus, "Tolkien, Modernism, and the Importance of Tradition," in Bassham and Bronson, 148.

5. "The same wisdom that his heroes use to escape from the evils of Middle-earth serves as a story that lets his contemporary readers escape, briefly, from the challenge of the modern. Middle-earth has enough landmarks to tell us that it will one day develop into our own, but it remains more magical" (Kraus, 149).

6. Petty, 256.

7. "His fiction reiterates an anti-'heroic' theme. The sorrows of the Elves in Beleriand, in *The Silmarillion*, stem from Féanor's vengeful decision to pursue the crimes of Melkor with war" (Rosebury, *Tolkien*, 163–164). "The heroes of the *Lord of the Rings* do not like the war, they morally win by rejecting this source." (Matthew Dickerson, *Following Gandalf* [Grand Rapids, MI: Brazos Press, 2003], 81).

8. "The seemingly inexhaustible ability of consumers of popular culture to experience personal identification with a tremendous range of heroes, from Spiderman to Obi Wan Kenobi to Neo to Van Fanel to Frodo, reveals a need for heroes that has never died away. Tolkien's books continue to supply a grand smorgasbord of heroes for generation after generation—his 'epic temperament,' as he described it, was not at all lost on readers accustomed to short attention span and novels that could be easily devoured in a few hours" (Petty, 259).

9. Ibid., 258.

10. Barker, "*The Lord of the Rings* and 'Identification.'"

11. "Aragorn is a fair king" (survey, male, 36–45, skilled manual). "His physical appearance and the role he plays as a king are very attractive to me" (survey, male, 36–45, self-employed). "He is the king who has to recover his throne. He is strong, brave and loyal" (survey, male, 26–35, creative).

12. It is worth noting that the largest proportion of complaints related to the suppression of Saruman.

13. Kayla McKinney Wiggins, "The Art of the Story-Teller and the Person of the Hero," in Croft, *Tolkien on Film*, 114.

14. Ibid., 121.

15. Petty borrows these terms from Northrop Frye's typology and applies them to these two characters, among others. See Petty, 252.

16. For this author, "Popular heroes are often public servants, such as police officers, fire-fighters, or co-workers in an office, who perform extraordinary acts of heroism while doing their regular jobs. When placed in life-threatening conditions or situations well beyond their previous experience, they rise to the task of helping others. They have no supernatural gifts, but their very nature allows them to respond heroically" (Porter, *Unsung Heroes*, 20).

17. "The recoil of the wounded hero is mainly, however, on Sam. He longs to stay with Frodo forever, but Sam has achieved true maturity; and as the Heroic Age passes, he longs to put down roots into the soil of the Shire and raise a family" (Marion Zimmer Bradley, "Men, Halflings, and Hero Worship," in Zimbardo and Isaacs, *Understanding*, 90).

TWELVE. THE FANTASY OF READING: MOMENTS
OF RECEPTION OF *THE LORD OF THE RINGS:*
THE RETURN OF THE KING

1. The authors wish to thank Ann Leysen and Philippe Meers, as well as the Ghent University Research Fund (BOF), for help and support with this project.
2. Vivian Sobchack, "The Fantastic," in Geoffrey Nowell-Smith, ed., *The Oxford History of World Cinema* (Oxford: Oxford University Press, 1996), 316.
3. Ibid., 319.
4. See Biltereyst and Meers, "Blockbusters and/as Events."
5. See, for example, David Morley, *The "Nationwide" Audience: Structure and Decoding* (London: British Film Institute, 1980); Thomas Lindlof, *Qualitative Communication Research Methods* (Thousands Oaks, CA: Sage Publications, 1995); Martin Barker, *From Antz to Titanic: Reinventing Film Analysis* (London: Pluto, 2000).
6. This analysis is based on the research project The Export of Fantasy: The Lord of the Rings, Global Film Culture and Blockbusters (2004–2005, BOF, Ghent University Research Fund). This project combined a political-economic analysis of the distribution, marketing, and exhibition of *The Return of the King*, with a discourse analysis of the press and media coverage in Belgium, and a wide-ranging audience and reception analysis of the movie. The research was also developed as part of the U.K. International Lord of the Rings Research Project. This chapter relies upon the Belgian data, out of the worldwide survey, as well as the qualitative audience (reception) analysis.
7. In terms of sociodemographics, the group consisted mainly of adolescents (the age group of sixteen to twenty-five years: 66.8 percent, followed by people in the twenty-six-to-thirty-five age group: 16 percent), with a slight overrepresentation of men (56.3 percent) and of higher-educated respondents (for example, 23.7 percent were university trained). Most respondents were still students (62.3 percent), were familiar with Tolkien's books (60.7 percent had read one or more of the books), and considered themselves film fans (92.5 percent). See Ann Leysen et al., *The Lord of the Rings: The Return of the King: A Quantitative Analysis of the Film Reception* (Ghent: Department of Communication Studies, 2005).
8. In total thirty-seven focus group interviews were conducted using a semistandardised format; see David Morgan, *The Focus Group Guidebook* (Thousand Oaks, CA: Sage, 1998). The interviewees were recruited from the survey respondents. The group of interviewees consisted of fifty males and thirty females. The data were collected as an ethnographic abstract and reported in a research paper: Ann Leysen et al., *The Lord of the Rings: The Return of the King: A Reception Study on The Lords of the Rings: The Return of the King in Relation to the Film Text, Film Experience and the Film Viewing Context* (Ghent: Department of Communication Studies, 2005).
9. See Daniel Biltereyst, "Resisting American Hegemony: A Comparative Analysis of the Reception of Domestic and US Fiction," in Denis McQuail, Peter Golding, and Els de Bens, eds., *Communication Theory and Research: An EJC Anthology* (London: Sage, 2005), 70–88; also Birgitta Höijer, "Studying Viewers' Reception of Television Programmes: Theoretical and Methodological Considerations," *European Journal of Communication* 5, no. 1 (1990): 29–56.
10. Hans Robert Jauss, *Literaturgeschichte als Provokation* (Frankfurt: Suhrkamp, 1997).
11. See also John Davenport, "Happy Endings and Religious Hope: *The Lord of the Rings* as an Epic Fairy Tale," in Bassham and Bronson, *The Lord of the Rings and Philosophy*, 204–217.
12. Elihu Katz, "The Ring of Tolkien and Plato: Lessons in Power, Choice, and Morality," in Bassham and Bronson, 5–20.
13. Elana Shefrin, "*Lord of the Rings, Star Wars,* and Participatory Fandom."

THIRTEEN. UNDERSTANDING TEXT AS CULTURAL PRACTICE AND AS DYNAMIC PROCESS OF MAKING

1. Tony Thwaites, Lloyd Davis, and Warwick Mules, *Introducing Cultural and Media Studies: A Semiotic Approach* (Basingstoke: Palgrave, 2002), 77.
2. Lothar Mikos, *Film- und Fernsehanalyse* (Konstanz: UVK, 2003); Richard Johnson, "What Is Cultural Studies Anyway?," in John Storey, ed., *What Is Cultural Studies? A Reader* (London: Arnold, 1996), 75–114; Mikko Lehtonen, *The Cultural Analysis of Texts* (London: Sage, 2000); Alan McKee, *Textual Analysis: A Beginner's Guide* (London: Sage, 2003).
3. Wolfgang Iser, *The Act of Reading: A Theory of Aesthetic Response* (London: Routledge and Kegan Paul, 1978).
4. John Storey, *Cultural Consumption and Everyday Life* (London: Arnold, 1999), 65.
5. John Fiske, *Television Culture* (London: Methuen, 1987) , 115.
6. Quoted in Hight, 6.
7. Hight, 12.
8. Alexander Böhnke, "Mehrwert DVD," *Navigationen* 5, nos. 1–2 (2005): 213–223.
9. Jim Taylor, Mark R. Johnson, and Charles G. Crawford, *DVD Demystified* (New York: McGraw-Hill, 2006), 17.
10. Thompson, "Fantasy, Franchises, and Frodo Baggins," 60.
11. Hight, 10.
12. Gerard Genette, *Paratexts: Thresholds of Interpretation* (Cambridge: Cambridge University Press, 1997).
13. Fiske.
14. Chin and Gray, "One Ring to Rule Them All," 1.
15. Ibid., 2.
16. Ibid., 15.
17. Jonathan Gray, "New Audiences."
18. Couldry, 69.
19. John Frow, "On Literature in Cultural Studies," in Michael Bérubé, ed., *The Aesthetics of Cultural Studies* (Malden, MA: Blackwell, 2005), 52.
20. Bennett and Woollacott, 64.
21. Couldry, 70.
22. Bennett and Woollacott, 64.
23. Matt Hills, *How to Do Things with Cultural Theory* (London: Hodder Arnold, 2005), 26.
24. Lothar Mikos and Elizabeth Prommer, "Das Babelsberger Modell," in Lothar Mikos and Claudia Wegener, eds., *Qualitative Medienforschung: Ein Handbuch* (Konstanz: UVK, 2005), 162–169.

FOURTEEN. OUR METHODOLOGICAL CHALLENGES AND SOLUTIONS

1. For a fine critical evaluation, see Milly Williamson, *The Lure of the Vampire: Gender, Fiction and Fandom from Bram Stoker to Buffy* (London: Wallflower, 2005).
2. Perhaps the most important attempt to follow in his footsteps has been Tony Bennett, Michael Emmison, and John Frow, *Accounting for Tastes: Australian Everyday Cultures* (Cambridge: Cambridge University Press, 1999).
3. Of course what counts as "mainstream" is inevitably heavily culturally defined, as the case of Latin American telenovelas well demonstrates. "Mainstream" to scholars from this region, this research

can appear exotic to others.

4. The signs of this weakness are to be found in the fact that still the most quoted book on the-atre audiences is Susan Bennett's entirely theoretical account (*Theatre Audiences: A Theory of Production and Reception* [London: Routledge, 1998]). Other works, such as Neil Blackadder's excellent historical/archival research into theatre riots (*Performing Opposition: Modern Theater and the Scandalized Audience* [Westport, CT: Praeger, 2003]), are rarely mentioned.

5. See, for instance, the four volumes of essays edited by Melvyn Stokes and Richard Maltby, *American Movie Audiences: From the Turn of the Century to the Early Sound Era* (London: British Film Institute, 1999); *Identifying Hollywood's Audiences: Cultural Identity and the Movies* (London: British Film Institute, 1999); *Hollywood Spectatorship: Changing Perceptions of Cinema Audiences* (London: British Film Institute, 2001); *Hollywood Abroad: Audiences and Cultural Exchange* (London: British Film Institute, 2004).

6. For a recent overview, see Leah Price, "Reading: The State of the Discipline," *Book History* 7 (2004): 303–320.

7. Michael Baxandall, *Painting and Experience in Fifteenth Century Italy: A Primer in the Social History of Pictorial Style* (Oxford: Oxford University Press, 1988).

8. See, for instance, Sarah Thornton, *Club Cultures: Music, Media and Subcultural Capital* (Cambridge, MA: Polity Press, 1995); Ruth Finnegan, The Hidden Musicians: Music-Making in an English Town (Cambridge: Cambridge University Press, 1989).

9. On this see Daniel Dayan's recent essay, "Mothers, Midwives and Abortionists: Genealogy, Obstetrics, Audiences and Publics," in Sonia Livingstone, ed., *Audiences and Publics: When Cultural Engagement Matters for the Public Sphere* (London: Intellect, 2005), 43–76.

10. On this see Livingstone.

11. See, for instance, David Buckingham, *The Making of Citizens: Young People, Media and Politics* (London: Routledge, 2000).

12. John Urry, *The Tourist Gaze* (London: Sage, 2002).

13. See, for instance, Russell W. Belk, Melanie Wallendorf, and John F. Sherry, Jr., "The Sacred and the Profane in Consumer Behavior: Theodicy on the Odyssey," *Journal of Consumer Research* 16, no. 1 (1989): 1–38.

14. See www.participations.org.

15. There are of course complex histories within mass communications research. Histories from the inside would note increasing sophistication in statistical methods, the growth of field studies, and the rise of particular theorisations (one thinks of the increasing influence of Dolf Zillman's theorisations—see, for instance, his essay "Dramaturgy for Emotions from Fictional Narration," in Jennings Bryant and Peter Vorderer, eds., *The Psychology of Entertainment* [Hillsdale, NJ: Lawrence Erlbaum, 2006], 215–238). Histories from the outside would note both the persis-tence in moral and political agendas and the lack of a real critical evaluation of past work, but also subtle shifts—as, for instance, the rise of "public health" metaphors within recent research.

16. Kim Schrøder, Kirsten Drotner, Stephen Kline, and Catherine Murray, *Researching Audiences* (London: Arnold, 2003), 16.

17. Natasha Walters, "A Hero for Our Time," *Guardian* (July 16, 2005), G2, 27.

18. A very good example of this is the fine study by Livingstone and others of the place of new media in the lives of young people. For all its great strengths as a study, its arguments are made almost entirely by its statistical enquiries. The role of quotations from interviews rarely rises above the illustrative, and they certainly never provide the grounds for any new discoveries of their own.

19. This research was published as "*The Lord of the Rings* and 'Identification': A Critical Encounter," *European Journal of Communication* 20, no. 3 (2005): 353–378.

20. One example: Ernest Mathijs uncovered a complex set of special interests in the film among those reporting themselves as creatives. These were presented under the title "Professional Activity and the Enjoyment of Popular Culture" at "The Art of Comparison: 6th ESA Research

Conference on the Sociology of the Arts" (November 3–5, 2004, Rotterdam).

21. Jerzy Neyman, "On the Two Different Aspects of the Representative Method: The Method of Stratified Sampling and the Method of Purposive Selection," *Journal of the Royal Statistical Society* 97 (1934): 558–625.

22. A good reference on probability sampling, for its completeness, is C. A. Moser and G. Kalton, *Survey Methods in Social Investigation* (London: Heinemann, 1971).

23. On theory-driven samples, see Barney G. Glaser and Anselm L. Strauss, *The Discovery of Grounded Theory: Strategies for Qualitative Research* (Chicago: Aldine, 1967), 45.

24. M. B. Miles and A. M. Huberman, *Qualitative Data Analysis* (Thousand Oaks, CA: Sage, 1994).

25. Alberto Trobia, *La Ricerca Sociale Quali-Quantitativa* (Milan: Franco Angeli, 2005), 32–35.

26. S. Sarantakos, *Social Research* (Basingstoke: Palgrave Macmillan, 2004), 169–170.

27. Richard Dyer, *Only Entertainment* (London and New York: Routledge, 1992).

28. Laura Mulvey, "Visual Pleasure and Narrative Cinema," *Screen* 16, no. 3 (1975): 6–18.

29. Jim McGuigan, *Cultural Populism* (London: Routledge, 1992).

30. Sadly, the one or two overviews of research tend to restrict themselves to these theoretical debates, and are hardly aware of empirical research contributions. See, for instance, Barbara O'Connor and Elizabeth Klaus, "Pleasure and Meaningful Discourse: An Overview of Research Issues," *International Journal of Cultural Studies* 3, no. 3 (2000): 369–387. See also Patricia McCormack, "Pleasure, Perversion and Death: Three Lines of Flight for the Viewing Body," available at http://www.cinestatic.com/trans-mat/MacCormack/PPDcontents.htm (accessed August 7, 2006).

31. Ien Ang, *Watching Dallas: Soap Opera and the Melodramatic Imagination* (London: Methuen, 1984).

32. Barker and Brooks, *Knowing Audiences.*

33. Austin, *Hollywood, Hype and Audiences.*

34. Aphra Kerr, Julian Kücklich, and Pat Brereton, "New Media—New Pleasures?", *International Journal of Cultural Studies* 9, no. 1 (2006): 63–82.

35. For interesting analyses of local struggles over meanings, see Colin Barker, "Social Confrontation in Manchester's Quangoland: Local Protest over the Proposed Closure of Booth Hall Children's Hospital," *North West Geographer* 1 (1997): 18–28; Chik Collins, "To Concede or to Contest? Language and Class Struggle," in Colin Barker and Paul Kennedy, eds., *To Make Another World: Studies in Protest and Collective Action* (Aldershot: Avebury, 1996).

36. See, for example, Elizabeth A. Clark, *History, Theory, Text: Historians and the Linguistic Turn* (Cambridge, MA: Harvard University Press, 2004); Victoria E. Bonnell and Lynn Hunt, eds., *Beyond the Cultural Turn: New Directions in the Study of Society and Culture* (Berkeley: University of California Press, 1999).

37. Two recent books have done a very good job of delineating the range of approaches currently available and showing something of the nature of the debates among them. The second provides a very helpful account of the different methods and illustrates the kinds of findings they produce. Margaret Wetherell, Stephanie Taylor, and Simeon J. Yates, eds., *Discourse Theory and Practice: A Reader,* and *Discourse as Data: A Guide for Analysis* (both Milton Keynes: Open University Press, 2001).

38. For these and other examples, see Carla Willig, ed., *Applied Discourse Analysis* (London: Sage, 1999).

39. On this, see Abigail Locke and Derek Edwards, "Bill and Monica: Memory, Emotion and Normativity in Clinton's Grand Jury Testimony," *British Journal of Social Psychology* 42 (2003): 239–256.

40. Michael Billig, *Banal Nationalism* (London: Sage, 1995).

41. In a forthcoming essay, Martin Barker has closely examined works of recent discourse analysis, to bring these two issues into view. See his "Discourse Analysis and the Problem of Researching

'Impossible Objects,'" in Mike Pickering, ed., *Cultural Studies Methods* (Edinburgh: Edinburgh University Press, 2008).

42. The exceptions to this general statement are those approaches that use computer facilities to study word frequencies and relationships. See the discussion of corpus analysis in Wetherell et al., *Discourse as Data.*

43. The early work in developing these ideas arose with the ideas of "ethnoscience." See, for instance, Jerome S. Bruner, Jacqueline J. Goodnow, and George A. Austin, "Categories and Cognition," and Charles O. Frake, "The Ethnographic Study of Cognitive Systems," both in James Spradley, ed., *Culture and Cognition: Rules, Maps and Plans* (Toronto: Chandler Publishing, 1956), 168–190, 191–205.

44. Thomas McLaughlin, *Street Smarts and Critical Theory: Listening to the Vernacular* (Madison: University of Wisconsin Press, 1996).

45. Rick Altman, *Film/Genre* (New York: American Film Institute, 1999).

46. Barker et al., *The Crash Controversy.*

47. Barbara Klinger, *Beyond the Multiplex,* 164–176.

48. The concept of *isotopy* (*iso* = "same"; *topos* = "place") was initially proposed by A. J. Greimas, in 1966, in order to define the recurrence, in phrases or texts, of group of words sharing certain semantic features. It refers to an idea of meaning as a "contextual effect," something that does not belong to words considered one by one, but as a result of their relationships within texts or speeches. See F. Lancia, *The Logic of a Textscope* (2002), available at http://www.mytlab.com/textscope.pdf. A typical technique that yields isotopies is Lexical Correspondence Analysis (LCA) (see below).

49. Because we wanted to be able to pursue these investigations deeply, we inevitably preferred those countries with large sets of responses. The advantage also was that these tended to be the countries in which we had active research groups, who could comment on and interpret our findings for us.

50. Again for practical reasons, we limited our choices here to English-language responses—which anyway generated a very large dataset. We returned to other languages, to explore similarities and differences, at a later stage of this set of searches.

51. For more details on cluster analysis, see B. S. Everitt, S. Landau, and M. Leese, *Cluster Analysis* (London: Arnold, 2001).

52. Trobia, 49–53.

53. L. Lebart and A. Salem, *Statistique Textuelle* (Paris: Dunod, 1994).

54. The description of these algorithms would require many pages and formulas and it's beyond the aim of this writing.

55. See http://eng.spadsoft.com, for SPAD, and http://www.tlab.it, for T-LAB.

56. J. P. Benzecri, quoted in Lancia, 14.

57. For further details, see Trobia, 55–62.

58. David Silverman, *Interpreting Qualitative Data: Methods for Analysing Talk, Text and Interaction* (London: Sage, 2001).

59. Sarantakos, 346. Tesch, instead, listed twenty-six different kind of approaches. See R. Tesch, *Qualitative Research: Analysis Types and Software Tools* (New York: Falmer Press, 1990), 77–102.

60. For instance, N. Blaikie, "A Critique of the Use of Triangulation in Social Research," *Quality and Quantity* 25 (1991): 115–136.

61. Wood, 1978; David Bordwell, "Textual Analysis Etc." *Enclitic* 10, no. 5 (1981): 125–136; Altman.

62. Janet Staiger, *Interpreting Films;* Janet Staiger, *Perverse Spectators: The Practices of Film Reception* (New York: New York University Press, 2000); Barbara Klinger, "Film History Terminable and Interminable: Recovering the Past in Reception Studies," *Screen* 38, no. 2 (1997): 107–128; Ernest Mathijs, "AIDS References in the Critical Reception of David Cronenberg: 'It May not

Be Such a Bad Disease after All.'" *Cinema Journal* 42, no. 4 (2003): 29–45.

63. "Content analysis is a research technique for the objective, systematic, and quantitative description of the manifest content of communication." Bernard Berelson, *Content Analysis in Communications Research* (New York: Free Press, 1952), 18.

64. See, for instance, the critical evaluation posed by Brian Winston, "On Counting the Wrong Things," in Manuel Alvarado and John Thompson, eds., *The Media Reader* (London: British Film Institute, 1990).

65. Content analysis is a technique that shows the inadequacy of the traditional separation between qualitative and quantitative methods of research. For a critical review of the definitions, see G. Shapiro and J. Markoff, "A Matter of Definition," in C. W. Roberts, ed., *Textual Analysis for the Social Sciences: Methods for Drawing Statistical Inferences from Texts and Transcripts* (Hillside, NJ: Lawrence Erlbaum, 1997), 9–31.

66. See F. Lancia, 5–6.

67. Karl Erik Rosengren, "Time and Culture: Developments in the Swedish Literary Frame of Reference," and Marcus Hudec and Brigitte Lederer, "A Text Model for the Content Analysis of Messages in the Print Media," both in Gabriele Melischek, Karl Erik Rosengren and J. Stappers, eds., *Cultural Indicators: an International Symposium* (Vienna: Verlag der Osterreichischen Akademie der Wissenschaften, 1984) 273–299.

68. Rosengren, 284.

69. Janet Wasko, "The Political Economy of Film," in Toby Miller and Robert Stam, eds., *A Companion to Film Theory* (London: Blackwell, 1999), 221–233; Dallas Smythe, "The Political Economy of Communication," *Journalism Quarterly* (August 1960): 156–171; Adam Smith, *An Inquiry into the Nature and Causes of Wealth of Nations* (London: Everyman's Library, 1904 [1776]).

70. Commentators tend to locate its earliest appearance in E. J. Webb, D. T. Campbell, R. D. Schwartz, and L. Sechrest, *Unobtrusive Measures: Nonreactive Measures in the Social Sciences* (Chicago: Rand McNally, 1966).

71. See his *The Research Act,* a book that has been through a number of editions (Chicago: Aldine, 1970, 1976, 1981, 1989, and so on), and in which the discussion of triangulation changes over time. Most notably it changes from being, in the earliest versions (in which he was closest to symbolic interactionism), very clearly an additional ground of *validity,* to a more limited and hermeneutic *multiplicity of possible accounts* (as Denzin moved closer to postmodernism). Compare: "My last criterion under the category of validity . . . is the triangulation of methodologies" (Denzin, 27) and "Triangulation is not a tool or strategy of validation, but an alternative to validation" (Norman K. Denzin and Yvonna S. Lincoln. *The Landscape of Qualitative Research: Theories and Issues.* Thousand Oaks, CA: Sage, 1998, 2).

72. See, for instance, the discussion in Michael Quinn Patton, *Qualitative Evaluation and Research Methods* (Newbury Park, CA: Sage, 1990), 467.

73. See especially Y. S. Lincoln and E. G. Guba, *Naturalistic Inquiry* (Beverly Hills, CA: Sage, 1985).

74. For a clear account of a number of these criticisms, see Alexander Massey, "Methodological Triangulation; or: How to Get Lost without Being Found Out," in A. Massey and G. Walford, eds., *Explorations in Methodology: Studies in Educational Ethnography,* vol. 2 (Stamford, CT: JAI Press), 183–197.

75. We are of course by no means alone in perceiving these problems within ways of conceiving the "cultural circuit." As just one example, take Ulrike Meinhof's statement of the problems of the relations among "the triad of communication between author . . . , text, and reader/recipient:" "it is the relative privileging of one interpretative focus over the other that influences the appreciation or denial of the power of an audience to assert his or her own readings. An emphasis on production rarely integrates textual analysis and variant readings. A textual analysis usually relegates the reader to that of an implied reader, who activates textual structures that impose their

own authority through the semiotic codes themselves. . . . Audience studies, on the other hand, tend to emphasise the multiplicity of meanings that are activated by readers. Attempts to analyse dynamic interactivity between production/author, the text, and reader/audience—though often asserted as desirable in theory—tend to privilege one perspective over the other'" (Ulrike Hanna Meinhof, "Initiating a Public: Malagasy Music and Live Audiences in Differentiated Cultural Contexts," in Livingstone, 115–116). Meinhof's solution is to find a relatively less complicated situation of live performance (a World Music performance in which musicians and audience directly exchange), and look at the "loops" between the three aspects within this special situation. We believe our solution may have wider application.

Bibliography

Abercombie, Nicholas and Brian Longhurst. *Audiences.* London: Sage, 1998.

Acland, Charles. *Screen Traffic: Movies, Multiplexes and Global Culture.* Durham, NC: Duke University Press, 2004.

Allan, Stuart. *News Culture.* Buckingham: Open University Press, 1999.

Allan, Stuart, ed. *Journalism: Critical Issues.* Maidenhead: Open University Press, 2005.

Altman, Robert. *Film/Genre.* London: British Film Institute, 1999.

Alvarado, Manuel and John O. Thompson. *The Media Reader.* London: British Film Institute, 1990.

Anderson, Benedict. *Imagined Communities: Reflections on the Origin and Spread of Nationalism.* London: Verso, 1991.

Ang, Ien. *Watching Dallas: Soap Opera and the Melodramatic Imagination.* London: Methuen, 1985.

Ang, Ien. *Living Room Wars: Rethinking Media Audiences for a Postmodern World.* London: Routledge, 1996.

Astin, Sean and Joe Layden. *There and Back Again: An Actor's Tale: A Behind the Scenes Look at The Lord of the Rings.* London: Virgin Books, 2005.

Austin, Bruce. "Portrait of a Cult Film Audience." *Journal of Communication* 31 (1980): 43–54.

Austin, Bruce. "Critics' and Consumers' Evaluation of Motion Pictures: A Longitudinal Test of the Taste Culture and Elite Hypotheses." *Journal of Popular Film* 10, no. 4 (1983): 156–167.

Austin, Bruce. *Current Research in Film: Audience, Economics, and Law.* Norwood, NJ: Ablex Publishing Corporation, 1985.

Austin, Thomas. *Hollywood, Hype and Audiences: Selling and Watching Popular Film in the 1990s.* Manchester: Manchester University Press, 2002.

Barker, Colin. "Social Confrontation in Manchester's Quangoland: Local Protest over the Proposed Closure of Booth Hall Children's Hospital." *North West Geographer* 1 (1997): 18–28.

Barker, Colin and Paul Kennedy, eds. *To Make Another World: Studies in Protest and Collective Action.* Aldershot: Avebury, 1996.

Barker, Martin. "News, Reviews, Clues, Interviews, and Other Ancillary Materials: A Critique and Research Proposal." *Scope: An Online Journal of Film Studies* (February 2004).

Barker, Martin. "*The Lord of the Rings* and 'Identification': A Critical Encounter." *European Journal of Communication* 20, no. 3 (2005): 353–378.

Barker, Martin. "Loving and Hating *Straw Dogs:* The Meanings of Audience Responses to a Controversial Film." *Participations: Online Journal of Audience and Reception Studies* 2, no. 2 (2005), and 3, no. 1 (2006).

Barker, Martin. "Envisaging 'Visualisation': Some Challenges from the International *Lord of the Rings* Audience Project." *Film-Philosophy* 10, no. 3 (2006): 1–25.

Barker, Martin, Jane Arthurs, and Ramaswami Harindranath. *The Crash Controversy: Censorship Campaigns and Film Reception.* London: Wallflower, 2001.

Barker, Martin and Kate Brooks. *Knowing Audiences: Judge Dredd, Its Friends, Fans and Foes.* Luton: University of Luton Press, 1998.

Barker, Martin, Kate Egan, and Ernest Mathijs. "Creative Viewing: Occupation, Status, and the Meanings of 'Enjoyment' of *The Lord of the Rings*." Annual Society for Cinema and Media Studies Conference: Institute for Education, London, April 3, 2005.

Barker, Martin and Ernest Mathijs. "Understanding Vernacular Experiences of Film in an Academic Environment. *ADCHE—Arts, Design and Communication in Higher Education* 4, no. 1 (2005): 49–71.

Barker, Martin and Julian Petley, eds. *Ill Effects: The Media Violence Debate,* 2nd ed. London: Routledge, 2001.

Barker, Martin with Thomas Austin. *From Antz to Titanic: Reinventing Film Analysis.* London: Pluto, 2001.

Bassham, Gregory and Eric Bronsson, eds. *The Lord of the Rings and Philosophy: One Book to Rule Them All.* New York: Open Court, 2003.

Basuroy, Suman, Subimal Chatterjee, and S. Abraham Ravid. "How Critical Are Critical Reviews? The Box Office Effects of Film Critics, Star Power, and Budgets." *Journal of Marketing* 67, no. 4 (2003): 103–117.

Baudrillard, Jean. *For a Critique of the Political Economy of the Sign.* St. Louis, MO: Telos Press, 1973.

Baxandall, Michael. *Painting and Experience in Fifteenth Century Italy: A Primer in the Social History of Pictorial Style.* Oxford: Oxford University Press, 1988.

Baym, Nancy. *Tune In, Log On: Soaps, Fandom, and Online Community.* Thousand Oaks, CA: Sage, 2000.

Beatie, Bruce A. "The Tolkien Phenomenon, 1954–1968." *Journal of Popular Culture* 3, no. 4 (1970): 689–703.

Beck, Ulrich. "The Cosmopolitan Society and Its Enemies." *Theory, Culture & Society* 19, nos. 1–2 (2002): 17–44.

Begg, Ean. *Lord of the Rings and the Signs of the Times.* London: Guild of Pastoral Psychology Paperback, 1975.

Belk, Russell W., Guliz Ger, and Soren Askegaard. "The Fire of Desire: A Multisited Inquiry into Consumer Passion." *Journal of Consumer Research* 30, no. 3 (2003): 326–351.

Belk, Russell W., Melanie Wallendorf, and John F Sherry, Jr. "The Sacred and the Profane in Consumer Behavior: Theodicy on the Odyssey." *Journal of Consumer Research* 16, no. 1 (1989): 1–38.

Bellin, Joshua David. *Framing Monsters: Fantasy Film and Social Alienation.* Carbondale: Southern Illinois University Press, 2005.

Bennett, Susan. *Theatre Audiences: A Theory of Production and Reception.* London: Routledge, 1998.

Bennett, Tony, Michael Emmison, and John Frow. *Accounting for Tastes: Australian Everyday Cultures.* Cambridge: Cambridge University Press, 1999.

Bennett, Tony and Janet Woollacott. *Bond and Beyond: The Political Career of a Popular Hero.* Basingstoke: Macmillan, 1987.

Bentele, Günter, Hans-Bernd Brosius, and Otfried Jarren, eds. *Öffentliche Kommunikation: Handbuch*

Kommunikations- und Medienwissenschaft. Wiesbaden: VS Verlag, 2003.

Bentele, Günter, Hans-Bernd Brosius, and Otfried Jarren, eds. *Lexikon Kommunikations- und Medienwissenschaft*. Wiesbaden: VS Verlag, 2006.

Berelson, Bernard. *Content Analysis in Communications Research*. New York: Free Press, 1952.

Bérubé, Michael, ed. *The Aesthetics of Cultural Studies*. Oxford: Blackwell, 2005.

Billig, Michael. *Banal Nationalism*. London: Sage 1995.

Biltereyst, Daniel and Giselinde Kuipers, eds. *Tijdschrift voor Communicatiewetenschap en Mediacultuur* 34, no. 1 (2006).

Biltereyst, Daniel and Philippe Meers. The International Telenovela Debate and the Contra-flow Argument: A Reappraisal. *Media, Culture & Society* 22, no. 4 (2000): 393–413.

Biltereyst, Daniel and Philippe Meers, eds. *Film/TV/Genre*. Ghent: Academia Press, 2004.

Blackadder, Neil. *Performing Opposition: Modern Theater and the Scandalized Audience*. Westport, CT: Praeger, 2003.

Blaikie, Neil. "A Critique of the Use of Triangulation in Social Research." *Quality and Quantity* 25 (1991): 115–136.

Bluestone, George. *Novels into Films: The Metamorphosis of Fiction into Cinema*. Baltimore, MD: Johns Hopkins University Press, 1957.

Böhnke, Alexander. "Mehrwert DVD." *Navigationen* 5, nos. 1–2 (2005): 213–223.

Bonnell, Victoria E. and Lynn Hunt, eds. *Beyond the Cultural Turn: New Directions in the Study of Society and Culture*. Berkeley: University of California Press, 1999.

Boose, Lynda E. and Richard Burt, eds. *Shakespeare the Movie: Popularising the Plays on Film, TV, and Video*. London: Routledge, 1997.

Bordwell, David. "Textual Analysis Etc." *Enclitic* 10, no. 5 (1981): 125–136.

Bordwell, David. *Narration in the Fiction Film*. London: Routledge, 1985.

Bordwell, David. *Making Meaning: Inference and Rhetoric in the Interpretation of Cinema*. Cambridge, MA: Harvard University Press, 1989.

Bordwell, David. *The Way Hollywood Tells It: Story and Style in Modern Movies*. Berkeley: University of California Press, 2006.

Bourdieu, Pierre. *Distinction: A Social Critique of Judgement of Taste*. London: Routledge, 1986.

Braudel, Fernand. *On History*. Chicago: University of Chicago Press, 1982.

Braudy, Leo and Marshall Cohen, eds. *Film Theory and Criticism*. New York: Oxford University Press, 2004.

Brodie, Ian. *The Lord of the Rings Location Guidebook*. London: HarperCollins, 2003.

Brooker, Will. *Using the Force: Creativity, Community and Star Wars Fans*. New York and London: Continuum, 2002.

Bryant, Jennings and Peter Vorderer, eds. *The Psychology of Entertainment*. Hillsdale, NJ: Lawrence Erlbaum, 2006.

Buckingham, David. *Public Secrets: 'EastEnders' and Its Audience*. London: British Film Institute, 1987.

Buckingham, David. *The Making of Citizens: Young People, Media and Politics*. London: Routledge, 2000.

Campbell, G. "Planet Middle Earth." *New Zealand Listener* (December 15, 2001), 18–24.

Carpenter, Humphrey. *J R R Tolkien: A Biography*. London: Allen and Unwin, 1977.

Carpentier, Nico, Caroline Pauwels, and Olga Van Oost. *The Un-graspable Audience*. Brussels: VUB Press, 2004.

Carter, Lin. *Tolkien: A Look behind the Lord of the Rings*. New York: Ballantine Books, 1969.

Cartmell, Deborah, I. Q. Hunter, Heidi Kaye, and Imelda Whelehan. *Trash Aesthetics: Popular Culture and Its Audience*. London: Pluto Press, 1997.

Centre for Contemporary Cultural Studies, ed. *Culture, Media, Language: Working Papers in Cultural Studies, 1972–79*. London: Hutchinson, 1980.

Chance, Jane. *The Lord of the Rings: The Mythology of Power*. Lexington: University of Kentucky Press, 1992/2001.

Chance, Jane. "Is There a Text in This Hobbit? Peter Jackson's *Fellowship of the Ring*." *Literature/Film Quarterly* 30, no. 2 (2002): 79–85.

Chaney, David. *Cultural Change and Everyday Life.* Basingstoke: Palgrave, 2002.

Chengzhi, Zhang. "The Eyes You Find Will Make You Shiver." *Inter-Asia Cultural Studies* 5, no. 3 (2004): 486–490.

Chin, Bertha and Jonathan Gray. "'One Ring to Rule Them All': Pre-viewers and Pre-texts of the *Lord of the Rings* Films." *Intensities: Online Journal of Cult Media* 2 (2001).

Clark, Elizabeth A. *History, Theory, Text: Historians and the Linguistic Turn.* Cambridge, MA: Harvard University Press, 2004.

Cohen, Jonathan. "Parasocial Break-Up from Favorite Television Characters: The Role of Attachment Styles and Relationship Intensity." *Journal of Social and Personal Relationships* 21, no. 2 (2004): 187–202.

Colebatch, Hal G. P. *Return of the Heroes: The Lord of the Rings, Star Wars, Harry Potter and Social Conflict.* Perth: Cyber Editions Corporation, 2003.

Communication Theory 14, no. 4 (November 2004).

Cooper-Chen, Anne. *Global Entertainment Media: Content, Audiences, Issues.* Mahwah, NJ: Lawrence Erlbaum, 2005.

Cormack, Patricia. "Pleasure, Perversion and Death: Three Lines of Flight for the Viewing Body." Available at http://www.cinestatic.com/trans-mat/MacCormack/PPDcontents.htm.

Couldry, Nick. *Inside Culture: Re-Imagining the Method of Cultural Studies.* London: Sage, 2000.

Croft, Janet Brennan, ed. *Tolkien on Film: Essays on Peter Jackson's The Lord of the Rings.* London: Mythopoeic Press, 2005.

Curran, James and Michael Gurevitch. *Mass Media and Society.* London: Arnold, 2000.

Curry, Patrick. *Defending Middle-Earth: Tolkien—Myth and Modernity.* Barrington, MA: Floris Books, 1997.

Dalton, Russell W. *Faith Journey through Fantasy Lands: A Christian Dialogue with Harry Potter, Star Wars and The Lord of the Rings.* Minneapolis, MN: Augsburg Fortress, 2004.

Davies, Máire Messenger. *Fake, Fact, and Fantasy: Children's Interpretations of Television Reality.* Mahwah, NJ: Lawrence Erlbaum, 1997.

Davies, Philip, ed. *Imagining and Representing America.* Stafford: Keele University Press, 1996.

Davis, E. "The Fellowship of the Ring." *Wired Magazine* (October 2001), 120–132.

Dawson, Anna. *Studying The Lord of the Rings.* London: Auteur Publishing, 2006.

Denzin, Norman K. *The Research Act: A Theoretical Introduction to Sociological Methods.* Chicago: Aldine, 1970.

Denzin, Norman K. and Yvonna S. Lincoln. *The Landscape of Qualitative Research: Theories and Issues.* Thousand Oaks, CA: Sage, 1998.

Dickerson, Matthew. *Following Gandalf.* Grand Rapids, MI: Brazos Press, 2003.

Donald, James. *Fantasy and the Cinema.* London: British Film Institute, 1989.

Dorfman, Ariel and Armand Mattelart. *How to Read Donald Duck: Imperialist Ideology in the Disney Comic.* New York: International General, 1973.

Dyer, Richard. *Only Entertainment.* London and New York: Routledge, 1992.

Dyer, Richard. *Stars.* London: British Film Institute, 2001.

Eaglestone, Robert. *Reading The Lord of the Rings: New Writings on Tolkien's Trilogy.* London: Continuum, 2005.

Elsaesser, Thomas. *Hollywood op Straat: Film en Televisie in de Hedendaagse Mediacultuur [Hollywood on the Street: Film and Television in Today's Media Culture].* Amsterdam: Amsterdam University Press, 2000.

Elsaesser, Thomas and Warren Buckland. *Studying Contemporary American Film: A Guide to Movie Analysis.* London: Arnold, 2002.

Erb, Cynthia. *Tracking King Kong: A Hollywood Icon in World Culture.* Detroit, MI: Wayne State

University Press, 1998.

Everitt, B. S., S. Landau, and M. Leese. *Cluster Analysis*. London: Arnold, 2001.

Fetveit, Arild. "Anti-Essentialism and Reception Studies." *International Journal of Cultural Studies* 4, no. 2 (2001): 173–199.

Field, A. *Discovering Statistics Using SPSS for Windows*. London: Sage, 2000.

Fielding, N. G. and R. M. Lee. *Computer Analysis and Qualitative Research*. London: Sage, 1998.

Finnegan, Ruth. *The Hidden Musicians: Music-Making in an English Town*. Cambridge: Cambridge University Press, 1989.

Fiske, John. *Television Culture*. London: Methuen, 1987.

Fiske, John. *Reading the Popular*. New York: Routledge, 1991.

Fiske, John. *Understanding Popular Culture*. New York: Routledge, 1994.

Flick, Uwe. *An Introduction to Qualitative Research*. London: Sage, 2006.

Flick, Uwe, Ernst von Kardorff, and Ines Steinke, eds. *A Companion to Qualitative Research*. London: Sage, 2004.

Flynn, G. "*Lord of the Rings:* Ringmasters." *Entertainment Weekly* (November 16, 2001), 36–46.

Gans, Herbert. *Popular Culture and High Culture: An Analysis and Evaluation of Taste*. New York: Basic Books, 1976.

Genette, Gerard. *Paratexts: Thresholds of Interpretation*. Cambridge: Cambridge University Press, 1997.

George, Sandy. "Gunning for a Bigger Stage." *Screen International* (November 12, 2004).

Giddings, Robert. *J. R. R. Tolkien: This Far Land*. London and Totawa, NJ: Barnes and Noble Books, 1984.

Giddings, Robert and Erica Sheen, eds. *The Classic Novel: From Page to Screen*. Manchester: Manchester University Press, 2000.

Gilbert, Nigel, ed. *Researching Social Life*. London: , 1993.

Glaser, Barney G. and Anselm L. Strauss. *The Discovery of Grounded Theory: Strategies for Qualitative Research*. Chicago: Aldine, 1967.

Gledhill, Christine and Linda Williams, eds. *Reinventing Film Studies*. London: Arnold, 2000.

Gordon, Andrew. "Science-Fiction and Fantasy Film Criticism: The Case of Lucas and Spielberg." *Journal of the Fantastic in the Arts* 2, no. 2 (1989): 81–94.

Götz, Maya, Dafna Lemish, Amy Aidman, and Hyesung Moon. *Media and the Make-Believe Worlds of Children: When Harry Potter Meets Pokemon in Disneyland*. Hillsdale, NJ: Lawrence Erlbaum, 2005.

Grant, Barry Keith. *Film Genre Reader II*. Austin: University of Texas Press, 1995.

Grant, Barry Keith. *A Cultural Assault: The New Zealand Films of Peter Jackson*. Nottingham: Kakapo Books, 1999.

Gray, Jonathan. "New Audiences, New Textualities: Anti-Fans and Non-Fans." *International Journal of Cultural Studies* 6, no. 1 (2003): 64–81.

Grossberg, Lawrence. *Bringing It All Back Home: Essays on Cultural Studies*. Durham, NC: Duke University Press, 1997.

Haber, Karen, ed. *Meditations on Middle-Earth*. London: Simon and Schuster, 2001.

Habermas, Jurgen. *Strukturwandel der Öffentlichkeit*. Frankfurt: Suhrkamp Verlag, 1962.

Hammond, Wayne G. and Christina Scull. *The Lord of the Rings: A Reader's Companion*. London: HarperCollins, 2005.

Harper, Sue and Vincent Porter. "Moved to Tears: Weeping in the Cinema in Post-War Britain," *Screen* 37, no. 2 (Summer 1996): 152–173.

Harris, Cheryl and Alison Alexander, eds. *Theorizing Fandom: Fans, Subcultures and Identity*. Cresskill, NJ: Hampton Press, 1998.

Harvey, David. *The Song of Middle Earth*. London: Allen and Unwin, 1985.

Helms, Randel. *Tolkien's Worlds*. London: Thames and Hudson, 1974.

Hesmondhalgh, Desmond. *The Cultural Industries*. London: , 2002.

Hight, Craig. "Making-of Documentaries on DVD: The Lord of the Rings Trilogy and Special Editions." *The Velvet Light Trap* 56 (2005): 4–17.

Hill, Annette. *Shocking Entertainment: Responses to Violent Movies.* Luton: University of Luton Press, 1997.

Hills, Matt. *Fan Cultures.* London: Routledge, 2002.

Hills, Matt. *How to Do Things with Cultural Theory.* London: Hodder Arnold, 2005.

Hoffner, C. "Children's Wishful Identification and Parasocial Interaction with Favorite Television Characters." *Journal of Broadcasting & Electronic Media* 40 (1996): 389–402.

Hofstede, G. *Culture's Consequences: Comparing Values, Behaviors, Institutions, and Organizations across Nations.* Thousand Oaks, CA: Sage, 2001.

Hofstede, G. and G. J. Hofstede. *Cultures and Organizations: Software of the Mind,* rev. and expanded 2nd ed. New York: McGraw-Hill, 2005.

Höijer, Birgitta. "Studying Viewers' Reception of Television Programmes: Theoretical and Methodological Considerations." *European Journal of Communication* 5, no. 1 (1990): 29–56.

Holub, Robert. *Reception Theory: A Critical Introduction.* New York: Methuen, 1984.

Horton, Andrew S. and Stuart Y. MacDougall, eds. *Play It Again, Sam: Retakes on Remakes.* Berkeley: University of California Press, 1998.

Horton, Andrew S. and Joan Magretta, eds. *Modern European Filmmakers and the Art of Adaptation.* New York: Frederick Ungar, 1981.

Horton, Donald and R. Richard Wohl. "Mass Communication and Para-Social Interaction: Observations on Intimacy at a Distance." *Psychiatry* 19 (1956): 215–229.

Innis, Harold A. *Empire and Communications.* Oxford: Oxford University Press, 1950.

Isaacs, Neil D. and Rose A Zimbardo, eds. *Tolkien and the Critics.* Notre Dame, IN: University of Notre Dame Press, 1968.

Isaacs, Neil and Rose Zimbardo, eds. *Understanding the Lord of the Rings: The Best of Tolkien Criticism.* London: Houghton Mifflin Company, 2005.

Iser, Wolfgang. *The Act of Reading: A Theory of Aesthetic Response.* London: Routledge and Kegan Paul, 1978.

Jakobson, Roman. *Essais de Linguistique Générale.* Paris: Editions du Minuit, 1963.

Jancovich, Mark, Antonio Lazaro-Reboll, Julian Stringer, and Andrew Willis, eds. *Defining Cult Movies: The Cultural Politics of Oppositional Taste.* Manchester: Manchester University Press, 2003.

Jauss, Hans Robert. *Literaturgeschichte als Provokation.* Frankfurt: Suhrkamp, 1974.

Jenkins, Henry. *Textual Poachers: Television Fans and Participatory Culture.* New York: Routledge, 1992.

Johnson-Cartee, Karen S. *News Narratives and News Framing.* Lanham, MD: Rowman and Littlefield, 2005.

Jowett, Garth S., Ian C. Jarvie, and Kathryn H. Fuller. *Children and the Movies: Media Influence and the Payne Fund Controversy.* Cambridge: Cambridge University Press, 1996.

Kay, P. and W. Kempton. "What Is the Sapir-Whorf Hypothesis?" *American Anthropologist* 86, no. 1 (1984): 65–79.

Kellner, Douglas. "Boundaries and Borderlines: Reflections on Jean Baudrillard and Critical Theory." *Illuminations, the Critical Theory Website.* Available at http://www.uta.edu/huma/illuminations/ke112.htm.

Kerr, Aphra, Julian Kücklich, and Pat Brereton. "New Media—New Pleasures?" *International Journal of Cultural Studies* 9, no. 1 (2006): 63–82.

Klinger, Barbara. "Film History Terminable and Interminable: Recovering the Past in Reception Studies." *Screen* 38, no. 2 (1997): 107–128.

Klinger, Barbara. *Beyond the Multiplex: Cinema, New Technologies, and the Home.* Berkeley: University of California Press, 2006.

Kreeft, Peter. *The Philosophy of Tolkien: The Worldview behind the Lord of the Rings.* New York: Ignatius

Press, 2005.

Kress, Gunther and Theo van Leeuwen. *Multimodal Discourse: The Modes and Media of Contemporary Communication*. London: Arnold, 2001.

Kuhn, Annette. *Dreaming of Fred and Ginger: Cinema and Cultural Memory*. New York: New York University Press, 2002.

Kuhn, Annette. "Heterotopia, Heterochronia: Place and Time in Cinema Memory." *Screen* 45, no. 2 (2004): 106–114.

Lam, Adam and Nataliya Oryshchuk, eds. *How We Became Middle-Earth: A Collection of Essays on The Lord of the Rings*. London: Walking Tree Publishers, 2007.

Lamb, David. "Preserving a Primitive Society: Reflections on Post-Wittgensteinian Social Philosophy." *Sociological Review* 25, no. 4 (1977): 689–719.

Lamont, Michèle. *Money, Morals, and Manners: The Culture of the French and American Upper-Middle Class*. Chicago: University of Chicago Press, 1992.

Lamont, Michèle. *The Dignity of Working Men: Morality and the Boundaries of Race, Class, and Immigration*. New York: Russell Sage Foundation, 2000.

Lamont, Michèle and Laurent Thévenot. *Rethinking Comparative Cultural Sociology: Repertoires of Evaluation in France and the United States*. Cambridge: Cambridge University Press, 2000.

Lancaster, Kurt. *Interacting with Babylon Five: Fan Performance in a Media Universe*. Austin: University of Texas Press, 2001.

Lancia, F. *The Logic of a Textscope*. 2002. Available at http://www.mytlab.com/textscope.pdf.

Lealand, Geoff and Helen Martin. "Aotearea/New Zealand." *Australian Screen Education* 39 (2004): 8–15.

Lebart, L. and A. Salem. *Statistique Textuelle*. Paris: Dunod, 1994.

Lehtonen, Mikko. *The Cultural Analysis of Texts*. London: Sage, 2000.

Lewis, Lisa A., ed. *The Adoring Audience: Fan Culture and Popular Media*. London: Routledge, 1992.

Leysen, Ann, Daniel Biltereyst, and Philippe Meers. *The Lord of the Rings: The Return of the King: A Quantitative Analysis of the Film Reception*. Research paper. Ghent: Department of Communication Studies, 2005.

Leysen, Ann, Sofie Van Bauwel, Daniel Biltereyst, and Philippe Meers. *The Lord of the Rings: The Return of the King: A Reception Study on The Lords of the Rings: The Return of the King in Relation to the Film Text, Film Experience and the Film Viewing Context*. Research paper. Ghent: Department of Communication Studies, 2005.

Liebes, Tamar and Elihu Katz. *The Export of Meaning: Cross Cultural Readings of Dallas*. Cambridge, MA: Polity Press, 1993.

Lincoln, Y. S. and E. G. Guba. *Naturalistic Inquiry*. Beverly Hills, CA: Sage, 1985.

Lindlof, Thomas. *Qualitative Communication Research Methods*. Thousands Oaks, CA: Sage, 1995.

Livingstone, Sonia. *Making Sense of Television: The Psychology of Audience Interpretation*. London: Routledge, 1998.

Livingstone, Sonia. "On the Challenges of Cross-National Comparative Media Research." *European Journal of Communication* 18, no. 4 (2003): 477–500.

Livingstone, Sonia, ed. *Audiences and Publics: When Cultural Engagement Matters for the Public Sphere*. London: Intellect, 2005.

Livingstone, Sonia and Moira Bovill, eds. *Children and Their Changing Media Environment: A European Comparative Study*. Mahwah, NJ: Lawrence Erlbaum Associates, 2001.

Lobdell, Jared, ed. *A Tolkien Compass*. New York: Open Court, 2002.

Locke, Abigail and Derek Edwards. "Bill and Monica: Memory, Emotion and Normativity in Clinton's Grand Jury Testimony." *British Journal of Social Psychology* 42 (2003): 239–256.

Loux, Michael M. *The Possible and the Actual: Readings in the Metaphysics of Modality*. Ithaca, NY: Cornell University Press, 1979.

Lowson, Iain, Keith Marshall, and Daniel O'Brien. *The World of the Rings: The Unauthorised Guide to the Work of JRR Tolkien.* Richmond, Surrey: Reynolds and Hearn, 2002.

Luthar, Breda. "Kulturna globalizacija, film in promocijski re im" ("Cultural Globalization, Film and Promotional Regime: The Case of The Lord of the Rings"). *Teorija in praksa* 43, nos. 1–2 (2006): 5–24.

Lutz, Catherine A. and Jane L. Collins. *Reading National Geographic.* Chicago: University of Chicago Press, 1993.

Machor, James L. and Philip Goldstein. *Reception Study: From Literary Theory to Cultural Studies.* New York: Routledge, 2001.

Magid, Ron. "Imagining Middle Earth." *American Cinematographer* 82, no. 12 (December 2001): 60–69.

Mannheim, Karl. *Essays on the Sociology of Knowledge.* London: Routledge and Kegan Paul, 1952.

Marshall, P. David. *Celebrity and Power: Fame in Contemporary Culture.* Minneapolis: University of Minnesota Press, 1997.

Massey, A. and G. Walford, eds. *Explorations in Methodology: Studies in Educational Ethnography,* vol. 2. Stamford, CT: JAI Press, 1999.

Massumi, Brian. *Parables for the Virtual: Movement, Affect Sensation.* Durham, NC, and London: Duke University Press, 2002.

Mast, Gerald, Marshall Cohen, and Leo Braudy, eds. *Film Theory and Criticism.* New York: Oxford University Press, 1992.

Mathijs, Ernest. "AIDS References in the Critical Reception of David Cronenberg: 'It May Not Be Such a Bad Disease after All.'" *Cinema Journal* 42, no. 4 (2003): 29–45.

Mathijs, Ernest. "Professional Activity and the Enjoyment of Popular Culture." The Art of Comparison: 6th ESA Research Conference on the Sociology of the Arts, Rotterdam, The Netherlands. November 3–5, 2004.

Mathijs, Ernest. "Watching Creatively: Profession, Status, and the Viewing Experience of the Lord of the Rings Audience." Conference paper. The Art of Comparison: 6th Conference of the ESA Research Network for the Sociology of the Arts, Rotterdam, The Netherlands. November 3–5, 2004.

Mathijs, Ernest. "Bad Reputations: The Reception of Trash Cinema." *Screen* 46, no. 4 (2005): 451–472.

Mathijs, Ernest, ed. *The Lord of the Rings: Popular Culture in Global Context.* London: Wallflower, 2006.

Mathijs, Ernest and Janet Jones, eds. *Big Brother International: Critics, Formats and Publics.* London: Wallflower, 2004.

Mathijs, Ernest and Murray Pomerance, eds. *From Hobbits to Hollywood: Essays on Peter Jackson's The Lord of the Rings.* New York: Rodopi, 2006.

McClain, Buzz. "The Lord of the Marketers." *DVD Exclusive* (May 2004), 20, 23.

McCormack, Patricia. "Pleasure, Perversion and Death: Three Lines of Flight for the Viewing Body." Available at http://www.cinestatic.com/trans-mat/MacCormack/PPDcontents.htm.

McDonald, Paul. *The Star System: Hollywood's Production of Popular Identities.* London: Wallflower, 2000.

McFarlane, Brian. *Novel to Film: An Introduction to the Theory of Adaptation.* Clarendon: Oxford University Press, 1996.

McGuigan, Jim. *Cultural Populism.* London: Routledge, 1992.

McKee, Alan. *Textual Analysis: A Beginner's Guide.* London: Sage, 2003.

McLaughlin, Thomas. *Street Smarts and Critical Theory: Listening to the Vernacular.* Madison: University of Wisconsin Press, 1996.

McQuail, Denis, Peter Golding, and Els de Bens, eds. *Communication Theory and Research: An EJC Anthology.* London: Sage, 2005.

McRobbie, Angela, ed. *Feminism and Youth Culture.* Basingstoke: Macmillan, 2000.

Mediana TGI, Institute for Market and Media Research. *Obiskovalci Kinematografov po Starosti in Izobrazbi. (Cinema Visitors according to Age and Education).* Ljubljana: Mediana, 2006.

Melischek, Gabriele, Karl Erik Rosengren, and J. Stappers, eds. *Cultural Indicators: an International*

Symposium. Vienna: Verlag der Osterreichischen Akademie der Wissenschaften, 1984.

Metz, Christian. *Psychoanalysis and Cinema: The Imaginary Signifier.* Basingstoke: Macmillan, 1990.

Mikos, Lothar. *Fern-Sehen: Bausteine zu einer Rezeptionsästhetik des Fernsehens.* Berlin: Vistas, 2001.

Mikos, Lothar. *Film- und Fernsehanalyse.* Konstanz: UVK, 2003.

Mikos, Lothar and Claudia Wegener, eds. *Qualitative Medienforschung: Ein Handbuch.* Konstanz: UVK, 2005.

Mikos, Lothar et al. *Im Auge der Kamera: Das Fernsehereignis "Big Brother."* Berlin: Vistas, 2000.

Miles, M. B. and A. M. Huberman. *Qualitative Data Analysis.* Thousand Oaks, CA: Sage, 1994.

Miller, Toby, Nitin Govil, John McMurria, and Richard Maxwell. *Global Hollywood.* London: British Film Institute, 2001.

Miller, Toby and Robert Stam, eds. *A Companion to Film Theory.* London: Blackwell, 1999.

Moran, Albert, ed. *Film Policy.* London and New York: Routledge, 1996.

Morgan, David. *The Focus Group Guidebook.* Thousand Oaks, CA: Sage, 1998.

Morley, David. *The "Nationwide" Audience: Structure and Decoding.* London: British Film Institute, 1980.

Morley, David and Charlotte Brunson. *The Nationwide Television Studies.* London and New York: Routledge, 1999.

Moser, C. A. and G. Kalton. *Survey Methods in Social Investigation.* London: Heinemann, 1971.

Mulvey, Laura. "Visual Pleasure and Narrative Cinema." *Screen* 16, no. 3 (1975): 6–18.

Munk, Nina. *Fools Rush In: Steve Case, Jerry Levin, and the Unmaking of AOL Time Warner.* New York: HarperCollins, 2004.

Naremore, James, ed. *Film Adaptation.* London: Athlone Press, 2000.

Neyman, J. "On the Two Different Aspects of the Representative Method: The Method of Stratified Sampling and the Method of Purposive Selection." *Journal of the Royal Statistical Society* 97 (1934): 558–625.

Nowell-Smith, Geoffrey, ed. *The Oxford History of World Cinema.* Oxford: Oxford University Press, 1996.

O'Connor, Barbara and Elisabeth Klaus. "Pleasure and Meaningful Discourse: An Overview of Research Issues." *International Journal of Cultural Studies* 3, no. 3 (2000): 369–387.

Orr, John and Colin Nicholson, eds. *Cinema and Fiction: New Modes of Adapting, 1950–1990.* Edinburgh: Edinburgh University Press, 1992.

Patton, Michael Quinn. *Qualitative Evaluation and Research Methods.* Newbury Park, CA: Sage, 1990.

Pawling, Chris, ed. *Popular Fiction and Social Change.* Basingstoke: Macmillan, 1984.

Penley, Constance. *NASA/Trek: Popular Science and Sex in America.* New York: Verso, 1997.

Petersen, Richard A. and Narasimhan Anand. "The Production of Cultural Perspective." *Annual Review of Sociology* 30 (2004): 311–334.

Petty, Anne C. *One Ring to Bind Them All: Tolkien's Mythology.* Tuscaloosa: University of Alabama Press, 2002.

Petty, Ann C. *Tolkien in the Land of Heroes.* New York: Gold Spring Press, 2003.

Pickering, Mike, ed. *Cultural Studies Methods.* Edinburgh: Edinburgh University Press, 2008.

Porter, Lynnette R. *Unsung Heroes of "The Lord of the Rings": From Page to Screen.* Westport, CT: Greenwood Press, 2005.

Powell, Sian. "Readers Choice." *The Australian* (October 15, 1997).

Price, Leah. "Reading: The State of the Discipline." *Book History* 7 (2004): 303–320.

Pryor, Ian. *Peter Jackson: From Prince of Splatter to Lord of the Rings.* New York: St. Martin's Press, 2004.

Radway, Janice. *Reading the Romance: Women, Patriarchy, and Popular Literature.* Chapel Hill: University of North Carolina Press, 1984.

Reese, Stephen D. et al., eds. *Framing Public Life: Perspectives on Media and Our Understanding of the Social World.* Mahwah, NJ: Lawrence Erlbaum, 2003.

Rescher, Nicholas. *A Theory of Possibility.* Oxford: Blackwell, 1975.

Richards, Jeffrey and Dorothy Sheridan, eds. *Mass-Observation at the Movies.* London: Routledge and

Kegan Paul, 1987.

Ripp, Joseph. "Middle America Meets Middle-Earth: American Discussion and Readership of J R R Tolkien's *The Lord of the Rings*, 1965–69." *Book History* 8 (2005): 245–286.

Roberts, C. W. *Textual Analysis for the Social Sciences: Methods for Drawing Statistical Inferences from Texts and Transcripts.* Hillsdale, NJ: Lawrence Erlbaum, 1997.

Rojek, Chris. *Celebrity.* London: Reaktion Books, 2001.

Rosebury, Brian. *Tolkien: A Cultural Phenomenon.* Basingstoke: Palgrave Macmillan, 2003.

Rossi, Lee D. *The Politics of Fantasy: C.S. Lewis and J.R.R. Tolkien.* Ann Arbor: University of Michigan Press, 1971.

Rubin, A. M. and M. M. Step. "Impact of Motivation, Attraction, and Parasocial Interaction on Talk-Radio Listening." *Journal of Broadcasting & Electronic Media* 44 (2000): 635–654.

Ruddock, Andrew. *Understanding Audiences: Theory and Method.* London: Sage, 2001.

Ryan, John S. *Tolkien: Cult or Culture?* Armidale, New South Wales: University of New England, 1969.

Sandler, Kevin S. and Gaylyn Studlar. *Titanic: Anatomy of a Blockbuster.* New Brunswick, NJ: Rutgers University Press, 1999.

Sandvoss, Cornel. *Fans.* Cambridge, MA: Polity Press, 2005.

Sarantakos, S. *Social Research.* Basingstoke: Palgrave Macmillan, 2004.

Schere, Klaus, R. "What Are Emotions? And How Can They Be Measured?" *Social Science Information* 44, no. 4 (2005): 695–729.

Schrøder, Kim, Kirsten Drotner, Stephen Kline, and Catherine Murray. *Researching Audiences.* London: Arnold, 2003.

Schütze, Marli. *Neue Wege nach Narnia und Mittelerde: Handlungskonstituenten in der Fantasy-Literatur von C.S. Lewis and J.R.R. Tolkien.* Berlin: Lang, 1986.

Serkis, Andy and Gary Russell. *Gollum: How We Made Movie Magic.* Boston, MA: Houghton Mifflin, 2003.

Shefrin, Elana. "*Lord of the Rings, Star Wars,* and Participatory Fandom: Mapping New Congruencies between the Internet and Media Entertainment Culture." *Critical Studies in Media Communication* 21, no. 3 (2004): 261–281.

Shippey, Tom. *The Road to Middle Earth.* London: Grafton, 1982.

Shrum, Wesley. *Fringe and Fortune: The Role of Critics in High and Popular Art.* Princeton, NJ: Princeton University Press, 1996.

Sibley, Brian. *The Lord of the Rings: The Fellowship of the Ring Insider's Guide.* Boston, MA: Houghton Mifflin, 2001.

Silverman, David. *Interpreting Qualitative Data: Methods for Analysing Talk, Text and Interaction.* London: Sage, 2001.

Silverstone, Roger and E. Hirsch, eds. *Consuming Technologies: Media and Information in Domestic Spaces.* London: Routledge, 1997.

Sinyard, Neil. *Filming Literature: The Art of Screen Adaptation.* London: Croom Helm, 1986.

Sklar, Robert. *Movie-Made America: A Cultural History of American Movies.* New York: Vintage Books, 1994.

Skopal, Pavel. "The Adventure Continues on DVD: Franchise Movies as Home Video." *Convergence* 13, no. 2 (2007): 185–198.

Smith, Adam. *An Inquiry into the Nature and Causes of Wealth of Nations.* London: Everyman's Library, 1904 [1776].

Smith, Jim and J. Clive Matthews. *"The Lord of the Rings": The Films, the Books, the Radio Series.* London: Virgin Books, 2004.

Smith, Mark Eddy. *Tolkien's Ordinary Virtues: Discovering the Spiritual Themes of the Lord of the Rings.* Downers Grove, IL: Inter-Varsity Press, 2002.

Smith, Murray. *Engaging Characters: Fiction, Emotion and the Cinema.* Oxford: Oxford University Press, 1995.

Smith, Murray and Carl Plantinga, eds. *Passionate Views: Film, Cognition and Emotion*. Baltimore, MD: Johns Hopkins University Press, 1999.

Smythe, Dallas. "On the Political Economy of Communication." *Journalism Quarterly* (August 1960): 461–475.

Sobchack, Vivian. *The Address of the Eye: A Phenomenology of Film Experience*. Princeton, NJ: Princeton University Press, 1992.

Sobchack, Vivian. *Carnal Thoughts: Embodiment and Moving Image Culture*. Berkeley and Los Angeles: University of California Press, 2004.

Speake, Tracie S. "The Power of the Ring: J R R Tolkien and American Popular Culture." *The Sextant* 1 (2003): 71–86.

Spradley, James, ed. *Culture and Cognition: Rules, Maps and Plans*. Toronto: Chandler Publishing, 1956.

Stacey, Jackie. *Star Gazing: Hollywood Cinema and Female Spectatorship*. London: Routledge, 1993.

Staiger, Janet. *Interpreting Films: Studies in the Historical Reception of American Cinema*. Princeton, NJ: Princeton University Press, 1992.

Staiger, Janet. *Perverse Spectators: The Practices of Film Reception*. New York: New York University Press, 2000.

Staiger, Janet. *Media Reception Studies*. New York: New York University Press, 2005.

Stam, Robert and Alesandra Raengo, eds. *Literature and Film: A Guide to the Theory and Practice of Film Adaptation*. Oxford: Blackwell, 2005.

Stanton, Michael N. *Hobbits, Elves and Wizards: Exploring the Wonders and Worlds of JRR Tolkien's The Lord of the Rings*. New York: St. Martin's Press, 2002.

Stempel, Tom. *American Audiences on Movies and Moviegoing*. Lexington: University of Kentucky Press, 2001.

Stokes, Melvyn and Richard Maltby, eds. *American Movie Audiences: From the Turn of the Century to the Early Sound Era*. London: British Film Institute, 1999.

Stokes, Melvyn and Richard Maltby, eds. *Hollywood Abroad: Audiences and Cultural Exchange*. London: British Film Institute, 2004.

Stokes, Melvyn and Richard Maltby, eds. *Hollywood Spectatorship: Changing Perceptions of Cinema Audiences*. London: British Film Institute, 2001.

Stokes, Melvyn and Richard Maltby, eds. *Identifying Hollywood's Audiences: Cultural Identity and the Movies*. London: British Film Institute, 1999.

Storey, John. *Cultural Consumption and Everyday Life*. London: Arnold, 1999.

Storey, John, ed. *What Is Cultural Studies? A Reader*. London: Arnold, 1996.

Straubhaar, J. D. (1991). "Beyond Media Imperialism: Asymmetrical Interdependence and Cultural Proximity." *Critical Studies in Mass Communication* 8, no. 1 (1991): 39.

Strinati, Dominic and Stephen Wagg, eds. *Come on Down? Popular Media Culture in Post-war Britain*. London: Routledge, 1992.

Stringer, Julian, ed. *Movie Blockbusters*. London: Routledge, 2003.

Sturken, Marita and Lisa Cartwright. *Practices of Looking: An Introduction to Visual Culture*. Oxford: Oxford University Press, 2001.

Taylor, Greg. *Artists in the Audience: Cult, Camp and American Film Criticism*. Princeton, NJ: Princeton University Press, 1999.

Taylor, Jim, Mark R. Johnson, and Charles G. Crawford. *DVD Demystified*. New York: McGraw-Hill, 2006.

Telotte, J. P. "The Blair Witch Project Project: Film and the Internet." *Film Quarterly* 54, no. 3 (2001): 32–39.

Tesch, R. *Qualitative Research: Analysis Types and Software Tools*. New York: Falmer Press, 1990.

Thompson, Kristin. "Fantasy, Franchises, and Frodo Baggins: *The Lord of the Rings* and Modern Hollywood." *The Velvet Light Trap* 2 (2003): 45–63.

Thornton, Sarah. *Club Cultures: Music, Media and Subcultural Capital.* Cambridge, MA: Polity Press, 1995.

Thwaites, Tony, Lloyd Davis, and Miles Warwick. *Introducing Cultural and Media Studies: A Semiotic Approach.* Basingstoke and New York: Palgrave, 2002.

Time Warner. *Factbook.* New York: Time Warner, Inc., 2003.

Trobia, Alberto. *La Ricerca Sociale Quali-Quantitativa.* Milan: FrancoAngeli, 2005.

Troost, Linda and Sayre Greenfield, eds. *Jane Austen in Hollywood.* Lexington: University of Kentucky Press, 2001.

Turner, Graeme. *Fame Games.* Cambridge: Cambridge University Press, 2000.

Urang, Gunnar. *Shadows of Heaven: Religion and Fantasy in the Writings of C.S. Lewis, Charles Williams, and J.R.R. Tolkien.* London: United Church Press, 1971.

Urry, John. *The Tourist Gaze.* London: Sage, 2002.

Verevis, Constantine. *Film Remakes.* Edinburgh: Edinburgh University Press, 2006.

Vorderer, Peter. *Fernsehen als Handlung: Fernsehfilmrezeption aus Motivationspsychologischer Perspektive.* Berlin: Edition Sigma, 1992.

Walton, Kendall. "Fearing Fictions." *Journal of Philosophy* 75, no. 1 (1978): 5–27.

Walton, Kendall. "How Remote Are Fictional Worlds from the Real World?" *Journal of Aesthetics and Art Criticism* 37, no. 1 (1978): 11–23.

Walton, Kendall. *Mimesis as Make-Believe.* Cambridge, MA: Harvard University Press, 1995.

Wasko, Janet. *Hollywood in the Information Age: Beyond the Silver Screen.* Cambridge, MA: Polity Press, 1994.

Wasko, Janet. *How Hollywood Works.* London: Sage, 2003.

Wasko, Janet, Mark Phillips, and Eileen R Meehan, eds. *Dazzled by Disney? The Global Disney Audiences Project.* Leicester: Leicester University Press, 2001.

Webb, E. J., D. T. Campbell, R. D. Schwartz, and L. Sechrest. *Unobtrusive Measures: Nonreactive Measures in the Social Sciences.* Chicago: Rand McNally, 1966.

Weber, R. P. *Basic Content Analysis.* Beverly Hills, CA: Sage, 1990.

Weitzman, E. A. and M. B. Miles. *Computer Programs for Qualitative Data Analysis: A Software Sourcebook.* Thousand Oaks, CA: Sage, 1995.

West, Richard C. *Tolkien Criticism: An Annotated Check List.* Kent, OH: Kent State University Press, 1981.

Wetherell, Margaret, Stephanie Taylor, and Simeon J. Yates, eds. *Discourse Theory and Practice: A Reader.* Milton Keynes: Open University Press, 2001.

Wetherell, Margaret, Stephanie Taylor, and Simeon J. Yates, eds. *Discourse as Data: A Guide for Analysis.* Milton Keynes: Open University Press, 2001.

White, H. *Figural Realism.* Baltimore, MD: Johns Hopkins University Press, 2000.

White, Michael. *The Life and Work of J. R. R. Tolkien.* Indianapolis, IN: Alpha Publishers, 2002.

Wilinsky, Barbara. *Sure Seaters: The Emergence of Art House Cinema.* Minneapolis: University of Minnesota Press, 2000.

Williams, Raymond. *The Long Revolution.* London: Hogarth Press, 1992.

Williamson, Milly. *The Lure of the Vampire: Gender, Fiction and Fandom from Bram Stoker to Buffy.* London: Wallflower, 2005.

Willig, Carla, ed. *Applied Discourse Analysis: Social and Psychological Interventions.* London: Sage, 1999.

Winch, Peter. *The Idea of a Social Science and Its Relation to Philosophy.* London: Routledge and Kegan Paul, 1958.

Worley, Alec. *Empires of the Imagination: A Critical Survey of Fantasy Cinema from Georges Mélies to The Lord of the Rings.* New York: McFarland and Company, 2005.

Wright, Greg. *Tolkien in Perspective.* Sisters, OR: VMI Publishers, 2003.

Wright, Greg. *Peter Jackson in Perspective: The Power behind Cinema's The Lord of the Rings: A Look at Hollywood's Take on Tolkien's Epic Tale.* Los Angeles, CA: Hollywood Jesus Books, 2004.

Wyatt, Justin. *High Concept: Movies and Marketing in Hollywood.* Austin: University of Texas Press, 1994.

Zimbardo, Rose A. and Neil D. Isaacs. *Understanding the Lord of the Rings.* New York: Houghton Mifflin, 2004.

Index

Because of the central themes of this book, a number of topics (notably, of course, J. R. R. Tolkien, and *The Lord of the Rings*) are mentioned throughout. In a related way, many names and topics are mentioned only in passing. In order to maximise its usefulness, we have limited this Index to those cases where a topic or a person's ideas receive some substantive attention. Also, because the authors of this book come from overlapping but differently configured research traditions, there are a number of slight differences in vocabulary even where related ideas are being discussed. We have therefore sought to group such references under a common term, again for ease of use of the Index. Italicised numbers indicate references within the book's endnotes.

Sut Jhally & Justin Lewis
General Editors

This series publishes works on media and culture, focusing on research embracing a variety of critical perspectives. The series is particularly interested in promoting theoretically informed empirical work using both quantitative and qualitative approaches. Although the focus is on scholarly research, the series aims to speak beyond a narrow, specialist audience.

ALSO AVAILABLE

- Michael Morgan, Editor
  Against the Mainstream: The Selected Works of George Gerbner

- Edward Herman
  The Myth of the Liberal Media: An Edward Herman Reader

- Robert Jensen
  Writing Dissent: Taking Radical Ideas from the Margins to the Mainstream

To order other books in this series, please contact our Customer Service Department at:

(800) 770-LANG (within the U.S.)
(212) 647-7706 (outside the U.S.)
(212) 647-7707 FAX

or browse online by series at:
WWW.PETERLANG.COM